The
Complete
Guide to
Performance
Appraisal

The Complete Guide to Performance Appraisal

DICK GROTE

American Management Association

New York • Atlanta • Boston • Chicago • Kansas City • San Francisco • Washington, D.C.
Brussels • Mexico City • Tokyo • Toronto

This book is available at a special
discount when ordered in bulk quantities.
For information, contact Special Sales Department,
AMACOM, a division of American Management Association,
1601 Broadway, New York, NY 10019

Library of Congress Cataloging-in-Publication Data

Grote, Richard C.
    The complete guide to performance appraisal / Dick Grote.
        p.   cm.
    Includes bibliographical references and index.
    ISBN 0-8144-0313-1
    1. Employees—Rating of. 2. Performance standards. I. Title.
HF5549.5.R3G64   1996
    658.3'125—dc20   96-33560
                                                        CIP

Printing number

10 9 8 7 6 5 4 3 2

Contents

Acknowledgments

A book that presumptuously proposes itself to be the "Complete Guide" to anything can never live up to its title, unless its topic is trivial. Performance appraisal is anything but trivial; it is one of the most important and substantial issues in all of management.

To the extent that this book comes close to living up to its title, the credit is due to the people who built the foundation on which it stands. An enormous number of writers, practitioners, and researchers are acknowledged throughout the text and in the notes.

Other people contributed more directly. Clients, colleagues, and associates from many different organizations were generous in sharing their insights and results: Linda Steger, Jerry Brady, Cindy Nosky, Chuck Mills, Bill Parker, Larrie Loehr, Thresa McDade, Peter Habley, Dick Moroukian, Richard Dauphine, Tom Peters, Chuck Canfield, Sylvia Pate, and Bill Combs.

Human resource professionals at two client organizations have been especially helpful over several years in provoking my beliefs and opinions about performance appraisal. At Alcon Laboratories, Jack Walters, Ed Brotman, Tom Faver, Jim Kuhn, Martin Vogt, Jay Jones, and Kay Cox; at E-Systems, Art Hobbs, Rick Huntley, Tom Coffey, and Tom Clark have challenged my thinking on performance appraisal.

In the specific area of employee development, Bob Eichinger has been a source of insight since we first met a quarter century ago. More recently, Carol Denton, Bill Evans, and Jeff Crawford have expanded my understanding of how to increase the effectiveness of individuals in organizations.

At the University of Dallas graduate school of management, where for almost twenty years I have had the privilege of teaching the concepts of organization behavior to an impressive roster of students from the United States and around the world, I owe a debt to Dean Ann Hughes and Professor Bruce Evans, who have added to my store of performance appraisal resources.

Without the help and contributions of Kayla Gingrich, marketing director for Grote Consulting, I could not have maintained the focus and concentration to produce this work.

Above all, one person is responsible for providing constant and unwavering support and sustenance. I am indebted to my wife, Jacqueline, more than I can express.

Introduction

Over the past fifty years, performance appraisal has become such a commonplace in organizational life that virtually every company has an appraisal system. The most obvious way for a mom'n'pop shop to proclaim that it is becoming a serious business is to institute a formal performance appraisal procedure. That it is a firmly established, middle-aged management technique, however, does not mean that it has achieved a comfortable place in organizations. In fact, no one seems satisfied with the system they have or content with the results it produces. "Performance appraisal systems are a lot like seat belts," a pair of writers assert. "Most people believe they are necessary, but they don't like to use them."[1]

Fortune editor Walter Kiechel, in an insightful, lighthearted one-page essay a dozen years ago, captured the universal opinion: "Let's be frank. Most managers hate conducting performance appraisals. If they think they can get away with it, they will skip such potential unpleasantness entirely. If compelled to go through the exercise, they tend to do so with bad grace, confusing the poor appraisee by mixing a kind of phony solicitousness with a candor that gives new meaning to the term, 'brutal.'"[2] The late quality guru W. Edwards Deming maintained that the annual performance review, as practiced in most companies, "leaves people bitter, dejected, depressed, and in despair for months."[3]

Performance appraisal is tolerated as a necessary evil at best—necessary, as the authors of a Conference Board study point out, because it seems to most managers to be impossible to manage an organization without good information on how well people are performing and how they go about meeting their responsibilities. The information is needed for critical management functions: maintaining control of current operations and planning for the future, making defensible decisions about compensation, deciding on promotions and transfers, and developing manpower plans and staffing requirements.

Certainly judgments about how individuals are performing will be made whether or not there is a formal system. People constantly make judgments about others. But since many of these informal, spontaneous judgments will be erroneous, some formal procedure is needed to mini-

mize the possibilities of bias and uninformed judgments. Abolishing performance appraisal systems will not stop people from appraising performance. Attacking the practice of performance appraisal, one manager said,
"will force companies away from formalized rating systems into unquali-
fied, subjective judgments. It would be a return to the smoke-filled room."

   This book contains everything that I have learned in a quarter century
of working with companies and their managers in helping them create and
use this nettlesome technique. Unlike most other professional or technical
books, it is intensely personal. I will be forthright in telling you what I
have found works and what I have found flops. I'll be frank—some of the
grand ideas or brilliant theories I have had over the years about performance appraisal have proven to be flops. I will highlight them and admit
them. You will profit from my mistakes.

   I make my prejudices known from the start. First, and most important,
I am neither neutral nor unbiased. I am an advocate of performance appraisal, a good, important, and necessary procedure. As difficult as it is
to do well, as flawed as the forms foisted on us may be, as ineptly as the
procedure may be used by clumsy managers, as scorned as it may be by
skeptics, it still is one of management's most valuable tools. That one hour
a year when supervisor and subordinate sit down face to face for a discussion of the twelve months gone by and the twelve months to come may
be the most significant conversation the two will have in that entire two-
year stretch.

   My second prejudice is that I believe that it is possible to create good
performance appraisal forms that make it easy for managers to capture
all of the important information about an individual's performance over
the past twelve months. Good forms can generate meaningful data for
making defensible decisions about compensation, potential, developmental needs, placement, and goals. They can separate chaff from wheat
and encourage discussions that are meaningful, accurate, and change producing. In this book I show a variety of forms from a variety of companies.
A few are ingenious—wisely constructed, cleverly designed, and enthusiastically accepted by everyone who is affected by them. Most are sufficient
to their purpose; they do what is asked of them. And a few are dreadful.
It is useful to see examples of the genuinely beastly; no matter how bad
our system may be, it is comforting to realize that others are worse.

   Here is my third prejudice: However shoddy the form may be, it
doesn't make much difference. What's important is not the form but the
conversation it generates. Give a talented and diligent manager a second-
rate form, and he will still do a good job of discussing performance and
setting goals despite its deficiencies. Give a mediocre manager a splendid
form, and his results will be only slightly better than if he were handed
nothing more than an antiquated trait-scale checklist.

   Although the form itself is not the critical component of a performance appraisal system, some forms are better than others (my fourth prejudice). Some techniques are more effective than other techniques, and some procedures do make more sense. In this book I tell you what I have found to work well and guide you away from approaches that may sound good in theory but somehow don't deliver the goods. I am not neutral and unbiased. "Often wrong; never in doubt": I'm comfortable with that for an epitaph.

Another bias is that I believe that performance appraisal done well, in an organization that takes the procedure seriously, can have a major impact on the corporate culture. The creation or renovation of a performance appraisal procedure can transform an enterprise from a best-effort environment to a results-driven climate. If a company is going to survive, let alone prevail, in the competitive climate that all face, performance appraisal, more than any other technique, has the power to generate incredible and sustained change throughout the organization. More than any other action management can take, the development or redevelopment of a performance appraisal procedure can focus the attention of every stakeholder on exactly those ends that must be achieved for the enterprise to survive. If exemplary performance is important to the organization—and I cannot imagine one in which a leader would say that good enough is good enough—then there is no faster or more controllable way to turn the organization in a different direction and cause performance to be improved more dramatically than by throwing out the existing performance appraisal system, appointing a team of the most knowledgeable and respected members of the enterprise to develop a procedure that is exactly right for their company in their market with their history and their people, and then insisting—upon pain of termination—that it be used in a totally committed fashion by every person in the institution.

Do you want culture change? Serious and major change? Then look to your performance appraisal system. It can be the source of the most significant organizational redirection possible.

About This Book

This book is aptly named. It is the *complete* guide to performance appraisal. Within these covers I will tell you everything that you need to know to understand the most important aspects of the subject.

Part I looks at the business of performance. It begins in Chapter 1 with an overview of performance appraisal. You will learn where performance appraisal came from, options that companies have for appraising performance, the expectations an organization can reasonably have of its system, and the kinds of forms that exist. I bring you up to date on the most current research about this topic.

Chapter 2 concentrates on an often overlooked question: Just what is performance? What motivates it? How do you measure it? How do you distinguish between good and bad? What's the difference between performance management and performance appraisal? Here we will determine the requirements for a total performance management system, exploring exactly what it takes for people to do a job right and what has to happen in order for the organization to get the performance it is paying for.

Chapter 3 briefly explains the only three elements that an appraisal system can measure: traits, behaviors, and results. It then provides a wealth of examples of performance appraisal forms from companies around the world.

Chapters 4 and 5 each consider one of the two critical areas in performance appraisal: the what and the how of job performance. Chapter 4 explores the results that an individual achieves on the job, the area of job outcomes. This is the domain of management by objectives, one of the most frequently used approaches to management. In Chapter 4 I show how objectives can be set and results can be measured.

Chapter 5 covers the other main area of performance: not what the person does on the job but how she does it. It concentrates on how to measure and appraise the person's actual performance: the behaviors that the individual exhibits while going about the job.

Part II focuses on how to use an existing performance appraisal system. Chapter 6 explains how to collect the data needed to do an honest evaluation, how to determine how well a person is actually doing the job, and how to avoid common (and uncommon) rating errors. One of the most valuable parts of this chapter is its explanation of how to fill out a performance appraisal rating form, whatever the form may look like.

Probably the toughest ten seconds in management arrive when a subordinate scheduled for an annual review knocks on the door, pops her head in the office, and says, "Here I am. Ready?" Chapter 7 provides everything a manager needs to be able to answer yes. It discusses how to create a discussion plan in advance and provides specific scripts to follow. This chapter explains how to prepare the individual in advance of the discussion, how to get it off to a good start, how to raise sensitive subjects and deliver unpleasant news, and how to wrap things up with a commitment to performance improvement and goal achievement. It also contains a highly workable and proven way to confront performance problems in the appraisal interview that will generate commitment on the employee's part to correct the situation and build individual responsibility and respect for the manager.

Chapter 8 wraps up the portion of the book devoted to how to make an existing system work as well as it possibly can. It explains how to get the maximum mileage from a system that everyone agrees is far from state-of-the-art.

Part III is devoted to an explanation of how to create and implement the ideal performance appraisal system. Chapter 9 looks at building management support—the most critical issue in ensuring that the new performance appraisal system will deliver the goods and keep making those deliveries long after initial installation is complete.

While every organization's forms and procedures may appropriately vary, what does not vary is the best way to create those forms and procedures. Chapter 10 reveals every step to take to create a system that satisfies all of the organization's needs and meets all of the organization's criteria, both professional and political. It explains every consideration in designing the operation of the system and every decision to be made in developing the form.

Just designing an ideal system isn't enough. Chapter 11 teaches everything you need to know to market the appraisal system. It reveals how to build organization-wide understanding, support, and acceptance.

The ultimate determinant of how well a new performance appraisal system succeeds in the long run may be the quality of the training received upon implementation by system users, both appraisers and appraisees. Chapter 12 explores all of the specific considerations that are involved in a successful training program whose topic is performance appraisal, both at the time of initial installation and for ongoing follow-up and refresher training.

Part IV looks at critical issues in performance appraisal. Chapter 13 concentrates on employee development. One mission of an effective performance appraisal process is to encourage the development of skills and capabilities required by the organization. How does development actually happen? What works? What doesn't? In addition to exploring the topics of development in detail, I explore 360-degree feedback: how it works and how it can be integrated into the appraisal and development process. Finally, I explain the individual management development procedure, which gives managers a workable tool to promote real employee development through the creation of on-the-job developmental experiences.

Chapter 14 explores the relationship between the appraisal and compensation systems, particularly as they apply to the idea of pay for performance.

No book today could fail to cover the legal aspects of performance appraisal. In addition to detailing exactly what the law requires and prohibits, Chapter 15 will be helpful in increasing the defensibility of any company's appraisal form or procedures. It also explores the advisability of providing an appeals process so that conflicts arising out of the performance appraisal process can be resolved internally without outside, third-party review. I am greatly indebted to and appreciative of the yeoman work done in reviewing this chapter and ensuring its accuracy by James W. Wimberley, Jr., of Wimberley and Lawson in Atlanta, Georgia.

The last chapter of the book looks at trends in performance appraisal: appraising team performances using computer-generated appraisals, and the impact of the total quality management philosophy on performance appraisal.

Two important appendixes complete this book. Appendix A contains the master performance appraisal form, a highly validated model performance appraisal form that places its emphasis where a majority of companies and research studies say it should be placed. This model approach allows for the analysis of both what was accomplished (results and job outcomes) and how it was accomplished (behaviors and job competencies). It is a logical starting point in efforts to create a performance appraisal system.

Appendix B contains the Individual Management Development form. This instrument identifies the primary competencies required for success in a professional or managerial position. More important, it provides behavioral indicators for each competency so that both the individual and the manager will be using the same yardstick to assess the need for development within this area. By adapting and modifying the instrument for its specific needs, any company can quickly inaugurate a tested and workable development process.

The ideas of many organizations are represented here, as are their performance appraisal forms, policies, and procedural guidelines. Many of them are not identified by name. Several companies that are doing an exemplary job in creating and administering effective performance appraisal processes believe strongly that their systems give them a source of competitive advantage. They would no more broadside their performance appraisal form than they would reveal their secret ingredient or give a competitor a tour of their R&D laboratory.

I have worked with a great many companies as a consultant to help them create or improve their system and procedures. In every case I have honored their request not to be identified by name or have a reproduction of their instrument shown. In other cases they gave me permission to use their appraisal form, or a particular part of it, with the understanding and agreement that it would not specifically be identified as theirs. In some cases I have had to disguise the identity of a company, but in no case is a performance appraisal form or procedure described in this book anything different from the way it actually is in practice.

One Final Bias

My final bias is that performance appraisal is here to stay. This management technique, more than any other, has the power to transform organizations and focus the energy of every organization member toward the achievement of organizational goals. A hundred years from now, in perhaps its eleventh edition, updated by my professional great-grandchild, managers may still be reading *The Complete Guide to Performance Appraisal.*

Notes

1. Gary P. Latham and Kenneth N. Wexley, *Increasing Productivity Through Performance Appraisal* (Reading, Mass.: Addison-Wesley, 1993).
2. Walter Kiechel III, "How to Appraise Performance," *Fortune* (October 12, 1987).
3. W. Edwards Deming, quoted in Nancy K. Austin, "It's Time for Your Review," *Incentive* (March 1994).

Part I
This Business of Performance

Chapter 1

Performance Appraisal: The State of the Art

Forty years ago in a classic *Harvard Business Review* article, "An Uneasy Look at Performance Appraisal," Douglas McGregor described the goals of an organization's performance appraisal program:

> Formal performance appraisal plans are designed to meet three needs, one for the organization and two for the individual:
>
> 1. They provide systematic judgments to back up salary increases, promotions, transfers, and sometimes demotions and terminations.
> 2. They are a means of telling a subordinate how he is doing, and suggesting needed changes in his behavior, attitudes, skills, or job knowledge; they let him know "where he stands" with the boss.
> 3. They are also being increasingly used as a basis for the coaching and counseling of the individual by the superior.[1]

McGregor's writings, including his influential *The Human Side of Enterprise*, mark a turning point in the way organizations viewed the process of performance appraisal. Before World War II, only a handful of companies and the military conducted regular formal performance appraisals. Most appraisals that were done concentrated more on an individual's personality and traits than on actual achievements against goals and formal analyses of the behaviors that produced those results.

Following the war, a few companies, heavily influenced by Peter Drucker's novel idea of management by objectives (MBO), moved from trait assessment to the development of a procedure that concentrated on goal setting, placed responsibility with the subordinate, and made the appraisal process a shared responsibility between subordinate and manager. McGregor used these early practices by such companies as General Electric and General Mills as models for his analysis of the appraisal process. McGregor's focus was on performance, not personality. The manager, he argues, must abandon the undesired role of therapist or psychologist and instead become a coach.

General Electric conducted a scientific study in the early 1960s to test the effectiveness of its approach. Called Work Planning and Review, this appraisal system combined a formal MBO-type procedure with the conventional once-a-year, comprehensive, supervisor-controlled appraisal that most of the company was using.

What GE Discovered

The GE studies began by acknowledging what every commentator on performance appraisal had observed: Although most people agreed that the idea of performance appraisal was a good one, in practice it is the extremely rare operating manager who will initiate an appraisal program. Typically, GE reported, most managers carry out performance appraisal interviews only when strong control procedures are established to ensure that they do so.

The study centered on analyzing the effects of the interview between the subordinate and the manager, because, the authors explained, "this is the discussion which is supposed to motivate the man to improve his performance." It found that:

- Criticism has a negative effect on achievement of goals.
- Praise has little effect one way or the other.
- Performance improves most when specific goals are established.
- Defensiveness resulting from critical appraisal produces inferior performance.
- Coaching should be a day-to-day, not a once-a-year, activity.
- Mutual goal setting, not criticism, improves performance.
- Interviews designed primarily to improve a man's performance should not at the same time weigh his salary or promotion in the balance.
- Participation by the employee in the goal-setting procedure helps produce favorable results.

The comprehensive annual review, the authors discovered, had little value for two reasons: Praise emerging during the discussion was discounted because "it was regarded as the sandwich which surrounded the raw meat of criticism," and criticism failed to produce results because it brought on defensive reactions that were essentially denials of responsibility for poor performance.[2] Thirty years later, no research has contradicted GE's initial findings.

Where Are We Today?

In 1991 writer Ron Zemke, exploring the current state of affairs in performance appraisal, observed that some managers would choose dental surgery or an IRS audit over another round of "playing God" with their employees' careers (without realizing, curiously, that the IRS was one of the first organizations to initiate and rigorously analyze the effectiveness of performance appraisal). Yet Zemke also asserted that although common wisdom holds that performance appraisal is a valuable management tool, "there is remarkably little evidence that this highly touted, widely used and much researched process actually improves employee performance."[3]

Although a multitude of cans have been hung on performance appraisal's tail, there still remain only two fundamental expectations for a performance appraisal system: (1) that it will substantially aid managers in the short term by improving employee performance and over the long term by contributing to employee development and (2) that it will serve as an effective and efficient bookkeeping system for the compensation and industrial relations departments. Whether performance appraisals actually improve performance is "one of those wonderfully simple, obvious questions that the literature does not address," says David L. De Vries, former vice president of the Center for Creative Leadership.[4] The only study he could cite that explored whether performance appraisal systems actually affect performance was conducted by Gary Latham and John Ivancevitch, who showed that a management by objectives (MBO) system can change people's performance if it is strongly supported by senior management. Without their support, there is no effect.

Latham, professor of organizational effectiveness at the University of Toronto, also worked with Edwin A. Locke of the University of Maryland to explore goal setting. Paralleling GE's findings two decades before, their 1984 book, *Goal Setting: A Motivational Technique That Works*, offers similar conclusions:

- Specific, challenging goals lead to better performance than do easy or vague goals, like "do your best."
- The most successful and motivating goals have two main characteristics. First, the goal should be as specific as possible, including a time limit wherever possible. Second, the goal should be challenging but reachable.
- Feedback on goal-directed performance motivates higher performance only when it leads to the setting of higher goals.
- Positive feedback on performance gives the worker a sense of achievement, recognition, and accomplishment.
- Feedback alone won't improve performance, but if it's missing from a performance system, performance can't improve.

▶ Both assigned and participatively set goals lead to substantial improvements in performance. Participation is important only to the extent that it leads to the setting of difficult goals.

▶ Competition—setting one group against another—affects productivity only in the sense that it encourages employees to commit to the goal. In other words, a competitive climate does not directly motivate performance. But it does persuade employees to accept the goals, which then leads them to strive to meet them.

▶ Productivity can be increased significantly if supervisors set a specific production goal and provide attention and support to workers.[5]

Since Zemke's 1991 overview, several major studies of performance appraisal have confirmed many of the conventional notions about performance appraisal and added a few unexpected insights. All of them are worth reviewing closely; here we look at some of their most arresting findings.

The DDI/SHRM Study: Critical Questions in Performance Appraisal

One of the most widely reported studies was conducted in 1993 by the Society for Human Resource Management (SHRM) and Development Dimensions International (DDI).[6] The respondents, 130 companies (a mix of SHRM members and DDI clients; two-thirds service companies, one-third manufacturing firms) participated in a survey exploring critical questions in performance appraisal: How satisfied are employees with their organization's performance appraisal system? How do they see performance management practices changing in the future? What factors cause performance management systems to succeed or fail?

The results, set out in *Performance Management: What's Hot; What's Not*, reported that managers and staff perceive performance management as a three-headed hydra: "One head wants to improve people's performance, another wants to help people grow, and the third wants to be a compensation and promotion mechanism." Rarely does a company succeed in merging all three heads into one productive system. Among the survey findings were these:

▶ Regardless of position, both managers and staff see a lot of room for improvement in performance management practices.
▶ Respondents give the lowest grades to feedback and coaching.
▶ Respondents don't see a clear link between their performance and their pay.

 ▶ Respondents describe performance management as a fragmented
system that lacks continuity.

The study designers consciously chose to use the term *performance
management* rather than merely *performance appraisal* to indicate that the
area of interest was the entire process, not just the once-a-year review.
The respondents nevertheless reported that performance management is
nothing more than a performance appraisal that happens only once a year.
In fact, little feedback occurs during the course of the year. Other findings
were that there is little opportunity for employee involvement in the appraisal process, performance isn't rewarded sufficiently, appraisals are late
and focus on the petty and negative, and managers don't follow up with
employees after appraising them. Finally, it takes too much time.

The report also found that many companies plan to initiate "upward
input" procedures—a maneuver that allows subordinates to turn the ta-
bles and evaluate the performance of the boss. Companies also expect their
use of peer and team approaches almost to double, though the total number
for each still is not particularly high.

Based on the report's findings, DDI and SHRM suggest that to improve performance management, organizations need to concentrate on
four areas:

1. **Organizational readiness** Top management must model appropriate behavior and reinforce the process. Involving employees in developing the system will build ownership. Clearly communicate to all employees
how the system works and how it reflects organizational values.

2. **Systems integration** The performance management system must
be fully integrated with other systems and organizational objectives. Alignment is critical since it ensures that all systems affected by the overall
performance management system (training, compensation, management
development, selection, manpower planning, strategic planning) support
it—or at least don't undermine it. Make sure that individual, team, and
department objectives link with the organization's overall business strategies and values.

3. **Training** The report encourages organizations to commit to a
high level of training for appraisers and appraisees alike. Managers and
employees must be taught how to allocate responsibility, set objectives,
identify key behaviors, and track and measure performance. Managers
need training in interpersonal and coaching skills.

4. **Evaluation** The effectiveness of a performance management system can best be ensured if managers are held accountable for using it
effectively. The quality and timeliness of performance reviews should be
spot-checked at a minimum. In addition to requiring midyear and annual

reviews, effective organizations demand that part of a manager's annual appraisal be devoted to how well he used the system with his subordinates.

Overall, the report offered no bombshells, few surprises, and a couple of unexpected predictions for the future, like a withering away of numerical ratings and a rise in subordinate-initiated appraisals of the boss.

The Bretz and Milkovich Study: Is Performance Appraisal Beneficial?

Bob Bretz and George Milkovich begin their report of a detailed survey of Fortune 100 firms (to which 70 percent of those surveyed responded) with the recognition that performance appraisal is widely considered by both academics and practicing managers as one of the most valuable human resources tools.[7] It is a vital component in recruiting and hiring employees where it is used to validate selection procedures. In the staffing arena, transfer, layoff, termination, and promotion decisions are based on appraisal results, and in compensation administration, performance appraisal forms the basis for the administration of merit pay systems. Most important, performance appraisal can serve as a motivational device to communicate performance expectations to employees and provide them with feedback. Finally, it is indispensable in training and development activities to assess potential and identify training needs. Nevertheless, debate continues about whether performance appraisal is truly beneficial. A significant number of managers firmly believe that the procedure may create more problems than it solves. Certainly, the process itself remains a largely unsatisfactory endeavor, and the systems suffer from design flaws. Moreover, managers receive poor training and are seldom rewarded for accuracy in appraisal. And, quoting Hunter Thompson's phrase, "both managers and employees tend to approach appraisal feedback sessions with fear and loathing."[8] The reasons are summarized in Figure 1-1.

Despite the assumption that performance appraisal is valuable, the study revealed that not a lot of time is devoted to it—an average of eight hours per employee per year for appraising executives and managers, six hours on professionals, and fewer than four hours on nonexempts. These figures include *all* of the appraisers' activities in observing and documenting performance, completing the evaluation form, and conducting the appraisal discussion.

Why isn't more time spent on appraisal? One reason is that managers are not commonly held accountable for how well they conduct performance appraisal on their subordinates, the researchers report, echoing directly one of the major findings of the SHRM/DDI study. "In only 22% of the Fortune 100 sample," Bretz and Milkovich write, "were managers

Figure 1-1. Factors Causing Antipathy Toward Performance Appraisal Systems

Ownership	Neither manager nor subordinate has any sense of ownership. They are not involved in the design or administration of the system; they frequently are not trained to use it, and their reactions to the system are rarely solicited or acted upon.
Bad news	Managers do not like to deliver negative messages to people with whom they must work and whom they often like. Employees do not like to receive them. Negative messages generate defensive reactions and promote hostility rather than serve as useful performance feedback.
Adverse impact	Both managers and employees know that bad reviews have an adverse impact on a person's career. Managers are conscious of the permanence of the paper trail that follows formal appraisal and are often hesitant to commit negative feedback to writing.
Scarce rewards	There are few formal rewards for taking the process seriously and probably no informal rewards. There are many informal rewards for *not* delivering unpopular messages.
Personal reflection	Managers hesitate to give unfavorable appraisals for fear that the appearance of unsatisfactory work by a subordinate will reflect badly on the manager's ability to select and develop subordinates. Lack of candor in evaluation is a way of hiding one's dirty laundry.

Source: Steven Thomas and Robert Bretz, "Research and Practice in Performance Appraisal," *SAM Advanced Management Journal* (Spring 1994).

evaluated on how well they conduct performance appraisal. Basic motivational theory as well as a common sense suggests that managers will devote little effort to a somewhat unpleasant chore for which they are not held accountable."[9]

While nine out of ten of the Fortune 100 companies reported that they provide rater training in how to conduct the appraisal interview and provide feedback, the researchers found that this training almost always occurred in conjunction with the initial development of the appraisal system itself, with few companies providing ongoing training. Since most of the appraisal systems in use were more than ten years old, an enormous number of managers had not received any help in making the system work successfully. And, once again paralleling the results of the SHRM/DDI study, Bretz and Milkovich found that virtually no training is provided to appraisal recipients on how to use the appraisal results and feedback information.

How do companies use the information generated by their appraisal systems? Bretz and Milkovich asked the question and tallied the results, shown in Figure 1-2. This list of uses for performance appraisal data points out one of the most serious difficulties faced by any performance appraisal system: One tool is expected to do a large number of extremely important but unrelated jobs. Demanding that performance appraisal do all of these tasks well would be like telling a plumber, a mortician, and a barber that they can use only one tool, that they must all use the same tool, and that it must serve every need each of them confronts.

More than three-quarters of the organizations surveyed reported

Figure 1-2. How Fortune 100 Companies Use Performance Appraisal Data, in Order of Importance

1   Improving work performance

2   Administering merit pay

3   Advising employees of work expectations

4   Counseling employees

5   Making promotion decisions

6   Motivating employees

7   Assessing employee potential

8   Identifying training needs

9   Better working relationships

10   Helping employees set career goals

11   Assigning work more efficiently

12   Making transfer decisions

13   Making decisions about layoffs and terminations

14   Assisting in long-range planning

15   Validating hiring procedures

16   Justifying other managerial actions

Source: Steven Thomas and Robert Bretz, "Research and Practice in Performance Appraisal," *SAM Advanced Management Journal* (Spring 1994).

Figure 1-3. Performance Distributions in Fortune 100 Companies

	Level 1: "Far exceeds objectives"	Level 2: "Exceeds objectives"	Level 3: "Fully meets objectives"	Level 4: "Partially meets objectives"	Level 5: "Unsatisfactory"
Executives	23	46	31	2	0
Managers	14	43	33	6	2
Professionals	13	43	34	8	1
Nonexempts	14	44	34	6	1

Source: Steven Thomas and Robert Bretz, "Research and Practice in Performance Appraisal," *SAM Advanced Management Journal* (Spring 1994).

skewed performance distributions to be a problem, and over two-thirds stated that these skewed distributions affected pay administration and their ability to reward the best performers. Are performance appraisal ratings actually skewed? It would be difficult to argue that the distribution of performance appraisal ratings in a given organization should approximate a bell-shaped curve (since organizations do not hire at random and are constantly, if not always successfully, trying to better the quality of the herd), how much of a skew actually exists? In one of the most intriguing aspects of their study, Bretz and Milkovich examined the distribution of performance ratings. They found that although most companies used a rating scheme that provided for five performance levels, only the three highest levels are actually used. As Figure 1-3 shows, only 2 percent of executives, 8 percent of managers, 9 percent of professional employees, and 7 percent of the nonexempts are rated in the bottom two levels. Clearly, they report, the norm has a "leniency bias," where employees are rated at the top end of the scale.

In summarizing the results of their research, Bretz and Milkovich offer five recommendations for improving the effectiveness of the appraisal process:

1. Get employees more involved in the design, development, and administration of the performance appraisal system. Participation creates ego involvement and a sense of commitment to the process.
2. Invest more heavily in training raters to use the system. Train managers not only to observe and document performance but also to communicate information effectively and deliver performance feedback.
3. Create an environment in which performance information is viewed as a resource that managers can use to develop subordinates. Top managers must create a climate in which accurate and

timely performance appraisal is expected of all managers, is taken seriously, and is rewarded.

4. Make performance appraisal the responsibility of the *ratee*, not the *rater*. This fundamental philosophical shift takes the burden to "be nice" from managers and frees them to be honest. As part of this philosophy, employees must be trained to use the feedback from the appraisal process to manage their own careers.

5. Use multiple perspectives (multiple raters), including peer evaluation, to reduce the reliance on a single source. This reduces sampling error by increasing the number of observations and makes raters more comfortable, since they are no longer solely responsible for what happens to the person as a result of the rating.

The Landy and Farr Study: Performance Rating

In a major research project published in *Psychological Bulletin*, Frank Landy and James Farr conducted a study of all research that had been conducted over a thirty-year period on one specific aspect of the entire performance management process: the performance rating.[10] They studied every aspect of performance ratings, including the effect of different rating formats and the influence of varying rater and ratee characteristics. "Typically," the authors say in describing the area that they chose to study, "a supervisor is asked to consider the past performance of one or more subordinates. The period of past performance is typically one year. During that period of time, the supervisor and the subordinate have interacted frequently and probably know each other reasonably well."

While a great deal of their study concentrates on issues that primarily interest only their fellow academicians, there is much practical wheat submerged in the academic chaff. First, they explored what personal characteristics of raters and ratees made a difference in how performance was assessed. What part did age and sex and race and education play? Here's what they found:

Sex   "In the majority of studies, there has been no consistent effect of rater sex on ratings obtained in various contexts." In other words, men are neither tougher nor more lenient than women. Nor do men rate women more gently or strictly than they do other men, or vice versa. Sex appears to be irrelevant.

Race   "Research conducted by the Educational Testing Service in conjunction with the U.S. Civil Service Commission found that in a majority of cases, supervisory raters gave higher ratings to subordinates of their own race than to subordinates of a different race." But the studies also indicated that the differ-

|Age|ence in ratings was on the order of only 2 percent—more important to the statistician or academician than to the line manager or human resources director. As far as peer ratings, the research showed that race had no effect.
Two studies explored whether age made any difference. One found that younger supervisors were less lenient than older ones; the other found no difference at all.|
|Education|Only one study indicated that the supervisor's education level has any effect on how supervisors rated subordinates. The researchers concluded that rater education was of no practical importance.|

Landy and Farr did repudiate one universally accepted piece of folk wisdom: Peers are not tougher than bosses, they discovered. Three different studies reported that "supervisors were less lenient in their ratings than were the peers of the ratee." Two other studies also found that supervisors were more consistent in their ratings than were peers. As they put it, there was "more interrater agreement with supervisory ratings than with peer ratings." On the other hand, while peers tended to be more lenient than supervisors, peers were more accurate in predicting promotions.

The Towers Perrin and William M. Mercer Studies: How Important Is Performance Appraisal?

In early 1995, Towers Perrin, the large consulting firm, released the results of a survey done with 300 senior executives at midsize and large companies.[11] As reported by *The New York Times,* nine out of ten senior executives told the researchers that people are a company's most important resource, and 98 percent said improved employee performance would boost the bottom line. No news here. Successful executives know how to parrot the company line. But given the chance to rank the strategies most likely to bring about organizational success, they ranked the two "people issues"—investment in people and people performance—near the bottom. The top three slots were assigned to customer satisfaction, financial performance, and product and service quality. Only quality of marketing was ranked lower than the two people issues.

"The executives' view of employees varied by their role," *The New York Times* reported. "The chairman and chief executive level were most likely to lapse into platitudes about people as assets and hiring the best and the brightest. The finance people saw people as strictly a cost to be contained. The line managers, who often are accused of forming a white collar wall of resistance to change, were most likely to see the connection between people and profits."

Patricia Milligan, managing principal in Towers Perrin's Stamford, Connecticut, office, said, "The good news is that line executives, the ones closest to customers, truly understand the relevance of managing their people. They are most likely to say it improves results. They are also the group most likely to correlate investment in people to business strategy."

Another large consulting firm, William M. Mercer, reported the results of a survey of 218 companies with employee evaluation systems. Half of the reporting companies said their evaluations were of only fair to poor value to employees or the organization. Colleen P. O'Neill, a principal in Mercer's Atlanta office, said that given this bleak assessment compared with the potential value of a good performance appraisal system, it is "not surprising that many survey participants are fine tuning and improving their employee evaluation processes." She noted that 44 percent of survey participants had revamped their evaluation processes in the past two years and another 29 percent had plans to do so.

In a summary of the William M. Mercer study, several results paralleling earlier studies were reported:[12]

- 84 percent of the responding companies reported that the results of performance appraisal directly affect merit raises.
- 64 percent said they had redesigned the evaluation process, or planned to so, with such changes as new rating scales.
- 49 percent reported adding new performance categories, such as customer satisfaction measures.
- 48 percent said they had increased, or would increase, their training of managers in how to observe, evaluate, and give feedback to employees. (While 72 percent of the companies said they held managers accountable for the evaluation process, only about half provided training in the use of the process.)

The trend toward more broadly based collection of assessment data, mentioned in almost all other studies, was also noted in the Mercer analysis. Nearly a fifth of the respondents ask some or all employees to rate peers or fellow team members; another fifth plan to start. Upward appraisal was also analyzed by Mercer: 14 percent currently ask employees to rate supervisors' performance; another 8 percent have plans to initiate the process in the future. Most of these multirater systems, they found, have come into being in the past two years.

Tying It All Together

No matter what the specific questions were, or the jobs of the people involved, or the kinds of companies, or even the country in which the study was done, these common factors appear in all the survey data:

1. Performance appraisal is here to stay. The overwhelming majority of organizations use the approach, and there is little discussion of abolishing it. There are probably few other management techniques whose projected life expectancy is so long.
2. There is widespread dissatisfaction with almost everything concerned with performance appraisal. Neither appraisers nor appraisees feel entirely comfortable with the process, and although organizations talk about its importance, they fail to give it the weight that they do to analyses of their financial or marketing situations.

In the early 1970s, David W. Ewing, executive editor of the *Harvard Business Review*, edited a collection of articles about performance appraisal that had appeared in the magazine in the preceding twenty-five years. "Performance appraisal," he wrote, "has come a long way since its origin as a simple, principally one-way communication between a boss and his subordinate. Judging from the articles in this series, the technique still has a way to go before most managers will be satisfied with it. It seems safe to conclude, however, that performance appraisal is not a passing fad. Any technique that can stimulate the kinds of experiment and inquiry described in this series should be around for many years to come."[13]

And, of course, it is. Many of the techniques described in the articles, some now approaching fifty years old, are still used by companies exactly as they were described. And for many companies, changing to some thirty- or forty- or fifty-year-old techniques would amount to a significant improvement in what they are currently doing.

Managerial dissatisfaction also remains, confirmed by the similarity of responses to the most recent studies and surveys. The complaints of managers from the earliest days of performance appraisal—the lack of training, the reluctance to "play God," the skepticism about the value of the form itself, and the use to which the results were put—still remain.

But over the past fifty years the performance appraisal process has matured to the point where it has so solidified itself as a part of organizational life that it is as fundamental as a profit-and-loss statement or a business plan. As James L. Hayes, former president and CEO of the American Management Association, wrote fifteen years ago:

> There are some ideas in management whose time comes and goes and comes again, depending on circumstances of economy or fashion. I have in mind such things as direct costing, the most profitable means of inventory valuation, and the eternal shift between centralization and decentralization. There are other ideas whose time is ever present and whose demands for effective practice are immutable. Of these perhaps the most pertinent for all managers anywhere in no matter what type

of operation—whether in the public or private sector, whether in a
market or socialist economy—is the need for effective performance
appraisal.[14]

Notes

1. Douglas McGregor, "An Uneasy Look at Performance," *Harvard Business Review* (May–June 1957): 5.
2. Herbert H. Meyer, Emanuel Kay, and John R. P. French, Jr., "Split Roles in Performance Appraisal," *Harvard Business Review* (January–February 1965): 81.
3. Ron Zemke, "Do Performance Appraisals Change Performance?" *Training* (May 1991).
4. Ibid.
5. Edwin D. Locke and Gary P. Latham, *A Theory of Goal Setting and Task Performance* (Englewood Cliffs, N.J.: Prentice-Hall, 1990).
6. Society for Human Resource Management and Development Dimensions International, *Performance Management: What's Hot—What's Not, A National Study of Current and Future Practices*, 1994. In addition to the report itself, the findings were analyzed and reported by *Compensation and Benefits Review* (May–June 1994); *Training and Development* (June 1994); *Training* (May 1994); and *Across the Board* (February 1994).
7. The results of the Bretz and Milkovich study appeared in Steven L. Thomas and Robert Bretz, "Research and Practice in Performance Appraisal: Evaluating Employee Performance in America's Largest Companies," *SAM Advanced Management Journal* (Spring 1994).
8. Ibid.
9. Ibid.
10. Frank J. Landy and James L. Farr, "Performance Rating," *Psychological Bulletin* 87 (1), reprinted in Lloyd S. Baird, Richard W. Beatty, and Craig Eric Schneier, *The Performance Appraisal Sourcebook* (Amherst, Mass: Human Resource Development Press), p. 134.
11. The Towers Perrin study was reported by Barbara Presley Noble in *The New York Times*, February 19, 1995.
12. *HRM News*, April 3, 1995.
13. David Ewing, ed., *Performance Appraisal Series: Reprints From the Harvard Business Review* (Boston, Mass.: Harvard Business Review).
14. James L. Hayes, Introduction to Donald L. Kirkpatrick, *How to Improve Performance Through Appraisal and Coaching* (New York: AMACOM, 1982).

Chapter 2
The Performance Management System

Performance appraisal is not an event. It is a process. Even the isolated incident we normally refer to as "giving somebody his performance appraisal" actually involves a large number of events. These events happen in a predictable and sequential fashion, with one completed before the next begins. The links vary from one company to another, but the following chain of events in well-managed companies is reasonably typical:

1. As performance appraisal time approaches, the manager reflects on how well each of his subordinates has done his job over the course of the year.
2. The manager assembles the various forms and paperwork designed by the organization to capture that information and fills them out.
3. The manager decides whether to recommend a compensation change and, if so, the amount of the increase.
4. The forms and recommendations are approved by the manager's supervisor, that person's supervisor, the organization's compensation administrator, and perhaps some other people. The manager then prepares for a discussion with the individual about his performance over the past year.
5. The manager and subordinate meet for about an hour. They talk about the past (how well the person did his job over the past twelve months), the present (the new amount of compensation the employee will now be receiving), and the future (what organizational goals and personal development plans the individual will be expected to achieve during the upcoming twelve months).
6. Both review the paperwork and sign the forms to acknowledge that the process has been completed.
7. The discussion complete, the meeting ends. The manager concludes the sequence by noting any additional comments and sending the paperwork to the personnel department for filing.

This arrangement is fairly typical of what happens at performance appraisal time in many companies. Reviewing the list demonstrates that it is indeed a process we are dealing with and not an individual event.

The Ideal Performance Appraisal Cycle

Among performance appraisal experts, there is a significant amount of agreement that there is an ideal cycle that, if followed, will generally produce superior results. Consultants who help organizations create effective performance appraisals, academicians who study the performance appraisal process as it is used in various organizations, and human resources managers and organizational development practitioners with companies that have successfully developed their own performance appraisal systems come to the same conclusion: Performance appraisal doesn't start with the form, it starts with the job—planning what needs to be done and figuring out how it will be accomplished.

An organization's overall performance management system begins with the development of organizational strategy. Before any assessment of individual performance can be made, the organization's direction must be articulated and communicated.

In some organizations, strategy development is a major responsibility of the company's senior management, who regularly engage in a SWOT analysis—a formal examination of the *strengths, weaknesses, opportunities,* and *threats* confronting the enterprise—or a similar strategy formulation process. In others, particularly smaller, entrepreneurial organizations, the strategy is in the mind of the owner or proprietor. Still other organizations deal with the strategy issue through the formulation of mission statements and the development of "vision and value" manifestos. But until the organization as a whole has defined its goals, neither the goals for organizational units nor individual performance objectives can possibly be created in any meaningful way.

Classic management by objectives (MBO) theory, the core philosophy behind most effective appraisal systems, begins with the requirement that the organization formulate long-range goals and strategic plans. These plans are then supported by developing overall organizational objectives. Derivative objectives are created for major operating units and departments. This cascading process continues until every organization member has set specific and measurable objectives, each of which can be ultimately related to the overall achievement of the organization's strategy.

Once the boss and the subordinate agree on what the job to be done is and how it should be achieved, the next step is straightforward: Do it.

The next step in the cycle is to assess how well the job was done. In the best systems, this appraisal is conducted not just by the supervisor but by the performer as well.

The appraisal of the individual's performance is then reviewed in a face-to-face manager-subordinate meeting—the classic performance appraisal interview. When the meeting is over, the process begins anew. New objectives are set and revised; updated development plans are put in place.

The ideal performance appraisal cycle is thus a five-phase process, beginning after the organization has established its corporate strategy and overall direction.

Phase I: Performance Planning

The appraiser and appraisee meet to plan the upcoming year. In their discussion(s) they come to agreement about five major areas:

1. The *key accountabilities* of the subordinate's job—the major areas within which the subordinate is responsible for getting results
2. The specific *objectives* the subordinate will achieve within each accountability area
3. The *standards* that will be used to evaluate how well the subordinate has achieved each objective
4. The *performance factors*, competencies, or behaviors that will be critical in determining how the results will be achieved
5. The elements of the *development plan* the subordinate will complete during the year

Phase II: Performance Execution

Over the course of the year the subordinate executes the plan agreed to in Phase I. During this time the supervisor is responsible for ongoing feedback and coaching. Elements of the plan that become obsolete are abandoned by mutual agreement; new objectives to respond to changing conditions are established.

Phase III: Performance Assessment

Appraiser and appraisee independently evaluate the degree to which the different elements of the plan were achieved. The manager completes an assessment of the subordinate's performance (the classic performance appraisal report card) and typically has it reviewed and approved by senior management and human resources personnel before discussing it with the subordinate. In an ideal system, the subordinate also completes a self-assessment, collecting data, if necessary, from customers, peers, subordinates, and others.

The subordinate may submit the self-appraisal to the manager to be used as part of the manager's overall assessment, or the manager and the subordinate may review each other's appraisal of the subordinate's performance concurrently as part of the Phase IV discussion.

Phase IV: Performance Review

The appraiser and appraisee meet to review their appraisals. They discuss the results that were achieved and the performance factors that contributed to their accomplishment. Phase III was the creation of the report card; Phase IV is its delivery and discussion. Their discussion includes:

- ▸ Results achieved (*what was done*)
- ▸ Performance or behavioral effectiveness (*how it was done*)
- ▸ Overall performance assessment
- ▸ Development progress

At this meeting the appraiser may discuss compensation changes, or this discussion may be held during a separate meeting at a different time. (Chapter 14 focused on the relationship between pay and performance appraisal and the benefits and disadvantages of combining the pay and appraisal discussions.)

Phase V: Performance Renewal and Recontracting

Phase V repeats Phase I, incorporating the additional data and insights gained during the previous appraisal process. The manager and subordinate revise any of the subordinate's key accountabilities that may have changed over the year and set new objectives and standards for the upcoming appraisal period. Finally, they create updated development goals and action plans. Figure 2-1 illustrates the ongoing and continuous nature of the performance appraisal cycle.

Performance Planning

The performance management model in Figure 2-1 reinforces a critical concept: Before even the most preliminary activities that are commonly considered part of the performance appraisal process can be undertaken, the organization must first have its mission clearly defined. If the organization doesn't know where it wants to go, herculean efforts on the part of organization members won't provide direction.

When the organization's mission and overall objectives are clear, the

Figure 2-1. The Performance Appraisal Cycle

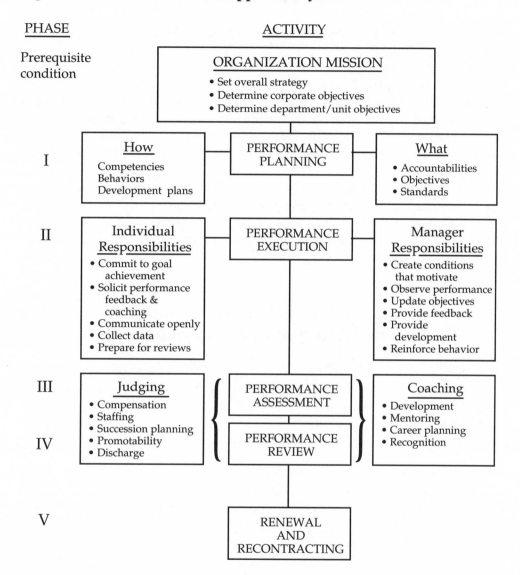

performance planning phase can begin. Performance planning involves completing two critical tasks: (1) establishing measurable objectives for the results or outcomes that the individual's efforts will produce (the *what* of the job) and (2) analyzing the way in which the individual will go about achieving those results or attaining the goals (the *how* of the job). The first task, establishing measurable objectives, is the subject of Chapter 4. The second task, analyzing the way the person goes about doing the job, is the theme of Chapter 5.

Performance Execution

Once accountabilities, objectives, competencies, and development goals have been established, the performance planning phase has been completed. Performance execution—the process of actually managing performance—now begins. The individual knows the results he will be expected to produce and the standards against which his production will be measured. In addition, he knows the important skills or competencies (teamwork, high quality, leadership, customer focus, resourcefulness) the organization expects him to demonstrate as he goes about achieving those goals.

Over the course of the year the individual will go about achieving those results and demonstrating those competencies; the manager's responsibility is to work with him as coach, boss, mentor, trainer, and guide. The activities of the individual and the manager in concert constitute the performance management process.

The Individual's Responsibilities in Performance Management

The primary responsibility for managing performance is borne not by the manager but by the individual. Over the course of the year he or she achieves the objectives and demonstrates the various skills and competencies required for success. Five major activities are involved in the management of personal performance in an organization:

1. Committing to goal achievement
2. Soliciting performance feedback and coaching
3. Communicating openly and regularly with manager
4. Collecting and sharing performance data
5. Preparing for performance reviews

Committing to Goal Achievement

Performance begins with goals, a new and different state of affairs that the individual actively commits to bring about. Note that a goal is neither a requirement nor a desire. If a manager announces to the troops that they must cut costs by 10 percent in the next quarter, this is not a goal, performance analyst Clay Carr points out.[1] Whatever words may be used, it is a requirement. It will not become a goal unless and until the members of the work group choose to expend the time and effort to achieve the 10 percent reduction.

Nor is a goal a desire. If the manager announces that the organization feels that it is important to achieve a 10 percent cost reduction, and all heads in the unit collectively nod, agreeing that this is highly desirable, it is still not a goal. It will not become a goal until the members of the unit commit themselves to seek it actively.

If individuals are going to perform successfully, they must know the answer to the fundamental question: "What goals does the organization expect me to *accomplish*?" This is a different question from, "What tasks does the company expect me to *perform*?" Tasks accomplished are *inputs*; goals achieved are *outputs*. The difference is critical.

To identify accurately the goals the organization expects the individual to achieve requires asking, "What do I produce that is important to my internal or external customer?" This is quite different from asking, "What does my boss want me to do or to know?"

A heavy emphasis on goals, particularly when that emphasis is accompanied by a performance planning process that involves the individual in setting goals and objectives, helps ensure the achievement of important organizational outcomes. It shifts the emphasis of performance management from a focus on tasks and work habits (cooperation, good communications, diligence, punctuality) to work outcomes—projects successfully managed, quality levels increased, greater customer satisfaction.

The literature on the effectiveness of goal setting is enormous and compelling. The evidence is in and it is convincing: The more that goals are clear, worthwhile, and challenging, the greater the chance is that the performer will be motivated to achieve them.

But goals alone won't motivate superior performance, even when these goals are clear, challenging, and worthwhile. Feedback and coaching are required.

Soliciting Performance Feedback and Coaching

While the manager is responsible for providing performance feedback and coaching, the individual is responsible for actively soliciting feedback and making use of the data to improve performance. A highly effective manager will provide a great deal of performance feedback and coaching, but even an individual who works for a weak manager can still solicit assistance and head off potential problems by initiating a coaching session with the manager in advance of a critical meeting or the commencement of a new project. The subordinate who runs her plans by the manager, describing the action she plans to take and soliciting assistance, may be surprised to discover that the manager has something worthwhile to contribute. Even if nothing beneficial directly results from this meeting, the individual will have prevented any surprises and eliminated any possibility of the manager's later complaining that an obvious problem was not foreseen.

Communicating Openly and Regularly with the Manager

Just as the manager is responsible for providing ongoing feedback and for revising work expectations as required during the course of the appraisal period, the subordinate also bears an obligation to communicate regularly.

Collecting and Sharing Performance Data

As projects are completed and goals achieved, the individual needs to advise the manager of the current status of the objectives that were set at the beginning of the period.

Preparing for Performance Reviews

When a review is approaching—whether an informal quarterly progress check or the annual formal performance appraisal discussion—the individual is not a passive subject. The advice for individuals is obvious: Be prepared. The work done in advance will enormously influence the success of the performance appraisal meeting. A new employee can ask coworkers what to expect. If the company uses a standard form, the individual can get a copy and write a personal appraisal, whether or not the procedures require this. He should be honest about his deficiencies and equally straightforward about his successes, writing the appraisal from his supervisor's perspective, as clearly as he can visualize it, so that when he gets the actual appraisal he can see where he has misread the supervisor's perceptions. He also can review his appraisal from a year ago to see how he has done at actually achieving the goals that were agreed to a year ago.

In organizations committed to using a comprehensive performance management process effectively, appraisees are trained on their responsibilities just as appraisers are.

The Manager's Responsibilities in Performance Management

For the manager, six major activities are involved in the ongoing process of performance management during the course of the appraisal period:

1. Creating the conditions that generate subordinate motivation
2. Observing and documenting performance
3. Updating and revising initial objectives, performance standards, and job competency areas as conditions change

4. Providing performance feedback and coaching when problems or opportunities arise
5. Providing developmental experiences
6. Reinforcing effective behavior and progress toward goals

Creating the Conditions That Motivate

The easiest way to discover what actually motivates people to perform is to ask them. Ask a person to recall the job that he had when he was the most motivated. When he has clearly recalled the specific job that generated the greatest feelings of motivation—job satisfaction, drive, enthusiasm, impetus to achieve, or whatever else his definition of motivation may be—ask him to recall the factors that generated those feelings of intense motivation.

What he will say is surprisingly predictable. The factors that are universally reported as the generators of high motivation are the same for almost everyone. Here are the typical answers:

"The job gave me the opportunity to achieve, the chance to accomplish something genuinely important or worthwhile."

"I was recognized for what I accomplished, both in raises and bonuses and in important nonmonetary ways."

"The job provided the opportunity for feedback—I knew how I was doing."

"I was given real [not a mere "sense of"] responsibility."

"The job offered the opportunity to learn and to grow. I was stretched by the job demands."

"I had a significant amount of discretion and a lot of autonomy and say in how the job was done."

"The work itself was stimulating and worthwhile. I got a kick out of what I was doing."

Now ask the same person to remember the time when he was most demotivated, when he was turned off by the job, when dissatisfaction prevailed. When you ask him to list the factors that generated those feelings, he will report these:

"The company's policies were out of date and were administered unfairly or haphazardly."

"The technical supervision I received was inept or incompetent."

"The salary was inadequate."

"The working conditions were shabby."

"The benefits were deficient."

"Interpersonal relationships were tolerable at best. I didn't like my
boss or respect the people I worked with."

The basic difference between the factors reported to be motivators
and those listed as dissatisfiers is that the motivators all deal with *job
content*. Achievement, discretion, feedback, recognition, responsibility, and
learning and growth are all functions of the work itself. Moreover, to a
large extent, they are controllable by the manager.

The dissatisfiers relate to *job context*. Policies, administration, salary,
benefits, working conditions, interpersonal relations, and supervision all
deal with the conditions under which the work is done. A change in any
of these factors will not change the nature of the work that an individual
does. For better or worse, only the conditions under which he does it are
changed. A job that is boring, pointless, and insipid will not be made
absorbing, engrossing, and stimulating merely by boosting the worker's
pay or offering the lollipop of a new dental plan.

Money is an oddity; it appears on both lists. The answer to the old
question about whether money is a motivator is that it depends on how
it is used. When someone includes pay or salary in his list of motivators,
he will usually describe the fact that the pay was not so much lavish but
rather commensurate with the responsibilities he was given. Or he will
talk about a large increase or unanticipated bonus he was awarded in
recognition of his achievements.

Dissatisfaction with pay usually springs from a different source. Demotivated people typically report feeling that they were paid less than
they were worth, or that they got the same pay as others who didn't contribute as much, or they resented the company's "one size fits all" salary
policy.

The factors that primarily influence the amount of dissatisfaction the
individual finds in the job tend to be the ones that individual managers
have the least amount of control over. Few managers can walk into their
work group on a Tuesday morning and tell a stellar subordinate that as
a result of her efforts they will immediately increase her salary 20 percent.
Nor can most managers significantly change the benefits or working conditions or other similar factors.

But managers have an enormous amount of control over the motivators. There are few managers who cannot delegate a high-level task to a
subordinate to increase the opportunity for achievement, or increase a
subordinate's level of discretion by allowing the individual to make decisions on his own, or assign a project that will cause learning and growth.
And there is no manager who does not have the complete power to recognize good performance on the part of a work group member—and recognition is usually the most frequently reported of all of the motivators.

While individuals bear the primary responsibility for managing their performance to achieve the goals and objectives that have been set and to do so in a way that reflects mastery of the job skills or competency factors, the manager bears a responsibility for creating the conditions that allow motivation to flourish. On an ongoing basis, the manager should be reviewing his area of operations, asking such questions as:

> "What high-level, important parts of my job that I am now handling competently myself can I delegate to a subordinate in order to enrich his or her job and increase the motivational opportunities that the job provides?"
> "Are there any decisions or activities that I am asking subordinates to get my advance approval for that I could allow them to handle on their own?"
> "What can I do to create developmental opportunities for members of my work group?"
> "Are there sufficient feedback mechanisms in place so that people can get accurate ongoing information on exactly how well they're doing?"

Observing and Documenting Performance

This least complicated of all performance management tasks involves little more than maintaining the familiar critical incident log, which may be nothing more than a piece of paper kept in the manager's desk. Whenever a critical incident occurs—perhaps a subordinate's performance was noticeably different from the norm, either praiseworthy or substandard—the manager makes a brief and informal note, recording the date, the facts and details about the incident, the specific behavior of the subordinate, and the effect on the work or the people involved.

In addition to serving as reminders of significant events during the year that might otherwise be forgotten when the time for constructing the appraisal comes, these notes can also be used for ongoing coaching during the appraisal period. By using them openly as coaching aids on a continuing basis, the manager gains an additional benefit: It eliminates concerns on the part of subordinates that the boss is "keeping book" on them. If the manager straightforwardly shares the observations recorded and the subordinate discovers that they contain a variety of both positive and negative performance situations that are used to spark coaching discussions, the manager will find that subordinates bring potential problems to his attention early, before challenges become crises.

Some managers use the performance appraisal form to record their critical incident notes. If the appraisal form has been effectively constructed to emphasize both results and behaviors, managers should find it easy to use the form as an informal record-keeping device. This record simplifies the ultimate writing of the formal appraisal itself, since a great deal of the work will have been done incrementally over the year.

Updating and Revising Initial Objectives, Performance Standards, and Job Competency Areas

Rarely will objectives and performance standards remain unchanged over a year. More typically, objectives are achieved and then replaced with new ones; objectives become irrelevant as conditions change and need to be revised or discarded; or business plans or opportunities change, and new objectives need to be added.

To succeed, the performance management system must be dynamic. One indicator of the commitment that an organization has to a performance management system (as opposed to its commitment merely to requiring every supervisor to fill out the form every year) is the degree to which the objectives appraised at the end of the year are unchanged from the objectives that were agreed upon at the start of the year. If they are, it's bad news.

That there will be changes in objectives is usually accepted as given. It does not take a great deal of sophistication to realize that conditions will change during the course of a year, making new and revised objectives necessary. What is more difficult for organization members to accept is that there may also be changes in performance standards over the course of the year. If the demands and challenges the organization faces change over the course of the year, the standards of performance expected from its members will also need to change.

Providing Feedback and Coaching

Few other ideas are as generally misunderstood as feedback. Too often we use it to mean, "I want to tell you something" (as in, "I want to give you some feedback on your performance"). This overly broad approach muddles the concept and degrades its usefulness. Feedback has one, and only one, useful meaning: *information on progress toward accomplishing a goal based on some standard.*[2] Without both a goal and a standard that defines success in accomplishing the goal, feedback is useless. If the information shared does not concern a goal or if there is no standard by which to measure performance, then it is not feedback; it is merely data or opinion.

Feedback is not information alone. It is information that has the ability to assist the performer to make midcourse corrections that increase the probability of goal attainment. When performance problems arise, developing workable solutions requires examining the goals, standards, and feedback the individual is using. Deficiencies in one or more of these areas are the frequent cause of large numbers of performance problems. If one factor is defective, no amount of good work on another can produce an overall acceptable performance improvement.

Coaching for improved performance is one of the critical skills in the performance management process.[3] The key points for conducting a coaching session are found in Figure 2-2.

In addition to coaching for performance improvement, there are two subtle opportunities for coaching a subordinate that managers often fail

Figure 2-2. Key Points for Conducting a Coaching Session

Before the Meeting

1. Determine desired and actual performance.
2. Determine the good business reasons that the problem must be solved.
3. Determine the logical consequences if the problem continues.
4. Determine the appropriate action step.

During the Meeting

1. Confirm that the planned action is appropriate.
2. Gain the employee's agreement to change.
3. Determine the action the employee will take.

After the Meeting

1. Document the discussion.
2. Follow up to make sure that the problem has been solved.

to take advantage of: coaching after a particularly successful experience and coaching in advance of an important event.

Coaching After Success

Management consultant and speaker Allan Weiss, in talking with fellow consultants about how they can improve their platform skills, makes a wise suggestion. He recommends that when someone says, "I really liked your presentation," instead of just thanking the person for the compliment and moving on, ask the individual, "What was it about the presentation that you liked?" By determining exactly what it is that the person liked about the presentation, Weiss emphasizes, you gain valuable data for improving future presentations.

Weiss's advice is applicable to a large number of situations unrelated to speechmaking. Too often managers offer a positive evaluation without discussing the factors that led them to form that opinion. If all the manager says is, "You did a good job," all the subordinate knows is that the manager is happy. If there is an explanation of the reasons behind the comment, however, the subordinate now knows what the manager takes into account in evaluating performance and is able to use that information to maintain performance at a high level. Otherwise all the manager may be doing is to generate superstitious behavior, reinforcing whatever random event the subordinate may assume the boss was referring to.

The Center for Creative Leadership confirms Weiss's recommendation. It reports, "Research on excellent learners indicates the following: They analyze successes minutely. They don't focus on what happened as much as why it happened. While they learn from mistakes and failures, they spend less energy on them because many times their mistakes are a reflection of their weaknesses and limits. It is more common for so-so learners to endlessly worry about their weaknesses and in effect beat a dead horse."[4]

Coaching Before an Event

The other frequently missed opportunity is to coach in advance of an event. For example, when both a manager and a subordinate will be attending an important meeting, the manager can have an pivotal impact on the subordinate's skill development by coaching the subordinate on what she should be aware of and the subtle cues and clues the manager will be reading.

Managers can often develop subordinates more effectively by coaching in advance of an event than by critiquing and debriefing afterward. Besides increasing the effectiveness of their subordinates, there are few better ways to demonstrate leadership than by this kind of preparation.

In addition to increasing the possibilities that the outcome will be successful, the manager builds an enormous amount of goodwill and respect.

Providing Developmental Experiences

Although individuals are responsible for their own development, managers bear a responsibility for making developmental opportunities available. At a minimum this means encouraging participation in training sessions and management development programs. Too often, though, organizations think exclusively about training programs when considering employee and management development.

Robert Eichinger, an adjunct faculty member of the Center for Creative Leadership and a consultant in executive development, strongly advocates abandoning the emphasis on "courseware" as a primary development tool. Together with Michael Lombardo of the CCL, Eichinger's research on executive development has focused on the question: What are the competencies that are supported by research as determinants of executive success?

Eichinger and Lombardo found sixty-seven competencies—such capabilities, traits, and aptitudes as strategic agility, decisiveness, integrity, written communication skills, and energy level. After identifying the research-supported competencies, Eichinger then analyzed the responses of three thousand successful executives to the question, "Where/how did you develop that competency?" Multiple reporting yielded over ten thousand replies to assess.

Whatever the competency, Eichinger found that very few could be developed through traditional training and educational programs. Most of the experiences that resulted in the development of competence were directly job related, and most of the rest were a function of special assignments. Few came as a result of traditional development efforts.

In meeting her responsibilities for developing subordinates as part of the organizational performance management system, the perceptive manager will go far beyond checking the class schedule issued by the training department or the offerings in the catalog of the local community college. Instead, she will be alert to opportunities for development in place that ultimately offer far more occasions for genuine development than any form of courseware can possibly provide—among them:

- Handling a difficult negotiation with a customer (or a typical negotiation with a difficult customer)
- Going to a college campus to be a recruiter
- Planning an off-site meeting or conference
- Serving at a booth during a trade show
- Managing the visit of a VIP
- Drafting a speech for a senior executive[5]

Chapter 13 explores the development process in detail.

Reinforcing Effective Behavior and Progress Toward Goals

The final requirement of an ongoing performance management process is to reinforce the subordinate's accomplishments in acting in effective ways and in achieving progress toward accomplishing the objectives that were set in the performance planning process.

Reinforcing desired performance may be the most neglected of all performance management activities. In his classic article, "On the Folly of Rewarding A While Hoping for B," Steven Kerr, former dean of the faculty at the University of Southern California and now vice president of corporate management development for General Electric, wryly notes: "Whether dealing with monkeys, rats or human beings, it is hardly controversial to state that most organisms seek information concerning what activities are rewarded, and then seek to do (or at least pretend to do) those things, often to the virtual exclusion of activities not rewarded. Nevertheless, numerous examples exist of reward systems that are fouled up in that the types of behavior rewarded are those which the rewarder is trying to discourage, while the behavior desired is not rewarded at all."[6]

Kerr offers abundant examples. Universities, he points out, hope for good teaching but reward professors almost exclusively for research and publications. Coaches laud the importance of teamwork and a one-for-all spirit but distribute rewards according to individual performance. Even the reporting of wrongdoing has been corrupted, Kerr notes, by an incredibly incompetent reward system that provides for whistleblowing employees to collect up to 30 percent of the total amount of a fraud without a stated limit. Thus prospective whistleblowers are actually encouraged to delay reporting a fraud—even to participate in its continuance—in order to run up the total and thus their percentage of the take. Kerr's message to managers is not only that effective performance during the year must be reinforced but also that a degree of caution must be used in determining exactly what performance to reinforce.

It is not uncommon in organizational life to hope for A and reward B. We hope for a commitment to quality; we then reward shipping on schedule, even with defects. We hope for candor and surfacing bad news early; we reward reporting good news and agreeing with the boss. We hope for teamwork and—most commonly in the performance appraisal process—reward exclusively individual effort.

Kerr admonishes managers to explore the types of behavior that are currently being rewarded. "Chances are excellent," he argues, "that managers will be surprised by what they find—that their firms are not rewarding what they assume they are. In fact, such undesirable behavior by organization members as they have observed may be explained largely by the reward system in use. This is not to say that all organizational behavior is determined by formal rewards and punishments. Certainly it is true that in the absence of formal reinforcement some soldiers will be patriotic, some players will be team oriented, and some employees will care about doing their job well. The point, however, is that in such cases the rewarder is not *causing* the behavior desired but is only a fortunate bystander. For an organization to *act* upon its members, the formal reward system should positively reinforce desired behavior, not constitute an obstacle to be overcome."

Completing the Cycle

Supervisor and subordinate, appraiser and appraisee have engaged in their performance management responsibilities during the year. At the end of the period, the comprehensive performance management system diagram calls for the formal performance appraisal—the comparison of results delivered with objectives set.

The performance management diagram (see Figure 2-1) illustrates the two primary functions involved in Phases III and IV in most organizations: judging and coaching. Not only are these different, but often they seem to be incompatible.

Judging means to assess performance: the preparation and delivery of the report card. In most systems a rating is assigned, and decisions about compensation change flow either primarily or exclusively from that rating. Chapter 6 explains how to assess an individual's performance accurately and equitably.

Coaching means to develop the individual in the current job and prepare the individual for the responsibilities the organization will expect this person to meet in the future. Chapters 7 (on the appraisal discussion) and 13 (on employee development) are particularly useful in this area.

The final phase of the ideal performance management system is renewal and recontracting, whereby the manager and the subordinate plan the next year's objectives, making all of the adjustments and revisions necessary to take into account the changes and accomplishments of the past twelve months. The process begins again.

Is the Approach Too Complicated?

This five-phase continuous performance management cycle may seem excessively demanding to organizations that still see performance appraisal as a once-a-year event, yet many of the processes and operations that I have described are already happening in most organizations right now. The only difference is that they are happening in an informal and unsystematic way. Additionally many managers—particularly strong and effective ones—are already using this approach with their subordinates. They are setting annual objectives and talking about performance factors, though they may not use those words. Making the process systematic will reinforce their approach and encourage other managers to become as effective.

But even if the approach in fact takes more time than whatever the organization is currently doing, the important question to ask is this: "Is this good use of the managers' and the organization's time?" Will the additional time spent turn out to be a cost or an investment? The additional time required by this approach is spent primarily in an increase in planning for the upcoming year and in periodic progress reviews. The activities involved in Phases III and IV—appraising the subordinate's performance and then discussing the results of that appraisal with the individual—are probably the same as the organization is doing now, except that the individual actions are made orderly, sequential, and visible.

The time spent in determining the organization's mission and in Phase I, Performance Planning, ensures the organization that the activities of each member are aligned with the organization's mission, and when variances do occur, they are caught and corrected quickly.

Periodic progress reviews based on preestablished performance objectives and targets, the essence of Phase II, are the surest means of reducing the concerns that both appraisers and appraisees feel when they begin a performance appraisal discussion without having talked in a planned and structured way about the subject since they met twelve months before. Periodic reviews give both people a clear notion in advance what will be contained on the form; in most cases, the document merely confirms what both of them have talked about all along.

Phases III and IV are at the heart of performance appraisal. The greatest emphasis of this book is on constructing systems and procedures to allow every individual with responsibilities for managing the performance appraisal system to fulfill those responsibilities at least at the level of "Fully Meets and Frequently Exceeds Expectations."

Phase V involves no activity. It serves as a simple reminder that performance management is a process, a system, a cycle. Once we believe we have finished with it, it all starts again from the beginning. That's just the way it should be.

Notes

1. Clay Carr, "The Ingredients of Good Performance," *Training* (August 1993): 51–54.
2. Ibid.

3. In *Discipline Without Punishment* (New York: AMACOM, 1995), I devote a chapter to the process of coaching when performance problems arise in order to forestall the need for a formal disciplinary discussion.
4. *Benchmarks: A Development Learning Guide* (Queensboro, N.C.: Center for Creative Leadership, 1994), p. 55.
5. These suggestions are among those found in Michael M. Lombardo and Robert W. Eichinger, *Eighty-Eight Assignments for Development in Place* (Queensboro, N.C.: Center for Creative Leadership, 1989).
6. Steven Kerr, "On the Folly of Rewarding A While Hoping for B," *Academy of Management Executive* 9, no. 1 (1995).

Chapter 3
Approaches to Appraisal

This chapter focuses on what most people consider to be the heart of the performance appraisal process: the appraisal form.

I often urge managers and human resources professionals to accept the idea that the appraisal form itself may be one of the least important elements of the whole appraisal process. And yet although I continue to be convinced that it is the process that is important and not simply the form, I understand that the form is the most visible manifestation of the entire process. Indeed, an organization's form tells a lot about where that company puts its energies and what it considers to be important.

The performance appraisal form serves as a report card for organization members. Just as we can gain some insights into the approach to education that different schools may take by examining the report cards they use to evaluate student achievement, so can we learn about the processes and behaviors and results an organization considers important by looking at its report card: the performance appraisal form it has chosen to use.

No organization is required to have a performance appraisal process. There is nothing in the law that says that a company must engage in performance appraisal. For companies that do choose to use a performance appraisal process (almost every single major company and the great majority of smaller ones), nothing in the law specifies what the form must look like or must contain or must proscribe. The law only prohibits companies from using performance appraisal—a test in the law's eyes—in ways that result in unlawful discrimination. Provided it does not discriminate illegally, a company is free to appraise performance in any way it chooses.

In this chapter we explore various approaches to performance appraisal and examine forms that reflect the approach under discussion. The chapter seeks to answer these questions: What alternatives are available? How good are they? How do they work? What kinds of problems do they create?

Appraisal Alternatives

To understand the essential differences in performance appraisal approaches, it helps to realize that different forms focus on different parts of the performance process. In this chapter we examine the small number of specific approaches, each one completely different from the other, that organizations use to appraise performance. Almost no organization uses any of these approaches to the complete exclusion of all other techniques for assessing performance; companies mix and match different approaches in order to design their unique form. But it is easier to understand the universe of alternatives available by understanding that although every company may have its own unique form, there are only a limited number of independent models that a company can draw on to make its own proprietary form.

For over twenty years I have been collecting examples of performance appraisal forms from organizations around the world. In that time I have found very few pure examples of any of the approaches I discuss; almost every form contains some mix of various styles. But if we can understand the broad areas that a performance appraisal system can focus on, then we can more appropriately combine different approaches to create one that is unique, appropriate, and effective for a particular organization's needs, culture, people, and history.

In several cases, I have removed the name of the organization from the form. Some companies were proud of the approach to performance appraisal they had developed and are happy to be identified. Others, either believing that their approach to performance appraisal provides them with a definite competitive advantage or concerned that their performance appraisal form does not accurately reflect the quality of their management processes as well as it might, preferred anonymity. But every example, unless clearly stated otherwise, is from an actual organization and is or was used as its primary performance appraisal tool.

A Job Performance Model

We will start with an uncomplicated model of job performance shown in Figure 3-1. In unadorned form, this diagram illustrates the four basic

Figure 3-1. The Job Performance Model

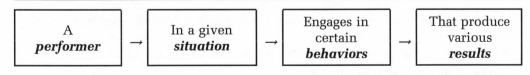

components that make up job performance: a performer, a situation, behaviors, and results—for example:

Performer	Susan Edwards, a secretary . . .
Situation	When the phone rang at 3:30 yesterday afternoon . . .
Behavior	Continued typing until it had rung six times before answering. She then picked it up and said, "Yeah?" After a pause, she said, "He's not here . . . no, I don't know when he's expected . . . sorry."
Result	Her manager later got a call from his manager complaining about the rude way in which he had been treated when he called.

Here is a somewhat more complex example:

Performer	Constance Bell, Ph.D., a senior R&D research scientist . . .
Situation	Was assigned to create and implement a business strategy to reduce the Food and Drug Administration approval time for new products. She was relieved of other responsibilities for four months, was assigned two junior team members, and was given a budget of $94,000.
Behavior	By means of a communications plan using colleagues in other industries and government, frequent visits to Washington, and participation in several conferences, . . .
Result	Bell and her team arranged for a joint industry-government approval roundtable to be held. The roundtable agreed to eliminate one and modify three approval procedures that industry analysis predicted would reduce average approval time from thirty-seven to thirty-two months.

These examples illustrate the four unrelated aspects of the job that must be examined when an individual's performance is evaluated.

Situation Analysis

The job situation is often critical to job success but almost never a primary focus of the performance appraisal form. Instead, almost every performance appraisal form concentrates on one of the other three factors: the performer, the behavior, or the results.

Evaluations of the situation as a formal part of the appraisal process are usually incorporated only into the appraisal summary when those situational elements are so extreme as to need discussion in order to understand the individual's performance or the appraiser's rating of it. Consider a salesman with an objective of selling 100 cases per week. At the end of the year, his weekly sales average 110 cases, placing him at 110 percent of his quota or objective. Is this good or a poor result? If we look only at results, he has certainly exceeded the objective, so it would seem that a strong case could be made for awarding him an above-average rating.

Next consider how he went about doing the job—the performance factors, competencies, or behaviors. Again, assume that he was at least fully satisfactory in the way he performed: He was diligent about making cold calls, regularly followed up with existing customers, prospected for new customers in his territory regularly, handled every request and complaint promptly and courteously, and studied all of the product brochures and technical advisories. Again an above-average rating seems justified.

Now assume that during the appraisal period his market grew by 40 percent. In spite of that growth, his sales exceeded quota by only 10 percent. With this information about the situation, even a rating of barely satisfactory performance might be difficult to justify. On the other hand, assume that four of his major outlets went out of business during the year. In spite of that, his sales exceeded the projection by 10 percent. Given this situation, a rating that reflects truly heroic performance might be appropriate.

In each of these situations, the performer, the behavior, and the results were identical; the only change was in the situation. For complete accuracy in appraisal, the situation must be taken into account, whether or not it is formally included on the form.

Figure 3-2 displays part of the appraisal form of a major British chemical company. It is a rare example of formal situation analysis being included on a performance appraisal form.

Performer-Focused Appraisals

The classic performer-focused appraisal approach is the trait scale. Organizations using this approach typically identify a constellation of traits or characteristics, qualities, or personal attributes, the possession of which is assumed to result in good job performance. Forget what he does; ignore the results he produces. Just ask the question, what kind of guy is he? That's the issue that a performer-focused appraisal form addresses.

Performance appraisal began with performer assessments. Early attempts at appraisal provided lists of traits assumed to be desirable in get-

Figure 3-2. Formal Situation Analysis

SECTION TWO REVIEW OF PERFORMANCE	Please tick in appropriate box. Where qualification/amplification to the assessment is necessary please use 'remarks' column.		
(A) Sales Targets	(Assessment should take note of competition, supply position, price trends, Government legislations, etc.)		Remarks
	While market size is:		
	Increasing	Stable	Declining
1. Exceeded sales target			
2. Achieved sales target			
3. Unable to achieve sales targets			

ting the job done and then asked the raters to assess the degree to which that trait was present or absent. After World War II, most large organizations and many sophisticated smaller ones began the routine assessment of supervisors, managers, and others in the middle of the organization. Top managers typically were exempt from the indignity of having their traits assessed, and except in some unusual cases, nonexempt and hourly personnel were also spared.

For the most part these were unsophisticated systems. A collection of traits was assembled—for example, loyalty, decisiveness, self-motivation, cheerfulness, adaptability, cooperation. (The list could include any characteristic that the form creator felt was useful to possess, frequently paralleling the Boy Scout creed: thrifty, brave, reverent, and kind.) Presented with the list of traits, the assessor would place a check mark in the accompanying box to indicate whether the individual undergoing evaluation possessed the trait in question. Slightly more sophisticated trait scale systems asked the appraiser to mark a rating scale to indicate the degree to which the trait was present.

Figure 3-3, an appraisal form from a large bank in Southeast Asia, represents the purest trait scale type of performance appraisal form that I have found. It contains thirty-one traits or attributes sorted into three categories, each attached to a 1 through 5 scale (Poor through Excellent). The only variation from absolute trait-scale purity is the addition of a column allowing the assessor to assign a weight to each element, to indicate the possibility that "Manner and General Appearance" or "Neatness and Efficiency" might have a different value to the organization than "Relationship with Customers" or "Handling of the Bank's Confidential Matters and Secrets."

Trait scales continue to be used in a number of organizations, fre-

Figure 3-3. Trait Scale Performance Appraisal Form

STRICTLY CONFIDENTIAL	STAFF APPRAISAL FORM	FOR OFFICERS ONLY

Name: ....

PART IV—ASSESSMENT OF PERSONAL QUALITIES AND PERFORMANCE
(To be completed by the Immediate Superior and countersigned by the Head of Department/Branch Manager/Head of Division/Regional Manager.)

	I	II					III	IV
	Weight (Max 5)	Excellent	Very Good	Good	Fair	Poor	Actual Scr. (Col. I × II)	Possible Scr. (Wt. Given × 5)
PERSONAL QUALITIES		5	4	3	2	1		
1. Manner and General Appearance								
2. Attitude Towards Work								
3. Drive and Determination								
4. Discipline and Compliance to Rules								
5. Willingness/Capacity to Learn								
6. Relationship With Customers								
7. Relationship With Fellow Employees								
8. Ambition and Self-Motivation								
9. Handling of Bank's Confidential Matters and Secrets								
10. Public Relations Approach								
Sub Total								
PERFORMANCE/KNOWLEDGE								
11. Reliability and Accuracy								
12. Work Speed/Productivity								
13. Quality of Work								
14. Neatness and Efficiency								
15. Knowledge of Job								
16. Ability on the Job								
17. Adaptability								
18. Problem-Solving Ability								
19. Decisiveness and Soundness of Judgment								
20. Oral Communication								
21. Written Communication								
22. Knowledge of Banking (Theoretical)								
23. Knowledge of Banking (Practical)								
Sub Total								
MANAGERIAL/EXECUTIVE ABILITIES								
24. Utilization of Office Hours								
25. Initiative and Creativity								
26. Planning and Organizing Ability								
27. Leadership Ability								
28. Development of Subordinates								
29. Exercise of Authority								
30. Delegation and Control								
31. Cooperation and Teamwork								
Sub Total								

Figure 3-4. Trait Scale Section of a Performance Appraisal Form

IV. ATTITUDE/PROFESSIONALISM
     Overall Rating   U   P   C   O
                                       □   □   □   □

     Mental position/feeling toward job and the company _____

     _____

     Interaction with coworkers and supervisor _____

     _____

     Cooperates and readily accepts changes in assignments and procedures

     _____

quently mixed in with measures of actual job behavior or skill. Figure
3-4, from a large finance company, seeks a measure of the trait of
attitude/professionalism, the final attribute assessed on the form after attendance, quality of work, and quantity of work.

Deficiencies of Trait-Based Systems

Vestiges of trait or performer appraisal remain in some performance appraisal systems, but for the most part, sophisticated approaches abandon
the focus on the traits the individual possesses and concentrate instead on
actual observations of behavior. The difficulty with trait assessment is not
that it is inaccurate (although a large body of evidence suggests that is
true) but that it is not predictive: The presence or absence of the trait tells
little about how well the person has done the job.

The few benefits of trait-based approaches—ease in construction, universal applicability—are illusory. There is almost universal agreement that
two primary purposes of a performance appraisal are to provide feedback
and to assist in setting goals. Trait-based appraisals contribute little of
value in either feedback or goal setting. To learn that my boss judges
me deficient in cooperation or attitude is not functional feedback; being
assessed as lacking in ambition and self-motivation is unlikely to produce
productive movement toward change. The trait scale assessment tells the
appraisee only what his boss's judgment is; it provides no usable data for
change.

Counterbalancing the benefit of trait scales' universal applicability is that while one size may fit all to some small degree, it fits no size well. What is critical or important in one job may be minor or irrelevant in another. Even allowing the appraiser to add different weights to the trait to indicate relative priorities or write comments to elaborate on any judgment does little to communicate the specific aspects of the job that are of crucial importance.

Trait assessment has a profound deficiency: It is doubtful that any unadulterated trait-based assessment would survive legal scrutiny. It is virtually impossible to prove the job relevance of a trait scale, particularly when those scales are used across various families of jobs. It is virtually impossible to demonstrate validity and reliability. Using a trait-based assessment instrument increases the possibility of common appraisal errors being introduced: halo effect, leniency, central tendency, and others. This is particularly true because managers are reluctant to rate an individual low on those traits that reflect vital personal qualities: maturity, creativity, and integrity.

The final flaw with trait-based assessments is that even when the judgment is accurate, it is not useful. It may well be true that the person who has been judged weak in professionalism or lacking in leadership or insufficiently adaptable is indeed so deficient. Now what? To tell someone that he lacks leadership, no matter how accurate that humiliating judgment may be, is to provide no help in ameliorating the situation. Performer-based appraisals compel the manager to rate what the employee *is*, not what he *does* or *achieves*. Although it may be possible to change what I am, it is far easier—and more defensible—for my boss to live with what I am and insist that I change what I do.

In his major work, *Management: Tasks, Responsibilities, Practices*, Peter Drucker puts the matter simply:

> An employer has no business with a man's personality. Employment is a specific contract calling for specific performance and nothing else. Any attempt of an employer to go beyond this is usurpation. It is abuse of power. An employee owes no "loyalty," he owes no "love," and no "attitudes"—he owes performance and nothing else.[1]

Where Performer-Based Assessment Is Appropriate

There are several places within the domain of human resources management where an assessment of an individual's traits and characteristics may well be a legitimate and valid subject of study. Certainly it is germane to ask, "What kind of person are we looking for?" when interviewing candidates, to make sure that they fit the culture of the company. When the issue is manager development, it is valid to assess the attributes and qualities of the individual in developing a prescription for improving the probability of long-term success. And in selecting candidates for promotion, assessment centers can help fill the gap in understanding who the individual is, to supplement the data on behaviors and results obtainable from a review of performance appraisals and other sources.

But here we are talking specifically about the appraisal of an individual's performance: How well did this person do the job he was paid to do? Personal qualities may well have had a beneficial or deleterious effect on the outcomes, but their assessment is not the supervisor's mission. The job here is to evaluate the performance regardless of the makeup of the performer.

Behavior-Based Appraisals

Trait scales focus on the performer. Far more valid and important is the approach that concentrates on the behaviors in which the individual engages in the performance of the job. In assessing behaviors, skills, and competencies, we are looking not at what the individual is but rather at what the person does. The question is not what kind of guy he is but how he goes about doing the job.

The most commonly used term for this aspect of the appraisal process is *performance factors.* In Chapter 5 I describe the complete procedure for identifying the performance factors that should be included on an appraisal form and the various alternative procedures for assessing them. Most organizations today include performance factors as part of their appraisal process. Many identify the specific factors to be assessed, together with a definition or description and a scale for the assessor to use in rating the quality of performance. Others simply list the performance factors to be considered and ask the appraiser to summarize and assess the individual's performance in this area.

BancOne Corporation, like most other organizations with effective appraisal processes, places the greatest emphasis on the assessment of results achieved. But it also requires analysis of performance factors, as Figure 3-5 shows. Similarly, a large manufacturing company lists seventeen performance factors for assessment, each with suggestions for aspects to be considered, as well as space for comments to be added. The first few items are shown in Figure 3-6.

A large oil company used a more sophisticated approach. It combines assessment of performance factors with the expectation that supervisors will generate formal standards of performance for the factor and then assess the individual's actual performance, in addition to merely indicating an assessment judgment on a scale, as shown in Figure 3-7.

Figure 3-5. Analysis of Performance Factors at BancOne Corporation

Section 2B—Important Performance Factors
The following are examples of factors that may be important to the employee's work performance. Provide comments in the space below only for the important factors that apply to this employee. Add your own factors as appropriate. Note the overall level of achievement.

PERFORMANCE FACTOR

MANAGERIAL PERFORMANCE FACTORS

A. Business and Operational Management
Financial planning/forecasting, controlling
Asset quality
Compliance and internal controls

B. Staff Management and Development
Staff planning, selection and development
Performance planning, counseling and appraisal
Teamwork (within department/across organization)
Communication (informing, impact, listening)
Affirmative Action/EEO

C. Quality Process
Solicits customer feedback/complaints
Measures key customer/financial indicators
Develops and reaches quality plan objectives
Reinforces reward and recognition efforts

OTHER PERFORMANCE FACTORS

A. Attendance and Punctuality

B. Customer Relations (internal/external)
Monitors customer/client feedback
Solicits/responds to employee suggestions
Develops new/improved customer relations

C. Teamwork and Staff Relations
Considers opinions and personal needs of others
Serves on cross-functional teams
Utilizes participative management techniques

D. Communication
Effective informing and listening skills
Quality written and oral communication
First impressions shops

E. Adaptability/Flexibility
Willingness/ability to learn and adapt
Demonstrates awareness of own strengths/weaknesses

F. Planning and Organizing
Makes plans that are realistic and thorough
Makes good use of time

G. Analytical/Decision Making
Identifies and distinguishes key issues
Makes quality decisions with information available
Utilizes IDEA system tools and techniques

H. Problem Resolution
Works toward best solutions
Recognizes agreements and generates consensus

I. Technical Job Knowledge
Understands department and function
Keeps current in field

J. Personal Development
Seeks increased responsibility
Attends quality training and utilizes self-development opportunities

OTHER:

COMMENTS (USE ADDITIONAL PAGES IF NECESSARY)

2B—Level of Achievement: ☐ Exceeds most ☐ Fully meets ☐ Meets the majority ☐ Performance unacceptable

Figure 3-6. Analysis of Performance Factors at a Manufacturing Company

Part II—Job Behaviors How well did this person:	Comments—Provide comments on job behaviors that will help the employee (a) understand what this company values, (b) recognize and capitalize on his/her strengths, (c) improve in needed areas.
1. KNOW THE JOB? (Demonstrated expertise? Handled unusual situations efficiently because of job knowledge and experience?) 2. PLAN AND ORGANIZE WORK? (Set objectives and priorities? Managed personal resources efficiently to meet objectives?) 3. ANALYZE PROBLEMS? (Identified relevant issues? Evaluated crucial issues? Clarified unknowns?) 4. INITIATE WORK? (Started assignments without prompting? Independently contributed ideas and projects?) 5. MAKE DECISIONS? (Used good judgment? Timely? Effective? Took appropriate risks?)	

Finally, GTE Telephone Operations not only identifies a host of performance factors clustered within many different domains (for example, motivation, support, work structure, and technical and professional knowledge) but then requires the assessor to indicate both the importance of the skill in the successful accomplishment of job requirements as well as the degree to which the individual applied the skill. Figure 3-8 illustrates the competencies included in the "Personal Effectiveness" category.

Behaviorally Anchored Rating Scales

Behaviorally Anchored Rating Scales (BARS), a notable departure from other appraisal methods, take the analysis of performance factors to a significantly higher level of sophistication. One major difference from the approaches I have just illustrated is that BARS is uniquely designed to

Figure 3-7. Analysis of Performance Factors at a Large Oil Company

Undesirable	Standard Below	Standard Average	Standard Above	Outstanding
Wastes supplies; mishandles equipment; never considers cost factors.	Tends to disregard cost considerations; not concerned.	Usually careful with supplies and equipment; tends to be cost conscious.	Cost conscious; makes attempts to control costs.	Always cost conscious; makes recommendations to reduce costs.

STANDARDS OF PERFORMANCE: _____

_____

_____

ACTUAL PERFORMANCE: _____

_____

_____

Figure 3-8. Analysis of Performance Factors at GTE

GTE Values

			Importance of Skill	Application of Skill
Q—Quality	I—Innovation			
B—Benchmarking	T—Technology			
P—People	E—Employee Involvement			
M—Market Sensitivity	and Teamwork			
	Ability to:		(C)(R)(M)(NA)	(S)(E)(G)(NO)

Do the right things to improve quality. (Q)

Produce top quality work for customers. (Q)

Set objectives about quality. (Q)

Be aware of what other companies/competitors are doing in area of responsibility. (B)

Identify and act on competitive benchmarks and gaps. (B)

Promote teamwork and establish cooperative and positive working relationships. (E) appraise a specific job. Unlike the assessments of performance factors that can easily be used across a multitude of positions (both the president and the sweeper can be rated in terms of their job knowledge or quality of work), the BARS technique concentrates on one job only. This turns out to be one of its greatest strengths and major shortcomings.

The BARS approach was developed in 1963 by psychologists Patricia Smith and Lorne Kendall for the National League of Nursing. Since the appraisal form would concentrate exclusively on one specific job, the consultants got both the workers and the supervisors together for an initial meeting to identify all of the important dimensions for effective performance for that job. Let us look at how to create BARS appraisal for the job of receptionist.

Step 1

Start by calling a meeting of all of the company's receptionists and their supervisors and ask them to make a list of the most important dimensions of the job. Fairly quickly the list will take shape:

Job	Receptionist
Critical Elements	Greet visitors to the office
	Answer the telephone
	Type
	Take messages
	Water the plants

Step 2

Once the group agrees on the critical dimensions of the job—the key tasks to be performed—they (or, in the most rigorous BARS development efforts, a different group) then generate examples of effective, average, and ineffective behavior. The facilitator will ask them to think about all the things they had ever seen a person holding the job under analysis do: good, bad, or indifferent. "Make no judgments about the quality of the performance," the facilitator would instruct the group as they struggled to describe specific examples of behavior without making any interpretations or using generalizations. "Just assume that you are observing the individual do something, and tell me exactly what it is that you see and hear." The result is a catalog of behavioral incidents.

Continuing with the receptionist example, the group might describe such behaviors as "Answered the telephone on the second ring," "Did not acknowledge a visitor's presence in the reception area until the individual had begun to speak," "Asked a fellow employee walking by if the coffee maker needed to be refilled," "Said 'sure' and smiled when a manager asked if she could help with overflow typing," and so on.

Step 3

The next step is to connect the various behaviors to the appropriate dimensions. Another group assembles, reviews both the list of job elements and the list of sample behaviors, and then attaches each behavior to the job dimension that it describes. In most cases, the assignment is obvious: "Answered the telephone on the second ring" belongs to the "Answer the telephone" dimension; "Did not acknowledge a visitor's presence in the reception area until the individual had begun to speak" fits neatly into the "Greet visitor to the office" category.

Step 4

The next step involves scaling. Each behavioral example is anchored to a rating scale at the point along the scale that represents its degree of "goodness" or "badness." Assume that a 5 rating indicates superior performance and a 1 abysmal performance. Within the job dimension of "Greet visitors to the office," the following scale might emerge:

Rating	*Behavior*
5	Smile, greet visitor by name, and offer refreshments if the person sought is not immediately available.
4	Say, "May I help you?" and then tell the visitor that the person sought would be free in a few minutes.
3	Look up from typing, say, "Hello," then wait for the visitor to state the reason for the visit.
2	Not acknowledge the visitor's presence until visitor asks for help and then say, "I don't know if he's here or not."
1	Walk out of the reception area as soon as the visitor enters, telling the visitor to wait in the hall until he or she returns.

Similarly, for the job dimension "Answer telephone," the scale might include the following behavioral anchors:

Rating	*Behavior*
5	Answer phone on first ring and so soothe an irate caller that he compliments her friendliness to the person called.

4   Identify self and department and route the caller to the
             appropriate department every time.
3   Answer the phone by saying, "Hello," and then wait
             for the caller to respond.
2   Immediately put the caller on hold and wait sixty sec-
             onds before returning to the call.
1   Answer the phone by saying, "Yeah?" and disconnect
             caller before getting a response.

In the examples, note that the behavioral anchors contain no judgments or generalizations about how well or poorly the incumbent did the
job. Instead, for each position on the scale, there is a specific and concrete
example of what a group of experts completely familiar with the job consider to be an example of performance at that level.

A performance appraisal system based on the use of BARS provides
the rater a form listing all important dimensions of the job to be assessed:
the primary accountabilities of the position. For each dimension, the form
contains a graphic rating scale. Instead of labels, definitions, or descriptions, each point on the scale contains an example of one specific behavior
that a person holding that job might be expected to engage in at that level.
The rater reads all of the behaviors listed on the form representing different
levels of performance, recalls the actual behaviors that he had observed
the job incumbent engage in over the rating period, and selects the one
that most closely approximated the actual behaviors observed.

Figure 3-9 is from a performance appraisal form for a supermarket
checkstand operator. Note that this example contains no judgments or
conclusions about the "goodness" or "badness" of the checkstand operator's performance. Instead, examples of actual checkstand operators doing
the job at various levels of quality are given.

The example in Figure 3-10 comes from the performance appraisal for
nonexempt salaried employees of a major pharmaceutical manufacturer.
Although the behavioral examples are not as elaborate as those in Figure
3-9, note that for the job dimension of "People Sensitivity," behavioral
examples are provided and the appraiser is asked to cite examples of observed past behavior to support the appraisal rating.

Strengths and Weaknesses of BARS Approaches

The creation and use of a formal BARS procedure has several significant benefits:

1. It has a high degree of rater and ratee acceptability; people feel that
   the system is fair. The process is specifically job related, and job

Figure 3-9. A Pure BARS Approach at a Supermarket

PERFORMANCE DIMENSION: ORGANIZATIONAL ABILITY OF CHECKSTAND WORK

Extremely Good Performance	7	This checker would organize the order when checking it out by placing all soft goods like bread, cake, etc., to one side of counter; all meats, produce, frozen foods, to the other side, thereby leaving the center of the counter for canned foods, boxed goods, etc.
Good Performance	6	
		When checking, this checker would separate strawberries, bananas, cookies, cakes, and breads, etc.
Slightly Good Performance	5	You can expect this checker to grab more than one item at a time from the cart to the counter.
Neither Poor nor Good Performance	4	
		After bagging the order and customer is still writing a check, you can expect this checker to proceed to the next order if it is a small order.
Slightly Poor Performance	3	This checker may be expected to put wet merchandise on the top of the counter.
		This checker can be expected to lay milk and byproduct cartons on their sides on the counter top.
Poor Performance	2	
		This checker can be expected to damage fragile merchandise like soft goods, eggs, and light bulbs on the counter top.
Extremely Poor Performance	1	

Figure 3-10. A BARS Approach Seeking Examples of Past Behavior

3. **People Sensitivity:** Being responsive to the needs and feelings of others
   (co-workers, supervisor, outside people). Using tact and consideration with
   others; being tolerant and courteous in interactions, etc.

Specific Examples   More Effective
of Past Behavior

- Can deal with others effectively even
  when he/she is frustrated or having
  a bad day.

- Courteous when speaking to others, and
  usually considerate of the feelings and
  thoughts of co-workers.

- Sometimes is moody and snaps at
  people who ask for help.

- Often gets irritated when asked questions.
  Can be rude to others over the phone.

Less Effective

incumbents and raters typically work together to create the instrument.

2. It has high reliability and validity. It measures what it sets out to measure, and different raters who are observing the same performance will come up with similar ratings.

3. It helps provoke good discussions. Since the focus of the appraisal is less on justifying the appraiser's subjective judgment and more on describing and analyzing actual examples of behavior, conversations tend to be less defensive and more likely to provoke behavioral change.

4. It tends to produce immediate performance improvements. People's performance typically improves once they are told exactly what the critical dimensions of their job are and are provided with some concrete examples of what the organization considers to be outstanding performance.

BARS is not without its problems—so many problems, in fact, that few performance appraisal systems use the formal BARS procedures as I described them above. Here are the reasons:

1. Although creating anchors for the extremes of the scale is relatively

easy, it turns out to be quite difficult to develop appropriate anchors for the central portion. Almost everyone is in agreement about what is terrific performance and what is terrible, and almost everyone can provide plenty of examples of each. Finding agreement and generating examples of job performance that is simply acceptable—neither good nor bad—is sometimes impossible.

2. It is difficult to develop job dimensions that are complete and contain no overlap. Independent dimensions are important so that the same examples of behavior are not rewarded or punished—rated high or low—in more than one category. If the differences between categories are not clear, the rater will tend to apply the same ratings from one category to another.

3. Raters often have difficulty in assigning the actual performance of the individuals they supervise to the highly specific behavioral examples used to anchor the various points on the form. In thinking back over Sally's performance in the course of the year, her supervisor may be able to come up with dozens of recollections of things that Sally actually did in the category of, for example, "Greets visitors to the office." But not one of the specific behaviors he has seen is captured precisely by the five or seven anchors listed on the form. The appraiser is still in the position of thinking about what he has seen and assigning it to a point on the scale from terrible to terrific—the same dilemma he would face if the scale were anchored with explanations or definitions rather than snapshots of typical behavior.

4. Although filling out a BARS form is relatively easy, the process requires the appraiser to keep an extensive diary of employee behaviors throughout the appraisal period. Few managers have the time, inclination, or discipline to do this.

5. A BARS performance appraisal system is enormously expensive to create. One organization can't use another's form; the system can't be purchased off the shelf or created by a consultant or human resources manager without the active and extensive involvement of both job holders and supervisors. A separate BARS form must be created for each discrete job.

6. As much as any other appraisal approach, BARS requires extensive appraiser training. Managers must become skilled in making fine behavioral observations, judgments, and opinions about what someone has done from the actual behavior itself.

7. The BARS approach is appropriate for jobs where the behavior of the incumbent, rather than the results achieved, is what is important. For such jobs as nurse, receptionist, flight attendant, or checkstand operator, it may be suitable to concentrate exclusively on what the individual does, as opposed to what he or she achieves. But there are few jobs where job behaviors are more important than results achieved.

8. No convincing body of evidence exists that a BARS approach is more accurate or valid than a far simpler graphic rating scale. A good deal of careful work has been done to assess the relative effectiveness of the BARS approach in relation to traditional graphic methods of rating. Although one early study concluded that "the BARS format yielded less method variance, less halo and less leniency in ratings," and another a year later "found that the BARS technique yielded ratings that were superior in reliability and rater confidence in ratings," it also reported that "simpler numerical formats resulted in less leniency and better discrimination among ratees."[2] Other studies have confirmed these gloomy findings. The general conclusion is that simply being involved in the development of the performance appraisal system is more important than the specific type of system developed.

In summing up the case for BARS, Landy and Farr conclude, "In general, the comparison of the BARS method with alternative graphic methods makes it difficult to justify the increased time investment in the BARS development procedure. In general, one must conclude that although enthusiasm greeted its introduction, the BARS method has not been supported empirically."[3]

Practical Applications of BARS-Type Appraisal Systems

While the problems involved in creating formal BARS systems are formidable, no one would argue with the wisdom of providing raters and ratees alike with a clear description of exactly what performance or behavior the organization desires. And even without involving academically complex construction methodologies, the performance appraisals of many sophisticated organizations incorporate behavioral observations into their appraisal system.

A dozen years ago, a group of hourly employees at a New England jet engine manufacturer asked management about the possibility of developing a performance appraisal process that would mesh with efforts in another area to build a culture of respect and responsibility. A task force of those employees, a consultant, and several of the plant's personnel and line managers created an hourly performance appraisal form based on behavioral observations. The example in Figure 3-11 of one of the major dimensions assessed by the form, "Quality of Work," demonstrates the incorporation of BARS technology into the form.

Combining Graphic Rating Scales With Behavior-Based Assessment

Almost ten years ago I worked with a task force from Houston's Utility Fuels to develop a new performance appraisal system. In examining the

Figure 3-11. BARS Assessment for Hourly Workers

---

1. **QUALITY OF WORK**
    <u>**The Accuracy, Skill, Thoroughness, and Neatness in Performance of Job
    Duties. The Care and Treatment Given to Equipment, Materials, and
    Procedures.**</u>

    ☐   Does not demonstrate enough concern about the quality of his/her
    work. Often wastes materials, makes numerous mistakes, improve-
    ment needed immediately.

    ☐   Has some difficulty in producing work of acceptable quality. Work
    often returned for rework. Work has to be constantly checked. Occa-
    sionally damages equipment or wastes materials.

    ☐   Produces satisfactory work. Generally accurate and neat. Work shows
    thoughtful preparation. Takes care of equipment. Not intentionally
    wasteful. Follows established procedures.

    ☐   Work is generally high in quality, checks and corrects own work.
    Shows pride in work. Rework seldom required. Takes good care of
    equipment. Does not waste materials. Looks for ways to improve pro-
    cedures.

    ☐   Gets highly effective results under varying conditions. Thorough;
    very accurate. Takes extremely good care of equipment and materials.
    Seeks out and suggests improved procedures.

---

corporate culture early in the process, I realized that although senior managers were willing to go along with a new appraisal system, the development of the system had to be rapid, and novelty in design would not
necessarily be considered a virtue. The old system had used only traditional performer-focused graphic rating scales. And although everyone
agreed on the importance of redirecting the focus toward results and behaviors and away from an exclusive focus on the performer, the new system needed to fall within the parameters of what would be considered an
acceptable, conservative corporate approach.

A significant breakthrough occurred during the course of one of the
team meetings. We had been struggling to find the appropriate words to
use for the various anchor points on the scale. Should the highest rating
be called Superior, or Distinguished, or Exceptional? Was the midpoint
Satisfactory, or Competent, or Fully Meets Standard? And what about
unacceptable performance? Would it be called Unacceptable, or would
Marginal or Unsatisfactory be more acceptable terms? Every team member
had an opinion; few were ready to move off their favorite terms and support someone else's choice. No one wanted to have the decision degenerate

into a winner-take-all, majority-rules vote, but it looked as if that would be the only way of resolving our multiple deadlocks.

Finally a team member had an insight. A crusty old-timer who had contributed little but skepticism and cynicism up to that point, he took the floor to explain that whatever terms we adopted, we would still be asking appraisers to make nothing more than absolute judgments about the quality of performance of the ratee. "Whether you call it superior or terrific or ducky if it's good," he said, "or marginal or rotten if it's bad, you're still not doing anything more than labeling the person. Good or bad, it's still a judgment call, a label you're sticking on. Instead of labeling the person, why don't we just describe what it is we want and then ask the manager to indicate how often the guy acts that way?"

As we started working through his suggestion, we realized that almost every performance appraisal rating form required the appraiser to make an absolute judgment about the subordinate. Whether the assessment of the subordinate's performance was positive or negative, the rating scale demanded that the individual be judged.

We also knew that one of the core problems in performance appraisal—one of the primary reasons it is so disliked by appraiser and appraisee alike—is that it forces the supervisor into the position of pinning a judgmental label on the employee.

Based on his insight, we devised a way to eliminate absolute judgments and replace them with descriptions of behavioral frequency. For each performance factor we had identified as being appropriate for inclusion on the appraisal form, we now asked, "What would someone who had a particular strength in this area be likely to do that someone who was not as effective would not do? How will we know it when we see it?"

We rewrote the text that accompanied each performance factor by eliminating formal definitions and replacing them with behavioral descriptions. We took "Adaptability" first. We believed that this competence or attribute in a person was highly important for managerial success but also found it impossible to develop a definition that satisfied everyone in the group.

We asked ourselves, How can we identify someone who really is highly adaptable? What would that person be likely to do? What should we look for? What would we accept as evidence? From that perspective, answers flowed easily. Far more indicators were suggested than we were able to use in the small space the form would provide. Here is the final description of "adaptability" the group developed: "Reacts to criticism objectively and positively. Deals with anger, frustration, and disappointment in a mature manner. Adjusts quickly and effectively to changing conditions. Maintains objectivity in conflict situations. Seeks solutions acceptable to all."

Then instead of asking the rater to judge whether the person was "Commendable" or "Fully Meets Standard" or "Unacceptable" (all judgmental phrases), we instead asked the rater to use a *behavioral frequency scale* to indicate how often the ratee acted in the way that we had described. Our anchors now became Seldom, Occasionally, Frequently, and Always. Each attribute was redefined to provide a behaviorally based description of ideal performance. The same four-point frequency scale was used for each attribute. Figure 3-12 illustrates the behavioral frequency assessment scale for several of the key performance factors that we developed.

Figure 3-12. Behavioral Frequency Scale

7. Decisiveness/Risk Taking — Identifies and analyzes potential problems before acting. Understands and accepts risks involved in decisions. Acts on the basis of limited but adequate data. Stands by decisions when challenged. Exercises good judgment about when to take risks. Willing to take appropriate risks.

| SELDOM | OCCASIONALLY | FREQUENTLY | ALWAYS |

COMMENTS/EXAMPLES: _____

8. Accountability — Displays professionalism in approach to work. Recognizes and accepts responsibility for all parts of job. Does not offer excuses for errors or mistakes. Does not blame others for mistakes. Displays corporate perspective in meeting job responsibilities.

| SELDOM | OCCASIONALLY | FREQUENTLY | ALWAYS |

COMMENTS/EXAMPLES: _____

9. Interpersonal Skills — Develops and maintains effective working relationships with all, including co-workers, supervisors and colleagues from other departments. Offers appropriate assistance to others. Maintains appropriate business demeanor and approach.

| SELDOM | OCCASIONALLY | FREQUENTLY | ALWAYS |

COMMENTS/EXAMPLES: _____

10. Innovation/Creativity — Seeks out, recommends and implements new approaches. Displays creativity in seeking solutions to problems. Integrates new ideas with current approaches.

| SELDOM | OCCASIONALLY | FREQUENTLY | ALWAYS |

COMMENTS/EXAMPLES: _____

After the new procedure had been fully implemented, Utility Fuels assessed the results and found these benefits:

1. *High rater acceptability.* Raters reported that they felt more comfortable in making and justifying their ratings. Because they were no longer required to cast absolute judgment on the appraisee but instead were asked how often the individual performed as desired, they felt more confident in discussing the appraisal results.

2. *High ratee acceptability.* Ratees, too, reported that the performance appraisal discussions were fairer and more useful since they were not subject to an absolute judgment.

3. *More effective discussions.* Both parties reported a significant reduction in the amount of defensiveness on both sides during the discussions, particularly when the rater had assigned a low rating to an attribute. It was much easier to have a good discussion about a problem area when they were able to describe the person as occasionally acting in a desirable manner and then discussing how to increase the frequency of desired behaviors than it was under the old system to have to judge someone as being marginal or fair and then defend the negative judgment.

4. *Improved development plans.* Since the form specified the desired behaviors for each attribute being rated, rater and ratee found it easier to construct development plans to increase effectiveness in an area. Writing the descriptions of the attributes as behavioral indicators rather than as trait definitions served to suggest areas where development efforts could most productively be applied.

Since the Utility Fuels implementation team developed the behavioral frequency rating scale approach a decade ago, I have used it with every organization I have worked with to create a new appraisal instrument. Organizations find that the benefits of replacing absolute judgments with statements of behavioral frequency are significant:

1. *High rater and ratee acceptability.* The reaction reported by the initial Utility Fuels group has continued. There is less defensiveness in the appraisal discussions. Instead of making an absolute judgment about the worth or value of a subordinate's performance, the rater describes how often the subordinate performs in a highly desirable way.

2. *Strengthening of corporate culture.* The activity of identifying the characteristics or attributes that the organization desires and then determining the behaviors it will accept as evidence that the individual is acting in that way is an effective way to make the corporate culture visible. No two organizations that I have worked with have chosen the same group of attributes to include on the assessment form. In Chapter 10 we examine

in detail the way in which the appraisal instrument can serve as a means to help senior management identify the essential elements of the culture and the specific behaviors that are expected.

3. *Increased reliability and validity*. Both reliability and validity are increased when job-related behaviors are identified and the rater is asked to describe the frequency with which these are emitted by the ratee.

4. *Reduced development cost*. The cost of developing a formal BARS appraisal is quite high, particularly because of the extensive development process required and the need for a separate BARS form to be developed for each job. Using behavioral frequency scales maintains the highly desirable focus on behavior provided by the BARS approach. In addition, the job dimensions or characteristics identified are usually appropriate and important across a range of jobs, so fewer forms have to be developed to account for differences in job content.

Numerous organizations have made use of behavioral frequency scales in the construction of their appraisal procedure. For example, a national real estate development firm that owned and operated several hundred apartment complexes constructed a performance appraisal form uniquely designed to assess the performance of the job considered to be the most important in terms of ensuring the organization's long-term success: the apartment complex's resident manager. Among fifteen different elements appraised, the instrument, a portion of which is shown in Figure 3-13, asks for an assessment of professionalism. A bakery placed a high premium on sanitation (Figure 3-14). A manufacturer of grooming products identified ten different elements for assessment, among them job knowledge (Figure 3-15). And a manufacturer of precision weighing equipment looked at adaptability (Figure 3-16).

Figure 3-13. Behavioral Frequency Scale in a Real Estate Development Firm

• **PROFESSIONALISM:** Shows discretion and loyalty in work relationships and with the public. Keeps company, employee and residents' business a private matter. Brings areas of concern to the attention of supervisors.

Employee ➡						
	SELDOM	**OCCASIONALLY**	**USUALLY**	**MOST ALWAYS**	**ALWAYS**
Evaluator ➡						

COMMENTS: _____

_____

_____

Figure 3-14. Behavioral Frequency Scale for a Bakery

6. Sanitation — Maintains personal appearance, grooming and hygiene at highest level. Seeks out opportunities to clean areas that require it. Recognizes importance of maintaining absolute sanitation in a food processing establishment.

| SELDOM | OCCASIONALLY | FREQUENTLY | ALWAYS |

COMMENTS/EXAMPLES: _____

_____

_____

Figure 3-15. Behavioral Frequency Scale for a Manufacturer of Grooming Product.

Job Knowledge: Possesses sufficient skill and knowledge to perform all parts of the job effectively, efficiently and safely. Relates current problems to historical ones. Provides technical assistance to others. Is consulted by others on technical matters. Makes active efforts to stay up-to-date.

INDIVIDUAL →																
	OCCASIONALLY			SOMETIMES			FREQUENTLY			ALWAYS						
APPRAISER →																

COMMENTS/EXAMPLES: _____

_____

_____

Figure 3-16. Behavioral Frequency Scale for a Manufacturer of Precision Weighing Equipment.

11. Adaptability — Reacts to criticism objectively and positively. Deals with anger, frustration and disappointment in a mature manner. Adjusts quickly and effectively to changing conditions. Maintains objectivity in conflict situations. Seeks solutions acceptable to all.

| SELDOM | OCCASIONALLY | FREQUENTLY | ALWAYS |

COMMENTS/EXAMPLES: _____

_____

_____

Results-Focused Appraisal Techniques

Management by Objectives

The most common results-based approach to performance appraisal is management by objectives (MBO). Most writers credit Peter Drucker with the creation of this approach.[4]

In his 1954 book, *The Practice of Management*, Drucker proposed a principle of management for business enterprise to harmonize the goals of the organization while allowing for full individual output. This principle was presented in terms of accountability for results achieved rather than in terms of human relations, the dominant approach at the time. "Perhaps Drucker's greatest contribution was that he did not assume that managers know what their goals are," point out John Bernadin and Richard Beatty, "but instead made goal setting explicit."[5]

MBO, its proponents argue, is more than simply a performance appraisal system. It is foremost a philosophy of management—a set of beliefs and ideas about how an enterprise should be organized, managed, and controlled. MBO is also a specific process for managing an enterprise, involving an orderly, step-by-step procedure for ensuring organizational excellence and desired results. Finally, MBO is a system for planning, evaluation, and organizational control.

As a philosophy, MBO emphasizes predicting and influencing the future rather than responding and reacting to the past. It concentrates on accomplishments and results. More than other management theories, particularly those prevalent in the late 1940s and early 1950s when MBO was developed, it places an unusual emphasis on increased participation by all members of the organization. Core elements of the MBO philosophy include the following:

- ▸ Formation of trusting and open communication throughout the organization.
- ▸ Mutual problem solving and negotiations in the establishment of objectives.
- ▸ Creation of win-win relationships.
- ▸ Organizational rewards and punishments based on job-related performance and achievement.
- ▸ Minimal use of political games, force, and fear.
- ▸ Development of a positive, proactive, and challenging organizational climate.

The MBO Process

The MBO process as described by most writers and practiced in most organizations that have adopted the approach involves goal setting, action planning, implementation, and periodic reviews. Within these broad areas, there are eight major steps to the process:[6]

1. Formulate long-range goals and strategic plans.
2. Develop overall organizational objectives.
3. Establish derivative objectives for major operating units.
4. Set realistic and challenging objectives and standards of performance for members of the organization.
5. Formulate action plans for achieving the stated objectives.
6. Implement the action plan and take corrective action when required to ensure the attainment of objectives.
7. Periodically review performance against established goals and objectives.
8. Appraise overall performance, reinforce behavior, and strengthen motivation. Begin the cycle again.

Step 1: Formulate Long-Range Goals and Strategic Plans

These are the statements of organizational mission: the development of goals and plans that result from a SWOT analysis conducted as part of an organization's strategic planning process. This planning process involves an investigation and analysis of the enterprise's strengths, weaknesses, opportunities, and threats. "Why do we exist?" "Where do we want to go?" "What kind of organization are we trying to become?" These are the fundamental issues that underlie all other organizational actions.

In recent years, the role of strategic planning has often been supplemented by the development of organizational mission statements and "vision and values" pronouncements. Whether called strategic planning or visioning (or whatever buzzword will replace these), the fundamental step of asking and answering basic questions—Who are we? Why are we here? Where do we want to go?—will be the foundation of all further activity. The statement of organizational mission determined in this first stage of MBO is often broad and abstract; it changes little, if at all, from year to year.

Step 2: Develop Overall Organizational Objectives

Once the organization is clear about what it is, why it is in business, and where it wants to go, senior management can begin determining how it will get there. The second step of the MBO process requires the development of objectives in key business areas: profitability, productivity, market share, and so forth. Based on the results of the strategic planning or mission development process, these objectives now become specific statements on an organizationwide basis about how the mission will be achieved. These strategic objectives are more often specific and quantifiable and are likely to be revised over time. For example, one objective that might be developed at this point in the process could be: "Increase our return on investment to 20 percent after taxes within the next three years."[7]

Step 3: Establish Derivative Objectives for Major Operating Units

Based on the broad organizational objectives just developed, each department or other organizational subunit now creates its own objectives, specifying how the broader objective will be achieved. At this level the process requires recognizing that creating objectives involves making trade-offs based on factors of risk and uncertainty. For example, departmental objectives that might flow from the previous example of increasing return on investment to 20 percent could be, "Increase sales to $20 million in three years"; "Raise gross profits to $4 million in three years"; "Reduce per-unit production costs by 8 percent"; or "Upgrade and maintain a skilled workforce to reduce cost of labor per sales dollar by 5 percent."

In Figure 2-1, steps 1 through 3 described here are described as the "Prerequisite Conditions" for a performance management system. The next step of MBO parallels Performance Planning, Phase I of the performance management system.

Step 4: Set Realistic and Challenging Objectives and Standards of Performance for Members of the Organization

Now each individual member of the organization becomes involved in the goal-setting process. Given the overall corporate mission and broad organizational objectives supported by the specific objectives set by the various departments, each individual determines key result areas and develops personal objectives that will help ensure the accomplishment of the departmental and organizational goals. Personal growth and developmental goals may also be included.

As psychologist Harry Levinson has pointed out, "Management by Objectives requires broad participation in the setting of objectives. When strategic and tactical objectives are established and implemented from the top down, MBO exists in name only. In such a situation, lower level managers and employees come to view MBO as a system of measurement and control, rather than one of planning and motivation."[8]

Some objectives must come from the top; some will be dictated. For example, the U.S. Environmental Protection Agency has forced companies to achieve environmental objectives within a specified period of time or pay stiff fines. Consequently top management may require department managers to set objectives relating to environmental hazards within their departments, even if they don't want to set these objectives or be held accountable for achieving them.[9]

Objectives provide the standards against which performance can be evaluated. To achieve the organizational or departmental mission, MBO participants develop both closed and open objectives.[10] For a sales manager, closed objectives (those with a specific and measurable result) might be, "Increase sales by 5 percent," "Maintain private label sales at 7 percent of total sales," or "Hold advertising expenses at last year's level." Open objectives might reflect such items as these: "Develop a quota system for all salespeople," "Prepare and recommend an incentive compensation system for regional managers," or "Shift the advertising emphasis from wholesalers to consumers."

Supervisor and subordinate work together to develop a series of objectives that the subordinate will concentrate on achieving over the course of the year. Ideally, they will agree on three things:

1. The objectives the subordinate will attempt to achieve in a specific period of time
2. The general actions to be taken or the tactics the subordinate will use in achieving the objectives
3. How progress toward the objectives will be measured and the specific dates for such measurements

Step 5: Formulate Action Plans for Achieving the Stated Objectives

In step 4, each individual, usually through a mutual negotiation process with his or her supervisor, determines what would be done. Now the focus shifts to how it will be achieved—a switch from ends to means.

The major activities required for action planning are reasonably straightforward:

1. Specify what is to be accomplished.
2. Determine the major activities and subactivities that must be accomplished in order to achieve the objective.
3. Clarify roles and responsibilities, and assign primary responsibility for each major activity.
4. Identify the resources (time, money, organizational support, technology, manpower, etc.) required to accomplish each activity.
5. Estimate the time requirements for each activity.
6. Create checkpoints and deadlines.

Steps 4 and 5 correspond to the Performance Planning element (Phase I) of the performance management system diagram.

Step 6: Implement the Action Plan and Take Corrective Action When Required to Ensure the Attainment of Objectives

Step 6 represents by far the greatest amount of time involved in the MBO process: the actual work of the organization and all of its members to achieve the predetermined goals through the execution of predetermined action plans. Tactical plans are translated into day-to-day action. Once the organization's mission or strategic plan has been determined, it may take only a few weeks of concentrated attention to develop all of the objectives and action plans described in steps 2 through 5. Once goals and plans have been reviewed and approved, the organization then concentrates on their achievement. During this period goals may be renegotiated and action plans revised as market forces and competitive pressures make change necessary.

It is in this step of the MBO process that the great benefits of the system emerge. As Hellriegel and Slocum explain, "Under MBO, managers give subordinates greater freedom in performing their tasks. Managers should be available to coach and counsel subordinates, as needed, to help them reach objectives rather than controlling their every movement. Managers must trust individuals to work effectively toward agreed-upon objectives. Conversely, employees must feel free to discuss problems with their superiors or others who can help them."[11]

Step 7: Periodically Review Performance Against Established Goals and Objectives

A major flaw with most appraisal systems is that performance appraisal is an annual occurrence and is seen as an event and not as part of a process. In MBO as prescribed, if not always as practiced, one fundamental element is the periodic review of performance against goals and the renegotiation of objectives and action plans.

Periodic reviews require the individual to review progress toward goals on a regular basis and provide relevant feedback to the performer, the supervisor, and the organization. Anthony Raia describes the essential functions that periodic reviews—*not* annual appraisals—serve:[12]

- *Remove obstacles*. The individual may be unable to achieve an objective because of unanticipated obstacles. The reviewing manager has a responsibility to clear the path for his subordinates so that they can achieve their goals when obstacles beyond their control arise.
- *Identify and solve problems*. The manager may not know the cause of the problem he's facing. By accessing the knowledge and skill of his boss on a periodic basis, he may be better able to recognize obstacles and distinguish between symptoms and causes. The re-

view may also indicate when it is better *not* to solve a problem—it may be too costly, too intractable, or simply easier to live with. Two heads often are better than one.

- ▸ *Plan for and take corrective action.* If objectives are not being met, the cause may lie in a deficiency in the original plan. Maintaining the objective but changing the action may be necessary.
- ▸ *Revise existing objectives.* Corrective action may include changing objectives that we agreed on months before. With changing conditions it may be appropriate to abandon an original objective based on new information. Similarly, it may be equally appropriate to toughen an original objective as changing conditions or new information reveal that the initial goal is now unreasonably tame.
- ▸ *Establish new objectives.* While the creation of new objectives is one of the primary functions of the end-of-year review, a great benefit of MBO is the expectation that periodic goal reviews will accelerate the development of new objectives and not delay them until a year has passed. Increased marketplace agility is a frequently reported benefit MBO provides.
- ▸ *Review performance.* Periodic MBO reviews also provide an opportunity for ongoing performance review. This feedback and counsel can prevent unpleasant surprises at the end of the review period and assure organization members that they are on track.

Step 8: Appraise Overall Performance, Reinforce Behavior, and Strengthen Motivation; Begin the Cycle Again

At the conclusion of the year, each individual's performance is appraised according to the person's success in achieving the objectives agreed on at the beginning of the period. As with any other appraisal, compensation adjustments and development plans may also be discussed as well as career planning and the other topics that invariably arise in the course of a performance appraisal discussion, whatever the approach itself may be.

But MBO has one more element that distinguishes it from the performer-based and behavior-based systems we have reviewed: the provision for the process to begin again with the development, negotiation, and acceptance of new objectives and action plans. In this way, MBO is not an event or a procedure. It is a cycle.

MBO Appraisal Forms

Most MBO forms are marked by their simplicity. For the most part, the form simply contains space for the objective to be entered at the beginning of the cycle and the analysis of performance at the end.

An international consumer goods company uses a pure MBO system for its managers. The form consists of four pages: a first page of instructions; two middle pages, each containing space for two objectives to be written and appraised; and a final page containing a narrative summary of the individual's overall performance, a space for the final performance rating, some lines for approvals, and space for the participant's acknowledgment. The instructions for using the appraisal form tend to be straightforward, as the first page of the form illustrates, and the middle pages are essentially blank sheets (Figure 3-17). A more unpretentious form could not be devised.

The procedure used by a large pharmaceutical manufacturer, shown in Figure 3-18, is simplicity itself. As the instructions indicate, the reviewer is to "list objectives or tasks that were established at the beginning of the review period, and indicate results achieved."

Finally, in the model performance appraisal form I have developed as a basis for helping client organizations create an approach tailored specifically to their culture, history, and needs, a results-oriented element is a critical component. Like the others, it incorporates space for the identification of the key result area together with a weighting if appropriate, allows for the results of an interim review together with a final review, and provides for a final appraisal rating for each objective. A copy of the master performance appraisal form is contained in Appendix A.

Accountabilities and Measures Approach

Common to every organization's MBO system is the provision that objectives and standards are negotiated and agreed on an individual basis as part of the overall process. Accountabilities and Measures is a results-based appraisal approach that provides for the objectives to be achieved by an individual, together with the measures or performance standards for each objective, to be determined, either completely or in part, by higher management.

Devising a Procedure

The Accountabilities and Measures performance appraisal procedure was developed at a Fortune 50 consumer goods company. An extensive analysis of the training needs of the company's district sales managers (DSMs) revealed that while all DSMs in the company were in agreement about the essential elements of their jobs, there was little correlation between their perception of the most important elements of the job and the opinions of region sales managers (their supervisors) or of senior management. For example, without exception DSMs believed that accurate and

Figure 3-17. MBO Appraisal Form

A. Instructions
MIDDLE MANAGEMENT
INCENTIVE PLAN

APPRAISAL OF
KEY OBJECTIVES

PARTICIPATION IN PLAN	
From:	To:

PARTICIPANT'S NAME:	POSITION TITLE:
ORGANIZATION LOCATION:	SUPERVISOR'S NAME:

Key Position Objectives were established at the time this individual became a participant in the Middle Management Incentive Plan. The purpose of this appraisal is to evaluate the participant's performance in achieving these objectives, thereby providing a basis for determining the amount of this participant's Incentive Award.

INSTRUCTIONS

Instructions for completing this appraisal are outlined below. For additional guidance, consult your supervisor or contact the Personnel Department.

- Present each key objective appearing in the participant's *Personal Statements of Award Opportunities*. List the objectives in order of importance.

- Measure and describe the participant's performance in achieving each key objective. Both the objective and the participant's accomplishments must be *quantified*.

- Rate the participant's performance against each key objective using the performance ratings indicated below.

Rating	Performance Factor (% of Standard Incentive Award)	Definition
Distinguished Performance	135%–175%	Results achieved far exceeded the expectations for the job. This year's contribution clearly moved the business forward.
Superior Performance	110%–135%	Results exceeded expectations. This year's contribution is clearly identifiable.
Competent Performance	90%–110%	Fully met expectations in all key areas. No major errors of execution or strategy.
Provisional Performance	70%–90%	Did not fully meet expectations.

Figure 3-17. *(continued)*

- Provide a summary statement on the participant's overall performance in accomplishing the key objectives.

- After completion, sign and forward this Appraisal to your immediate manager for review and approval.

- Personally review this Appraisal with the participant when you present the approval Incentive Award.

B. Statements of objectives and analysis of results

OBJECTIVE:
ACCOMPLISHMENTS: _____
PERFORMANCE: _____

OBJECTIVE:
ACCOMPLISHMENTS: _____
PERFORMANCE: _____

Figure 3-18. MBO Appraisal Form for a Pharmaceutical Manufacturer

**Performance Management
and Career Development**

Appraisal Form

Name _____   Please Indicate: ☐ Supervisor Copy ☐ Employee Copy
      Last   First   Initial
ID# _____ SS# _____   Appraisal Date _____
                              Mo.   Day   Yr.
Job Title _____   Performance Period _____ to _____
                                  Mo/Yr   Mo/Yr
Division/Group _____   Date Entered Present Position _____
                                          Mo.   Day   Yr.

I. Results Achieved—List objectives or tasks that were established at the beginning of the review period, and indicate results achieved.

    Objectives or Tasks: *Results:*

timely submission of paperwork was a paramount priority. Upper-level managers, while not denigrating the importance of accurate reports, believed strongly that the DSMs' most important mission was spending time with their salespeople and building customer relations.

The project team realized the implications of the needs analysis data: No sales training program could possibly be effective given the gap between the DSMs' clear view of their job and their supervisors' equally clear and totally contradictory understanding. The need was to resolve the perceptual difference. There needed to be a common ground among all parties and agreement on the job of the DSM before anyone could be trained to do it successfully. The result was a "training program" that consisted of three elements: a new job description, a new weekly activity report, and a new performance appraisal form.

An experienced group of line managers, headquarters senior staff, and consultants developed a new job description that described specifically what the company had determined the DSM's job to be. This new job description consisted exclusively of a list of thirteen separate and specific accountabilities, allocated into three primary areas: supervisory, sales development, and administrative.

The district sales manager weekly activity report was then redesigned. Previously it had been open-ended, with only a few topic headings to guide DSMs in reporting where they had spent time over the previous week. The new activity report went the opposite direction: It exactly paralleled the new job description and was entirely data driven. The job description had thirteen accountabilities; the weekly activity report required reporting in each accountability area. There were no blank lines or open spaces; instead the report called for specific and quantitative reporting on each accountability.

The most significant change was the development of the new performance appraisal system. It, too, exactly paralleled the new job description and the weekly activity report. The DSM performance appraisal form was entirely job specific; it applied only to the job of the district sales manager. It consisted of two parts: a four-page performance appraisal worksheet that contained each accountability from the job description, the specific predetermined measures that were to be used to assess the individual's performance of that accountability, space (in a few cases) to describe any external conditions that influenced the results that the individual had achieved, and a five-point rating scale.

The performance appraisal form thus consisted of the thirteen accountabilities and only the thirteen accountabilities, together with the specific and predetermined measures that region managers were to use in assessing the performance of the district sales manager in meeting each accountability. Like a classic MBO system, it was entirely results oriented. Unlike an MBO system, however, there was no negotiation of objectives, standards, or key result areas. Instead these were decided entirely by senior management and dictated to the DSMs.

At the end of the year, the region sales manager accumulated all of the weekly reports that each DSM had submitted and then plugged in the numbers in the appropriate blanks on the performance appraisal form. For example, one accountability required the DSM to perform direct supervision of route salesmen three days per week. The performance appraisal worksheet required the regional managers to answer the following questions:

1. How many days were planned for the DSM to supervise salesmen on their route?
2. How many days did the DSM actually supervise salesmen on their route?
3. How many days did the DSM replace route salesmen on open routes?
4. How many days did the DSM replace route salesmen on vacation routes?

After responding to an open-ended question asking the regional manager to describe the district manager's ability to help route salesmen take advantage of sales development opportunities on their routes, the regional manager evaluated performance against that accountability as marginal, fair, competent, superior, or distinguished. Figure 3-19 shows the first page of the DSM performance appraisal worksheet.

After entering the data required to assess the first accountability, making whatever comments the worksheet required, and evaluating the DSM's performance using the five-point scale, the RSM then entered the thirteen individual appraisal assessments onto the performance appraisal summary. There is no narrative explanation, simply a rating of the thirteen individual performance values assigned for the accountabilities. Figure 3-20 shows an example of the performance appraisal summary.

Implementing the new system provoked some fully anticipated grumbling about the job's being recast into rigid categories. More important, however, the effect of providing absolutely clear direction on what management expected the DSM to do (the new job description), combined with the reinforcement of that expectation by requiring each job incumbent to report regularly on his or her performance in each component of it (the weekly activity report), followed by the creation of a performance evaluation system that focused exclusively on the specific accountabilities that had been determined, redirected the efforts of the sales management team in way that no sales training program could hope to achieve.

Among other organizations, GTE Directories has implemented a form of accountabilities and measures for its division managers. A part of its form is shown in Figure 3-21.

Figure 3-19. District Sales Manager Appraisal Worksheet

DISTRICT SALES MANAGER'S NAME		SOCIAL SECURITY NUMBER
LOCATION CODE	NO. OF YEARS IN PRESENT LOCATION	NO. OF YEARS WITH THE COMPANY

PRINCIPAL ACCOUNTABILITIES:

SUPERVISORY

1. ACHIEVING THE DISTRICT SALES FORECAST
    A. Actual sales - last four quarters $_____
    B. Sales forecast - last four quarters $_____
    C. Percent of forecast achieved   [_____%]
    D. Describe conditions which influenced achieving the forecast:

_____
_____

A B C D E F G H I J K L M N O P Q R S T U V W X Y Z
MARGINAL | FAIR | COMPETENT | SUPERIOR | DISTINGUISHED   **PERFORMANCE VALUE** [ ]

2. CONTROLLING AND VERIFYING STALES ACCORDING TO PLAN
    A. Percentage of stales to sales - last four quarters

	MOST RECENT QUARTER	PREVIOUS QUARTER	2nd PREVIOUS QUARTER	3rd PREVIOUS QUARTER
ACTUAL %				
PLAN %				

    B. Describe conditions which influenced achieving the plan:

_____
_____

A B C D E F G H I J K L M N O P Q R S T U V W X Y Z
MARGINAL | FAIR | COMPETENT | SUPERIOR | DISTINGUISHED   **PERFORMANCE VALUE** [ ]

3. SELECTING AND EMPLOYING ROUTE SALESMEN IN HIS DISTRICT
    A. How many Route Salesmen are assigned to the district?_____
    B. Number of Route Salesmen employed during the last 13 periods:_____
    C. During the last 13 periods how many quit?____ were discharged?____
    State the general reasons for the above terminations?

_____
_____
_____

A B C D E F G H I J K L M N O P Q R S T U V W X Y Z
MARGINAL | FAIR | COMPETENT | SUPERIOR | DISTINGUISHED   **PERFORMANCE VALUE** [ ]

Figure 3-20. District Sales Manager Performance Appraisal Summary

DISTRICT SALES MANAGER'S NAME	REPORTS TO
ORGANIZATION UNIT	LOCATION

PRINCIPLE ACCOUNTABILITIES:

SUPERVISORY

PERFORMANCE VALUE

1. Achieving the district sales forecast. ☐
2. Controlling and verifying sales according to plan. ☐
3. Selecting and employing Route Salesmen in his district. ☐
4. Conducting the Route Salesman Training Program and continuous training activity. ☐
5. Performing route supervision three days per week and motivating Route Salesmen to increase productivity by communicating on progress and problems. ☐

SALES DEVELOPMENT

1. Selling, implementing and maintaining the space management program. ☐
2. Selling, improving present customer relations and developing new sales distribution. ☐
3. Coordinating and controlling all promotions and market development activities. ☐
4. Inspecting the market to assure proper service, merchandising effectiveness to evaluate competitive activity and overall market conditions. ☐

ADMINISTRATIVE

1. Assuring timely and accurate submission of order invoices, monies and daily reports by Route Salesmen, certifying inventory and reconciling discrepancies. ☐
2. Preparing the District Activity Reports for the Region Sales Manager and the Division Sales Manager. ☐
3. Compiling appropriate information and making recommendations to the Region Sales Manager concerning route revisions, route adjustments and route additions. ☐
4. Inspecting route vehicles on a scheduled basis and assuring cleanliness and proper servicing according to the preventive maintenance program. ☐

PERFORMANCE APPRAISAL:
Consider the Performance Values for all the accountabilities and rate the District Sales Manager's overall performance.

A B C D E	F G H I	J K L M N O P Q R S	T U V W X Y Z
MARGINAL	FAIR	COMPETENT	SUPERIOR	DISTINGUISHED

OVERALL PERFORMANCE VALUE ☐

Figure 3-21. Accountabilities and Measures Form for GTE Directories

APPRAISAL SHEET - Division Managers, District Sales Managers - Premise and Telephone

NAME _____ SS# _____

FOR DIVISION MANAGERS

YEAR	SALES TURNOVER FOR DIVISION		REGIONAL SALES TURNOVER %	DIVISION YEARLY		REGION YEARLY		DOLLAR ADJUSTMENTS	NUMBER OF SHOWPROOFS
	NO. OF SEPARATIONS	%		% OF BUDGET	% B.N. INC. TO REV. HANDLED	% OF BUDGET	% B.N. INC. TO REV. HANDLED		
19									
19									
19									
19									

FOR DISTRICT SALES MANAGERS AND DISTRICT TELEPHONE SALES MANAGERS
UNIT AND PERSONAL SALES RESULTS

YEAR END STANDING - PERCENT OF BUDGET

YEAR	19	19	19	YEAR TO DATE	Comments:
UNIT					
PERSONAL					

CUSTOMER COMPLAINT HISTORY

	MANAGER'S TOTAL		UNIT TOTAL	
YEAR	19	19	YEAR TO DATE	Comments:
NO. OF 3006 COMPLAINTS				
NO. OF ADJUSTMENTS				
AMOUNT REVENUE LOST				

NO. REPS BELOW 100% OF BUDGET YEAR TO DATE _____

NO. REPS BELOW 100% OF BUDGET YEAR END STANDING _____

NO. REPS TERMINATED PAST YEAR _____ PAST THREE YEARS _____

ORGANIZATION AND TERRITORY CONTROL

Percent of all directories worked by the unit on which at least 90% of assigned territory (advertisers and non ads) was completed when 90% of assigned days had passed.

YEAR	19	19	YEAR TO DATE	Comments:
PERCENT OF 90/90				

Advantages and Disadvantages of Results-Based Appraisal Approaches

A results-based system has some solid benefits to offer an organization:

1. *It produces improved short- and long-term planning.* With MBO, the process begins at the highest level of the organization with the determination of organizational mission, vision, and values combined with the set-

ting of broad organizational objectives for their achievement. This objective-setting process cascades throughout the organization until every member has completed the process of identifying, developing, and committing to the achievement of personal goals that will support the broad organizational mission. With Accountabilities and Measures, the process requires at least the senior management of the enterprise and, in most cases, the job incumbents themselves and their supervisors to identify the critical components of the job and, equally important, to determine how the individual's performance within that dimension will be measured.

2. *The focus on results communicates the importance of achieving measurable results to all members of the organization.*

3. *The system encourages more effective performance.* It specifies to organization members what the organization is seeking and thereby reduces the probability that time and resources will be committed to the successful achievement of unimportant ends.

4. *Both appraisers and appraisees accept the approach as fair.* While some may prefer a less demanding system, there is little objection that can be made to the message the organization sends when it creates a results-based system: "This is what we are paying you for; this is what we expect you to accomplish."

5. *It results in increased commitment to the organization.* The participation of employees may result in increased motivation and loyalty.

6. *Results-based approaches lead to improved clarity of the individual's role and priorities.*

7. *Results-based systems are highly defensible.* The process is completely job specific and, in the case of MBO, directly involves the participation of the subordinate in the development of goals and objectives.

A results-based system does have limitations and potential problems, too:

1. *It may be excessively results oriented.* If results are the only thing that counts—if ends are everything and means are irrelevant—we are likely to find an enormous emphasis placed by participants in the system on achieving short-term results at the expense of long-term prosperity. A maintenance manager operating under a system that places almost exclusive emphasis on cost reduction as the primary objective may well be tempted to defer needed repairs with the hope that he will be promoted away before the roof caves in.

2. *It may be inflexible.* In MBO, so much energy and time may have gone into the original development and negotiation of objectives that there is great reluctance to tamper with what was originally established, even

when market conditions suggest that the original goals may no longer be appropriate. The Accountabilities and Measures approach may be even more rigid, since the procedure focuses entirely on one job. In the example given, if only one element of the district sales manager's job changed, the entire form would have to be revised.

3. *It is neither easy to create nor easy to use.* A great deal of organizational commitment is required to make them work. A great deal of training is required for everyone affected by the system, and organizational controls must be in place in order to ensure that the various steps of the system occur as designed.

4. *The approach may not provide adequate personal incentives to improve performance.* The emphasis is on the benefits to the organization; little attention is paid to the development of the individuals involved.

5. *It may not fit all aspects of a job.* Not all critical aspects of a job are amenable to quantifiable and objective measurement. In the Accountabilities and Measures example, the team was frustrated in its efforts to create definite, precise, and valid measures for the accountability that included "improving customer relations." The alternatives are unappealing: Abandon important objectives because they do not permit easy measurement or settle for inadequate measures whose only value is being quantitative.

MBO in particular is seen by some as an organizational panacea. It is not. It cannot provide all of the data required for making valid personnel decisions on compensation, promotion and training, and development. It cannot be used for those critical job functions where results measures are either nonexistent or are secondary in importance to the way the job is done. Results-oriented systems alone provide insufficient information on how a job was done. They focus only on what was achieved, and that is rarely sufficient.

Global Performance Appraisal Approaches

There is one type of performance appraisal form that focuses on nothing in particular. Perhaps the simplest of all appraisal systems, it is the narrative essay. In a typical essay-type performance appraisal, the rater is asked to describe in writing an individual's strengths and weaknesses, achievements and potential, and development needs. "The assumption underlying this approach is that a candid statement from a rater who is knowledgeable of a ratee's performance is just as valid as more formal and more complicated appraisal methods."[13]

The form shown in Figure 3-22, from a British-based chemical company, is an example of an essay-type performance appraisal in its purest form. The reverse side of the form provides three more essay questions: "Thoughts on Future Development," "Overall Comments," and "Discussion with Individual." The performance appraisal here is absolutely global; there is not one box to be checked or specific piece of information to be entered. Whatever the rater wants to discuss becomes the subject of the performance appraisal, in the rater's discretion entirely.

When done well, narrative essays can provide the most detailed and most intimate feedback an individual can receive from a boss. Unrestrained by required structure, the appraiser can use the appraisal to highlight those areas of genuine accomplishment and discuss areas where improvement is needed, giving each appropriate weight.

The global or essay-type appraisal is also the simplest and easiest to construct. Nothing more than a blank piece of paper is required, with perhaps some broad guidelines on what is to be covered. Appraisers are given enormous latitude in deciding what to include and what to ignore. But essay appraisals have serious limitations:

1. Unlike other types of performance appraisal, two entirely unrelated skills are required. First, like all other methods, appraisers must be schooled in how to observe behavior, how to assess and appraise it, how to communicate effectively with the appraisee, and all of the other performance appraisal skills. But essay-type appraisals also demand that appraisers be skilled essayists. They need not only the ability to appraise but also the unrelated faculty for turning those behavioral observations and assessments into finely crafted sentences that convey the precise meaning they intend the appraisee to comprehend. Few managers have the proficiency required.

2. Essay-type appraisals suffer from a complete lack of reliability and validity. No two appraisers will construct the same narrative report on an individual's performance; no two raters will even select the same behaviors or results to discuss.

3. No other approach is more susceptible to rater error. Leniency, halo effect, first-impression error, similar-to-me effect, and many others are routine in essay-type appraisal results.

4. A well-constructed essay may be of enormous value to a particular ratee, but it is of almost no value to anyone else. Cross-department comparisons are impossible. Basing compensation decisions on a comparison of different essay appraisals is indefensible.

5. Essays focus on only the qualitative aspect of the individual's performance; no quantitative data are demanded. But for the purpose of mak-

Figure 3-22. Essay-Type Performance Appraisal Form

EXECUTIVE PERFORMANCE REVIEW
Malaysia, Singapore, Thailand

Name..	Review period .... to ....

		Yrs.	Mths.
Job Title..	Age: } as at		
	Service: Total		
Department	Present Job		

1. REVIEW OF PERFORMANCE

(Tick to indicate whether by Individual ☐ or by Reviewer ☐)

Highlight most noteworthy achievements against objectives of job, and the extent to which the individual was accountable to these achievements (inclusive of external factors which helped or hindered the individual, the application of talents, judgment, discretion, human relations skills on-the-job, etc.)

ing personnel decisions or to be compared objectively one with another, some form of rating that can be quantified is essential.

Although an entire performance appraisal based exclusively on essay is rare, the use of global appraisal is common as part of an organization's complete system. Regardless of whether they are performer, behavior, or results based, almost every performance appraisal form concludes with a narrative section requiring the appraiser to summarize and draw final conclusions regarding the individual's overall performance.

Analysis of Performance Appraisals

In this chapter we have looked at three significantly different and independent approaches to performance appraisal used by organizations: performer based, behavior based, and results based, together with the global or essay approach. Examples of systems that use one of these procedures to the exclusion of all others are rare. Virtually every organization uses some combination of these methods.

Many combine all three. The organization's overall performance management procedure may be based on a results-based MBO-type system, and the appraisal form may provide a section asking the appraiser to evaluate how the individual went about achieving the results as well as enumerating the results themselves. And virtually all appraisal forms, whatever their primary focus, provide for a narrative summary—a global essay—at the end.

Understanding the different approaches to appraisal is useful in two major respects. First, when an organization is creating or revising its existing system, it is useful for all involved in the effort to know the available choices and options. Second, when an organization or one of its managers wants to increase the effectiveness of an existing system in improving the performance of organization members without making any substantive changes to the prescribed forms or mandated procedures themselves, it helps for him to know what he's dealing with.

In the next two chapters we examine closely the two components that make up the preponderance of assessment items in the great majority of appraisal forms: the results to be achieved and the performance factors that lead to their accomplishment.

Notes

1. Peter F. Drucker, *Management: Tasks, Responsibilities, Practices* (New York: Harper & Row, 1973), p. 424.

2. J. P. Campbell, M. D. Dunnette, R. D. Arvey, and L. V. Hellervik, "The Development of Behaviorally Based Rating Scales," *Journal of Applied Psychology* 57 (1973): 15–22; W. C. Borman and W. R. Vallon, "A View of What Can Happen When Behavioral Expectation Scales Are Developed in One Setting and Used in Another," *Journal of Applied Psychology* 59 (1974): 197–201.

3. Frank J. Landy and James L. Farr, "Performance Rating," *The Performance Appraisal Sourcebook* (Amherst, Mass.: Human Resources Development Press, 1982), p. 144.

4. Peter F. Drucker, *The Practice of Management* (New York: Harper & Row, 1954).

5. H. John Bernadin and Richard W. Beatty, *Performance Appraisal: Assessing Human Behavior at Work* (Belmont, Calif.: Wadsworth, Inc., 1984).

6. The description of the MBO process is drawn largely from Anthony P. Raia, *Managing by Objectives* (Glencoe, Ill.: Scott Foresman, 1974).

7. This example is drawn from Don Hellriegel and John W. Slocum, Jr., *Management* (Reading, Mass.: Addison-Wesley, 1989) and based on G. A. Steiner, *Strategic Planning* (New York: Free Press, 1979).

8. Harry Levinson, "Management by Whose Objectives?" *Harvard Business Review* (July–August 1970): 97.

9. H. Weihrich, *Management Excellence: Productivity Through MBO* (New York: McGraw-Hill, 1985).

10. The discussion of closed and open objectives is based on Hellriegel and Slocum, *Management*.

11. Ibid., p. 316.

12. Raia, *Managing by Objectives*.

13. Wayne Cascio, *Applied Psychology in Personnel Management*, 4th ed. (Englewood Cliffs, N.J.: Prentice-Hall, 1990).

Chapter 4
Objectives, Accountabilities, and Standards

The most emotionally demanding task managers face in performance appraisal is conducting the appraisal interview. The most intellectually demanding task, however, may be determining accountabilities and objectives, key results areas, and standards and measures.

In Chapter 3 I provided a model for understanding job performance: A performer, in a given situation, engages in certain behaviors, in order to achieve desired results. Of these four elements, the situation is rarely identified as a specific component of the appraisal (though it is often an important determinant of success). And evaluations exclusively of the performer, independent of what the person does and achieves, are also rarely the basis of most appraisal processes.

So for an appraisal system, two legitimate areas for assessment remain: behaviors and results. The following chapter is devoted to ways in which behavior can be identified and assessed for performance appraisal purposes. This chapter concentrates on what most managers see as the most important factor to consider in any performance appraisal process: results.

Assessing Results

In order to appraise the results of a person's efforts, we must answer three questions:

1. What are the different areas in which this individual is expected to focus efforts? (*accountabilities*)
2. Within each area, what goals or objectives do we expect the person to achieve? (*objectives*)
3. How will the results that the person produces be measured? How

will we distinguish good performance from bad? (*performance standards* or *measures*)

In an effective performance appraisal system, the manager and subordinate meet at the beginning of the appraisal period to review the accountabilities, set objectives, and come to agreement on how the individual's performance will be measured. They decide the primary areas in which the subordinate will concentrate attention, the various results or outcomes that should be achieved as a result of efforts in that area, and the yardstick against which the quality of performance will be measured.

Accountabilities

Accountabilities are the broad areas within a job that change little from year to year. One of the most common sources is an individual's job description. Scott Parry of Training House described a project his firm had undertaken to help identify the accountabilities of a college professor.[1] The faculty was resistant to the idea that the job of college professor could be codified, since so many different activities and academic areas were involved. Nevertheless, the task force working on the project handily identified the specific accountabilities that might appear in the job description of virtually every college professor:

► Teaching
► Research
► Writing
► Counseling students
► Professional development
► Service to the university

Although an individual professor might place greater emphasis on one area than another and exemplary performance in some areas was of greater importance than in others, almost every job-related activity undertaken by any professor would be fairly easily assignable to one of these six categories.

As the list demonstrates, accountabilities function as labels: They identify the areas within which a person is responsible for achieving results and sorting the broad areas of the job into more discrete chunks. They are not objectives—statements of the outcomes or results that will be achieved within each accountability area. For the most part, accountabilities are stable and change little from year to year; objectives vary significantly and are revised at least annually.

Sources of Accountabilities

The majority of accountabilities are found in the job itself, either listed in the job description or obvious simply by asking what are the most important things that the person does.

The first step is to read the job description. The job description of any human resources manager, for example, reveals several discrete and independent areas in which a human resources director is expected to achieve results:

- *Staffing*—employment, recruitment, interviewing, staff planning
- *Employee relations*—union negotiations, contract interpretation, grievance handling, conducting union-free or decertification campaigns, handling disciplinary problems and terminations
- *Employee development*—administering the tuition refund program, scheduling training programs, engaging outside training consultants, conducting needs assessments
- *Compensation*—conducting wage surveys, determining merit increase procedures

Although there certainly may be other areas in which the human resources manager will have responsibility, note that each of these accountabilities is simply a label: staffing, employee relations, employee development, compensation. We do not know yet what the organization or supervisor expects this manager to do within each of these areas, nor do we know how his performance will be measured. All we are doing at this point is identifying his accountabilities—the broad areas of the job that constitute the major areas within which he will be expected to achieve results.

Is the list complete? Not yet. Are there other areas where we will expect him to concentrate efforts? Certainly. But the process begins by identifying the broad areas within which results are to be achieved, most of which are—or should be—contained within the job description.

Job descriptions tend to be static documents; the nature of jobs is that they change. And although the basic responsibilities of human resources managers would probably have been present in a job description for a personnel director written forty years ago (and probably will still be on the job description of a person charged with the people management function forty years from now, whatever the job then will be called), there are still changes in jobs that create new areas of accountability that may not be immediately reflected in the job description. An example is "Equal Employment Opportunity," or "Managing Diversity," or "Regulatory Compliance," or however else the organization may choose to phrase it. The job description of a personnel manager written in the early 1960s would not have contained anything about ensuring compliance with civil rights and antidiscrimination legislation because it didn't exist. Today it would be unusual for the job description of a human resources manager not to contain a specific accountability for ensuring a balanced workforce.

Note that the specific objectives to be achieved within this particular accountability area would probably change frequently over the years, while the actual accountability area, phrased perhaps as "EEO Compliance," might remain unchanged. With the passage of the first civil rights laws in the late 1960s and early 1970s, the objectives to be achieved might involve such activities as conducting sensitivity training for supervisors and managers, ensuring that all employment advertising and interviewing are free of discriminatory statements, negotiating goals and quotas with government agencies, and developing voluntary affirmative action programs. Today the specific objectives would probably be significantly different. Items like conducting workshops in managing diversity and locating and dismantling perceived glass ceilings might be included in the objectives. But the point is clear: Although the specific objectives within a given accountability are likely to change from year to year, over a period of forty years the accountability of "EEO Compliance" could remain unchanged.

A similar situation might be true in the area of managing technology. Ten years ago probably no one in an organization had any responsibility for the management of computer technology except for the programmers, systems analysts, and mainframe hardware technicians, often located in the bowels of the finance department. Today almost all managers have an accountability for managing technology within their area. And although the objectives that may be set for this year's appraisal period regarding managing technology may be obsolete even before the close of the appraisal period, the overall accountability is likely to remain for decades.

That's why it's important to look beyond the job description in determining what the accountabilities of the job are. Another source for accountabilities is simply to look at what the person does. What are you responsible for doing? is the question to ask. Where do you spend your time? The answers to these questions may suggest areas of accountabilities that are not spelled out in the job description—for example:

If the person spends significant time:	*Then an accountability might be:*
Managing special projects	Project management
Writing reports	Providing information
Interacting with customers	Customer satisfaction
Interviewing applicants	Employment
Managing the work of others	Supervision

To search for important accountabilities, particularly in senior management jobs, is to consider the business problems that face all organizations and make sure that no major area has been left unconsidered. In a pithy and succinct article, Tom Kramlinger, senior design consultant with Wilson Learning Systems, urged performance appraisal designers or consultants or users to make sure that the accountabilities within the performance appraisal of each organizational member contain those genuine business responsibilities that have an ultimate impact on the success or failure of the enterprise as a whole.[2] It is in this area that the whole genuinely is greater than the sum of its parts. If everyone who is primarily concerned with success within a given function restricts his view of his accountabilities only to those that are specifically function-related without exploring how that job and that function affect the success of the business as a whole, then the health of the entire operation is in jeopardy.

Kramlinger proposes four primary business issues that are core concerns in any organization: acquiring customers, satisfying customers, capacity (maintaining adequate resources), and productivity (controlling costs). Although these elements may not appear as accountabilities in the performance appraisal of every member of the enterprise, there are several reasons that everyone's objectives should be tested to see if the core issues of the business are being addressed:

▸ If the senior leaders of the organization do not have each of these areas clearly and directly specified as an accountability, the probability of ultimate business success will be small. In other words, in addition to ordering the merchandise and stocking the shelves and sweeping the floor and greeting the customers; hiring the clerks and checking the inventory and handling all the other hundreds of miscellaneous minor detail required to make even the smallest mom-and-pop operation succeed, if everyone connected with the enterprise (especially mom and pop) isn't aware of and to some extent responsible for the fundamentals for ensuring business success, mom and pop and all their minions will end up on the breadline.

▸ The more that the accountabilities of each member of the organization can be directly related to one or more of these fundamental business issues, then the higher is the probability that the efforts of that person will lead to significant and measurable business outcomes and results.

▸ The more that everyone in the organization understands how his or her job relates to the four fundamental business issues, the greater is the likelihood that when confronted with a decision involving insufficient data and unpredictable outcomes, the individual will make a choice that supports ultimate business success.

Accountabilities, or key results areas, describe in the simplest words or phrases the reason that a job exists. They are not long statements of outcomes that are expected to be produced or results to be achieved; they are labels.

Accountabilities are limited in number. As a general rule, it would be unusual for any job to have fewer than three accountabilities or more than seven. If there is a very small number of accountabilities, probably some important job areas have been overlooked. It might also mean that the job is one of such limited scope that the accountabilities should be reassigned to another position and the job abolished. With more than seven accountabilities listed, the chances are great that what has been generated is a task inventory or a list of goals. Accountabilities are not tasks or goals; they are the basis for setting specific objectives and broad statements of the areas within which the jobholder is expected to produce results.

Accountabilities remain stable over a long period. They are independent of the person who is doing the job. If the job incumbent is replaced or the job itself transferred from one function to another, the accountabilities of the position are unlikely to change.

Accountabilities serve to define the broadest duties and responsibilities of the position. It is within accountabilities that actual objectives are set.

Accountabilities Lists

Perhaps the easiest way to understand the essentially simple nature of accountabilities is to provide a list of common accountabilities that might logically appear in various jobs. These certainly will vary from one organization to another, but listed below are accountabilities for various positions and functions. Reviewing these can serve two purposes: demonstrate the point that accountabilities function more as labels designating major job areas than they do statements of what is to be accomplished by individuals, and suggest areas where important accountabilities may have been overlooked.

General Management or Senior Executive

- Internal operations
- Market development
- Profitability
- Organizational structure
- Organizational climate, culture, and mission
- Asset and liability management
- Board of directors relationship
- Productivity
- Financial strategy
- Business development
- Technology
- Customer satisfaction

- Community relations
- Regulatory compliance

Finance and Accounting

- Credit approval
- Management information
- Capital expenditures
- Security
- Financial analysis
- Cost control
- Internal audit
- Government reporting
- Collection
- Risk review
- Financial records
- Competitive analysis
- Cash forecasting
- Cash management

Sales

- New business acquisition
- Territory management
- Customer education
- Lead generation
- Lead qualification
- Account development
- Customer retention
- Selling skills
- Product knowledge
- Sales forecasting

Manufacturing

- Inventory control
- Maintenance
- Labor relations
- Waste
- Yield
- Safety
- Quality
- Production
- Record keeping
- Inventory control

Human Resources and Personnel

- Staffing
- Labor relations
- Employee development
- Compensation planning and administration
- Policy development
- Benefits administration
- Executive development
- Career development
- EEO/affirmative action compliance
- Human Resources Information Systems (HRIS) administration

Marketing

- Advertising
- Promotional strategy
- Pricing
- Market research
- Field support
- Marketing materials
- Media relations
- Sales support
- Agency relations

Secretarial, Clerical, and Administrative

- Correspondence
- Filing
- Records management
- Administrative support
- Internal customer service
- Equipment maintenance
- Forms administration
- Scheduling
- Supply maintenance and purchasing
- Telephone coverage
- Project support

Finally, there are overall accountabilities appropriate for consideration by every individual in the organization:

- Personal development
- Professional development
- Internal and external customer satisfaction
- Public relations
- Communications
- Interdepartmental relations
- Project management

Once it appears that all of a job's accountabilities have been identified, three final tasks remain before beginning the process of formulating the specific objectives in each accountability area:

1. Review the list to make sure that each accountability deals with a discrete and nonoverlapping part of the job. In other words, refine the list to eliminate duplications or mere rephrasing of the same broad issue.
2. Review the list to make sure that no significant issues or responsibility areas have been overlooked.
3. Review the list to make sure that the accountabilities assigned to the job are appropriate. A frequent source of organizational political squabbling arises when the same accountability is assigned (or allowed to exist) in two different jobs.

Objectives

If the accountabilities of a job have been thoroughly and comprehensively determined, the objective-setting process is enormously simplified. A frequent problem in the development and administration of results-based appraisal systems, however, is that the objective-setting process begins before all accountabilities have been identified. If people start setting objectives before there is clear definition of the areas in which these objectives should be set, the consequence is that the objectives will not be directly connected to the strategic goals of the enterprise. Individual objectives may well be important and worth pursuing, but they will not directly relate to the broader organizational purpose.

In his influential book, *The Seven Habits of Highly Effective People*, Stephen Covey points out a common flaw in the way people frequently approach the goal-setting process: They set their goals independent of their roles. Covey asserts that truly effective people begin the goal-setting process by first determining the roles that are truly important in their lives, in both the personal and work arenas.[3] For example, I might identify my primary work roles as these:

Writer	Creating books and articles for professional journals and popular magazines on how to help people become more successful in their work lives
Speaker	Giving keynote addresses and conducting management seminars on issues involving the management of people at work
Consultant	Helping client organizations create more effective performance appraisal systems and other management consulting activities
Marketer	Marketing my consulting and speaking services
Business manager	Running an enterprise (people to supervise, bills to pay, technology to keep abreast of, rent to pay, and a score of other business details to manage)

These are my primary business roles. In my personal life I also have important roles that I play: husband, family member, community volunteer, gardener, and athlete.

Covey makes his point clear: Set your goals within your roles. If we engage in goal setting without reference to the important roles we have chosen to play, then those goals will exist in a vacuum with no bedrock of support. With the first breath of adversity, we will give them up and move on. But if our goals are rooted in those parts of our lives we have chosen as important to us, then that grounding will support the likelihood of our continuing our labor when adversity emerges. Our goals in that case will not be mere wishes and good intentions; they will be carefully constructed statements of highly desirable outcomes that will further the satisfaction of those bedrock roles genuinely important to us.

The same situation prevails with regard to accountabilities and objectives. The function of an accountability is similar to that of a role: It is one of a small number of supremely important areas where we concentrate our efforts in order to ensure those successes that will be the most meaningful and satisfying. Objectives and goals differ only in terminology. Call it a goal or an objective or a target; its function is the same. It is the statement of an important and measurable outcome that, when accomplished, will help ensure success within the broad area represented by the accountability or role.

Characteristics of Effective Objectives

Objectives are set within each accountability area. Having established or been given a list of job accountabilities, the individual, in consultation with her superior, determines the goals or objectives that will be accomplished within that accountability during the appraisal period.

Several guidelines will help ensure that objectives are comprehensive and complete.

Focused on Specific Results to Be Achieved

A worthwhile performance objective concentrates on outcomes, not on activities. Effective objectives do not describe the routine activities involved in doing a job or the tasks and duties that the jobholder will engage in. What is important is not the activities engaged in to come up with the end product but the product itself. To achieve any worthwhile objective, a great deal of activity will be put forth. But the activity is not the issue; the result is.

Let's say that the public relations director of a professional services firm has as one of her accountabilities "client awareness." Within this accountability area she decides to concentrate her efforts during the course of the year on greatly increasing the number of times the firm and its services and successes are mentioned in the various media that current and potential clients are likely to be exposed to. The objective would not be stated as, "Identify all publications potential clients are likely to read" or "Send a press kit and follow-up letter to . . . ," with a list of publications. These are activities, not objectives. A well-stated objective might be, "Create and implement a plan to increase the number of favorable mentions within target media."

Written in Crisp and Concise Statements

Objectives should avoid irrelevant information, excessive descriptions, or elaborate background detail. The longer an objective statement is, the greater is the likelihood that activities and actions are being described instead of measurable results.

Stated Forcefully

Each objective should contain an action verb identifying exactly what will happen as a result of activity in this area.

Significant

Performance objectives should be limited to those that are of the greatest importance to the organization. Obviously in any job, a great number of objectives could be set. Some would involve little more than simply continuing the activities and minor improvements expected of anyone in the organization. The purpose of objective setting, however, is to concentrate on identifying a limited number of highly important results that, when achieved, will have a dramatic impact on the overall success of the organization or the specific unit in which the performer works.

In generating a final list of objectives, ask this question of each one: "If I achieve this objective completely, will it make a critical impact on the overall success of the business?" If the answer is no, strike it from the list of primary objectives, and keep it simply as part of the ongoing responsibilities of the position.

Prioritized and Weighted

Not all objectives are of equal importance. As writer and consultant Bill Swan notes, "Common sense suggests that when you send an employee off to meet seven complex performance objectives it would be a good idea to at least list them in order of importance (weight). It would also be a good idea to mention which should be done first, if they're not going to all be done simultaneously (prioritize). Each employee should know at the beginning of the year not only what is expected, but the priorities and weightings of these performance objectives so he or she can make decisions independently on a daily basis at every fork in the road."[4]

Placing weights on objectives also serves two other purposes. First, it gives the individual some guidelines for where the greatest amount of effort should be expended. All objectives are important; otherwise, they wouldn't be on the list at all. But if one objective is more important than all of the others, this information needs to be clearly communicated so that the individual can make good decisions when time pressures prohibit working on everything. Weighting and prioritizing objectives communicates the relative urgency of each.

In attempting to achieve all of our objectives, we often feel as if we're in the position of the person who is trying to put twelve bottles on a shelf built for ten. Although it may not be possible to get every bottle on the shelf, we certainly need to know if some bottles are more important than others and the sequence they should be placed in.

A second reason for prioritizing and weighting is to make sure that the ultimate performance appraisal accurately reflects the actual contribution that the individual made. It may well be that one person, who achieved only one of four assigned objectives, actually contributed more to the success of the organization by fully accomplishing that one task than another individual who completed four out of five but neglected the one that was singularly the most important.

Limited in Number

If the objectives that are set are truly important, there is only a limited number that any individual can accomplish. Once more than seven objectives are assigned, the likelihood grows that many will be neglected because of the excessive number of directions in which efforts are to be focused.

Fully Communicated

More than the person who is responsible for achieving the objectives needs to know what they are and how performance will be measured. Everyone who will be affected by that person's activities in accomplishing the objectives also needs to be aware of them: peers, colleagues in other departments, and subordinates.

If objectives are communicated broadly, the chances are better that information that can influence the accomplishment of the objective will be brought to the attention of the responsible person by others who encounter it.

Another benefit of cross-department communication of objectives is that it minimizes the possibility that two people in different sections will be working to accomplish the same end unaware of the other's efforts, promoting rivalry and unnecessary competition rather than collaboration and maximization of resources.

Written in Quantifiable Statements That Can Easily Be Measured and Reported

One of the greatest challenges in writing objectives is to develop statements that are capable of accurate measurement. The objective, "Increase customer perceptions that our products are of high quality," is certainly a laudable and important goal. The problem is not its importance; the dilemma is discovering a yardstick that can be used to determine exactly how well it has been achieved. What will we accept as evidence?

The ideal approach to writing measurable objectives involves ensuring that four elements are present:

1. An action verb
2. A statement of results
3. A time target
4. A standard of performance

While it may not be possible to include all four elements in every objective statement, the chances that the objective will be achieved increase when they are present: People know what they are expected to achieve, by what date, and at what cost.

Generic Objectives

From the start, we have talked about the importance of tying the process of setting goals and objectives into the process of determining the accountabilities within which these goals fit. There are, however, generic objectives that are potentially appropriate for any job done by any individual.

In *How to Measure Managerial Performance,* Richard Sloma observes that there are some objectives that are always applicable, always relevant, but alarmingly often overlooked.[5] Among the objectives that might fall into this universal category are these:

- Supporting the company's ethical standards as expressed in the mission statement
- Boosting profits
- Streamlining interdepartmental cooperation and communication
- Maintaining the highest possible quality
- Delivering better customer service to both internal and external customers

The list could easily go on with dozens more examples of objectives to which every member of the enterprise would be expected to contribute in any possible way: lowering costs, streamlining procedures, decreasing delays, and so forth.

There is obviously no shortage of objectives that could be set for any position. The important consideration is setting a small number of highly important objectives that will concentrate the available energy, commitment, and talent of each member of the organization on that small number of critically important outcomes that will positively affect the success of the business as a whole. It is entirely possible that in the course of the performance planning discussion, the manager might say to the subordinate, "Jerry, we have come to agreement on five critically important objectives for you to concentrate on over the course of the upcoming year. And while these five are by far the most important, and the factors that will be of greatest importance in your ultimate performance appraisal, I don't want you to forget that there are certain expectations we have of everybody who draws a paycheck from this place," and then go on to review them.

Establishing Performance Standards

We know now what the individual is accountable for and, within each accountability area, what goals or objectives we expect him or her to achieve. The remaining question is, What yardstick can we use to determine how well the job has been done?

Direct Measures of Output

The last criterion for effective objectives was stated as, "Written in quantifiable statements that can easily be measured and reported." Although not every objective may be immediately amenable to direct, quantitative, objective measurement, the more that unambiguous measures are available, the easier it will be for both the individual and the appraiser to assess accurately how well the individual performed in achieving the objective.

In seeking ways to measure the degree to which an objective or goal has been achieved, it is helpful to recognize that there are only four direct measures of output: quantity, quality, cost, and time. If an organization is using measures that are not directly related to one of these four, it is measuring something other than output or results.

Quality

Improving quality of performance is one of the primary goals of the entire performance appraisal process. In this case, we are looking more specifically for indicators that will provide information on how well the goal is achieved.

Quality measures can be objective and subjective. The quality of a sales representative's performance can be assessed subjectively through the responses customers write on feedback forms. The same sales representative's level of quality can be assessed more objectively by determining the number of customer complaints, customer referrals, customer retention, and other specific measures.

The more that subjective measures of quality can be made objective, the stronger the data are for use both in the appraisal interview itself and in any subsequent decisions based on those data. For example, the fact that a customer complained about poor service without providing any factual information to support the assertion is certainly a subjective piece of data; it's one person's opinion. But if 62 percent of customer feedback forms indicate that they felt they received less than excellent service, those subjective judgments are now an objective indicator of a serious service problem.

Here are some possible measures that can be used in determining the quality of goal or objective achievement:

> ▸ Customer complaints and compliments
> ▸ Error rate or rejects
> ▸ Compliance with specifications
> ▸ Returned goods
> ▸ Internal feedback and reports

Quantity

Quantity may be the easiest of the four outcome measures to work with, since all it requires is counting: How much? How many? How often? The risk, however, is that the quantity measures created do not provide an accurate assessment of the quality of goal achievement. The quality of a surgeon is not measured by the number of operations performed; the quality of a priest is not determined by the number of confessions heard.

The number of quantity measures is enormous. Although the challenge in assessing quality lies in finding accurate and direct measures that unerringly indicate the actual quality of the product made or service delivered, the challenge in assessing quantity is in sorting through the excessive number of possible measures to isolate those that genuinely make a significant difference.

Among the hundreds of quantity measures available, following are some examples:

> ▸ Number of units produced
> ▸ Calls per hour
> ▸ New products introduced
> ▸ Garbage cans emptied
> ▸ Grievances per 100 employees
> ▸ Mileage per replacement tire

Note that quantitative measures may generate valuable data about quality. In the last example, "Mileage per replacement tire," the data may indicate that on identical vehicles, one brand may need replacement at an average of 27,000 miles, while another brand wears out at 34,000 miles. Other things being reasonably equivalent, obviously there is a quality difference.

Cost

This is the domain of expenditures and budgets. To measure cost, explore such items as these:

- ▸ Variance against budget
- ▸ Dollars spent
- ▸ Ratio of product cost to maintenance cost
- ▸ Waste
- ▸ Overtime incurred
- ▸ Profit per item

Time

Consider both clock time and calendar time. Due dates, adherence to schedule, cycle times, and deadlines are all measures of time and timeliness. Other measures of time include:

- ▸ Reduction in number of class-days required for certification
- ▸ Deadlines and schedules met
- ▸ Average call response time
- ▸ Projects completed per month
- ▸ Number of minutes before initial contact with physician

Again, the measures focus on the timeliness of the result, even though they are countable and thus equally within the domain of quantity. The point is not to create rigid separations among the four measures of output. Instead, it is to make clear that there are four aspects that can be measured and to encourage appraisers and goal setters to consider all four in answering the question, "How will I know how well I have done in achieving the results I want?" If feelings or suppositions are the only way of telling, then there will be little justification to support any assessment made.

Determining Fully Satisfactory Performance

At this point in the process, most of the work has been done. Accountabilities have been determined, objectives have been set, and measures have been determined. The only question remaining unanswered is, "What will be considered fully acceptable performance?" In Chapter 3 I described a situation in which a sales representative had an objective of selling 100 cases per week. At the end of the year his weekly sales averaged 110 cases, placing him at 110 percent of his quota or objective. Is this good or bad? In discussing this case, I indicated that situational variables could well influence the performance appraisal rating. If the market significantly contracted during the year, 110 percent might be extremely good performance; if the market dramatically expanded, 110 percent might be rated unacceptable.

But without considering the external situation, the underlying assumption in this case is that selling 100 cases per week is fully satisfactory performance, since that is the quota that the sales representative has been assigned. To express it in terms that we have used throughout this chapter:

Accountability   =   Sales
Objective   =   Sell product to new and existing customers
Measure   =   Cases per week

The final dimension is added when the sales manager determines what "fully satisfactory performance" will be: 100 cases per week. The sales representative then knows that during those weeks when he sells more than 100 cases per week, he is exceeding the fully satisfactory level; in the weeks when case sales slip, he knows his performance is less than fully acceptable.

The benefit is that the sales representative is now capable of measuring his own performance against the organization's standard. And at performance appraisal time, he can be assured that unless there have been dramatic changes in his market situation, his achievement of selling an average of 110 cases per week will likely bring him a rating of at least Fully Satisfactory or perhaps the next rating higher.

For the sales representative, it's easy. It's easy not only because we are comfortable in thinking in terms of sales quotas but also because sales are so easily quantifiable. It's easy, too, because there are so few intervening variables between the behavior of the sales representative (his sales efforts) and the resulting outcomes (number of cases sold).

In an ideal performance management system, the sales representative's situation is replicated with every performer, for every objective. In addition to determining the major areas of accountability, assigning appropriate objectives for each, and determining how performance will be measured, the final requirement is to specify fully satisfactory performance as precisely as possible. This will provide a benchmark for each individual to measure his or her own performance on an ongoing basis throughout the appraisal period.

Many organizations and managers make the mistake of trying to determine in advance the level of performance that will earn a rating at each position on their scale from highest to lowest. This is unnecessary. Only the core requirements for Fully Satisfactory Performance need be identified. Most organizations use a rating scale with anywhere between three and seven categories into which different levels of performance can be assigned. It is impossible to specify in advance what the performer must do in order to be considered Superior or Distinguished or Exceptional. Similarly, it is unnecessary to specify the performance derelictions that will result in one's being branded Marginal or Unacceptable.

The reason is that, particularly for the higher levels of performance, it is impossible to know in advance exactly what will need to happen to cause a skilled assessor to decide that the performance he is evaluating is indeed distinguished. He will know it when he sees it, but until he sees it, he can't tell you what it looks like. The old joke about the three baseball umpires applies here. The first one said, "I calls 'em as I sees 'em." The second counters, "I calls 'em what they are." The third umpire settles the issue: "Boys, they ain't nothin' till I calls 'em!"

Probably the classic example of the unpredictability of higher levels of performance involves the now-familiar story of the 3M scientist who invented Post-It notes. Certainly product development would be one of his accountabilities, and "Develop a marketable adhesive-based paper product for the office supply market" might be a very specific objective. But can you imagine listening in to the performance planning discussion at the beginning of the appraisal year when the scientist's supervisor is reviewing accountabilities and objectives and measures. According to the story of how the product was developed, the supervisor would have said something like: " . . . and in order to get a rating of Outstanding, what you will need to do is develop a product that does not currently exist, on your own time, the only initial use for which is replacing bookmarks in hymnals, using an adhesive of such poor adhesive ability that it has been rejected as having no market potential, and continue developing it clandestinely after we have specifically instructed you to abandon all work on the project, and create a $300 million market all by yourself." It is not necessary to specify what Distinguished or Outstanding performance will look like. The results will speak for themselves. In addition, much of what we consider to be distinguished performance is a function of innovation, which by definition cannot be predicted.

Nor is it necessary to specify the conditions that will earn someone an Unacceptable rating. Over the course of the appraisal period, as the manager or appraiser becomes aware that the individual's performance is in fact not acceptable, they will discuss the problem and develop strategies for overcoming it well before it is time for the performance review. (They will be able to do this because, in addition to having set a specific objective, they will also have discussed and agreed on both the ways the objective will be measured and the checkpoints along the way when they will discuss progress toward the goal.)

What the performer needs to know is what his boss considers to be fully satisfactory performance: a good job, well done. Once that is clarified, the performance alone will speak for itself.

Objectives, Accountabilities, and Standards: A Summary

There are ten key steps in creating results-based assessment in an existing or new performance appraisal system:

1. Identify the key accountability areas for the position. Typically five to seven major accountabilities is a workable number.
2. Within each accountability, draft a series of possible objectives that, if achieved, would significantly increase organizational effectiveness and success within that accountability area.
3. Test each potential objective to make sure that it:
   ▸ Supports the overall strategic goals, values, and mission of the entire organization
   ▸ Is possible to achieve but demands some significant challenge and stretch
   ▸ Does not conflict with or inappropriately overlap the objectives set by another individual or department
   ▸ Is capable of completion given the availability of resources and the realities of organizational life
   ▸ Is capable of being measured on both an ongoing and ultimate basis
4. Based on the outcome of the tests in step 3, select a smaller number of significant goals or objectives to be achieved within the appraisal period. Again, five to seven is a workable target for the number of objectives to establish.
5. Write each objective in a clear, concise, and unambiguous statement of the end result to be achieved.
6. For each objective develop complete and appropriate mechanisms to measure goal attainment.
7. For each objective determine the level of performance required to achieve a performance rating of Fully Satisfactory (or similar organizational equivalent).
8. Determine appropriate mileposts or checkpoints for assessing progress toward goal achievement over the course of the appraisal period.
9. Communicate these objectives to all other individuals (subordinates, peers and colleagues, customers, vendors, etc.) who may be sources of information or assistance in achieving or revising the objective.
10. Begin the process of achieving the objectives, reviewing progress at predetermined checkpoints, and revising objectives as conditions and requirements change over the course of the appraisal period.

Notes

1. Scott Parry, "27 Ways to Increase Transfer of Training," speech at the National Speakers' Association Convention, Atlanta, Georgia, 1995.

2. Tom Kramlinger, "A Trainer's Guide to Business Problems," *Training* (March 1993): 47.
3. Stephen Covey, *The Seven Habits of Highly Effective People* (New York: Simon and Schuster, 1989).
4. William S. Swan, Ph.D., *How to Do a Superior Performance Appraisal* (New York: John Wiley & Sons, 1991), p. 75.
5. Richard Sloma, *How to Measure Managerial Performance* (New York: Free Press, 1980).

Chapter 5
Skills, Behaviors, and Competencies

Chapter 4 explored one of the two critical components that appears in almost every performance appraisal: the assessment of results. In this chapter we look at the other side. Here we focus not on what was done but on how the person went about doing what was done.

Even in an area like sports where results and output measures abound, more than results data are necessary for individuals to improve their performance. Performance outcomes by themselves do not inform employees of what they need to do to maintain or increase their productivity. Gary Latham and Kenneth Wexley in *Increasing Productivity Through Performance Appraisal* point out: "Telling a baseball player that he struck out will not come as a surprise to him. What the player needs to know, and what a good appraiser-counselor will be able to tell him, is exactly what he must do to at least get on first base and possibly hit a home run."[1]

Results measures can never tell the full story. If you know that $A + B + C = 19$, points out Peter Scholtes of Joiner Associates, you still do not know the value of C.[2] With performance appraisal, you may know the sum of the outputs (tons per day, sales, profits, machine up-time, etc.), but you do not know the value of any part of the sum. Individual performance is not the sum. It is only one part, and measuring only the outputs or results will provide a skewed and incomplete picture of the individual's overall performance.

What Are Competencies?

Call them what you will: skills, knowledge, behaviors, performance factors, competencies, success factors, values, quality concepts. All of these terms have been used by writers on performance management and by companies in their performance appraisal forms to identify those attributes of the individual that are important in achieving the results desired and in being a good corporate citizen.

Some of the terms are straightforward. *Skills* refers to the measurable and observable abilities that have been developed through practice, training, or experience. The individual has learned to do something and to do it well: solve quadratic equations, negotiate contracts, play "Dixie" on the tuba. *Knowledge* refers to what is in a person's head: a familiarity, awareness, and understanding of a topic or issue. Job knowledge, for example, is an area for assessment that appears on a large number of performance appraisal forms.

Competencies is the term currently in vogue to refer to the broad area of skills, abilities, and behaviors. The most comprehensive and complex definition of *competency* is this: "an *underlying characteristic* of an individual that is *causally related* to *criterion referenced effective and/or superior performance* in a job or situation."[3] The authors of this definition provide some help in understanding the words that they emphasized. By an "underlying characteristic" they mean that the area in question is a fairly deep and enduring part of an individual's personality. It is an aspect that can predict behavior in a wide range of situations. For example, the competencies they describe as critical to achieving success as a technical professional include such factors as achievement orientation, initative, analytical thinking, and concern for order. All pass the test of deep and enduring characteristics. "Causally related" means that the competency causes or predicts behavior. If I know that Jane has a strong concern for order and Joe does not, I can predict with reasonable confidence the things that Jane will do and Joe will avoid. "Criterion referenced" means that the competency predicts who does something well or poorly, as referenced to a specific criterion or standard. Examples of criteria are the dollar volume of sales for salespeople or the number of clients who stay sober for alcohol abuse counselors.

Whatever they may be called, we are looking here at the performance factors of the job. We will be considering the questions that deal with how the individual went about doing the job, not with what results were achieved.

Determining the Performance Factors for a Job

Whatever term we choose, our issue is the method and the manner through which a person achieves success on the job. Consider the performance factors used by four very large but significantly different companies in their performance appraisal forms for exempt employees: E-Systems (a defense contractor), ICI Paints (the parent company of Glidden Paints), Mobil Oil, and Coca-Cola. In each case, the greatest emphasis in their performance appraisal process is on the achievement of predetermined

Figure 5-1. Management Performance Factors

ICI Paints	E-Systems	Coca-Cola	Mobil
Core Competencies	*Management Skills*	*Performance Factors*	*Competencies*
Flexibility	Leadership	Communication	Teamwork
Initiative	Teamwork	Job knowledge	Technical
Concern for	Technology	Problem solving/	knowledge
impact	Human resources	decision	Effective
Concern for	development	making	communications
standards	Community	Budgeting/fiscal	Setting high
Self-development	relations	management	standards
orientation	Continuous	Work	Concern for
	improvement	relationships	accuracy
	Ethics and	Leadership/	Taking initiative
	regulatory	development	Concern for
	compliance	of others	effectiveness
		Planning,	Flexibility
		organizing,	Innovation
		and executing	

objectives. For all four of them, the first, and more important, part of their appraisal form is devoted to an assessment of results.

Each one of them, however, also identifies the performance factors that they want managers to assess in order to evaluate how the individual went about doing the job. Figure 5-1 lists the performance factors identified by each of the four organizations. The four companies do not list the items in any particular order; position is not an indicator of relative importance. What the list does indicate is that for management employees in these four organizations, there are common competencies that the organization expects its members to display independent of the results the individual is able to achieve.

Choosing the Competencies to Assess

There will always be a far greater number of important skills, behaviors, or competencies that an organization expects its members to display than there will be space on an appraisal form for them to be evaluated. Just a review of the competencies or performance factors in Figure 5-1 demonstrates that although the list of items to be assessed varies between five and eight, fewer than half of the items appear on more than one appraisal form, and not one item appears on more than two of the forms. Even such presumably obvious managerial competencies as effective communication skills, leadership, teamwork, and people development appear on only half of the appraisal instruments.

Competencies and Performance Factors vs. Objectives and Work Outcomes

The process for determining performance factors is exactly the opposite of that for objectives or work outcomes. With the latter, the manager and the subordinate have an enormous amount of work to do. They must determine the specific accountabilities of the subordinate's job or the varying roles the subordinate is expected to play. For each of those roles or accountability areas, they must determine what objectives should be set. In some cases the objective will be merely a maintenance one: to keep things running as smoothly in the future as they have run in the past. In other cases the objective will involve significant stretch and growth.

Having determined objectives, they will set checkpoints along the way, establish measures, and determine what acceptable performance will look like. Over the course of the year, they revise objectives as missions are accomplished and strategies change.

The opposite is true for performance factors. Look at the list of core competencies or management skills listed in Figure 5-1. Try to imagine the circumstances that would cause a manager to approach a subordinate and tell him that one of the items included on the form is being eliminated because of changed business requirements. It is easy enough to visualize Mr. Dithers rushing up to Bumstead to tell him to drop work on landing the new Fosdick project; all efforts must be redirected toward retaining existing accounts. It is ludicrous to envision Dithers telling Dagwood that "Effective Communications" and "Flexibility" have been taken off the appraisal menu and that, from now on, obfuscation and rigidity will be the order of the day.

Objectives change. Performance factors do not.

Choosing the Performance Factors to Include

Objectives are ephemeral; performance factors tend to be permanent. As a result, it is more important for the organization to choose wisely when it selects the items in this area against which managers will assess subordinates. In putting forth the performance factors or competencies for assessment, the organization is telling its members that these are the single most important attributes that they seek from members of the team. There will certainly be other important attributes expected of corporate citizens; no one will argue that any list of competencies, no matter how long, is exhaustive. But whatever items do not make the list must necessarily be less important than those factors that do make the cut. Although the organizations listed in Figure 5-1 may not have gone through a specific exclusionary exercise of deciding what gets on and what goes off the list, it is a reasonable assumption to conclude that at E-Systems and Coca-Cola, leadership (however it may be defined or assessed) is a more important organizational value than it is at ICI Paints or at Mobil, while flexibility is significantly more important to ICI Paints and to Mobil than it is to E-Systems or Coca-Cola.

By demarcating the competencies to be assessed, the organization is sending a clear message to its members that these competencies, more than any others, are the ones that they particularly esteem. An employee with enormous leadership ability who is not particularly flexible would be better served by seeking employment at E-Systems or Coca-Cola than at ICI Paints or Mobil.

Is that the message the organization wants to send? It had better be, since through its selection of a limited list of performance factors on the appraisal form, the company is advising its constituents that the way to get raises and promotions is to excel at these behaviors. If the behaviors listed are not the ones desired, then an enormous amount of both counter-productive effort and organizational cynicism will result.

Determining the Performance Factors to Be Assessed

The identification of objectives and work outcomes is an individual task, one that requires each member of the enterprise to set goals for the upcoming appraisal period. The identification of competencies or performance factors typically is a corporate undertaking, since these will usually remain constant regardless of the individual's job. When an organization embarks on determining which competencies should be included in the list for appraisal, there are several considerations that will help ensure an appropriate list:

- ► Number of job families
- ► Relevance to the nature of the job
- ► Impact on job success
- ► The organization's mission
- ► Senior management direction
- ► Need for change and organizational redirection

Number of Job Families

The first decision for a company to make is whether more than one set of performance factors is necessary. Most organizations find that the critical determinants of success in a nonexempt job are sufficiently different from those in an exempt position that two different sets of performance factors are required (though many of the same items will appear on both lists).

Although it is common to have different performance appraisals for the exempt and nonexempt populations, companies may decide to create additional forms in order to take into account the fact that the performance factors important in other job families may be sufficiently distinct as to require a separate form. The most common example is sales. Obviously the behaviors, skills, and competencies that make an individual a good salesperson are likely to be different from those that make for a good clerical employee, just as the attributes of an ideal clerk may differ from those of an ideal supervisor or engineer.

And what about technical specialists? Should they have a separate form with a separate list of competencies critical to success in their specialty? What about supervisors or any of a host of different jobs?

The list of performance factors for general managers of defense contractor E-Systems was provided above. But "General Management" is only one of seven job families for which the company has identified a specific set of performance factors to be assessed in determining how well the individual has done the job. In the exempt or management category, separate appraisal forms were created for four additional groups: supervisory, exempt professional, exempt technical professional, and managerial. For nonmanagement positions, two more sets of appraisal forms were developed to respond adequately to differences in the jobs: nonexempt salaried and nonexempt secretarial/clerical.

Whatever the job category, each E-Systems appraisal form contains nine performance factors. In almost every case the identical factors appear on every form. The core set of competencies, taken from the managerial appraisal form, includes the following:

- Job knowledge
- Work habits
- Planning and organizing
- Control and accountability
- People development and leadership
- Communication
- Interpersonal relations
- Problem solving
- Work results

Only minor changes in the list of competencies to be assessed can be found in the other forms. In the forms for exempt professional and technical employees, "People Development and Leadership" is replaced by "Influencing Others." For both categories of nonexempt employees, the

"Work Results" and "Work Habits" factors are supplemented with the addition of an assessment of "Ethics."

Through its construction of its appraisal forms, the company is communicating its deliberate decision that, with only the most minor variations, the nine most important competencies that it wants displayed by a vice president are the same that it expects to find in its engineers, its shop coordinators, and its typists. What constitutes a high degree of "Job Knowledge" or skill in "Interpersonal Relations" may be very different for those on the top of the heap than those in the middle or at the bottom; there is no difference, however, in what the company expects.

One of the subtle advantages in the approach used by E-Systems is the reduction in the likelihood of a perceived caste system, where people at lower organizational levels find themselves appraised under a different set of rules or guidelines from those at the top. With this approach, the company can demonstrate that although there are seven discrete appraisal forms (counting the headquarters general management form), the company's message to its members about what is desired is the same. The difference is not in expectations but in the opportunities the job allows each person to demonstrate that he or she is doing exactly what is expected.

Relevance to the Nature of the Job

The E-Systems approach—with all employees, regardless of the nature of their work or their position in the hierarchy, assessed according to a single set of criteria—is not the one taken by most organizations. Most companies believe that the performance factors that lead to success as a sales representative have little relationship to the behaviors that make a supervisor successful. Those individual contributors whose work involves the use of technical knowledge—software debuggers, research scientists, systems analysts—may need an entirely different set of competencies from those whose work requires marshaling the efforts of others—drill sergeants, marriage counselors, schoolteachers.

Since jobs are significantly different, it stands to reason that the performance factors used to measure effectiveness in those jobs should also be different. How do you determine the number of sets of criteria (and, as a result, the number of different appraisal forms) required to assess everyone in the organization by an appropriate collection of performance factors? One way of coming up with an answer is to look at the jobs inside one's own organization. What are the obvious family groups? One logical separation is provided by law, the Fair Labor Standards Act, which separates all of a company's employees into exempt and nonexempt classifications.

Another way is to look for significant differences in the nature of the work itself. Certainly the jobs of training coordinator, industrial engineer, staff attorney, and financial analyst are entirely different. The job incumbents will have majored in different subjects in college (and may well have gone to quite different schools), and they will probably score quite differently on personality tests. They will interact with significantly different people in the organization and face entirely different problems, which they must solve. Nonetheless, each one of them is a professional individual contributor. They are knowledge workers who make their contributions to the organization based on exercising their craft and skill in achieving organizational purposes. They supervise no one. They make decisions by themselves about the best way to approach a problem; they operate independently without close supervision. Although not one of the four might be successful if reassigned to one of the other's jobs, one performance appraisal form that includes both specific objectives and performance factors describing the work of technical or professional specialists would probably cover the dimensions of all four jobs with ease.

Sales jobs are frequently singled out to be assessed on unique appraisal forms. Two arguments support this approach. The first is that more than most other jobs, the sales position is highly measurable, and success is a direct function of the effort and skill of the individual in the position. The second is that most appraisers believe that they know what it takes to be a good salesperson and can spot one when they see one.

That last consideration is often more myth than fact, however. Even Tom Gilbert, one of the strongest advocates of competency-based learning, cautions against assuming that a high degree of consistency exists between the way exemplary performers do their jobs and the results that they achieve. Gilbert tells the story of three superb salespeople working for the same manufacturer of forklifts. One of these exemplary forklift sales representatives spent his time cruising through the countryside looking for abandoned warehouses that might be opening in the future. Another spent his morning on the telephone tracking down leads. The third top salesperson, who hated telephones, waded through all manner of paperwork—new building permits, business section articles in local newspapers, help wanted ads—looking for prospects. All three, Gilbert points out, were distinguished from the rest of the sales force by the exellent quality of their prospecting. It led to sales, the outcome the company desired. Gilbert summarizes his findings simply: "In 30 years of observing exemplary (and non-exemplary) performers I have found a surprisingly low consistency in how exemplary performers do their jobs. In other words, two exemplars are likely to exhibit quite different behaviors in the course of producing their masterful results."[4]

Impact on Job Success

Certainly there are specific competencies for success in different positions that can be determined. Although the three sales representatives Tom Gil-

bert describes had strikingly different ways of going about finding potential forklift purchasers, all three were highly skilled at the competency that
might be labeled "Prospecting."

In their book, *Competence at Work*, Lyle Spencer and Signe Spencer
report the research they have conducted exploring whether there is a common set of competencies that are predictive of success in various jobs.
They determined that it is possible, based on the structured interviews
they conducted in the course of their research, not only to identify the
specific competencies required for success in major jobs but also to determine the relative importance of each competency in distinguishing superior from average performers. "Achievement Orientation is the single most
frequent distinguishing characteristic of superior technical contributors,"
they found.[5] Better than anything else, technical professionals with a strong
achievement orientation—individuals who measure their own performance, improve outcomes based on results, set challenging goals, and
innovate—are the ones who most distinguish themselves from the mediocre. If I want to succeed as a technical professional, is there any one thing
that I should do? Yes, answer the Spencers unequivocally: Develop your
achievement orientation.

What else is important for the technical specialist? The Spencers provide a list in descending order of the importance of the competencies that
distinguish the truly superior from the merely pedestrian:

Relative Weight	*Competence Requirements for Technical Specialists*
6	Achievement Orientation
5	Impact and Influence
4	Conceptual Thinking
4	Analytical Thinking
4	Initiative
3	Self-Confidence
3	Interpersonal Understanding
2	Concern for Order
2	Information Seeking
2	Teamwork and Cooperation
2	Expertise
1	Customer Service Orientation

Curiously, two competencies that might have been expected to be
near the top of the pile show up at the bottom: "Expertise" and "Customer
Service Orientation." Another, "Impact and Influence," normally associ-
ated with success in jobs requiring a gret deal of persuasion and individual
interaction, ranks only behind "Achievement Orientation" as the most
important.

For salespeople, the Spencers find that "Impact and Influence" is at the top of the chart of key competencies—and not only at the top but exactly twice as important as the next two key factors on the list. Following these three, the rest of their list also provides some additional surprises:

Relative Weight	Competence Requirements for Salespeople
10	Impact and Influence
5	Achievement Orientation
5	Initiative
3	Interpersonal Understanding
3	Customer Service Orientation
3	Self-Confidence
2	Relationship Building
2	Analytical Thinking
2	Conceptual Thinking
Threshold	Technical Expertise

Curiously, "Technical Expertise"—product knowledge—makes the list at the very bottom, and then only as a threshold factor.

Finally, their generic managerial model is based on thirty-six different types of managerial situations, running from first-line supervisors to general managers in organizations as diverse as production, education, human services, health care, finance, and marketing. There are no changes in the top two; "Impact and Influence" and "Achievement Orientation" once again come out as the two most important determinants of job success. Some, like "Initiative," that were on both of the sales and technical professional lists drop off; others, like "Developing Others" and "Directiveness/Assertiveness," appear for the first time:

Relative Weight	Competence Requirements for Managers
6	Achievement Orientation
6	Impact and Influence
4	Teamwork and Cooperation
4	Analytical Thinking
4	Initiative
3	Developing Others
2	Self-Confidence
2	Directiveness/Assertiveness
2	Team Leadership
2	Conceptual Thinking

In determining which competencies to include in the performance appraisal for various jobs, this analysis will help the organization emphasize the abilities that have been demonstrated to be the most accurate predictors of job success. In addition, providing a tested and validated list will prevent appraisers from merely measuring that which is easy to measure (for example, giving high performance appraisal grades to salespeople who are the acknowledged experts in product knowledge without recognizing that the mere possession of product knowledge has little to do with the mastery of the sales position).

The Organization's Mission

In almost every speech or major presentation I make to groups of managers representing different organizations, I ask, "How many of you have committed to writing a statement of vision and values for your company—written a corporate mission statement?" In almost every case, about 90 percent of the hands go up. And the larger the size of the organizations they represent, the greater is the likelihood that they will have created a mission statement.

The creation of a mission statement can be one of the most important undertakings of any organization. The effort expended in determining exactly who we are and what we stand for can marshal and direct the energies of organization members toward the achievement of the broad calling the organization has set for itself. Creating mission statements is not an endeavor to be undertaken lightly. A study reported a few years ago by *Fortune* magazine noted that of all managerial tools and techniques, fads, and quick fixes, the two that organizations found to have the greatest significant positive impact on success were the inauguration of TQM efforts and the development of a corporate mission statement.

The question to raise in the area of performance appraisal is an obvious one therefore: To what extent does the performance appraisal form reflect the elements contained in the mission statement? If providing exemplary customer service or dealing with employees with dignity and consideration are values embodied in the mission statement, is the assessment of those values also included in the appraisal form? If not, then management may be seen as speaking with a forked tongue: pronouncing one set of values appropriate for the plaque on the reception area wall but discounting the actual importance of those values by ignoring them when it comes time to assess the actual performance of organization members.

GTE Telephone Operations has consciously included its corporate values as part of its appraisal process. GTE has identified seven core values for its telephone operations:

1. Quality
2. Benchmarking
3. People
4. Market sensitivity
5. Innovation
6. Technology
7. Employee involvement and teamwork

In the appraisal form, the section devoted to performance factors lists several dozen short statements of expected performance. The assessor is asked to indicate both the importance of the skill (C = critical; R = a regular part of the job; M = a minor element; and NA = an element that is not applicable to the job being assessed) and the employee's level of performance (S = strength; E = effective; G = skills in need of development; and NO = items not observed during the appraisal period). As the short excerpt from the GTE appraisal form in Figure 5-2 indicates, each performance factor is directly keyed to one of the GTE values.

Some organizations, including PepsiCo, General Mills, and Bank of Boston, in creating a 360-degree feedback assessment instrument for employee development purposes, base the items to be assessed directly on the company's mission statement. The same process applied to the development of performance factors to be assessed on the formal performance appraisal instrument will help reinforce the importance of mission statement values throughout the enterprise.

Figure 5-2. Performance Factors and Values

GTE Values		Importance of Skill (C)(R)(M)(NA)	Application of Skill (S)(E)(G)(NO)
Q—Quality	I—Innovation		
B—Benchmarking	T—Technology		
P—People	E—Employee Involvement		
M—Market Sensitivity	and Teamwork		
	Ability to:		
Do the right things to improve quality. (Q)			
Produce top quality work for customers. (Q)			
Set objectives about quality. (Q)			
Be aware of what other companies/competitors are doing in area of responsibility. (B)			
Identify and act on competitive benchmarks and gaps. (B)			
Promote teamwork and establish cooperative and positive working relationships. (E)			

Senior Management Direction

Several years ago a group of senior executives from one of America's most successful multinational consumer goods companies assembled for a weekend retreat to identify a success profile for the organization. Over the course of many hours, they struggled to identify the traits and attributes, skills, and competencies that were predictable determinants of success at general management levels in their firm. They sought to generate a list of the specific requirements needed to be successful as the head of one of the corporation's businesses or a senior executive on the corporate staff. The list that they generated would be used for making recruitment decisions, planning developmental opportunities, and selecting individuals for highly compensated, highly demanding posts.

Suggestions of attributes and competencies were made and debated. Finally the group arrived at a list of the twenty most important factors deemed as the determinants of success in their organization. In order of importance they listed the following:

1. Leadership
2. Results orientation
3. Analytical skills
4. Planning/organizing
5. Communication skills
6. People evaluation skills
7. Judgment/street sense
8. Negotiation skills
9. Initiative/resourcefulness
10. Conceptual planning skills
11. Drive/energy
12. Decisiveness
13. Interpersonal skills
14. Competitiveness
15. Assertiveness/toughness
16. Maturity
17. Adaptability
18. Intuition
19. Innovativeness/creativity
20. Language skills/facility

This list was the product of that group of managers working at that point in time. A year later, given a different set of senior executives working in changed market conditions and corporate realities, the list generated would unquestionably be different. But what this group of top executives did was define the performance factors that to them made the difference between being highly successful and just meeting the standards of the job.

Having invested the energy and resources required to generate this list, it would be wasteful not to use it in one other arena: the organization's performance appraisal. Certainly not every member of the company, even of its management staff, would be a contender for the sparse number of senior executive positions they were concentrating their search on. But using these attributes as the performance factors incorporated on the performance appraisal would produce two important benefits: It would send a clear signal to all members of the organization about what the top executives felt were particularly important, and it would assist in the development of these capabilities since organization members would know that these were the ones most prized and rewarded.

In the course of creating a new performance appraisal, one of the most valuable activities can be to assemble the organization's leaders and charge them with determining the most important five or seven or nine performance factors that they want to see encouraged among the organization's members. Including these factors on the appraisal form, together with the explanation that these attributes were not chosen at random, picked by personnel, or culled from a generic list by the implementation team but instead were determined by senior management after intensive study as representing the ones that were the singularly most important, will mobilize organizational energy toward their achievement.

Need for Change and Organizational Redirection

Dick Moroukian, a manager with experience running industrial operations on three continents, was describing the situation he encountered when he was named the general manager of Milltronics, a manufacturer of precision industrial ultrasonic weighing equipment. "I arrived to find a best-effort culture," Moroukian explained. "There were no problems in the organization with people not working hard or giving their best effort. But the attitude was that working hard and doing your best was sufficient, and if that didn't produce the results, well, there was nothing more that we could do about it—we had given it our best shot."[6]

One of the ways that Moroukian chose to redirect the Milltronics management team was through the means of performance appraisal. The previous system, concocted years ago by corporate headquarters in Canada, had been little more than an antiquated trait scale. Keith Sinclair, the new Canadian human resources chief, visited the Milltronics operation to help set up a more results-based, MBO-type approach. Moroukian embraced it but felt it didn't go far enough.

Each individual at Milltronics generated specific results-based objectives at the beginning of the appraisal period. Moroukian then added exactly a dozen performance factors, each with a definition of what he considered to be ideal performance. Even more than the change from a trait-based system to an MBO approach, the addition of specific skills and attributes Moroukian considered important for the company's success, together with his definitions, had a significant impact in redirecting Milltronics' "best-effort" culture into a results-oriented one. Among the attributes, together with their behaviorally based definitions, Moroukian demanded that his managers use to assess their subordinates were these examples taken from the company's performance appraisal form:

- *Organization Support/Teamwork.* Supports management decisions even when personally in disagreement. Communicates enthusiastic support of our goals and activities. Works effectively as a team member and encourages teamwork in others.

- *Decisiveness/Risk Taking.* Identifies and analyzes potential problems before acting. Understands and accepts risks involved in decisions. Acts on the basis of limited but adequate data. Stands by decisions when challenged. Exercises good judgment about when to take risks. Willing to take appropriate risks.

- *Accountability.* Displays professionalism in approach to work. Recognizes and accepts responsibility for all parts of job. Does not offer excuses for errors or mistakes. Does not blame others for mistakes. Displays corporate perspective in meeting job responsibilities.

- *Productivity.* Produces quality, desired results in an efficient (input per output) manner. Accomplishes and produces higher quality and quantity than co-workers. Manages resources (time, manpower, money, etc.) efficiently.

Where is the organization failing? Where does the organization need shoring up? What attributes are missing that are critical to future success? Incorporating these concepts in the company's set of performance factors can have a major impact in getting both managers and appraisees to start paying more attention to the items that truly make a difference.

Defining the Competencies to Be Assessed

The most effective way of defining competencies is to describe each competency or performance factor in behavioral terms, as Milltronics did with the four factors listed above. Note that what Milltronics provides is not a definition; instead it is a description of the behavior that an exemplary performer could be expected to engage in during the performance of tasks involving this area.

The more that competencies can be described (in behavioral terms) rather than defined (in dictionary terms), the more useful the appraisal form will be to both appraisers (in telling them the kinds of things that they should be looking for in determining how well a person has performed in the particular area) and appraisees (in suggesting to them the things that the organization will smile upon when they do them).

Mobil further enriches the process. Figure 5-1 lists the nine competencies that apply to most jobs at Mobil and appear on its annual performance and development summary. In the explanation of the process that all system users receive, Mobil devotes a full page to a description of each competency. The description includes four elements:

1. A definition
2. A description of specific behaviors that can be observed when someone demonstrates a competency effectively
3. A description of behaviors that are likely to occur when someone does not demonstrate a competency effectively
4. A list of suggestions for developing the competencies

What is most interesting—and unique—about the elaboration on competencies is the third item: the description of behaviors that are likely to occur when someone does not demonstrate a competency effectively. Setting off performance failures in relief against successes makes it far easier for both subordinate and supervisor to understand not only what is wanted but also what is *not* wanted. Each of the nine competencies contains four to six examples of counterproductive behavior within that area, along with at least as many specific examples of desirable performance. For the competency labeled "Flexibility," for example, the user's guide explains that individuals who do not demonstrate this competency focus on why things can't be done, invest so much energy in their own ideas that they fail to hear the merits of others, view disagreements as contests and defend the correctness of their ideas even in the face of evidence to the contrary, and find change threatening because generally they feel their way is best.

Providing not only behavioral descriptions of what the competency is but also, equally important, what it is not helps appraisers identify the behaviors that are strong exemplars of highly competent performance.

Choosing the Number of Performance Factors for the Appraisal Form

The Milltronics performance appraisal form had twelve factors for assessment, in addition to the specific objectives each individual in the company created at the beginning of the appraisal year. ARCO provides for seventeen to be evaluated; Mobil provides nine. American Airlines asks for eighteen performance factors to be assessed; Sprint asks for only six. Baxter Laboratories and Utility Fuels both present eleven items for the assessor to appraise.

The temptation is usually to include too many items to be assessed rather than too few. The consumer goods company referred to earlier in this chapter for its development of the twenty critical success factors ultimately elected to include none of them on the formal performance appraisal form. Its appraisal form was entirely results oriented. Appraisals were made on the successful achievements against accountabilities of the individual's job and that person's success in meeting predetermined objectives, not against performance factors. The performance factors or success profile that the top executives developed at their retreat was used for informal promotability assessments, job reassignments, and the determination of development needs.

Once the appraisal form includes more than perhaps a dozen items, several problems arise. The most important is a loss of impact for any one item. If everything is important, then nothing is important, and if appraisers are faced with a laundry list of twenty or thirty factors to be assessed, they will tend to give the list less time and attention than if there were only a few.

The second problem is more a mundane physical difficulty. Performance appraisal forms are notorious for trying to cram an enormous number of words onto a single piece of paper. Certainly it is possible to use very small type and virtually nonexistent margins to cram a stupendous number of assessment items on a single page. But the effect of including a stupendous number of items is to stupefy the assessor, who ends up giving minimal attention to the process just to get it over with.

A dozen performance factors, perhaps one or two fewer, is certainly sufficient. It is the rare organization whose mission statement or organizational condition or plans for the future require that more than a dozen broad areas of skill or competency on the part of organization members be assessed. As in so many other areas of organization life, less is more.

Trainability

In developing a list of performance factors to incorporate on the appraisal form, a consideration almost always overlooked is the issue of trainability. If an individual does not have street sense, or maturity, or innovativeness, or adaptability, no annual development plan or seminar participation will provide it. One great benefit of considering trainability in developing the list of performance factors is that it points out where the organization should be placing its emphasis: on selection, not on development.

The easiest way to understand the distinction between selection issues and development issues is to ask a CEO whether she feels that leaders are born or made. The answer will indicate whether for that person, leadership is a development issue or a selection issue. If she says that leaders are born, not made, then eliminate leadership as a performance factor on the appraisal form. Leadership, in this CEO's eyes, is not a characteristic amenable to development; this organization needs to fine-tune its recruitment process to make sure that it unearths a sufficient cadre of these born leaders since they cannot be home-grown. It should stop sending staff out to leadership training; cancel their Tom Peters seminar tickets; not hold employees accountable for something they had the genetic misfortune not to be born with. But should a CEO say that anyone who tries hard enough can be a leader, the organization should load up its appraisal form with leadership factors and sign everybody up for ropes courses, sensitivity sessions, Outward Bound, and whatever else the leadership fad of the month may be.

In generating a list of performance factors, it is essentially unfair to organization members to assess them on something that is basically untrainable and unchangeable. Several highly validated studies demonstrate that the best predictor of success in any job is the possession of a high IQ. Whatever the job, it turns out, the smarter the performer, the better the performance. But including intelligence as a performance factor is inappropriate—not because it isn't a critical determinant of job success (it is). But in spite of the accuracy of the manager's assessment of an underling's wits and the yearning of the subordinate to improve, IQ remains a fixed quantity that no training effort or development plan will significantly ameliorate. Move intelligence from an assessment characteristic to a recruitment requirement. Concentrate performance appraisal efforts exclusively on those performance factors about which something can be done.

A Separate Supervisory Assessment?

One area where creating a separate form covering specific skills, competencies, and behavior could be valuable is in the assessment of supervisory skills. When Houston's Utility Fuels was creating an appraisal form, it quickly determined that there would be two basic versions of the instrument: one for exempt employees and one for the company's nonexempt workforce.

As it began to develop the performance factors for assessment in the exempt area, however, it ran into two problems. One was the large number of unrelated but critically important supervisory skills that needed to be assessed. The other was that a large number of exempt employees were professionals, technicians, and other individual contributors. None of the items in the supervisory skills area applied to them.

The solution was straightforward and one that is easily adopted by other organizations: a separate, one-page assessment of supervisory skills that would be completed by the appraiser if the subordinate being appraised had supervision of others as a major job requirement. A total of twenty-nine discrete supervisory skills were presented for assessment followed by a section in which the appraiser was asked to prepare a narrative summary of the individual's overall performance as a supervisor. A copy of the first few items on the supervisory skills appraisal appears as Figure 5-3.

Other companies have also separated out supervisory skills from other performance factors in order to concentrate on those critical items that comprise a supervisor's responsibility. Mobil identifies twelve specific factors to be assessed for employees with direct supervisory responsibility:

1. Coaching
2. Effective communications
3. Encouraging teamwork
4. Establishing high standards and getting results
5. Effective delegation
6. Rewarding performance
7. Developing and releasing employees
8. Building consensus
9. Supporting reasonable risk taking
10. Forward thinking
11. Improving the organization
12. Managing diversity

By separating out the components of effective supervision, the organization gains several benefits:

- ▸ Without a great deal of additional burden, it allows appraisers to concentrate on assessing the individual components of the supervisory job.
- ▸ It provides an organization's supervisors information on precisely the areas where the company expects them to expend efforts and achieve success.
- ▸ It allows the individual who has supervisory responsibility as only part of the job to be appraised separately on both elements of performance: as an individual contributor and as a supervisor of the performance of others.

Figure 5-3. Supervisory Skills Appraisal

INSTRUCTIONS TO THE SUPERVISOR

NAME: _____   DATE: _____

1. Review each supervisory skill listed below.
2. If a "Job Requirement" is not part of this individual's supervisory duties, check the box "Not Applicable."
3. If the individual's performance is completely unacceptable for a particular "Job Requirement," check the box "Unacceptable."
4. For all other "Job Requirements," circle the number which best describes the extent to which the individual meets the requirements of the job.
5. Write a narrative summary of the individual's overall performance as a supervisor.
6. Provide an overall appraisal of this individual's performance as a supervisor using the UNSATISFACTORY, FAIR, GOOD, EXCELLENT or OUTSTANDING rating system.

			Extent to Which Individual Meets Job Requirements				
Job Requirements	*Not Applicable*	*Unacceptable*	*Great Improvement Needed*	*Some Improvement Needed*	*Fully Meets*	*Somewhat Above*	*Well Above*
1. Training employees	☐	☐	1	2 3	4	5 6	7
2. Coordinating subordinates' work	☐	☐	1	2 3	4	5 6	7
3. Scheduling subordinates' work	☐	☐	1	2 3	4	5 6	7
4. Controlling quality	☐	☐	1	2 3	4	5 6	7
5. Completing administrative reports	☐	☐	1	2 3	4	5 6	7
6. Complying with safety program	☐	☐	1	2 3	4	5 6	7

▸ The activity involved in determining the list of appraisal items for supervisors is useful in generating a thorough understanding of the job and may highlight areas where additional training and development efforts are needed.

Including Optional Performance Factors

In every case, the list of performance factors or competencies, no matter how long, is finite. Unlike the setting of objectives or work outcomes, where one employee may have as few as three and another as many as nine, virtually every company that chooses to include performance factors in its appraisal process generates a list of exactly so many, no more and no less, that the individual appraiser can neither delete nor add to.

Is this appropriate? In most cases, probably yes. In a well-designed appraisal process, the organization has invested a great deal of emotional energy and managerial deliberation in ascertaining exactly what competencies it wants to see exhibited among organization members and has valid reasons for wanting these to be consistently applied—if not across the entire organization, certainly throughout the different job families for which they were developed. Allowing individual appraisers to pick and choose among which competencies they will assess flirts with organizational anarchy.

But should appraisers be able to add a competency or two to the list when they realize that either there is a skill deficiency on the part of a subordinate that needs to be addressed or a particular strength that is worthy of formal recognition? The only organization I have encountered that not only permits but encourages the inclusion of an additional performance factor is one of the most successful and profitable of all of E-Systems' divisions. Nine performance factors make up the core appraisal form for all six of the different job families in the corporation. In addition to those nine, every appraiser is given the opportunity to add a tenth performance factor in the event that the nine listed do not allow the appraisal of one aspect of a subordinate's performance that is, for better or worse, particularly noteworthy. Figure 5-4 displays this part of the form.

As the figure illustrates, using this additional performance factor is demanding. The appraiser must give it a title, describe behavior that is fully competent, provide behavioral examples of the individual's performance, provide a rating with narrative justification, and then complete the assessment by adding objectives and comments.

Few E-Systems managers take advantage of the opportunity the company presents to enhance the performance factors section of the form, but the opportunity is there. All the company asks is that the manager create that individual assessment of a performance factor at the same level of quality and thoroughness as the rest of the form has been constructed.

Weighting Performance Factors

Some performance factors are more important than others. But few appraisal forms allow for various performance factors to be weighted in order to reflect their importance, to either the organization as a whole or the individual appraiser. With only one exception, in every performance ap-

Figure 5-4. An Optional Performance Category

10. SPECIAL PERFORMANCE DIMENSION (SD)

Title of Performance Dimension: _____

Meets Expectations When: (Describe performance that is Fully Competent.)

_____

_____

_____

Behavioral Examples (Critical Incidents): (Give two examples of behaviors observed during the rating period.)

1. _____

   _____

2. _____

   _____

Rating: _____
   Behavior Justifications of Rating: If the rating is a "3," the rating is already justified under the topic "Meets Expectations When." If the rating is "4" or "5," describe how the behavior exceeds "3" behavior. If the rating is "1" or "2," describe how the behavior is less than "3" behavior.

Objectives and Comments: _____

_____

praisal form I am familiar with, there is no distinction made on the form regarding the relative weights or importance of the various performance factors. Just its appearance on the form is sufficient to indicate that this is a behavior or skill or attribute that the organization values highly; to refine the process further by allocating weights is seen by almost all organizations as excessive.

The one exception is a large defense contractor. As Figure 5-5 indicates, each of the ten performance factors is rated on a 1 to 5 scale and

Figure 5-5. Weighting Performance Factors

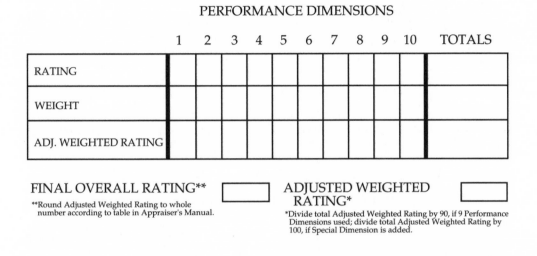

APPRAISAL SUMMARY

Summary of Rating Factors

PERFORMANCE DIMENSIONS

	1	2	3	4	5	6	7	8	9	10	TOTALS
RATING											
WEIGHT											
ADJ. WEIGHTED RATING											

FINAL OVERALL RATING** ☐
**Round Adjusted Weighted Rating to whole number according to table in Appraiser's Manual.

ADJUSTED WEIGHTED RATING* ☐
*Divide total Adjusted Weighted Rating by 90, if 9 Performance Dimensions used; divide total Adjusted Weighted Rating by 100, if Special Dimension is added.

then weighted in terms of its overall importance. Using the mathematical formula shown, a final overall rating, as well as an adjusted weighted rating score, is generated.

Integrating Performance Factors and Work Outcomes

The final question in the determination of competencies or performance factors brings us to the assessment process as a whole: Where will the organization place the weight? Is it appropriate to allocate half of the entire performance appraisal rating to the individual's success in the area of skills, behaviors, and competencies, with the other half of the report card grade determined by that person's success in meeting the objectives that were set and the job outcomes that were achieved, or is some other allocation wiser?

Allocating the final grade fifty-fifty will certainly make it easier to generate a final score, but this rarely is consistent with the needs of the business. What is important is results, most managers agree, and the emphasis therefore needs to be more on job outcomes and objectives than on behaviors and performance factors. If the greatest emphasis is placed on the achievement of results, the organization avoids rewarding those individuals who try hard and work hard and put forth great effort, but achieve little. This is the way it should be.

As management consultant Tom Gilbert points out, "The term *competencies* can lead people to err by focusing on behaviors instead of on accomplishments. It is really the accomplishments of the job performer—the results the person produces—that have value to the organization. The specific behaviors that go into producing those accomplishments are important, but they are a secondary concern."[7] Worthy performance, Gilbert would agree, is evidenced by people's accomplishments, not by their behaviors.

Notes

1. Gary P. Latham and Kenneth N. Wexley, *Increasing Productivity Through Performance Appraisal*, 2nd edition (Reading, MA: Addison-Wesley, 1994), p. 55.
2. Peter R. Scholtes, "An Elaboration on Deming's Teachings on Performance Appraisal," in *Performance Appraisal: Perspectives on a Quality Management Approach* (ASTD, 1990), p. 51.
3. Lyle Spencer and Signe Spencer, *Competence at Work* (New York: John Wiley, 1994), p. 9.
4. Timm J. Esque and Thomas F. Gilbert, "Making Competencies Pay Off," *Training* (January 1995): 47.
5. Spencer and Spencer, *Competence at Work*, p. 162.
6. Private conversation with author.
7. Esque and Gilbert, "Making Competencies Pay Off," p. 44.

Part II
Making the Performance Appraisal System Work

Chapter 6

How to Write a Fair Performance Appraisal

Get a copy of your company's performance appraisal form, take out your pen, and write Joe's appraisal. For many managers, this task is one of the most distasteful parts of the job—the element that they most would like to have eliminated.

The best way to approach the task is to look beyond the merely clerical responsibilities of checking off the boxes, playing with numbers, and writing comments on the lines and spaces provided. Writing performance appraisals is made much easier, and the end products are of far higher quality, if the manager sees the operation of generating a performance appraisal document as a three-step process:

1. Collect the data.
2. Evaluate the performance.
3. Write the review.

The first task—collecting data about the individual's performance that is accurate, representative, objective, and complete—is by far the most challenging and time-consuming. The better the manager does at data collection, the easier will be both completing the form and conducting the appraisal discussion.

Step 1: Collect Appraisal Data

The first piece of information needed has nothing to do with how well the employee is doing the job; instead, it describes the job itself. The formal job description for the employee's position is the basis for evaluating how well the employee did the job. Start by asking whether the official job description still accurately reflects the key responsibilities of the job. Does this piece of paper accurately reflect what Sally is doing and should be doing on a day-to-day basis? Is she doing important things that aren't discussed in here? Does the job description describe activities that are no longer as important as they were when it was written?

Cross outdated requirements out; add in new responsibilities. The official job description may have been written to serve many purposes. The goal now is to develop a working document that reasonably reflects the reasons the job exists, the most important activities the job requires, and the objectives and results the jobholder is expected to achieve.

If there is no formal job description, draft an informal one by filling in the blanks:

The reason the company created this job is to _____.

The most important ways a person doing the job should spend time are _____.

The two or three most important duties of someone in this position are _____.

If someone asked me what it takes to be successful in this job, I would say, _____.

The easiest way to determine whether this job is being done well is by _____.

Questions like these have nothing to do with the performance of the specific individual doing the job; they deal with the job itself. Answers to these questions give a standard against which to compare the performance of the person who's getting paid to do the job with what the manager and the organization as a whole expect to get for their investment. Before anyone can ask how well the person is doing he or she needs to determine what it is that you want to get done.

Data on the Jobholder

Once you have identified the requirements of the job itself, you can gather the data you need to tell you how well the jobholder is performing. There are three different kinds of information needed:

1. Objective data
2. Critical incidents
3. Behavioral observations

Objective Data

"Objective data" means facts—for example:

- Number of calls per hour made
- Average response time
- Number of patient complaints
- Average sales volume per customer
- Number of articles written
- Number of days absent and late
- Projects completed on time
- Number of errors

Objective data are quantifiable. The information is countable, factual, and objective. It is, to use a term we will use frequently in discussing both how to prepare fair performance appraisals and later in discussing how to conduct effective appraisal discussions, unarguable. There is no judgment or opinion involved. The employee made an average of 6.3 calls per hour; she missed five days of work; he wrote 122 lab reports. Is 6.3 calls per hour good or bad? Does missing five days of work reflect an exemplary attendance record or a terrible one? Should the lab technician be proud of generating 122 lab reports or ashamed?

Objective data do not reveal whether the performance was good or bad. They simply tell us what it was. The decision about the quality of performance depends on having a standard. In some cases the standard will be established. If agents are expected to handle 4 calls per hour and Harvey handled 6.3, he's doing better than expected. But if the standard is 9 calls per hour, Harvey's average of 6.3 is lower than expected.

In other situations a standard is assumed. The hospital assumes that no employees will act in a way that provokes a formal patient complaint. One complaint is unacceptable.

In some cases the standard will involve a comparison with others. Is Norma's attendance record of five days of absence good or bad? If the average absence rate of all employees is three days, her five days of absence is worse than average. If the office average is ten days, she's doing much better than most others.

Objective data are usually the easiest to collect and discuss. That's the good news. The bad news is that objective data are rarely the most useful of the three kinds of information managers need to gather to make defensible and fair appraisal judgments about their subordinates. Objective data give the facts, but the facts by themselves rarely tell the whole story. For example, although Harvey handled 6.3 calls per hour compared with a standard of 4, he achieved that apparently excellent result by cutting customers off, rudely terminating conversations, telling callers to call another number rather than looking up the information, and ignoring opportunities that could have led to major sales. Objective data tell only what the individual did, not how he or she did it, and frequently the *how* is the primary concern.

Critical Incidents

The second type of information to collect involves critical or significant incidents—situations in which employees acted in ways that were either especially effective or especially ineffective in accomplishing parts of their jobs. Note that critical incidents are not negative incidents. The situation described can be positive as well as negative. A critical incident can also describe what the person didn't do as well as what he did. For example, in describing the performance of a police officer chasing an armed robbery suspect down a busy street, a supervisor recorded the following: "June 22, officer Mitchell withheld fire in a situation calling for the use of weapons where gunfire would have endangered innocent bystanders."

Using critical incidents is ideal for performance appraisal purposes, since the rater is focusing on actual job behavior rather than on vaguely defined traits. Performance, not personality, is being judged. Not only do individuals receive meaningful feedback on their performance, they understand exactly what they need to do differently in the future. The employee may not agree with the supervisor's standards, but there is no question about what the expectation is.

Collecting critical incidents is difficult and time-consuming. First, you need to pay sufficient attention to the performance of every employee that you recognize critical incidents when they occur. Many managers are not sensitized to look for incidents when an individual's performance is significantly better or worse than usual. If the employee were to do something absolutely heroic or utterly odious, the manager would certainly notice, but heroic and odious examples of performance are rare. Managers may let noteworthy incidents of good and poor performance go by simply because they are not trained or skilled to notice anything but the most extraordinary.

Using critical incidents in performance appraisal presents a second challenge. In addition to recognizing that the performance just observed is indeed significant—whether particularly better or worse than normal—the manager must also make a record of it. It seems time-consuming and burdensome to keep regular records on a daily or weekly basis of the performance of a group of subordinates. But most managers are already using some system to keep track of appointments, deadlines, projects, and other work items. Frequently what is required is not creating a new system but adding observations to the in-place schedule-tracking system. Another only slightly more involved process is to create a file with a manila folder for each employee. Get into the habit of noticing examples of particularly strong or ineffectual performance, write a quick summary of the incident, and drop it into the subordinate's "critical incident" file. Making regular entries will generate a wealth of data to use when the time comes for completing the annual appraisal.

A final, more subtle difficulty in using critical incidents in the performance management process involves the question of whether to discuss the incident at the time of its occurrence with the individual or wait until the annual review. Positive incidents are not a problem; subordinates are happy to hear about them at any time. But when the incident involves a performance failure, the manager faces a two-edged sword. If she decides to wait until the annual review to discuss it, she will be accused of sandbagging the employee—delaying the discussion of an important aspect of performance until it could be used against the subordinate at the time of formal appraisal. "Why didn't you tell me at the time, when I could have done something about it?!" is a legitimate complaint on a subordinate's part. On the other hand, if the manager raises the incident at the time of its occurrence and discusses it with the individual, the employee may feel that he has been a victim of double jeopardy if it is again raised during the performance appraisal, particularly if he has worked to correct the problem.

Behavioral Observations

Almost twenty years ago Tom Peters codified the practice of MBWA: management by walking around. It's still a good idea.

As you walk around your operation, observing your employees performing their jobs and interacting with them in all of the normal day-to-day transactions between supervisor and subordinate, you will get a thorough understanding of how each person goes about doing the job. You'll notice how the person interacts with coworkers and customers; you'll see examples of good corporate citizenship; you'll find an abundance of data about each individual's successes and shortcomings in achieving the objectives of the enterprise. Make note of them.

When the time comes for performance appraisal, these day-to-day observations made over many months will give you the examples and evidence you need to move from general judgments of your opinion of how well an employee is doing to actual examples of specific behavior that provide evidence to support the judgment you have made.

Data About the Person

What about the employee? It is also important to know the individual's history. Unless the individual has recently joined the organization and is coming up on her very first formal appraisal, there is a history that you should examine. Pull out Carla's appraisal from a year ago and read it. How does her performance this year compare with how she was doing a year ago? Has she corrected problems that were noted in the "Needs Improvement" section of the prior year's form? Has she kept pace with the changes in technology and expectations? Your appraisal of her will be more valuable and easier to discuss if you have a broad perspective of her entire history with the company, not just the isolated facts about the previous twelve months. And if there has been specific improvement in important areas of deficiency noted on previous appraisals, recognizing that improvement will almost certainly have a positive motivational effect.

Self-Appraisal

The final piece of information to collect is the individual's own perceptions of his or her job performance. If your organization uses self-appraisal as a formal part of the performance management process, follow whatever specific procedures your company's policy outlines. If your organization does not provide for self-appraisal as a prescribed part of the process, it is rare that managers would not be permitted to do this on their own. It's a good managerial practice. The best way is to begin far in advance of the time when the official appraisal is due. As part of your regular performance management interactions with your work group, tell them that you will be adding a new element to the standard performance appraisal process this year. Explain that you want to get their input and insights into the way they see their job performance, and you want to do that in a more thoughtful way than just by asking for their reaction to what you have written on their annual appraisal. For that reason, you explain, when performance appraisal time comes around this year, you'll be asking each of them to prepare and submit a self-appraisal. Ask them to think about this as they go about their jobs over the upcoming months and keep track of any information they feel would be important to include on the appraisal they'll be writing.

Step 2: Evaluate the Performance

Now that you have collected all of the information you need to evaluate the person's performance and fill out the evaluation form, put the facts and the form aside for a moment and think about the individual. What is the core message you want to communicate?

The performance appraisal documentation will be used for many purposes: determining who gets raises and how much they get, determining who gets promoted and who gets fired, pinpointing where the company needs to provide training and recruit talent. The discussion you will have about the appraisal will cover many topics: your assessment of the individual's performance over the previous year—what was done well and what needs improvement; what the individual should concentrate on during the next twelve months; where the individual's development efforts should be concentrated; how much of an increase the person will get and why that amount is the right amount.

In all the clutter of conflicting messages, it's easy for the central point to be missed. What is the central point? That's your job to figure out.

By now you've probably determined the overall level of performance. If the individual's performance is well above that of others, you may not have decided exactly whether to rate it as superior or distinguished, but you know that it will be somewhere above the middle category. For most people, you'll have confirmed that the middle rating is appropriate, and for a few you'll have come to the conclusion that a lower-than-average rating is correct.

Before you start checking off the boxes and writing down your comments and examples, however, it's wise to start by getting the big picture clearly in mind. The purpose of the performance appraisal form and your upcoming conversation with the person is to communicate a message. If you have not determined the precise message that you want to send, it's unlikely that the individual will learn what you want him to learn from the performance appraisal experience.

Therefore, start with the end in mind. When all the boxes have been filled out, when all of the personnel and administrative requirements have been completed, when the conversation is finished, what do you want the result to be? Should the employee know that you consider his performance to be well above your expectations and that you want to see this level of effort and accomplishment continued? Is the message that the performance is well above average but, given your experience in working with him and others, that he is capable of even greater things next year? Are you dealing with a person in a noncritical position who sees the job as simply a way of making a living, whose performance is fully competent, and you will be satisfied if the current level is maintained for the future? Or is the central message: "Shape up or ship out"?

In considering the message you want to send, keep the employee's career goals in mind. One writer points out, "Whether the employee's motive is to move up the company ladder, be the top performer in the department, or merely hold on to his or her current position, there are skills and expectations required to reach each objective that coincide with what superiors need to manage a successful team. For the purpose of performance appraisal, identifying these skills in terms of the employee's goals—rather than the supervisor's—will have the most enduring impact."[1]

Begin with the end in mind. Recognize as you write the appraisal that it will be used for many purposes. What is the core communication to be? Assume that a month has passed since the performance appraisal was completed and discussed with the employee. What are the one or two, at most three, things you want the individual to remember?

Once you have determined the core message about performance, you are ready to begin writing the appraisal. If company policy provides for all appraisals to be written at the same time, it's usually easiest to start with those whose appraisals will be the easiest to justify and discuss: the high performers. Starting with this group gives you a benchmark when you consider the performance of others. While it is much more important and valid to compare an individual's performance to a predetermined standard than it is to the performance of others, starting with high performers sharpens your ability to recognize what you want from all members of your staff.

The Meaning of Fair

Writing a person's performance appraisal, more than almost any other activity performed by a manager, requires the individual to be fair, unprejudiced, and objective. But the fairness requirement does not mean that the manager can use only quantitative, numerical resources in completing the assessment. The manager's opinions, feelings, and judgments are what is demanded by the appraisal process. Managers are paid to make judgments even when—or particularly when—all of the facts are not available. In every other area of managerial activity, the ability to act appropriately on the basis of limited and occasionally conflicting data is celebrated and rewarded. Only in the case of performance appraisal are we uncomfortable about the fact that nonquantitative, subjective, experience-based information is used.

If you approach the appraisal writing process with certain beliefs and assumptions, you will have little difficulty in generating an appraisal that is fair, unprejudiced, and objective. Your assumptions need to be these:

- ▸ The purpose of the performance appraisal is to further the organization's purposes by strengthening the performance of every member of the organization.
- ▸ You will never have all the facts and, in spite of that you must still do the job.
- ▸ The bar is rising every year. What was good enough last year is no longer good enough this year.
- ▸ People genuinely want to know what their boss thinks of their performance.

- People are capable of handling the truth about their performance, even when that truth is unpleasant.
- It is better to demand more of people than it is to settle for whatever level of performance they choose to give.
- The ability and willingness of any individual to perform is unrelated to that individual's race, sex, religion, or any other non-job-related factor.

Many people will argue that their jobs can't be measured. R&D scientists, software engineers, designers, and graphic artists cry out the loudest when you suggest that performance appraisals can be constructed for their jobs. The key is *describing* good performance with words, not measuring it with numbers. In every case, a good job can be described in such a way that it can be verified. Measurability is not the goal; verifiability is. Not everything can be measured with numbers; some numbers are meaningless, and sometimes the most meaningful aspects of the work can only be described. Aim for verifiable performance standards. Numbers just happen to be easy to verify.

Rating Errors

In spite of a manager's good-faith efforts to maintain a fair, objective, and impartial manner in writing every appraisal, errors in judgment can arise when one individual observes and evaluates another. Psychologists define rating errors technically as, "the difference between the output of a human judgment process and that of an objective, accurate assessment uncolored by bias, prejudice, or other subjective, extraneous influences."[2] What makes rating errors so difficult to correct is that raters are unaware that they are making them. The result is an employee who is inappropriately retained, terminated, promoted, demoted, or transferred.

Psychologists and academicians studying the performance appraisal process have identified nine common appraisal errors:

1. Contrast effect
2. First impression error
3. Halo/horns effect
4. Similar-to-me effect
5. Central tendency
6. Negative and positive skew
7. Attribution bias
8. Recency effect
9. Stereotyping

Figure 6-1 identifies, defines, and provides an example of each error. Of all of the errors, contrast effect (comparing one person against another

Figure 6-1. Common Appraisal Errors

Error	Definition	Example
Contrast effect	The tendency of a rater to evaluate people in comparison with other individuals rather than against the standards for the job	Think of the most attractive person you have known. Rate this individual's attractiveness on a scale of 1 to 10. Now think of your favorite glamorous movie star. Rerate your acquaintance. If you rated your friend lower the second time around, contrast effect is at work.
First impression error	The tendency of a manager to make an initial positive or negative judgment of an employee and allow that first impression to color or distort later information	A manager new to a work group noticed one employee who was going through a divorce performing poorly. Within a month the employee's performance had returned to its previous high level, but the manager's opinion of the individual's performance was adversely affected by the initial negative impression.
Halo/horns effect	Inappropriate generalizations from one aspect of an individual's performance to all areas of that person's performance	Jeff was outstanding in his ability to get delinquent customers to pay up. His excellence in this important area caused his manager to rate him highly in unrelated areas where his performance was actually mediocre.
Similar-to-me effect	The tendency of individuals to rate people who resemble themselves more highly than they rate others	Carol, a single mother of four small children, had prevailed in her efforts to succeed and had been promoted to manager. She unwittingly rated several women who were also single mothers higher than their performance warranted.
Central tendency	The inclination to rate people in the middle of the scale even when their performance clearly warrants a substantially higher or lower rating	Out of an erroneous belief that the law required companies to treat all employees the same and a conscious desire to avoid confrontation, Harold rated all seven of the employees in his work group as "Fully Meets Standard."
Negative and positive skew	The opposite of central tendency: the rating of all individuals as higher or lower than their performance actually warrants	Susan rates all of her employees higher than she feels they actually deserve, in the misguided hope that this will cause them to live up to the high rating they have been given. Carlos sets impossibly high standards and expectations and is proud of never having met a subordinate who deserved a Superior rating.

Figure 6-1. *(continued)*

Error	Definition	Example
Attribution bias	The tendency to attribute performance failings to factors under the control of the individual and performance successes to external causes	Harriet, a manager with a mixture of both excellent and mediocre performers in her work group, attributes the successes of the former group to the quality of her leadership and the failings of the latter group to their bad attitudes and inherent laziness.
Recency effect	The tendency of minor events that have happened recently to have more influence on the rating than major events of many months ago	Victoria kept no formal records of the overall performance or critical incidents of her work group of twelve people during the course of the year. When she began writing their appraisal, she discovered that the only examples she could provide for either positive or negative performance had happened in the last two months.
Stereotyping	The tendency to generalize across groups and ignore individual differences	Waldo is quiet and reserved, almost meek—about as far from the conventional cliché of a salesman as can be imagined. His sales record, however, is one of the best in the company. But his boss rated his performance lower than that of other salespeople since he didn't fit the mold, ignoring the results that Waldo had produced.

instead of against a standard) and recency error are probably the two most common. The one that may have the most damaging effect on an organization, however, is central tendency or its even more pernicious cousin, leniency.

Too many supervisors fail to evaluate the negative aspects of employee performance honestly, asserts Professor Barbara H. Holmes.[3] They may justify their leniency—giving a rating higher than deserved—by arguing that it avoids the hurt feelings, hostility, arguments, and potential demotivational effects that may result from a negative appraisal. Supervisors fear that employees will take their dissatisfactions to court. And besides, they rationalize, "nobody really gets hurt." In fact, lenient appraisals, whether motivated by cowardice or kindheartedness, do hurt. They hurt the supervisor, the employee who is undeservedly awarded a higher-than-justified rating, other teammates and coworkers, and the organization as a whole.

Although the overrated employee is as unlikely to complain about the erroneous appraisal as the student who has earned a B will complain about getting an A, the worker, like the student, is being shortchanged. Besides being a mechanism for allocating salary increases, the procedure is also a mechanism for providing feedback. Employees whose supervisors fail to give them accurate information on their performance deficiencies and shortcomings have little motivation to improve. The status quo will continue, the performance will remain unchanged, and the employee is likely to be passed over for opportunities he might have had if he had honestly been confronted with the need for change and had taken advantage of the honest feedback, or he may be placed into a situation he is unable to handle and experience the bitterness of failure. Short-term kindness—the supervisor's reluctance to identify and discuss performance shortcomings—may produce long-term harm to the deficient performer.

The organization suffers even more if inadequate performers are not confronted. Inflated appraisals result in the organization's being stuck with a cadre of less-than-optimal individuals. Organizational deadwood will proliferate. Worse, when the organization finally does realize that survival depends on cutting loose the noncontributors and begins eliminating those whose contribution is marginal, it will be haunted by a history of above-average appraisals given to below-average performers. The peril of wrongful-termination litigation cases may cause the organization to act far more slowly than competitive and market conditions demand, ameliorating the appraisal process to build accurate records of deficient performance that accurately contradict the erroneous appraisals of years past.

The employee's thought process, as attorney Jonathan A. Segal illustrates, is easy to follow: "For years I have received nothing but stellar appraisals. Now suddenly I am discharged. It can't be because of my performance. Otherwise, my evaluations would not have been as good as they were. There must be another reason. And it must be an illegal reason. It must have been because of my _____."[4] Fill in the blank with any protected group the employee happens to belong to.

By giving employees a false sense of security and depriving them of an opportunity to improve, inflated performance appraisals provide the individual with an incentive to sue. They provide more than just an incentive, Segal argues; they are a strong arsenal in litigation. Supervisors who rate all employees as satisfactory are not only not doing their jobs but are putting their employer at risk.

The most insidious costs of inflated appraisals may be on the organization's other employees—the ones who have genuinely earned stellar ratings. "It is a simple fact of life," Holmes points out, "that organizations have limited money and positions that employees compete for. If some employees are given inflated performance appraisals, it is likely that when management is distributing pay raises and promotions, the inflated employees will receive more of these resources than they really deserve."[5]

How will good performers react once they discover, as invariably they will, that the organization is permitting inflated appraisals to be accepted? *Equity theory* provides an answer. It proposes that individuals are concerned not only with their own situation in an absolute sense (How much money am I making?) but also with how their situation compares with others in the organization (How does what I am making compare with the amount that others are making?). Employees make judgments about the fairness or equity of their situations and then make appropriate adjustments in their behavior. To determine if their situation is "fair," employees compare how much they are giving (effort, time, skill, dedication) with how much they are getting (pay, recognition, promotions, special privileges). They then compare their situation to that of others. The good performer, observing that a lackluster and apathetic coworker is receiving the same performance appraisal and thus the same organizational rewards for a far lower contribution, perceives her situation as unfair.

Equity theory predicts that the good performer will act to change the situation so that it becomes equitable, with the giving and the getting balanced. The obvious way—demanding higher raises and greater access to promotions and privileges—will probably not work. The good performer therefore decides to reduce his effort—to coast—so that the rewards he receives are in proportion to the efforts he makes. Alternatively, he will decide to leave the organization and find another where equity prevails.

The Need for Courage

The key requirement is courage. All the training in the world will be to no avail if supervisors lack the internal courage to make the tough judgment calls. The organization must demand that they honestly assess performance and deliver negative appraisals when they have been earned.

Peter Habley, Vice President, Employee Resources, Pfizer Hospital Products Group, makes the point clearly: "Any system/process/design will work if the fundamentals of good performance management are used. But the place where performance management breaks down is at the moment of truth when a supervisor has to sit in judgment on the performance and behavior of a subordinate. How do you get an average, good-guy, competent supervisor to muster the courage to confront? All systems depend on the ability to give immediate, frequent, and, yes, positive and supportive evaluation of subordinates. But if they don't have the courage to confront, then forget it."[6]

Tom Peters is equally adamant on this point: "Employee evaluations should reflect perform-or-else principles." Peters acknowledges that organizations are routinely asking people to do more than they have ever done in the past. Simply showing up and doing what you're told, the expectation of yesterday, has been replaced by a new requirement: "Now you must: (1) become darn good at something, since expertise is the basis of all value-added services and products; (2) become pretty good at lots of things—everyone must be a well-rounded businessperson; (3) be a first-rate team player; and (4) exercise initiative daily in solving customer problems. Performance must take a front-row seat. These days we must put every employee—for their own good and their firm's good—on an up-or-out trajectory."[7]

Supervisors, each the captain of an individual ship that en masse makes up the organizational flotilla, must ask of each member of their crew: "Is this person a sail or an anchor?" Sails must be rewarded and retained; anchors must be confronted and, in the absence of immediate and dramatic change, eliminated.

Step 3: Write the Review

With all data at hand and the resolve to avoid ratings errors and avoid leniency, you are now ready to use the appraisal form to rate the performance of the individual.

Start by examining the form to determine whether its structure allows you to appraise performance appropriately. Every appraisal of an individual is a balance of two factors: behaviors and results. Does the form your company provides allow you to describe and evaluate both what the person accomplished and how she went about doing the job? Is it merely a trait list? Is it a totally unstructured essay format? "The more inadequate and haphazard the form, the more latitude you are probably given in applying it," performance appraisal consultant Bill Swan argues. "If your organization's performance appraisal system is inadequate to the tasks it must perform, the chances are you have room to take action to repair faults in the system. Where the criteria for the appraisal are lax, vague, or insufficiently job-related, you can use those criteria but define them for yourself in a concrete, job-related way."[8]

The problems inherent in deficient forms or systems can usually be overcome in several ways:

- ▸ Attach additional documentation to the formal performance appraisal form.
- ▸ Hold goal-setting meetings with employees at the beginning of the year, and appraise their performance against those goals as part of the organization's standard appraisal procedure.
- ▸ Review the traits listed on the appraisal form with members of your work group, and jointly define what behaviors could be used as evidence of good performance of each.
- ▸ Specifically define the work outcomes and behaviors that you will include in appraising performance using a global essay form.

Moving From the General to the Specific

In actually writing the performance appraisal itself, a useful guideline is to move from the general to the specific and use a one-two-three format. If the form allows for only a few lines of comment for each item being assessed, begin with an overall statement summarizing how the person did within the broad area. Then continue with a second sentence, a more specific example supporting the overall assessment from the data you have collected. The third sentence can set a higher goal for the next period, encourage the individual to continue performing at the already fully acceptable level, or set a specific target for needed performance improvement.

Highlighting the Best Evidence

Remember that not everything has to be written on the performance appraisal form. The data on the form itself should be as close to unarguable as possible: objective, factual, accurate, and bias free. Often, however, particularly when you are rating someone as deficient in a certain area, you will have half a dozen varied pieces of evidence. Should all of them be included?

Usually not. Pick out the two or three that are the most telling, the most convincing. Use these for the actual document. Then in your notes jot down reminders of the others so that when you discuss the issue with the individual, you will have complete ammunition to explain the reasons behind a low rating.

Providing More Evidence for Particularly High or Low Ratings

When you rate one part of the appraisal form particularly high or low compared to the other portions, increase the amount of information to support the assessment. It's inevitable that these are the parts of the appraisal that will get the most attention, from both the individual being appraised and those who have to approve the appraisal before it is delivered or defend it later if the appraisal rating is challenged. While requiring any ratings above the midpoint to be justified with additional data runs the risk of encouraging central tendency, one of the most common rating errors, failure to provide reasonable explanations for ratings at either extreme, can raise questions about the appraisal's overall accuracy.

One way to help yourself generate the information needed to defend ratings at either end of the scale is to assume that you are being challenged about the accuracy of your rating. You know that the appraisal is absolutely accurate, but your questioner does not, since he has not worked with the individual but has only read the words on the paper. The questioner points to a rating that is far from the midpoint and asks you, "How do you know that? What led you to come up with that judgment? Why do you feel that way? Can you give me an example?"

If you find it difficult to answer these questions to yourself in advance of reviewing the appraisal form with your supervisor or getting approval from your personnel department (let alone justifying it to the employee or his lawyer), it does not mean that you should change your rating to one that is less likely to be questioned. That is an example of central tendency at work. Instead you should think through exactly why that appraisal rating is in fact accurate, and go back through your records and experience so that you can comfortably defend what you know to be right.

Determining the Final Rating

The most difficult part of the process may be determining the final report card rating of the individual's overall performance. Three factors will help in coming up with the most accurate final rating:

1. Review all of the interim ratings you have made in preparing the appraisal. An ideal process will allow you the chance to assess a significant number of performance factors or work behaviors, each independently rated. Similarly, the form may provide for the inclusion of several work outcomes or results, each with its own assessment. The final rating does not have to equal the mathematical sum of all of the interim ratings in the form, but there should be strong consistency between the individual ratings and the final rating. Only in the case where one performance factor was performed so well or poorly that it overshadowed all of the others, or one important objective was so met or missed that everything else is secondary, should one factor have major influence on the final result.

2. Review the core message you determined when you began the evaluation process and thought about what you wanted the employee to remember a month or two after the appraisal process was completed. Make sure that the final appraisal rating confirms the core message you want to send.

3. Consider weighting the various parts of the appraisal. If your form or procedure already provides for predetermined weights, then this part of the job has been done for you. But if no weights are specifically assigned by the form, there's no reason that you can't decide, for example, to allocate one-third of the overall performance appraisal rating to how well the individual did in the work behaviors portion and two-thirds to the degree to which work outcomes or objectives were achieved.

Whatever weighting system you determine to be appropriate for providing the most accurate possible picture of a subordinate's performance, be sure to let the person know that—well in advance of the appraisal, in time that the person can put his efforts where you are expecting successes.

Putting It Away

The final step, once you have finished writing the appraisal and making all of the evaluations required, is to put it away for a period of time. A week or two is ideal, but even allowing a weekend to pass between the time you complete the appraisal and the time you take action on it—sending it to your supervisor for approval or reviewing directly with the subordinate—will allow you to step back and perhaps see areas that might be improved before the document becomes official.

Kay Cox, director of human resources for a large division of Alcon Laboratories, created an appraisal writing checklist to help line managers in her organization make sure that they had completed the job of writing appraisals at the level of *good solid performance* and perhaps *superior*. Cox's checklist, adapted for use by managers in any organization, appears as Figure 6-2.

Figure 6-2. Appraisal Writing Checklist

☐ Is my written description of performance clear and to the point? If this appraisal were given to me, would I understand exactly where I exceeded and where I fell short of expectations?

☐ Have I analyzed and described performance honestly, factually, and accurately? Did I tell it like it is?

☐ Have I praised a solidly good job where appropriate and avoided nitpicking relatively insignificant items?

☐ Have I used actual examples to describe performance, especially when dealing with technical, managerial, or interpersonal skills?

☐ Is my performance assessment consistent with other feedback I provided the employee during the year?

☐ Are the developmental plans I have outlined specifically tied to identified development needs?

☐ Have I prioritized and focused on specific developmental needs, so that efforts at improving skills can be concentrated on areas of greatest importance?

☐ Have I reviewed the performance rating definitions to make sure that my rating is consistent with the guidelines?

☐ Have I outlined my plan for the discussion to make it a learning experience and not a one-sided judgment?

Source: Checklist developed by Kay Cox, director of human resources, Ophthalmic/Vision Care, Alcon Laboratories.

The last item on the checklist is, "Have I outlined my plan for the discussion to make it a learning experience and not a one-sided judgment?" Once you are satisfied that the appraisal you have written is the best possible analysis of the individual's performance and any necessary approvals have been obtained, you are ready for the most challenging and important step of all: conducting the performance appraisal discussion. Creating the plan for that discussion will be one of the key points in ensuring success.

Notes

1. Mary Ann Hahn, "Writing the Effective Performance Appraisal," *Supervision* (September 1994).
2. M. L. Blum and J. C. Naylor, *Industrial Psychology: Its Theoretical and Social Foundations* (New York: Harper & Row, 1968).
3. Barbara H. Holmes, "The Lenient Evaluator Is Hurting Your Organization," *HR Magazine* (June 1993).
4. Jonathan A. Segal, "Firing Without Fear," *HR Magazine* (June 1992): 126.
5. Holmes, "Lenient Evaluator," p. 76.
6. Peter Habley, private communication, 1995.
7. Tom Peters, "Employee Evaluations Should Reflect Perform-or-Else Principles," *Dallas Business Journal*, January 6, 1994, p. 20.
8. William S. Swan, Ph.D., *How to Do a Superior Performance Appraisal* (New York: John Wiley & Sons, 1991), p. 108.

Chapter 7

How to Conduct an Appraisal Discussion

Writing the evaluation document has served as the primary preparation for the central element of the performance appraisal process: the one-on-one, face-to-face discussion between the supervisor and the subordinate.

This chapter sets out the most effective ways to prepare for the meeting, then guides you through exactly how to conduct a performance appraisal discussion that allows you to get the core message across to the individual. You will learn how to handle the discussion so successfully that the subordinate walks out knowing what you think of his performance, what he needs to do to improve, what strengths he has that can be capitalized on, and what objectives he needs to accomplish in the next appraisal period. Finally, this chapter tells you what you need to do when the meeting is over in order to maximize the ongoing effectiveness of the appraisal discussion.

Before the Meeting

You have already completed the most important premeeting preparation step: writing a fair and thorough performance evaluation. In order to get maximum mileage from the investment you've made, however, you can't just call the subordinate in, ask her to read it, and discuss any items that she has questions about. More preparation will produce significantly greater results.

Meeting Logistics

Begin by arranging all of the details and logistics for the meeting. Set a time convenient for both of you. If the subordinate is in the middle of an important new venture, she will face a conflict between wanting to spend time discussing her performance and wanting to get back to work on an important assignment. If the meeting is scheduled for late in the day, the need to wrap things up may preclude extended discussion of important points.

Where will the meeting be held? If your office allows for privacy, that might be the ideal location. Otherwise find a conference room or even a remote table in the cafeteria.

Conduct the discussion in a business setting. There are stories of managers' holding performance appraisal discussions with subordinates while the two of them were driving to a customer's location or reviewing the appraisal over coffee in a doughnut shop. Neither of these locations is conducive to a businesslike discussion of an important concern. The reason for the selection of these clumsy locations was probably the manager's awkwardness about conducting the appraisal at all. Yet by choosing to do it in an inappropriate locale, he undoubtedly raised the level of awkwardness while simultaneously reducing the value of the discussion.

Advising the Employee

If performance appraisal is an annual organizational rite, conducted perhaps one month after the books are closed, all members of the organization will be aware that evaluation time is approaching. In other organizations, particularly when appraisals are scheduled throughout the year, the employee may not know exactly when to expect the evaluation. In either case, doing a professional job of advising the individual of the upcoming appraisal can set the tone and help ensure an overall successful experience.

The first consideration in advising the employee about the upcoming appraisal is whether the organization—or you as an individual manager—will be using self-appraisal as part of the process. Even if writing a self-appraisal is not a formal organizational requirement, the benefit of asking the individual to reflect on her contributions to the company over the past year, think about career goals, and set some objectives for the upcoming twelve months are so powerful that I strongly recommend it.

If Self-Appraisal Is an Organizational Requirement

If preparing a formal self-appraisal is a regular part of the company's performance evaluation process, as it should be, you may have been provided with specific guidelines on how to handle the mechanics of arranging for subordinates to complete this part of the process. If guidelines don't exist, start by meeting with each subordinate well in advance to explain the process and your expectations. Two different schedules are possible for employee self-appraisals. In one, the employee completes the appraisal and sends it to the manager before the manager writes the official appraisal. The two of them may meet to discuss the employee's appraisal of her own performance at the time the employee submits it, or, more frequently, the review of the employee's self-appraisal is one part of the overall discussion once the manager's appraisal has been written. If it is submitted in advance, the employee's self-appraisal forms one important source of information for the manager to use in writing the official appraisal form.

The other approach is for the manager and the individual to prepare their appraisals separately. The employee completes a self-evaluation; the manager, without seeing what the employee has to say about her own performance, writes the supervisory appraisal, has it approved, and schedules the review meeting. When the two of them meet, they read for the first time what each has written. Although the appraisal created by the manager remains the official one, the discussion of the employee's perception makes the overall meeting more valuable.

The greatest benefit to the second approach is that it requires the manager to write the evaluation without his judgment being colored, positively or negatively, by the perceptions of the subordinate. It also keeps the subordinate from feeling that she has been inappropriately asked to show her hand so that the manager can use this information in constructing the final appraisal without her being able to respond. Finally, it eliminates the possibility that the subordinate will feel that the manager is simply asking the subordinate to do his job for him. Both of them start out at the same point.

The great disadvantage is that by waiting until the actual appraisal discussion to review the subordinate's self-evaluation, the manager denies himself an important source of information. People invariably have insights and perspectives about themselves that are valid and worthwhile; denying oneself access to this information makes the appraisal process a little less valuable than it might otherwise have been. Another shortcoming of waiting until the official review meeting to examine the subordinate's self-appraisal is that the manager will not be aware of any glaring differences between the manager's evaluation of the subordinate's performance and the individual's personal assessment of her own performance. The manager may be caught off-guard if a marginal performer sees herself as a distinguished contributor.

The most effective way to resolve this conflict requires self-discipline on the manager's part: writing a draft of the formal appraisal before the employee submits her own. If the manager writes a preliminary appraisal first and then uses the employee's insights to flesh out his perceptions and correct any obvious gaffes, he has made legitimate use of the subordinate's information without asking the employee to do his job for him or co-opting the individual's ability to get a fully unbiased assessment.

If Self-Appraisal Is the Manager's Decision

Even if there is no organizational requirement for individuals to conduct a self-evaluation, it would be the rare company that would frown on individual managers' asking their troops to review how they've done over the past year as a way to improve the performance of the unit.

The best way is to hold individual meetings a few weeks before formal appraisal time with each subordinate. Have a copy of the company's appraisal form, a copy of the employee's job description, copies of the objectives that the two of you agreed to at the beginning of the appraisal period, and any other information that would be useful in creating an appraisal document. You might follow the script provided in Figure 7-1.

If Self-Appraisal Is Not Part of the Process

If asking for a subordinate's self-appraisal is not to be part of the overall performance appraisal procedure, it is even more important that the individual be well prepared for the meeting so that both the employee and the supervisor can gain maximum benefit.

Figure 7-1. Supervisor's Script for a Preappraisal Meeting

Mary, in the next few weeks I'll be preparing your annual performance appraisal. As I'm writing it, I'd like you to spend some time thinking about your own performance and writing an evaluation on yourself. I have a copy of our appraisal form for you. Let's go over it and see what the key points are. [*Reviews the form with the individual and highlights those areas where most attention should be paid.*]

Over the next two weeks, I'd like you to write a formal appraisal of your own performance, writing down your comments the same as I will in the appraisal of your performance that I'll be writing. I'd also like you to rate your performance using the rating categories. As you're completing the form, be thinking about your objectives for the upcoming year, as well as your development plans.

EITHER: While you are writing your appraisal, I will be preparing the official appraisal document. I'd like you to send me your form on ___[*date*]___ so that I can incorporate your insights on your own performance. We will get together to review your appraisal [after I receive it from you] / [as part of our regular performance appraisal discussion].

OR: While you are writing your appraisal, I will be preparing the official appraisal document. I'd like you to bring your self-appraisal to our meeting when we review the appraisal that I've written.

Here are copies of the information I'll be using: your job description and the list of objectives we set at the beginning of the year [*and anything else*]. Use these as resources as you write your personal evaluation.

I believe that the performance appraisal process, particularly the self-appraisal, is one of the most important parts of our jobs here. Take it seriously, and give it some real thought.

A meeting with the individual a week or two before the formal appraisal discussion will encourage the employee to think about her performance over the past year, even if a formal analysis of personal performance is not required. To get the greatest return on the investment made in performance appraisal, an adroit manager will also send a memo to the individual, confirming their discussion and asking the employee to prepare to get the most out of the session. Figure 7-2 provides a sample memo.

Creating a Discussion Plan

Writing a fair, honest, and complete appraisal is the best preparation for the meeting. The second most important act of preparation is to create a discussion plan in advance of the actual meeting with the subordinate.

Figure 7-2. Sample Preappraisal Memo

This memo is to confirm our plans to meet on [date] at [time] to review your annual performance appraisal, to set goals and objectives for the upcoming year, and to create a plan for your personal development.

Your input will be an important part of the meeting, so I'd like you to look over the questions below and write down your responses, as well as any other thoughts you might have that can help me better understand your concerns and priorities.

You can either bring your responses to the meeting, or return this worksheet to me before we meet. Thanks.

1. Do you have any questions about what's expected of you on the job? Are there any areas that are unclear?

2. What do you consider to be your most important accomplishments in the past twelve months?

3. What do you feel you need to do in order to improve your performance? What can I or this organization do to help you improve?

4. Please tell me about any special accomplishments, awards, activities, or recognition that I should be aware of.

One or two days before the face-to-face transaction, assemble all of the material you will need for the review:

- ▸ Your completed and approved performance appraisal form
- ▸ A copy of the employee's self-appraisal or responses to the memo set out in Figure 7-2
- ▸ Actual work materials, files, project documents, or status reports that support statements in the appraisal
- ▸ A copy of the employee's job description
- ▸ A copy of the objectives set at the beginning of the appraisal period

Look all of these over and then write down your specific plan for what you want to accomplish during the meeting. Without an orderly plan, the agenda for the appraisal meeting will be set by chance. Discussions may lead down blind alleys, and nothing of genuine profit is likely to result.

The most important part of the plan involves determining the one or two—at most, three—messages you want the individual to receive, remember, and act on as a result of the performance appraisal discussion. Performance appraisal research consistently shows that individuals tend to retain little of the totality of information communicated during a performance appraisal discussion. What they do remember is often either irrelevant or just the opposite of what the appraiser meant to say.

In the previous chapter on writing a fair performance appraisal document, I urged appraisal writers to start by determining the core message that they want to get across. Determining the core message for the conversation is equally important.

In developing your plan for the meeting, start by asking yourself, "Given all that we will discuss in the upcoming session, what is the one thing I would have the employee remember a month after the meeting is over?" Once you have whittled your response down to one clear statement, then ask, "If I could have her remember just one more thing, what would it be?"

Here's a way to appraise your own performance in conducting a performance appraisal discussion. Assume that a month after your appraisal discussion, someone says to your subordinate, "What do you remember from the performance appraisal conversation you had with your manager last month?" If the employee accurately and unhesitatingly responds with the two statements you picked, your accomplishment is worth evaluating at least at the Good, Solid Performance level. If the individual can accurately recall any more than those two messages, your performance can be rated at the Superior level.

Since the quantity and accuracy of information retained from performance appraisal discussions is discouragingly low, make sure that what is remembered is important and correct. Rather than talk about ten different things in the course of the discussion, it is wiser to talk about two things in five different ways and at five different times during the course of the meeting.

What should that core message be? Figure 7-3 provides a chart that is useful in determining what the core message and the objective of your discussion with the subordinate should be.

The first column, "Final Rating," asks the rater to determine the overall level of the subordinate's performance: superior, satisfactory, or unsatisfactory. Whatever terms may be used on the actual appraisal form (and even if your form doesn't provide for any final report card rating), virtually every supervisor knows which of the three performance categories a subordinate's performance falls into: The work is much better than average, acceptable, or unacceptable.

The second column asks about the likely future of the individual over

Figure 7-3. Appraisal Discussion Models

Final Rating	Most Likely Prospect	Discussion Objective
Superior	Promotion	Review opportunities
	Growth in present assignment (vertical load)	Make development plans
	Broadened assignment (horizontal load)	Review possibility of extending responsibility
	No change in responsibilities	Decide how to maintain current level
Satisfactory	Promotion	Review opportunities
	Growth in present assignment	Make development plans
	No change in responsibilities	Decide how to maintain/ improve current level
Unsatisfactory	Performance correctable	Plan correction/ gain commitment
	Performance uncorrectable	Consider reassignment and/or prepare for termination

the course of the next year. Recognize that there is little relationship between the first column and the second. Just because a person's work is outstanding doesn't mean that he is going to be promoted. The company may be downsizing, or the individual may have a particular technical skill that is invaluable in the job she currently has but is of no use in any other position. The individual's prospects for the upcoming year may involve remaining exactly where she is but taking on new tasks and learning new skills ("Growth in present assignment") or doing even more of the work she currently is doing ("Broadened assignment"). Finally—and probably the case for most people—her responsibilities are not likely to change much in the upcoming year.

The same dynamic is at work for the satisfactory and the unsatisfactory performer: Determine the level of performance; then determine the most likely prospect for the upcoming year.

The third column recommends a discussion objective. If the individual's performance falls into the satisfactory area (whatever the actual term used in your company's rating scheme may be) and you foresee no change in the person's responsibilities in the next twelve months, your primary goal in the appraisal discussion is to focus on how the individual can maintain and hopefully improve her performance over the next twelve months. Similarly, if the final assessment is unsatisfactory and you do not believe that the person will be able to correct her performance to a fully acceptable level, your objective during the meeting will be to set the stage for reassignment or, more likely, termination.

The Night Before

The final part of advance preparation happens the night before the appraisal meeting, and perhaps again as you are commuting to work that morning: the visualization of the way the meeting will go. Managers who operate exclusively on the basis of logic, rationality, analysis, and cognitive reasoning will be skeptical, but one of the most effective techniques for making sure that the meeting goes the way you want it to go is through the use of guided fantasy or creative visualization:

> *It's the night before the appraisal meeting. You are in bed, starting to drift away.*
>
> *As sleep approaches, you visualize tomorrow's meeting with Sally, one of your subordinates. You see her walking into your office. You see the two of you smiling as you sit and begin the discussion. You hear the two of you speaking—not the actual words but the tone of voice used in the discussion: the tints and hues and shadings as the two of you professionally and securely discuss her performance over the past year.*

You hear her ask you difficult questions. In your mind's eye you see yourself sitting quietly while she asks the complete question that is on her mind, waiting out her pauses, nodding while she struggles to find exactly the right words. You then hear yourself, without distinguishing the exact words of your answer, responding in a comfortable and untroubled way to the most intricate issues and sensitive areas that arise.

During the visualization of the upcoming interview, you hear yourself sending the core message to Sally. You can hear yourself saying the actual words to her that you will be saying in your meeting the next day.

As you finally drift off to sleep, you envision the meeting drawing to a close. The aura of confidence and control, poise and self-possession is manifest, almost tangible. You are barely able to complete the image of the two of you shaking hands and smiling before sleep overtakes you.

Scoff and scorn, gibe and jeer if you must. Nevertheless, creative fantasy or guided visualization can be a powerful, if nonrational, tool in bringing to pass the kind of successful appraisal meeting you want to have with each of the individuals on your team who looks to you for leadership. By visualizing supreme success, the unconscious mind will operate to guide you to its achievement.

During the Meeting

Before the meeting actually begins, make sure the arrangements are fitting. If you are planning to meet outside your office, make sure that the space is reserved and private. Arrange for work coverage, have your telephone covered, and turn your pager off. Don't schedule your next appointment too tightly.

Get yourself ready, too. Review the core message or messages that you want to send. Say the words out loud so you'll gain practice in saying exactly what you want to say.

Think about the employee's likely reaction to the appraisal. What's her emotional response going to be? A useful device for understanding emotional reactions is to recognize that there are only four emotions: mad, sad, glad, and scared. How is Sally likely to react to the appraisal, particularly if it is not good news? Are you more likely to encounter a reaction of mad, where she becomes angry and you will need to prepare yourself for a hot-under-the-collar hostile reaction and bitterness toward you and the evaluation you've written? Or is she more likely to be sad: depressed, uncommunicative, and likely to react to suggestions for improvement as futile and vain? You probably won't get a glad reaction from a negative appraisal, but be prepared for it. If the person reacts to what you've written by thanking you for the opportunity to find out where she stands and praises your candor in shooting straight, you may be encountering denial. The employee may seem to be reacting very maturely but is actually pushing the appraisal's bad news under the cerebral rug. Finally, is the person scared? Is the reaction to criticism fear of losing the job or never making any progress in the company? Is the individual nervous about her future?

Preparing Physically

If you anticipate a difficult session in which you will be bringing an individual's shortcomings to her attention, particularly when you feel she may be unaware of the seriousness of the situation, get yourself in good physical condition for the meeting. Taking a brisk walk and practicing deep breathing can increase your physical ability to handle stress. If you anticipate a stressful discussion, prepare.

Completing the Final Logistics

Most managers hand a copy of the appraisal to the individual at the start of the review meeting. That is not an effective procedure. The employee is forced to read through the appraisal quickly with her supervisor breathing down her neck, waiting for her to finish so that the discussion can begin. She may feel pressured and may not take the time to go back and reread important parts of the appraisal. She certainly won't have the chance to think about what has been written and reflect on the questions she wants to ask.

A much better alternative is to give a copy of your appraisal to the individual an hour or two before the meeting. Explain that you want her to be able to read it carefully and be fully prepared to discuss it when the two of you get together. If the employee has been asked to write a self-appraisal and bring it to the meeting, pick it up now so that you can read it and prepare before the actual discussion begins.

Opening the Discussion

Have a specific plan in mind for how you will open the meeting. It is fully appropriate to write a script for yourself or at least a list of key points and refer to it openly to kick things off. In your opening words, lay out a road map for the individual, describing your agenda for the conversation and the order in which you plan to cover things. Figure 7-4 provides a script that can be adapted and tailored to your needs.

Discussing the Appraisal

Beginning by asking the individual about the self-appraisal accomplishes one important thing quickly: It puts the conversational ball in the employ-

Figure 7-4. A Script for Starting the Meeting

Introduction

Thanks for coming in, Sally. I've been looking forward to the chance to go over this past year with you. I'd like to go through the process carefully, since this will be one of the most important things that we do together all year.

Setting the Agenda

I'd like to start by having you tell me about the appraisal that you wrote of your own performance—what you felt were the most important items and how you came up with the evaluation that you did. Then I'd like to talk about the appraisal that I wrote.

I think the most productive way to proceed is for us to cover the areas where we both agree first, and then move into those areas where we don't see exactly eye to eye. I want to explain how I went about evaluating your performance the way I did and give you the chance to ask me any questions you have.

The most important part of the appraisal is the review of your specific job accountabilities and the objectives of your job. I'd like to start our discussion there, and then move on to discussing the performance factors—the way you went about doing the job.

When we've finished that, I'd like to talk about my overall rating and how I arrived at it.

When we've finished reviewing last year, I'd like to talk about your development plans for the upcoming year. I have some ideas on things you might do to increase your skills, and I'm sure that you have some feelings in this area, too.

Compensation

Either: At the end of this meeting I'll be reviewing the salary increase you'll be receiving. I'll explain how I arrived at the amount and answer any questions you have about how our compensation system works.

Or: Individual performance is one of the primary factors in determining each person's salary. When we get together for our review meeting, I will be able to tell you about the specific salary action we'll be taking.

Or: As you know, pay changes in our company are based on job classification and seniority. While your pay won't change as a result of this review, I think it's important to know how you're doing and what you can do to get ahead.

Planning for the Next Appraisal Cycle

Either: The other thing I'd like to do at the end of this meeting is to talk about your plans for next year and set some specific goals and objectives for the next appraisal period.

Or: When we're done with this review, Sally, I'd like to set a date for us to get back together to update your key accountabilities and objectives for next year, and also talk about your development plans and goals.

Starting Things Off

Why don't you start by telling me how you feel this past year has gone?

ee's court. Your job in this opening part of the meeting is primarily to understand the employee's point of view. There is no need for any arguments or disagreements during this section of the appraisal interview, even if your perception of the employee's performance is radically different from her own. Later, when you discuss the appraisal you have prepared, it will be appropriate to explain why the way you see things is different from the way she sees them. At this point, however, your primary task is to understand the other person's point of view.

The effectiveness of the conversation is also increased by beginning with areas of agreement. Unless the employee is oblivious to the value (or the lack of value) of the contributions she has made to the organization in the past year, the two of you will find far more areas of agreement than disagreement.

It's important to talk about and understand those areas where you and the subordinate agree. The results of the General Electric study of performance appraisal thirty years ago, described in Chapter 1, have been consistently confirmed since. The GE researchers found that criticism has a negative effect on achievement of goals, while praise by itself has little effect one way or the other. Defensiveness resulting from a critical appraisal produces inferior performance; mutual goal setting, not criticism, improves performance. Finally, performance improves most when specific goals are established; participation by the employee in the goal-setting procedure helps produce favorable results.[1]

Good Intentions Matter

The performance appraisal conversation with the supervisor may be the most important transaction of the year for the individual. Everything of importance is tied up in this forty-five-minute to one-hour discussion: the employee's future with the organization, the opportunities that are open to her, the amount of money that she will make, the security of her employment. While you may look at it as merely an administrative chore, for the subordinate it is very serious business. Take it seriously.

Encourage the individual to talk by actively listening to what she is saying. There are four fundamental rules for listening:

Look	Maintain eye contact. Lean toward the individual and look at her. If maintaining direct eye contact becomes awkward, use the old actor's trick of looking at the spot directly between the eyes where the eyebrows merge.
Nod	Move your head up and down while the other person is

	talking. This is one of the most powerfully reinforcing behaviors anyone can engage in.
Grunt	In addition to the nonverbal communicators of looking and nodding, use verbal encouragers. Sounds and statements like, "uh-huh," "oh," "really," "I see," "yeah," can indicate that you are paying close attention.
Pause	Don't interrupt. Be quiet and let the other person talk. Wait until the other person fully completes a thought before responding.

Don't get distracted and let your mind wander while the other person is talking. A basic structural problem with the human communications process is that people usually speak at a rate of 145 to 175 words per minute but can intelligently listen at a rate of 600 to 800 words per minute. Don't let your mind drift in the interim. Play good-listener games with yourself. Try to guess what word is coming next. Guess what the individual's point is going to be before she gets to it, and then confirm or adjust your prediction.

In discussing areas where you and the individual agree in your assessments, supplement the employee's evaluation with observations of your own. Be particularly alert to any situations where the two of you have used different data to come to the same conclusion. Beginning with areas where you both agree helps you understand how the employee went about making judgments about her own performance and shows her your thought processes.

For items where you disagree, start where your opinions have the least divergence and gradually move toward those where the discrepancy is the greatest. Make sure you have facts and specifics to back up your judgments. While you have the right to interpret the facts and performance details you have observed (that's your job as a manager), the employee certainly has the right to know the basis on which you made the judgments that you did. If your only response in answer to a question about how you came up with a particular rating is something like, "I dunno. I just felt that way. I'm the boss. It's my opinion," you will have difficulty building an effective working relationship or sustaining your position if ever you are challenged.

Resolving Discussion Difficulties

Of all discussion difficulties, dealing with the defensive subordinate is the most common. When people are under pressure, they adopt one of two different coping mechanisms: fight or flight. The individual who is upset about an unexpectedly negative review of her performance may react to the stress generated by engaging in either fight behavior (standing her ground, raising her voice, shaking her finger or pounding the desk, arguing for points that have clearly been refuted, or finding someone else to tag with the blame) or flight behavior (looking away, changing the subject, speaking softly, agreeing even when it is obvious that she doesn't agree, or accepting whatever is said).

When defensiveness arises, active listening remains the most effective strategy for coping with the response. To the four simple listening techniques described above, add another: Check and reflect. Check that you have accurately understood the other person's position and reflect the feelings and concerns expressed.

Whether the defensive reaction is showing up as a fight response or a flight response, your reaction of maintaining eye contact, nodding, using verbal encouragers ("uh-huh," "I see") to communicate that you are paying attention, and pausing to allow the other person to fully vent her displeasure over the rating or pausing to encourage the other person to express her feelings will be highly effective in coping with the defensive reaction. Along with these, asking questions to understand the other person's reactions and feelings is critical.

Let's say Monica is upset because her customer relations skills, which she felt were excellent, were rated as Needs Improvement. She responds angrily: "How could you rate me as Needs Improvement in customer relations? Customers specifically ask for me when they come in. Nobody has ever complained about my service. Other people ask me how they should handle difficult customers. This is wrong!"

There's no question about which reaction she's displaying: it's fight. She's upset, and she's letting you know about it.

A typical reaction is to mirror her defensiveness and immediately argue back: "That's not true. There have been customer complaints; they just don't make them directly to you. And while our young customers may seek you out, I've noticed that you deliberately avoid helping older people. Just last week I saw you . . . "

This discussion is shaping up as unproductive. Monica isn't listening, you're not listening, and the problem isn't getting solved.

Start by letting Monica vent her feelings. It may take every ounce of maturity you've got to hold back from responding and instead let her speak her piece in full. Maintaining eye contact, nodding, using verbal encouragements, and waiting until she has finished will start the process of resolving the issue.

Then check and reflect. Restate Monica's position and ask if you have accurately reflected her concerns: "Monica, let me make sure I understand. You are angry about the rating of Needs Improvement because you feel that dealing with customers is one of your strengths. You've noticed customers seeking you out and other employees asking for your help. You feel that I haven't taken this into account in coming up with my evaluation. Is this correct?"

Notice that you have not agreed with anything that Monica has said. You simply have restated her position to demonstrate understanding. The first step in dealing with the defensive individual is to demonstrate that we understand—but not necessarily agree with—the other person's point of view.

Monica may continue to produce additional evidence, accurate or erroneous, to bolster her assertion that she has been misappraised. If she does, you will continue listening actively, nodding, waiting, and reflecting as accurately as possible exactly what Monica's position and feelings seem to be.

Eventually Monica will have completely expressed her position. If you consciously and sincerely listen to Monica actively, this point will usually come fairly quickly. Eventually all of the steam compressed inside the boiling kettle that is Monica will have been expelled, and although the kettle remains hot, the steam has been discharged.

Now the door is open to discuss the rationale behind the low rating. Had you tried to explain your position earlier, anything that you said would have been dismissed by Monica, if she even heard it at all. But now she has been fully heard. More important, she has discovered that instead of criticizing her for the outburst or rebuking her for becoming upset, she has been treated with dignity and respect and listened carefully to.

Begin by seeking areas of agreement. "Monica," you tell her calmly and maturely, "many of the things you have said are true. I have noticed some customers, particularly the younger ones, seeking you out, and I know that occasionally other employees ask your help when they run into problems. I have noticed that, and I do appreciate it."

Having been fully heard, and now having had several of her points acknowledged, Monica is probably much more willing to listen to what you will say next.

"Several of the things you mentioned are correct, and I did take them into consideration in coming up with my rating. There are other things that I also considered. [*Pause*] I have noticed that while the customers who approach you are our younger ones, you seem to avoid approaching older people. We have received several complaints about your service. In the past two weeks . . . "

You continue explaining the reason for the rating. It is likely that from time to time Monica will interrupt, to challenge a point or argue about an observation. Whenever she does, immediately go directly back to the active listening mode, hearing her out, nodding, and asking questions and restating her arguments to make sure that you fully understand her.

Why Bother?

Why go to all this trouble? managers ask. Why put up with all the arguments when the end is not going to be any different? The rating of Needs Improvement is accurate and is going to stand.

If the manager's only objective is to deliver a performance appraisal rating and then get back to work, there's no reason for active listening. There's probably not even the need for a meeting; he can just mail the appraisal to the individual with the instructions to read, sign, and return. But the goal is not merely to deliver a rating. It is to improve performance. And the investment made in the meeting to engage in active listening will pay dividends many times over.

How much time does active listening actually take? If you took a stopwatch to the conversation described above and clocked the additional time expended to hear Monica out fully, restate her position and feelings, listen again and perhaps a third time to her rejoinders, respond appropriately to each and then explain the reason for the unexpected rating, perhaps a total of five additional minutes, and ten maximum, will have been spent in the discussion.

That ten-minute investment produces a disproportionate positive return. You have confronted a serious gap between desired and actual performance on a subordinate's part and demonstrated, through patience and maturity, willingness to listen and understand employee concerns. Monica still may not like the Needs Improvement rating at the end of the meeting, but she is far more likely to understand what caused you to decide that was the appropriate rating and, more important, be willing to take active steps to act more responsively to all of the company's customers.

The more effort and attention managers devote to understanding what the subordinate is feeling and how the individual is reacting to the appraisal, the greater the likelihood is that they will be able to bring about a genuine commitment to change and improvement. The rule is simple: Seek first to understand, then to be understood.

Solving Performance Problems

Many times in performance appraisal discussions managers will be required to bring a specific problem to an employee's attention and begin the process of getting that problem solved. The greatest challenge facing most managers who are confronted with an employee whose performance must improve is identifying the specific gap between desired and actual performance. Answering the questions, What do you want? and, What do you get? without resorting to unsupported judgments, undocumented generalizations, or wails about attitudinal deficiencies is arduous for many managers.

Respect and Responsibility

The performance appraisal discussion is frequently the venue in which managerial concerns about the performance of subordinates are first formally brought to their attention. Although egregious violations of rules or procedures are usually confronted at the instant they occur or shortly after, these infractions are the exceptions. More frequently the manager's concern is not about an outrageous violation of an established regulation but a minor failing that informal discussions or words in the ear have failed to correct.

Since confronting inappropriate behavior or unsatisfactory performance is a task that few managers savor, many postpone dealing with the issue until the formal performance review leaves them no choice. Now the revelation that a gap exists between the organization's expectations and the employee's performance is unavoidable. The manager is responsible for bringing to the individual's attention that, in at least one area of her job responsibilities, performance is deficient, and correction must be immediate.

The reluctance managers feel in confronting performance deficiencies results from a failure to understand that every performance improvement discussion with an employee has two goals, both of which need to be achieved if a lasting correction is to occur: Solve the problem and maintain the relationship.

The reason so many attempts to get employees to redirect their behavior and return to fully acceptable performance miscarry is that the manager fails to achieve both goals. Heavy-handed threats, mean-spirited browbeatings, and miserly raises can certainly convince an individual to change her ways, but at what cost? By using punishment, managers solve the problem at the expense of the relationship. The possibility of commitment is sacrificed for the surety of compliance.

You can punish people into compliance. You cannot punish people into commitment. And commitment is what organizations genuinely need.

Managers dislike punishment. Few people relish donning the black hat and being the bad guy. They find it easier to let sleeping dogs lie, to assume that this too shall pass, and to hope that eventually the employee will shape up. Often they are right. And when they are right, they have achieved the other of the two goals. By avoiding a distasteful confrontation, they have maintained the relationship. But when they are wrong and the problem continues despite their hopes that time alone will bring about a correction, then they must act.

Having sanctioned the employee's shortcomings through their silence, they find it even more difficult to confront the issue during the appraisal discussion, knowing that the subordinate can justifiably demand, "Why didn't you tell me about this a long time ago?"

The best approach is to deal with problems at the time they arise in a way that clearly delineates the gap between desired and actual performance and secures the individual's agreement to correct the deficiency. That opportunity often first arises in the course of the performance appraisal discussion.

Preparing for a Productive Discussion

When the manager realizes that one aspect of the appraisal discussion will be the review of a need for specific performance improvement, there are a few additional steps to take to ensure a successful resolution. In addition to the standard chores involved in preparing the appraisal and handling the administrative requirements, when a specific need for correction is going to be on the appraisal agenda there are four steps to take to make sure he is fully prepared for a productive discussion:

1. Identify the specific gap between desired and actual performance.
2. Determine the good business reasons that the problem must be solved.
3. Determine the consequences the employee will face if she fails to correct the situation.
4. Determine the appropriate action to take.

Identify the Gap

The first step is to delineate clearly the difference between what is expected and what is delivered in the individual's performance. Instead of relying on easily challenged generalities and judgments, a more effective way is to ask yourself how you would respond to two situations:

1. Assume that the employee says, "I know you're not happy with something I'm doing, but I'm not sure exactly what it is that I'm doing wrong. What exactly is it that I'm doing that concerns you?" How would you respond?
2. Assume that the employee says, "I want to make sure that I'm doing the job the way you want it done. What exactly would you have me do in order for you to say that at least in this area, I'm doing a good job?" How would you respond?

While you are answering those questions, assume that the individual, in a courteous and respectful manner, asks, "Could you give me an example?" or, "What would that look like?" or, "For example . . . ?" Answering those questions will force you to zero in on both the precise performance concern you have and the specific steps the employee needs to take to correct it.

Determine Why the Problem Must be Solved

Most people will agree to solve a problem once it has been brought to their attention. In most cases, simply making the employee aware of the specific gap between what you want and what you get during a performance appraisal discussion will generate an agreement to change. Nevertheless, sometimes managers meet resistance. Particularly if the issue of concern involves a continuing minor deficiency that you are only now getting around to discussing, the subordinate's response may be to resist immediate acquiescence with your request and instead argue that the issue is insignificant.

Managers are often nervous about raising the need for performance change, even when they are able to specify clearly the difference between desired and actual performance. They fear that they will be seen as focusing on the trivial, particularly when the issue is not a major transgression but a small but still important matter. "What's the big deal?" they hear the employee muttering and are unsure of how to respond.

Completing the second step of premeeting preparation, determining the specific reasons why the problem must be solved, gives you the appropriate response. After specifying the difference between desired and actual performance, ask yourself the question, "Why is this really important?" Ignore the fact that it may be a rule or accepted performance standard and seek the rationale behind it. "What would happen if we didn't have this rule or expectation? What are the good business reasons for requiring this of members of the organization?"

Whatever the issue, you will quickly discover that there are indeed good business reasons and that there will be a significant impact on the business if the expectation is regularly flouted. If the employee responds to the request for a performance change with a statement like, "Oh, come on. That's not important . . . what's the big deal?" it will be easy to explain exactly what the big deal is.

Determine the Consequences

Most of the time, people will agree to change their behavior after the specific change required has been discussed and the good business reasons behind the requirement have been enumerated. But if the employee fails to agree to change or fails to understand the seriousness of the need, be prepared to discuss the consequences if the employee fails to comply.

One possibility is formal disciplinary action. Managers tend to view the prospect of disciplinary action as sufficiently dire to provoke immediate acquiescence on an employee's part, but far fewer employees will be cowed into submission by the threat of a written warning or similar action. The likelihood of a professional or exempt employee's actually receiving a formal warning notice is slim; even lower-level employees know that when it comes to formal disciplinary action, most supervisors are more bark than bite.

What will have a significant influence on the individual's decision to change and perform more effectively is the recognition that the adverse consequences for failure to do so are both real and likely. Vague threats of "I'm gonna write you up" will have far less leverage than a specific explanation of the reluctance you would have in justifying a merit increase, an assignment to a special task force, a transfer to a more desirable location, or the approval for attendance at a professional development seminar if a problem is not corrected.

The purpose is not to bludgeon the individual into submission through threats of adverse action. It is to point out, clearly and directly, that the choices the employee makes affect the choices that you make. If the employee, in spite of knowing that something she is doing (or failing to do) creates a problem for the organization, decides to continue the recalcitrant behavior, that decision has consequences. The employee has the right to know exactly what those consequences are so that she can make an informed decision to change.

Determine the Appropriate Action

Now that you have clearly defined the specific dimensions of the problem itself, determined the good business reason that it must be solved, and assessed the consequences to the individual if change is not forthcoming, you can make a prudent decision on the specific way to handle the issue during the appraisal discussion. In terms of increasingly serious action, the options might include these:

- ▸ Discussing the issue during the appraisal interview without making written reference to it on the appraisal form
- ▸ Including a reference to the issue in the written narrative of the appraisal document
- ▸ Including a reference to the issue and lowering the appraisal rating in the particular segment of the document affected by the poor performance

▸ Including a reference to the issue in the overall summary of performance and lowering the final appraisal rating for the overall performance

In addition to these actions, the need for change (and the consequences of failure to change) can also be included in the narrative section covering development needs. Finally, if the issue is of major importance and the need for correction is critical, you may decide to attach a separate memo to the employee as part of the appraisal form to emphasize unmistakably the need for immediate change.

Managing the Appraisal Interview

The agenda for the meeting was set out in your opening remarks. The most effective pattern is to start with the areas where you and the subordinate agree and move toward those where opinions diverge. Your objective is to understand the employee's perceptions, to reinforce areas where performance is effective, and to communicate those where development is required. If there is a specific performance problem to be addressed, approach it with the dual goal of solving the problem and enhancing the relationship with the individual. If necessary, review the impact of the problem and the consequences to follow if correction does not occur, all with the goal of gaining the employee's agreement to change. Throughout the process, listen to the employee and work to convince her of the soundness of your point of view.

By the time the components that make up the overall appraisal document have been discussed, there should be little argument about the appropriateness of the final appraisal rating. Even if the employee began the meeting with an inflated view of her own contributions, the discussion should have produced a good understanding of exactly how the organization evaluates the performance of its members and why her performance was so rated.

If a merit increase is to accompany the performance appraisal, this is usually the time to reveal the amount along with the rationale and administrative considerations underlying the decision: "Based on your work over the past year, Jane, I have recommended that you receive an 8 percent increase. That is almost exactly in the middle of the guidelines for employees whose performance is rated Superior. It will bring your annual salary from $39,000 to $41,040. Since you are still under the midpoint of your salary range, you will be eligible for another merit review in nine months."

Some sophisticated managers use a different timetable for discussing the merit increase with excellent results. Instead of waiting for the end of the performance appraisal to reveal the amount of the salary increase, they deliver the news right at the beginning: "Jerry, I know that you're interested in how I view your performance. I also know that you want to know about how much of a raise you'll be getting. Let's get that part out of the way first. We'll discuss all the reasons when we get into the appraisal itself, but starting with your next paycheck you'll be receiving an increase of 7 percent. Your annual salary will be going from $64,000 to $68,400. Now that you know that, let's put the money issue aside and concentrate on what's really important: how you've done over the last year and where you want to go from here."

Particularly with subordinates whose performance is rated at least Fully Satisfactory, getting the money question answered right at the start allows the two of you to concentrate on the performance without the subordinate's wondering "What will that mean in my paycheck?" to every statement you make.

Planning for the Future

After completely discussing the appraisal document and the rationale behind it and covering any salary administration requirements if these happen at the same time as the appraisal interview, you need to bring the discussion to a productive close. The easiest way is to follow the past-present-future model:

> ▸ The appraisal interview has primarily concentrated on the *past*—how well the individual has done over the last twelve months.

Figure 7-5. Script for Planning for the Future

Based on what we talked about in your performance appraisal discussion, Jack, there are several areas for development we might focus on. Some relate to improving your effectiveness in your current role, while others might represent areas you might want to work on to meet the demands of the future. There may be opportunities you see that you want to take advantage of.

Let's come up with a list of goals or objectives for your development activities for next year. Then we can plan ways in which we can make them happen.

When you consider development activities, I'd like you to think about specific skills you need to acquire, not just about things you should learn or courses you might want to take. Think about what you'll be able to do better and how it will benefit the department and the company.

I'd also like you to review all of the key accountabilities and objectives we've just talked about and revise them so that they will be appropriate for next year. I'll do the same. Let's get back together on [*date*].

▶ The salary issue deals with the *present*—how much pay will change starting today.

▶ The final issue is the *future*—what the individual will need to do in the next twelve months to maintain and enhance the current quality of performance.

There are two key issues here: (1) updating the current performance objectives and setting new goals for the future and (2) creating a personal development plan to increase the individual's knowledge, skill, and competence to perform even more effectively in the future.

Even if the two players in the appraisal drama have each given competent performances in discussing the past and the present, expecting them to immediately begin considering the future may be excessive. Both parties need time to digest what was said and think through all the information that was communicated. You might bring the meeting to a close by setting a date and the agenda for a meeting to cover issues dealing with the future. Figure 7-5 provides an effective script.

Wrapping Things Up

Once the date has been set for discussing the upcoming year's objectives and the employee's development plans, you need to wrap up the appraisal

Figure 7-6. Script for Wrapping Up the Appraisal Discussion

Now that we've reviewed the complete appraisal, Jack, let's summarize the key points we've discussed. In general, you feel that [general statement of employee's reaction to complete performance appraisal]. Is that an accurate summary?

In reviewing the entire appraisal, there are two areas in which I think your performance has been outstanding: [describe two specific areas of strength that should be continued and enhanced].

There is also one area in particular that you need to immediately work on improving. That area is [describe the single most important weakness in the employee's performance and explain why improvement is necessary].

Finally, when you think about your development plans for next year, the one area I'd like you to give some serious thought to is [discuss most important developmental need].

That pretty well sums it up for me, Jack. Are there any other questions I can answer for you? [Listen and respond appropriately.]

As a final matter, it's our policy to ask you to sign the performance appraisal to make sure that you've had a chance to read and understand it. If you'd like to add any comments, feel free to do so. [Give appraisal to employee to sign.]

This session has been extremely valuable to me, Jack, and I'm sure it has been for you, too. I'll look forward to discussing plans for next year on [date for meeting set to discuss objectives, accountabilities, and development plans].

discussion professionally. Throughout this chapter and the previous one, I have cautioned against having unreasonable expectations of what an appraisal interview can do or how much an individual will even remember a month after the discussion is over. I have stressed the importance of determining a limited number of highly important core messages and concentrating on the clear communication of these during both the writing of the appraisal and the discussion of the narrative.

The closing remarks should not only wrap the meeting up on the appropriate tone; they should communicate one more time the limited number of core messages that you want the subordinate to remember. Figure 7-6 provides a script that covers all of the key points in wrapping up a performance appraisal discussion successfully.

The meeting closes; the players depart. The meeting to discuss the employee's development plans and objectives for the upcoming year is still to come, but the most difficult—and rewarding—part of the performance management process has been completed.

Note

1. Herbert H. Meyer, Emanuel Kay, and John R. P. French, Jr., "Split Roles in Performance Appraisal," *Harvard Business Review* (January–February 1965).

Chapter 8
Optimizing Your Existing Performance Appraisal System

Frequently a line manager or human resources executive is faced with a dilemma: The existing system isn't as good as it might be, but there is no license to make substantive change. You're not allowed to develop the system the way you'd like it to be and must use the system you've got. How do you make the best of a bad—or, at the least, imperfect—situation?

There are many things that a savvy and clever manager can do when confronted with the need to use an appraisal system that is less than ideal. Whether you're a line manager or a personnel administrator, it is quite possible to play by the organization's rules *and* use the existing system, flawed though it may be, to achieve the same objectives that a far superior system would.

As Bill Swan contends in his short manual, *How to Do a Superior Performance Appraisal*, "The more inadequate and haphazard the system, the more latitude you probably have in applying it."[1] If the formal system is seriously deficient, it is likely that you will be able to supplement it in informal ways to suit your needs and purposes. Few organizations object to additional documentation being appended to whatever appraisal form is mandated. As long as whatever is added—an addition to the procedures or a supplement to the documentation—meets all of the tests of defensibility and legality, the manager who gets more than the minimum from the system is likely to be noticed and rewarded. And even if individual efforts to improve a mediocre system are ultimately thwarted, the old maxim still applies: It is easier to gain forgiveness than permission.

Chapters 6 and 7 described how to write a fair performance appraisal and conduct an effective discussion regardless of the kind of form provided or the organizational procedures specified. This chapter examines ways to make the best use of an existing system without altering the core procedures and mandated forms.

We consider the task from two perspectives. First we discuss what an operating manager whose goal is to use the organization's existing performance appraisal process to increase the effectiveness of his own work group can do to make that happen. (This section is also useful to human resources professionals who need to help line managers make best use of an imperfect system.) Second, we explore the issue from the perspective of the human resources specialist who might lack the mandate to replace the company's existing system but recognizes the need to make the current procedure more effective.

Optimizing the Appraisal System: The Line Manager's Perspective

Where to Begin

To optimize an existing system, start by analyzing what it is that you're dealing with right now. Is your current system an MBO approach that pays too little attention to how the results were obtained? Is it a complex BARS or other behaviorally based system that rewards well-intentioned efforts but ignores the results of those behaviors? Are you stuck with a trait scale that spotlights characteristics of the performer without paying attention to what that person achieves or how he goes about doing the job? Or is it simply a global essay form where you can appraise anything you want?

It will be rare that the system your company uses will take one approach to the complete exclusion of all others. In most cases, when you review your form you'll find that the problem is that it is out of balance, concentrating too much on one aspect and not enough on another.

The simplest way to create a significant improvement is to start by identifying the primary deficiency in the existing procedure. Basically effective performance appraisal forms and processes concentrate on two critical aspects: work outcomes (results) and performance factors (behaviors).

The ideal form or process should strike an appropriate balance between work outcomes and performance factors, depending on the specific duties and requirements of the job you're appraising. An MBO-type form for a customer service representative might be excessively results oriented. On the other hand, a graphic rating scale by itself would be insufficient to capture the most important aspect of a sales representative's job: sales results.

Begin by determining which of the two elements needs to be amplified more: results or performance factors. Do you need to put more emphasis on how the person went about doing the job or the results achieved?

Improving a Behavior- or Performer-Focused Form

If your procedure needs work in the area of increasing the emphasis on results or work outcomes, get your employees involved with goal setting. Use the goal-setting techniques discussed in Chapter 4, and help each person set three or four reasonable targets or expectations. Let your subordinates know what your goals for the unit or department are, and ask them what goals they can set for themselves that will help achieve those objectives. Tell them that you will hold them accountable for these goals and that you'll include them as part of the annual review. Provide a simple form for them to write down their goals with space for the results to be described.

It will probably take two or three sessions with your group, either individually or with the team as a whole, to get the process working smoothly. First you'll need to be sure that you can explain your goals simply and understandably. You'll probably need to give most team members help in arriving at specific, worthwhile, and measurable goals, particularly if this is a new experience for them.

In effect, you'll be creating a personal, individual mini-MBO system within your department or unit. Whether or not the informal form you created to record goals and results is submitted along with the official paperwork at the conclusion of the annual appraisal, you'll be increasing your managerial effectiveness without changing the official performance appraisal.

Another way to make a trait based appraisal system more effective is to make the traits or characteristics assessed on the form more meaningful and measurable to your work team. Ideally, if the performance appraisal form requires that a person be assessed on cooperation, teamwork, initiative, and attitude, it provides examples of the desired behaviors. In the absence of examples—real examples, not just trait definitions—what one person might accept as evidence of initiative might be considered obnoxious aggressiveness by another.

What does it look like? is the question to answer. How will we know it when we see it? What will you accept as evidence that someone displays initiative, excels in communication, or is deficient in teamwork? Well in advance of the time for completing the performance appraisal, sit down with a blank copy of the appraisal form and review the characteristics that you will be called on to appraise. For each, tell your subordinates what kinds of behaviors you will be looking at when the time comes for you to complete the form. Ask for suggestions to measure the abstract traits or characteristics listed on the form.

Improving a Results-Based or Global Performance Appraisal

The opposite situation may also be present: Your organization may use a procedure that concentrates on results achieved but slights or ignores the performance factors. In this case, adding a separate form to cover performance factors—the *how* of the job—is probably not a good solution. Instead, make sure you discuss the importance of means as well as ends both during the initial objective-setting process and certainly when you review performance.

The task of tailoring a performance appraisal to increase its usefulness is easier if the form is primarily an essay-type, global approach. In this case, since almost anything goes, you can feel free to write the essay to provide exactly the appropriate balance between results and performance factors that the job you're appraising requires. The same procedures and recommendations apply: Talk to your group well in advance of the appraisal period, explain that both results and performance factors are important, and help group members set goals and define exactly what behaviors are examples of the traits or characteristics listed on the form.

Understanding the Power of Self-Appraisal

Probably the most powerful technique available to any manager who wants to increase the effectiveness of performance appraisal in building superior performance among a work group is self-appraisal. Adding a self-appraisal component to the performance appraisal process can be instituted without changing any other procedures or adding or revising any forms.

Self-appraisal allows managers to emphasize the most important aspects of the existing appraisal form and downplay those parts that don't apply well to the job being appraised. Most important, it brings the individual into the appraisal process and ensures that there will be genuine two-way communication. Figure 7-1 provides a sample script for introducing the self-appraisal. This same script can be adapted to maximize the potential of even the feeblest appraisal system.

Changing the Event to an Ongoing Process

In most organizations, the most serious imperfection with the existing performance appraisal system is that the procedure has become merely an event and not a process that involves a year-round series of important activities and processes. Once a year the personnel department sends out the forms, managers scramble to get them written up and approved and delivered, and everybody breathes a collective sigh of relief when the last form is returned, knowing that eleven months can now pass before the performance appraisal fiend rises from the grave again.

A shrewd manager always follows personnel's marching orders re-

Figure 8-1. Script for Introducing a Different Appraisal Process

Most of you know that every year at this time we complete a performance appraisal process. Most people think of performance appraisal as a chore to be endured, but I think the idea of looking at how we've done over the past year and planning for what will be different next year is a pretty good idea.

This year we're going to be doing things a little differently. We'll still be using the same form that we have in the past, but the form isn't the important thing. What is important is the work we do as a team to make next year better than this year has been.

I'll be asking each of you to do a self-appraisal. I think doing a self-assessment is important in figuring out where we are right now and where we want to go next year. I'll also be asking each of you to set a couple of goals for next year. A year from now, when you look back over the past twelve months, what do you want to have achieved? We'll talk about that.

Finally, I don't want to wait twelve months to find out how we're doing. I think every couple of months we should get together and see how we're doing against the goals that we've set. Spending an hour or so every few months talking about how things are going will help all of us know exactly how we're doing and highlight any areas where a mid-course correction needs to be made.

In the next week or two I'll be meeting individually with each of you for the formal performance appraisal. When we get together, I'd like you to come in with some ideas on goals that you want to achieve next year and some possible dates during the year for us to get together for a review.

garding completing, discussing, and returning the forms. But since her concern is with actually improving the performance of her work group, and not just filling out a bunch of forms, she uses the annual event to initiate a year-long cycle of performance improvement. She might gather her group of subordinates together and use the script in Figure 8-1 as a model.

By introducing the new procedure in a group meeting, the manager has made sure that every team member has received the identical message. During this meeting she can go into more detail about the self-appraisal or wait for individual meetings with employees to talk about how that should be done. She can simply mention goal setting or use this meeting as a training session and spend ten or fifteen minutes helping the team improve their goal-setting skills and begin the process of drafting some actual and substantive goals for the next year. She may choose to allow team members to decide for themselves whether review meetings should be held every three or four months and when those meetings will be scheduled or announce to the group what the schedule will be.

Whatever specific decisions you make about the logistics of the process, the following key elements have been covered:

- ▸ The company's performance appraisal form will be used again this year as it has in the past. But whether the form is good or bad is irrelevant, the important thing is the process itself.
- ▸ Next year's process will be different from this year's process in three significant ways:
  - — Each member of the team will complete a self-appraisal and discuss it with the manager.
  - — Each member of the team will be responsible for setting goals to be achieved during the upcoming year.
  - — There will be regularly scheduled review meetings during the course of the year.

Optimizing the Appraisal System: The Human Resources Perspective

All of the recommendations made to line managers can be used by an organization's human resources managers as coaching suggestions they can make to help individual operating managers increase the effectiveness of their work groups. These suggestions can also be valuable for the personnel manager confronted by a line manager who points out some obvious deficiencies in the organization's form or procedure and asks the personnel representative what he's going to do about it. Instead of responding defensively to the line manager's accurate observation (the system may indeed be out-of-date, obsolete, and passé) he might choose to use the challenge to reinforce the fact that performance appraisal is a line manager's responsibility. The following response might be appropriate:

> At this time, Matt, I'm not going to do anything about it. Revising the company's appraisal system, which is probably a worthwhile thing to do, is just not one of our top priorities at present. But even if we did revise the system, managing people and appraising performance would still be your responsibility, not ours. Let's talk about some ways that you can use our current process, even if it isn't as good as it might be, to do a better job of managing and appraising your staff. I can think of a couple of things you might do that will make the system work much better for you, even if the form remains the same.

In this way, the human resources manager remains in the appropriate role of coach and consultant. Accepting the fact that the system may not be as good as it might be, he provides assistance to the line organization by offering counsel about how to meet their responsibilities even if all the tools they have to do the job are not state of the art.

But this is still a reactive posture. There are several other ways that the human resources manager can increase the probability that the performance appraisal process will have a greater beneficial impact on the organization as a whole and each of its members individually.

Providing Appraiser Training

One obvious way of increasing the effectiveness of an existing system is to offer training to appraisers in how to get the most benefit from the system. Even highly effective managers often feel that their specific performance appraisal skills are deficient, primarily because they use them only once a year. The situation is similar to filling out income tax forms. By April 14 we have become genuine experts on the various forms, the data required, and the various strategies that will provide differing results. But having completed the form and dropped it in the mail, we rapidly lose those skills since we do not use them in other parts of our lives. When the next year's forms arrive after the beginning of the new year, we must start the skill development process from scratch.

Human resources managers usually find that the response rate is high when they offer a three- to four-hour workshop on how to complete the company's performance appraisal forms, conduct an effective interview, and follow all of the administrative procedures. The workshop does not have to be sophisticated or particularly polished. If it is presented in a nuts-and-bolts manner with the primary objective to help busy managers get a difficult chore completed as painlessly as possible, it will succeed.

A workshop like this can be pulled together in a short period of time. Since virtually all operating managers are aware that performance appraisal is an area that can expose them to legal challenge, the appeal of the workshop will be increased if the session is presented as a way to help them stay out of legal hot water.

In planning for this workshop, the human resources manager should consider the following issues.

Common Problems

The task here is to review the previous year's appraisal forms to identify the most common mistakes, and then enumerate them to the group. Common examples include failure to obtain the employee's signature, using a non-exempt form to evaluate an exempt employee, and leaving sections blank without explanation.

Senior Management Concerns

The relevance of the workshop can be increased if the personnel manager can act as a conduit through which the senior executives can speak to the line managers of the organization about their commitment to and concerns with performance appraisal. No matter how large the organization or how remote the top management group, a resourceful training specialist is probably going to get a positive response if she calls the top dog's secretary a few weeks before the session and says, "On October 4 I'm going to be conducting a half-day workshop for all the managers in the finance division on how to do a good job of completing the company's performance appraisal system with their subordinates. I don't know whether Ms. Atkinson has any feelings or opinions about the importance of performance appraisal, but if she does, I'd like to know them so I can pass them on to the people who'll be there. Can I give you a couple of questions that she might want to respond to?"

Count on it: There is no subject that senior managers of most organizations don't have feelings and opinions about, and they love to be solicited to deliver them. Sending the secretary four or five questions that are likely to provoke a feeling or opinion and the date the response is needed will probably be successful and may even get a request from the chief honcho to appear at the seminar so she can deliver her performance appraisal pronouncements personally.

The questions to ask the top executive might include ones like these:

- Do you honestly think that performance appraisal is a good idea? Does it really make any difference?
- How important is it for people to get feedback on how they're doing? Do you think they want to know? Do you think they want the truth or just to be told to keep up the good work?
- In your career, did you ever have a supervisor who did a poor job of giving you a performance appraisal? What went wrong—bad information, wasn't prepared, prejudiced? How did that affect you?
- If a new manager came to you and asked, "What's the most important thing I should keep in mind when I'm doing somebody's performance appraisal?" how would you respond?
- In your career, how important has it been to you to have managers who shot straight with you, telling you what you were doing well and what your problems were?

Obviously, there are managerial softballs—questions that senior managers can hit out of the park. And that's exactly what is needed: a ringing endorsement of performance appraisal and the importance that getting solid performance information has had on their careers.

Written Instructions

No matter how sharp their memories and how many notes they take, participants in your performance appraisal workshop will forget many critical points about the company's performance appraisal process if you don't hand out written instructions on exactly how the form is to be completed and the procedure observed.

If there is a formal calendar for the completion of various performance appraisal events, hand it out. If there is no formal calendar, make one up and call it "Recommended Sequence of Performance Appraisal Events." In the calendar, include both personnel's responsibilities and those of senior management, as well as the duties that must be performed by appraisers. This will position the calendar as a checklist for everybody who is involved with the process, not just as a task list for line managers. In addition, include items that may not be part of the organization's official system but are ways of increasing the overall effectiveness of the company's performance appraisal process. For example, the calendar shown in Figure 8-2 contains some items that were included by the human resources organization even though they are not mandated by the formal policy of the organization.

Providing Appraisee Training

In addition to training the managers in the organization who will be conducting performance appraisals, consider providing training to those who will be the recipients of a performance appraisal (many people in the organization fit into both categories). While the need for appraiser or rater training is fairly well accepted and widely conducted, it is the unusual organization that provides any formal mechanism for those who are the subjects of the system to maximize the benefits they receive from it. If one of the primary purposes of performance appraisal is to help people do a good job, one important element of ensuring that will happen is to teach people how to use the information they will receive during the appraisal to improve their personal development and contribution to the organization.

A caution belongs here: Don't offer training to appraisees without appraisers at all levels being fully informed and knowledgeable about what you are doing. It is not unusual in some organizations that mandate that every person will receive an annual performance appraisal to discover that there are still some people who don't get one. In some cases this results from organizational obstacles: The appraiser is out on extended leave; the employee changed jobs just before the appraisal process began; the individual's supervisor was fired and the subordinate was a self-managed individual contributor when the time for appraisal came. In other cases, however, managers simply avoid doing a task they find distasteful. With either the willful collaboration or neglectful oversight of their supervisors, the performance appraisals in some departments just don't get done.

The human resources manager runs a political risk in offering training to appraisees on how to make the most of their performance appraisal if

Figure 8-2. Performance Appraisal Checklist and Calendar

Week Ending	Responsibilities	Completed
Friday, September 10	Human resources half-day training session completed (optional but recommended).	☐
Friday, September 17	All forms, compensation worksheets, and written guidelines distributed by human resources to operating departments.	☐
Friday, September 24	Operating managers give blank copies of appraisal forms to subordinates and request completion of self-appraisal (optional).	☐
Friday, October 15	Operating managers complete written appraisal forms on each subordinate and submit to immediate supervisor for review and approval.	☐
Friday, October 22	All performance appraisals and compensation change requests sent to corporate human resources.	☐
Wednesday, November 3	All appraisals and compensation change requests returned to department heads for distribution.	☐
	Managers schedule performance appraisal interviews with subordinates after approved appraisals received.	
Friday, November 12	All performance appraisal interviews completed.	☐
	All compensation changes announced.	
	Meeting date to establish goals and review dates for next year set (recommended).	

there are pockets of resistance in the line organization. The training effort may be seen by insecure managers as a ploy on personnel's part to coerce everyone into compliance: If they can't get their way directly, managers will assume, then they do it by stirring up the troops and fomenting discord at lower levels.

One way around this obstacle, if it is or could be present, is to make the announcement of the training through the line organization and its managers, not through a broadside originating in personnel. Another is to make it part of the performance appraisal procedure for the upcoming assessment cycle, clearly announced well in advance and supported at the top.

Chapter 12 provides a specific model for appraisee training.

Seeking Small Successes

Even in organizations with both very ineffective appraisal processes and a great deal of organizational inertia for inaugurating change, sensitive human resources managers can usually find one department or unit open to experimenting with the status quo. Offering one department the opportunity to be the informal pilot-test site for a different form, procedure, or sequence can build organizational interest and support after managers in that department become advocates for their new approach.

The key is to determine where there is pressure for change. After only one or two appraisal cycles, the human resources manager will begin to recognize the departments or sections that do the job in a competent, straightforward way, just as they would follow any other organizational directive. He will also spot those that tend to resist, either actively by complaining about the process or passively by missing deadlines and doing the minimum that the organization will tolerate.

Finally, there will be those few units that not only do the job as expected but perhaps a little more. Individual managers in this department tinker with the system. They add an extra page to the appraisal, experiment with asking for self-appraisal without direction from outside, initiate a goal-setting process on their own. It is with these exceptional groups that the seeds of change can take root.

Talk to one of the managers in this group who has been around for a while about the performance appraisal process. Ask her what changes she would like to see. Take a form from last year that included more than what was required—a listing of agreed-on goals, perhaps, or a well-developed development plan—back to the manager who created it and ask her what the results were since the appraisal discussion months ago. What would you like to see different this year? Who else feels the same way you do? How can human resources support your efforts?

In several organizations, skillful human resources practitioners have

taken advantage of the fact that there is always much open territory between that which is mandated and that which is prohibited. Creating an
informal MBO-type process for the marketing department to use to supplement the company's trait based appraisal system, as long as it is marketing's idea and not forced on anyone else, will probably meet with no
resistance. If marketing then gets significantly better performance and
measurable outcomes from the informal experiment, it is easier to convince
more recalcitrant departments to consider implementing the same change.
The results will speak for themselves.

Making Resources Available

If nothing else, the human resources function can make resources available
to help the line organization achieve its performance appraisal mission in
a fully competent way. To start, it would be fairly simple to provide examples of both good and (far more interesting) bad performance appraisals
from previous years.

Since the personnel department usually functions as the traffic cop
for the performance appraisal system and human resources administrators
regularly read at least a sampling of performance appraisals, most personnel managers can usually remember and lay hands on both superb and
slipshod illustrations of performance appraisals from real managers about
real people in their organization. Reading these (with the names and any
identifying details blacked out) can give managers an illustration of what
they should be striving to achieve and the comfort of knowing that, no
matter how bad a job they feel they do in creating performance appraisals,
there are certainly people who do worse.

If genuine examples are not available or political sensitivities preclude
their use, a model performance appraisal can be made up. Another approach is to annotate the organization's performance appraisal form to
make it serve as a job aid. In addition to whatever instructions appear on
the front of the form and are provided in the course of training, each
section of the form can list the kinds of information that should be provided
and items that should not be included.

To do this, assume that a new manager walked into your office and
said, "Can we go over that performance appraisal form I'm supposed to
fill out on my staff? I've read the instructions, but I'm still not sure exactly
what to put where." Take each section or component of the form and write
down exactly what the appraiser should include in that section. Indicate
where to find the data he will need. In the ratings section, give some
guidelines on how to distinguish average from above average or differen-
tiate between competent and superior performance.

One piece of information that appraisers usually are eager to get is
the ratings distribution for past performance appraisals. Giving managers

this information—data they would love to have but are afraid to ask for—as a means to reinforce the company's commitment to open communication and high standards of performance can pay enormous benefits. It will make authentic those elements of the company's mission statement or declaration of vision and values that speak to such issues as trust, openness, honesty, and full disclosure. It will position the human resources department as an ally to the line, not as an obstacle. It will demonstrate that "no secrets, no surprises" is a reality, not a slogan.

Telling the Truth: A Caution

Before being disclosed, all data must be worthy of disclosure. If the organization has been practicing deceit—talking about tough standards but actually approving undeserved high ratings since they are easier for a manager to deliver than honest and candid ones—then it had better take pains to keep its managers in the dark and the truth behind closed doors.

If the organization has engaged in the folly of requesting A while rewarding B or if it talks a tough performance game but rewards merely showing up, people will catch on. In cases like this, the data are better hid.

But usually the data regarding the distribution of performance appraisal ratings are consistent with the company's message that to get a superior rating an employee must perform in a superior way; that high ratings are in truth available but will be awarded only when deserved. By frankly revealing how many people last year were rated competent or superior or marginal or distinguished or whatever else the label may be, the organization thereby earns the right to demand that the managers who assign those ratings apply the standards both fairly and toughly. The alternative is to create an organizational Lake Wobegon, where all the members are above average, and no one has any incentive to do better because they already are.

Note

1. William S. Swan, Ph.D., *How to Do a Superior Performance Appraisal* (New York: John Wiley & Sons, 1991), p. 108.

Part III

How to Create a Performance Appraisal System

Chapter 9
Building Management Support

Creating a new performance appraisal system is one of the most important but difficult jobs an organization can undertake. No other organizational system affects as many people as the performance appraisal does or affects them in such important ways. The performance appraisal system itself, combined with the way in which it is administered, affects how much money people will be paid, their relationship with their supervisor, their opportunities for promotion and growth, and ultimately their membership in the organizational family.

Everybody has a stake in the mechanics and operation of the system. And if a change in the system is going to be successful, the attitudes, opinions, and anxieties of everyone affected by it will need to be considered and resolved.

This chapter explores the process for building senior management support for creating a performance appraisal system that works. By saying "a system that works," I mean that the end result once the system has been designed, implemented, explained, used, and reflected on by all affected by it will be that there is common consensus that the way performance is managed in the organization is better than the way it used to be, whatever that way may have been. Specifically:

- The enterprise's senior managers find that the approach focuses organizational energy on the attainment of strategic business objectives.
- Corporate lawyers and human resources management professionals recognize that the system gives them powerful ammunition in the event a personnel action is challenged.
- Line managers find that the system:
    — makes it easier to talk to subordinates about their performance, both good and bad.
    — helps them identify and communicate the things their subordinates should do more of and less of.

— makes it easier to explain decisions that they make that directly affect subordinates: promotions, reassignments, raises, and assignment to training or special projects.

— provides a return on their investment of time, effort, and emotional energy that is well justified by the results.

▸ Appraisees discover that to a greater extent than before they:

— know where they stand.

— know what to do to improve their performance and increase the likelihood of receiving an increase in pay.

— know where to concentrate their self-development efforts.

— know what possible career paths may be available to them in the organization.

▸ Throughout the organization, among appraisers and appraisees alike, there will be agreement that the approach is appropriate, reasonable, and fair.

Where to Begin

Developing a new performance appraisal system that provides the benefits that most organizations want is an undertaking that will consume many months of intensive work. If the entire period is considered as the time between the organization's decision to create a new appraisal system and the time that a full appraisal cycle has been completed and the results are available for review, between eighteen and twenty-four months may elapse. If that time frame seems excessive, consider what "from start to finish" involves:

▸ The recognition that there is a need for an appraisal system where one doesn't exist or a new system to replace one that no longer is seen as satisfactory

▸ The persuasion of senior management to commit the resources to creating a system

▸ The analysis of the current state of performance management in the organization and the changes that need to be made

▸ The design of an appraisal form or forms that are accepted as appropriate and meet the needs by policymakers, human resources professionals, appraisers, and appraisees

▸ The development of procedural guidelines that are understood and accepted

▸ The possible testing of the planned new system with a pilot group to ensure that the design works as expected in field practice

▸ The revision of forms and guidelines based on field tests and user feedback

► The training of all appraisers on how to use the system
► The orientation of all appraisees on the purpose and operation of the system
► The formal implementation of the system: collecting performance data, writing appraisals, getting them approved, conducting discussions, making development recommendations, setting goals and objectives for the upcoming period
► The review of the degree to which the first pass at using the new system was successful and the correction of any obvious problems coming out of the first round of appraisals
► The actual performance of organization members during the time from the conclusion of the initial appraisal and goal-setting discussion to the beginning of the next appraisal cycle—typically one year
► The completion of the performance appraisal process for the second time, this time based on the use of the new system for goal setting and performance management initiated a year before
► The review of results from the first complete performance management cycle and the correction of any faults and flaws discovered
► The establishment of maintenance procedures to ensure that new appraisers are trained, new appraisees are oriented, forms keep pace with changes in strategic objectives, and procedures remain appropriate with internal and external changes

The time frame described includes one full year in which the new performance management system is used after its initial introduction to the organization. Only after a full appraisal cycle has been completed using the new procedure can its effectiveness be fully assessed. The question, "When will we know for sure that our new system is working effectively?" can be answered only after every element of it has been used as intended.

Creating a new performance appraisal system involves four major components:

1. Gaining senior management support
2. Designing the system and the administrative procedures
3. Implementing the system
4. Training the users

In this chapter I explain how to build management support for creating a sound and sophisticated performance management process. I start at the absolute beginning: Someone has decided that perhaps a better way of managing performance might be found. The chapter closes with the decision by senior management to commission an implementation team responsible for designing the system, the forms, and all accompanying procedures.

Working Assumptions

In describing how to create a performance appraisal system, I make certain assumptions about the organization and its members:

▸ The intent is to create an entirely new system from scratch, not merely to tune up or tinker with an existing system. I realize, of course, that the majority of organizations have a performance appraisal system in operation. They are not in the perhaps enviable position of creating a system and presenting it to people who had never used one before—people who brought with them neither biases nor preferences regarding how it should and should not work. There is almost invariably a great deal of corporate memory and organizational history that will need to be unearthed, analyzed, and understood if the new system is to prove successful. No matter how appalling the existing system is, there will always be at least one person whose interests are best served by keeping it exactly the way it is. People will have strong feelings about performance appraisal from the very start.

For example, if the existing system has been used as the basis for layoffs or reductions in force, there will be a great deal of emotional baggage surrounding any new approach. Implementation will be longer, users will be suspicious, training program participants will be less enthusiastic and more apprehensive than usual, and the central tendency rating error will be much more likely to appear. Similarly, if the previous performance appraisal system had only a marginal relationship with the compensation system—raises were based primarily on hanging around and getting along—expect organizational insurgency if the new system is highly leveraged toward pay for performance.

▸ The organization is large—perhaps a thousand employees or more. Smaller organizations will be able to accelerate or combine (but not eliminate) many of the steps I describe. The larger the organization is, the more important it is that every step required for ultimate success be taken and completed. In a very small organization, the personnel director will undertake almost all of the responsibilities of the implementation team singlehandedly. In a larger organization, tasks will be shared.

▸ The organization is not just going through the motions to meet minimum requirements. I assume that the company is in fact committed to creating a superior system that is demonstrably more productive in achieving senior management's strategic objectives. It wants to create a system it can be proud of. The process I describe will involve a major investment but will produce the greatest results. In creating a performance appraisal system, as in most other areas of life, one gets what one pays for. There are certainly ways in which significant savings in time and money can be realized without unduly compromising the ultimate product, and I will point these areas out. But don't be deceived: A new Lexus cannot be had at the price of a used Pinto.

▸ I make no assumptions about the nature of the business, whether it manufactures a product or provides a service.

▸ I make no assumption about whether the organization is in the private or public sector. The steps required to create an effective performance appraisal system are not significantly different whether the organization is a manufacturer of coffee spoons, a not-for-profit hospital, a city government or federal agency, or the administrative staff of a symphony orchestra or religious body. If the organization is to succeed in achieving its mission—producing spoons, restoring health, collecting garbage, entertaining audiences, or saving souls—its members must engage in certain behaviors and avoid others; they must generate predetermined results and accomplish desired objectives. Whatever the organization, this process will work. When I call the organization a company, recognize that I could just as easily have said agency, enterprise, department, business, firm, or bureau.

Getting Started

The decision to create a performance appraisal system usually begins when one person of influence in the organization comes to the realization that the existing process—or the absence of a process—is not fostering the success of the organization. That person may be a powerful operating manager who becomes frustrated after filling out the same old forms one more time and resolves that things will be different next year. A senior executive may have had his performance appraisal consciousness raised following the experience of being stung by a disgruntled former employee's wrongful-discharge suit when nothing in the file supports everyone's clear recollection of the departed as a flagrant goof-off and goldbrick. A personnel manager or human resources executive, in the course of her own personal development and professional growth, may realize that what the organization is doing right now in performance management is dangerously obsolete or ominously inadequate.

Whatever the trigger, no action to change the performance appraisal system can proceed without the active support and involvement of top management. Performance appraisal involves policy decisions, and policy comes from the top. Even in decentralized organizations, where the human resources function has been empowered to act autonomously or line management has been allotted the authority to manage people as it sees fit, senior management support is still critical to success. The development of a performance appraisal system is invariably a political process; there will always be hidden agendas, private objectives, and preconceived notions. Wise (or once-burned) organizational consultants and change masters will insist on getting as a minimum a charter from top management to proceed with the project and report back at regular intervals. Unless the CEO or other senior manager is the instigator of the decision to change the system, getting top management support is the first step.

Where change efforts often fail is in asking too broad a question too early in the process. When individuals or groups in the organization start to become dissatisfied with the existing performance management approach and open to considering alternatives, asking the top for authority to create a new system is premature. The case for change needs to be compellingly made before one can ask for the order. Thus the first step is to assemble the evidence that making the investment in creating a new performance appraisal system is not merely justified but unarguable.

The question to ask at this point in the process therefore is not, "Should we develop a new performance appraisal system?" but, "Should we get the information we need in order to determine whether developing a new performance appraisal system is a good business decision?" In other words, the jury is still out on whether a new system is needed. The important question at this point is whether this is an area to give serious attention to.

Approaching the development process in this way provides several benefits. First, in a straightforward way it provides the data that top management needs to justify making the business decision to commit a portion of the enterprise's resources to creating a performance appraisal system. Resources are always scarce; in the corporate nest there are always more mouths to feed than worms available. Big bird must decide which nestlings will be fed and which will be ignored. Asking initially only for license to collect the data on which a later decision will be based is an easy one for executives to accede to.

A second benefit of this approach is that it allows for top management participation in the data-gathering process. In addition to surveying appraisers, appraisees, and administrators of the system, top management can also be included. Later, when the results of the data collection activity are reviewed and the decision to proceed with the development of a new appraisal system is requested, top management's data will be part of the whole that justifies the investment. If the opinions of senior executives about the existing performance management process closely parallel those of other groups (as they usually do), the case for making a substantial investment in managing performance will be easier to justify.

A third benefit of starting the process by collecting data about the need for system redesign is that it permits biases and prejudices to emerge early and their effects later in the process to be anticipated.

Although collecting data on the need for a new performance appraisal system may inappropriately raise expectations of change before the actual commitment to change has been made, it does provide the benefit of increasing organizational awareness of performance management issues before any decisions have been made.

Finally, it is possible that once the data have been collected, they demonstrate that the case for changing the system is in fact a weak one and that corporate resources would be better allocated somewhere else. This finding will be disappointing to those with a stake in proceeding with a redesign of the system, but if the investment ultimately will produce no benefit, it is always better to learn that sooner rather than later. There are times when the wisest course of action is to leave well enough alone.

The Data Collection Process

Once the organization has decided to proceed with the development of a new system, a great deal of data will be collected through surveys, interviews, focus groups, and other means. The purpose of this data collection is to answer the question, "Should we create a new performance management system?" not to decide all of the details and specifics that will be determined once the decision to proceed has been made. The purpose of initial data collection is to make the internal sale to begin the project, not to make any substantive decisions about what the final product will look like.

Figure 9-1 contains a survey form to help companies determine the areas where a new performance management system may offer some of the greatest returns. Using a survey like this at the beginning of the project and then resurveying after the first round of appraisals with the new system has been completed (or a resurvey after a year's experience with the new system) will provide data that can demonstrate the system's impact on the organization and indicate areas where additional work may be necessary.

Similarly, conducting a preliminary paperwork audit and interviewing a small number of system users at various levels will help to confirm or reject the need for a new system. Once the need has been confirmed, a comprehensive paperwork audit and extensive interviews and focus groups may be required to determine all of the needs and expectations the system should meet.

The interviews and surveys provide feedback on people's feelings about the current process; the paperwork audit answers questions regarding the use of the system:

- Are forms completed properly? Are the formal mechanics of the system being followed?
- Are forms used effectively? Is there evidence of thoughtful consideration and analysis in the written comments? Are judgments and generalizations backed up by specific examples?

Figure 9-1. Performance Management Survey

1. In our organization, supervisors and subordinates agree on what constitutes good performance:

Totally Disagree	1	2	3	4	5 Neutral	6	7	8	9	Totally Agree

2. Employees who do their jobs well are sufficiently recognized and rewarded for their achievements:

Almost Never	1	2	3	4 Occasionally	5	6	7	8	9	Almost Always

3. Employees who don't do their jobs well are confronted with the need for change:

Almost Never	1	2	3	4 Occasionally	5	6	7	8	9	Almost Always

4. Most people have a thorough understanding of how the performance appraisal system operates:

Totally Disagree	1	2	3	4	5 Neutral	6	7	8	9	Totally Agree

5. Current performance appraisal procedures provide accurate and sufficient feedback to individuals:

Totally Disagree	1	2	3	4	5 Neutral	6	7	8	9	Totally Agree

6. In our organization, performance appraisals are fairly and honestly done:

Totally Disagree	1	2	3	4	5 Neutral	6	7	8	9	Totally Agree

7. Employees display a high degree of personal commitment to the organization and its goals:

Totally Disagree	1	2	3	4	5 Neutral	6	7	8	9	Totally Agree

8. In our organization salary decisions are made on the basis of performance appraisal:

Totally Disagree	1	2	3	4	5 Neutral	6	7	8	9	Totally Agree

9. In our organization, promotion decisions are made on the basis of performance appraisal:

Totally Disagree	1	2	3	4	5 Neutral	6	7	8	9	Totally Agree

Figure 9-1. *(continued)*

---

10. When I have to conduct a performance review or coaching session with an employee, I feel confident with my ability to say and do all the right things:

Totally	1	2	3	4	5	6	7	8	9	Totally
Disagree					Neutral					Agree

11. The forms that we use to appraise performance are complete and appropriate:

Totally	1	2	3	4	5	6	7	8	9	Totally
Disagree					Neutral					Agree

12. Managers who do a good job of performance management are recognized and rewarded for their efforts:

Totally	1	2	3	4	5	6	7	8	9	Totally
Disagree					Neutral					Agree

13. It wouldn't make much difference to our business if performance appraisals were not done:

Totally	1	2	3	4	5	6	7	8	9	Totally
Disagree					Neutral					Agree

14. When I need to conduct performance appraisal discussions or coaching sessions, I get all the help I need from my boss and/or human resources:

Totally	1	2	3	4	5	6	7	8	9	Totally
Disagree					Neutral					Agree

- ▸ Are the forms as currently completed legally defensible?
- ▸ Are there any employee comments? What do employees say? Are there any patterns?
- ▸ In a given department, what percentage of employees have current performance appraisals in their personal files? Is the information up to date?

When the data have been collected, ask the key question: Do they support the case for revamping the system so strongly that even a skeptic would agree that there is merit in proceeding?

Relating Performance Appraisal and Strategic Business Outcomes

Data alone cannot make the case. More important in ensuring top management support is the ability to demonstrate a relationship between improving the performance management system and achieving strategic business objectives.

Almost a quarter century ago, consultant Malcolm Warren passed along an insight about training and development that remains unsurpassedly useful: "The training business," Warren observed, "is a lot like the dog food business. The initial purchaser is rarely the ultimate consumer."[1] Warren's aphorism reveals the dual nature of the audience for training, management development, and other human resources management systems. Human resources professionals lose credibility and effectiveness when they fail to recognize that the benefits senior management expects from a system may be entirely different from the benefits to system users. In the area of performance appraisal, arguing that creating a new system may increase the feedback between supervisor and subordinate, increase the accuracy of performance appraisal data, build more effective relationships, and help set better development plans may be accurate but irrelevant, since these are not strategic business issues.

Even if you prepare a formal cost-benefit proposal and demonstrate a positive return on investment, you are more likely to get a patronizing nod over the nice numbers than a solid commitment to proceed. To address business problems on a level that truly commands top management's attention, the project can't just be about making money. It has to be about solving the problems that challenge the health of the business as a whole: problems that affect the overall balance of revenues over expenses.

Ask, in what direction is the senior management group of the organization trying to take the company? Then ask whether the current procedure for managing and evaluating performance is a support or an interference to that effort. Is it likely that changing the system that guides the performance of organization members will cause a redirection of the organization toward the attainment of senior management's goals? Those are among the strategic concerns that a performance appraisal system revision can address.

Building Senior Management Support

A formal executive overview is one of the major milestone events in the process of creating and installing a new performance management system. It provides the charter under which those who will be involved in creating the new system will work and marks the official beginning of the project. The executive overview, particularly when conducted by an external expert on performance appraisal, can also provide top managers with a concentrated dose of executive education on what their role and expectations of a system should be. This meeting will build top management political support for the creation of a new system, determine any constraints on system acceptability, and confirm the appropriateness of the planned design process.

Beginning the Creation Process

Once top management has approved the creation of a new system, they do not need to be involved with the day-to-day details and decisions involved in designing the system. That task is the responsibility of three other groups or individuals:

1. *Consultants or technical specialists.* Their role is to serve as the technology experts on performance appraisal, ensuring that the system incorporates the expertise gained from other organizations and academic research, as well as ensuring full legal compliance.
2. *Human resources representatives.* They are responsible for administering and maintaining the system once it has been implemented. They bear the responsibility for making sure that the system effectively integrates with all other people management systems (compensation, promotion, management development, and so forth).
3. *Users of the system.* This group is charged with ensuring that the ultimate design is appropriate for their needs.

One group of academics and consultants in performance appraisal has observed that there are three distinct sets of beliefs about the best approach toward designing organizational systems: the rational, the political, and the participative.[2]

The *rational approach* argues that the design of the system is best done by those who are experts in the field of performance appraisal. There is a body of knowledge regarding the discipline of performance management, and if a performance appraisal system is going to be effective, it must incorporate the learnings from research and avoid the pitfalls that the unwary can blunder into.

The *political approach* recognizes that no matter how academically sound and research based an appraisal system may be, if it is not supported by powerful people in the organization, it will fail. Proponents of taking a political approach to system design argue that as long as there are no legal landmines or glaring deficiencies in design, the critical factor in system success is top management support. The role of those who are charged with designing the new system is primarily to determine the kind of approach preferred at the summit and, without violating basic constraints, to give them what they want.

The third approach is *participative*. Designs cannot be forced, by specification or imposition, on the people who must eventually use them, this group points out. "To force a design courts the risk that people will somehow tailor it to their own purposes and perhaps undercut its original intent. This approach argues that the best way to ensure the acceptability of a design and lessen the possibility of its being subverted is to let users participate in its design. The participative approach assumes that the final participants will alter things to their own purposes anyway, therefore, why not involve them in the design process?"[3]

The ideal procedure for designing a performance appraisal system incorporates all three of these approaches. Top management's concern is with business strategy, corporate goals, and the setting of overall objectives. It is not only appropriate but necessary for those at the top to make sure that the approach is aligned with and supports corporate strategy. The specific role of the senior management team is not to be involved in the day-to-day process of designing all the forms and guidelines but to be advised of the evolution of these elements on a regular basis and make sure that they fit with the broad organizational direction. In this way the political requirement is met.

In the rational domain, there is a great body of expertise and experience available about performance appraisal; experts have much to contribute. But experts, whether internal human resources and organizational development specialists or outside consultants specializing in performance management, cannot be expected to be equally familiar with the strategic concerns of senior management. The job of the performance appraisal subject matter expert is to understand the purposes that top management wants the system to serve and the needs and preferences of system users, and then integrate his expertise with the demands of business strategy.

Finally, almost all specialists in organizational design and the development of performance management systems agree with one simple observation: People support what they help create. The more that ultimate users are involved in the process of designing the system, the greater is the likelihood that they will ultimately use it and see it as being appropriate for their needs.

An Effective Design Process

An effective design process combines the political, rational, and participative approaches. Technical expertise is provided from either an external authority or an internal specialist together with administrative expertise provided by active participation of human resources specialists. Users of the system are involved in the tailoring of the process to meet the needs of the various functions and departments that will be using it. And senior management is involved in direction setting at the start of the project and regular check-ins and course correction meetings during the entire development and implementation process.

In smaller organizations, many of the roles required for effective system development can be filled by one individual. The head of human resources is likely to be a member of the senior management team setting the direction for the new system, the resident expert on performance appraisal technology, and the project manager involved, together with a group of users from various line departments, in the day-to-day development of the system and forms.

In larger organizations the roles are more likely to be discrete. For the rest of this discussion on the most effective way to create a performance appraisal system, I assume that the organization is sufficiently large to require the use of an implementation team to develop the new system, oversee its installation, and ensure its success. Over the years of working with organizations I have consistently used an implementation team–task force approach with success, since it combines the rational, political, and participative approaches.

Top management's role in the performance appraisal design and implementation process involves these activities:

- Appointing the members of the implementation team who will develop the system
- Determining the overall parameters that the system must meet
- Designating one or several members of the senior management group to serve as the primary interface or review board with the implementation team
- Providing guidance to the implementation team as questions arise and decisions are approaching the point of being made final
- Actively supporting the design and implementation process through being available for consultation when problems or difficult issues arise, being actively involved in the communications process, and participating appropriately in appraiser training and appraisee orientation
- Actively supporting the organization's performance management process itself through using the system to make appraisals of subordinate managers, demanding that subordinate managers use the process as designed with their subordinates, using data from the system to make promotion, development, and termination decisions, and making the appropriate use of the performance management system a priority for all members of the organization

Determining the System Parameters

Although the implementation team will be assigned the responsibility of creating the system itself, the organization's senior management must provide the specifications. Setting the parameters of the performance management system involves making broad decisions about the overall operation of the process. A useful analogy is that of building a new house. Senior management is in the position of the homeowner, deciding such major issues as where the house will be built, the overall style, the budget, and the design parameters. The implementation team functions as the architect, taking the broad goals of the homeowner and translating them into specific blueprints and designs that will meet all of the homeowner's wants and needs and ensure a strong foundation and a safe and efficient structure. Finally, the system users are the contractors and workers, carrying out the plans of the architect to produce exactly what the homeowner wanted to build.

Some system parameters that might be appropriate for most organizations include decisions like these, each of which needs to be reviewed for its appropriateness in the reader's organization:

- The performance management process will include a formal performance planning process as well as a performance evaluation process.
- Every employee will receive a performance appraisal (or, for example, all employees up to and including the level of vice president will receive a performance appraisal).
- Employees will receive performance appraisals at least once a year. (When they receive them is a matter more appropriately decided by the implementation team.)
- The appraisal process will include the evaluation of both work results and work behaviors. (The balance between outcomes and behaviors is another decision best left to the implementation team or perhaps to individual appraisers.)
- The organization will use a pay-for-performance philosophy, and the performance appraisal will be the primary determinant of compensation changes.
- Every appraiser will be trained.

Creating an Implementation Team

Once the decision has been made at the top to begin the development of a new appraisal system and the basic parameters determined, senior management's next task is to appoint an implementation team charged with the responsibility of developing the system.

This task force usually includes between six and sixteen people, depending on the size of the company, the availability of talented participants, and the anticipated complexity of the task. Although the members of the team will include human resources or personnel specialists and perhaps a representative from the legal or training functions, or both, the core group is system users from all major departments. The team represents a cross section of the organization in terms of demographics and organizational level. The one common criterion, particularly among the representatives from user departments, is that they possess a great deal of internal credibility with their peers.

The implementation team is headed by a project manager, usually either the senior human resources representative on the team or a senior line manager. The project manager may also be the technical expert on performance appraisal if the organization is not using an outside consultant or expert. The project manager usually has a designated member of the senior executive group with whom he keeps in regular contact about the direction of the team and the decisions that are being recommended. In this way the organization's senior management remains aware of the progress of the project and understands that it is operating within the broad constraints set out.

The implementation team's responsibility is to create and implement the new performance appraisal system. To do that they first must become mini-experts on performance appraisal procedures and techniques, sufficiently knowledgeable about the subject that they can come up with a design that fits their needs and satisfies all of their customers' demands.

The success of the initial meeting of the implementation team will have a significant impact on the success of the overall effort. In most cases, the task force is asked to spend at least one full day in this initial meeting and often, depending on the complexity of the project, the commitment of the organization, and the availability of team members, two full days.

Being requested—or directed—to serve on the implementation team is an important form of recognition and a career-enhancing grooming opportunity. Selection of members and their orientation is critical. If team members assemble and discover themselves to be one of a group of busy, smart, ambitious fast-trackers, the perceived importance of the assignment will be significantly different than if they find themselves with a bunch of also-rans and retreads who could easily be spared.

Regardless of the degree of premeeting communication, it is certain that members will arrive for this first meeting with significantly different understandings of the purpose of the project, its importance, the amount of time that will be involved, and the goals of senior management in commissioning it. In addition to a presentation from the senior manager who will serve as the primary interface between the executive group and the chairman of the implementation team, a number of procedural and human dynamics issues need to be addressed and resolved early in the process:

- ► Are members there as representatives of their departments (to protect its interests) or as independent thinkers (with the corporate good as the overriding goal)?

- ▸ What are the ground rules? What rules and expectations will the group set about attendance, work in between team meetings, degree of participation, decision making, conflict resolution, confidentiality, and other issues?
- ▸ Why has this particular group been chosen? What specific skill set is each member expected to bring to the table?
- ▸ What are the logistics?
- ▸ Is there a deadline?
- ▸ How often will the team meet?
- ▸ How will membership on the implementation team be balanced with their other job demands?

The first day of the initial implementation team meeting usually begins with a kickoff from senior management, a short introduction to the task ahead, and the exploration and resolution of the logistical and group dynamics issues. The greatest amount of time is spent in a training session conducted by the external consultant or internal subject matter expert on performance appraisal to bring everyone on the team up to full understanding of the topic as quickly as possible.

It is useful during this presentation for the group to share their own experiences with performance appraisal, as both appraiser and appraisee, with their current employer and in earlier jobs. How does the system actually work in their department? they need to be asked. Everyone knows that there are two performance appraisal systems: the one on the books and the one that is actually used. What actually happens? The policy and all of management's pronouncements may say that there is no quota for ratings; members of the team may know differently. The policy may require pay for performance; the reality may be that appraisers deliberately skew appraisal ratings to reward favorites regardless of results achieved.

Once the team knows why it has been assembled and has gained a basic understanding of the operation in both theory and practice of a performance management system, the team chairman then explains the two critical tasks they must accomplish:

1. Design the system itself: all forms, procedural guidelines, and policy statements, together with appropriate maintenance and monitoring systems.
2. Develop organization-wide understanding, support, and acceptance of the new approach.

With the knowledge they have gained on the technology and research about performance appraisal from the technical expert or consultant, they are ready to begin work on their two assignments: designing the system and ensuring its successful implementation. To carry out these roles, the most effective approach is to assign members of the larger implementation team to serve on one of two task forces, each with its own mission: the design task force and the communications task force.

Although the implementation team as a whole is responsible for the overall development and implementation of the new performance appraisal system, the primary mission of the design task force is to develop the forms, procedures, and policy statements for review by the implementation team as a whole and ultimate approval by senior management. Their role is to use the expertise they acquire in working with the consultant or technical expert to design a comprehensive performance appraisal system uniquely tailored to the needs, culture, and goals of their organization.

Their counterparts on the communications task force have a different role. Their work approximates that of an advertising agency. Their product is the performance appraisal system that their colleagues on the design task force are developing. Their market is everyone inside and outside the organization who will be affected by the new system, and their mission is to create a communications plan that will ensure complete understanding, support, and acceptance.

Chapter 10 concentrates on the work required of the implementation team in designing the system, including the forms and procedures. Chapter 11 then describes how to ensure a successful implementation.

Notes

1. Private conversation with author.
2. Allan M. Mohrman, Jr., Susan M. Resnick-West, and Edward E. Lawler III, *Designing Performance Appraisal Systems* (San Francisco: Jossey-Bass, 1989).
3. Ibid., p. 14.

Chapter 10

Designing the Performance Appraisal System

Before the implementation team can help the organization decide where it needs to go, it first needs to ascertain precisely where the organization is right now. Several approaches are useful in generating data and beginning the communications process that will lead to smooth implementation. If a *paperwork audit* was not done earlier as part of the initial process to determine the investment of resources in creating a new system, it should be undertaken as one of the implementation team's initial steps. If the organization currently has a system that will be replaced, appraisal forms from all departments should be reviewed to determine the way in which the existing system is being used and the areas where major improvements are required. Is there a significant difference in the average rating from one department to another? How great is the spread in the use of the rating scale? Are there any obvious problems with central tendency, negative skew, or leniency? Does everyone who is due a performance appraisal get one?

Personal interviews, conducted by members of the implementation team, can sensitize all members to the perceived needs and problems among the user groups. Asking both appraisers and appraisees a common set of questions about their reactions to the current performance management system and their expectations of an ideal system can highlight common concerns and also any significant differences in perceptions among executives, managers, and appraisal recipients.

Focus groups of employees throughout the organization can be useful in the initial process of assessing the current state of performance management in the company. Their reactions can serve to confirm other data and allow concentrated attention on specific issues.

As the development process continues, focus groups of users will be particularly helpful in making sure that the implementation team does not venture too far from what others in the organization who are less involved in the development process would consider a reasonable outcome. It frequently happens that as the implementation team learns more about the impact a comprehensive performance management system can have on an organization, they come up with a process that the majority of users are unprepared for. Frequent discussions and draft reviews with users help ensure ultimate acceptance.

In addition, when the team presents the drafts of the new performance appraisal forms and operating guidelines to senior management, they will usually be asked whether other people in the organization unconnected with the implementation team have had a chance to review them. Continuing use of focus groups to consider drafts and offer suggestions on the process will increase the probability of ultimate approval.

As we were creating a new performance appraisal system for the sales force of a major consumer good company a few years ago, the vice president of sales was adamant in his demand that we run everything that we were developing by a group of field sales representatives and sales supervisors before presenting it to him or any of his lieutenants for approval. He had started his career with the company thirty years before as a route salesman and was highly sensitive to the tendency of headquarters to come up with some new policy or procedure without subjecting it to close field scrutiny in advance. His insistence on extensive field review slowed the development process to some degree, but any time lost was more than made up for when the new system, a radical departure from what had been done before, was installed with virtually no field resistance.

Employee opinion surveys tailored to the specific issues of concern in the organization can generate useful data and prepare the organization for change.

Once the team has assembled and reviewed the data about the current state of performance management as it exists in the organization right now, they are ready to begin developing a system that will move the organization to where it needs to be.

Determining the Purposes the Appraisal System Will Serve

Virtually every performance appraisal system has as its fundamental purpose the assessment of how well the individual performed the job over the appraisal period. Most add to that a second expectation: that the system will assist in improving performance by giving the employee a clear future direction.

Another common purpose is to allocate salary dollars according to the quality of performance. Still another is to justify layoffs or reductions in force. Another expectation the organization may have of its performance appraisal process is that it provide the data the enterprise needs for planning its manpower needs in the future. And the training department expects the process to serve as a training needs analysis, identifying the areas where developmental expenditures will have the maximum impact. Operating managers want the system to have a motivational impact and improve the overall level of performance. Employee relations specialists and company lawyers want the form to serve as a basis for terminations and defending those terminations when challenged. Finally, with employees and employers today recognizing that lifetime employment is becoming less and less likely, everyone would like the appraisal system to provide data that the individual can use for career planning.

Stop! It's just too much.

One of the primary reasons performance appraisal systems are frequently held in disrepute is that they are unable to deliver the goods for all the unrelated expectations we have of them. We want this one system, which too often lies sleeping for eleven months, to provide information on how well the individual did his job over the previous twelve months (historical data), tell us how much we should change his salary (a decision in the present), and then help set goals and plan developmental endeavors (future activities). No wonder so many performance appraisal systems are out of whack. Three entirely unrelated demands in three different time frames are loaded into one procedure.

The solution is not to create more forms to address different purposes. A better approach is to provide for a greater separation of the various subsystems involved in the overall performance management process.

The implementation team must establish exactly what purposes the organization expects the new system to achieve. The more importance the enterprise places on having the performance appraisal system serve as the basis of a pay-for-performance program or as the primary determinant of assessing training and development needs, the stronger the argument will be for separating these discussions from the review of how well the person did over the past twelve months. (Chapters 13 and 14 provide more information on these topics.)

If the implementation team is starting from scratch—the organization has never had a performance appraisal system—the development of a system with its forms and procedural guidelines should be fairly straightforward. But in most cases a performance appraisal system is already in place. It frequently has been used for a number of years, and organizational frustration with its failure to meet all needs thoroughly (or at all!) has been growing. Finally the organization is ready to throw out baby and bath water both and start over with something unsullied and pristine. In this case the implementation team has to identify clearly the gaps that exist between management's expectations and the ways in which the current system fails to deliver.

In developing all the elements of the new system, the implementation team increases the probability of success if it can clearly identify all of the expectations that the new system will be expected to meet and identify how existing procedures are failing. This, at least, will minimize resistance from those whose favorite argument against change is, "But we've always done it this way!"

This is the reason that senior management must be clear about the system parameters. It is not the job of the architect to decide what kind of house the client wants, or where to build it, or how much it should cost. Even less are those decisions the responsibility of the contractors and workers. They are the responsibility of the homeowner. Similarly, top management, the owner of the performance management system, must make the broad decisions. The implementation team then creates the plans; the organization's appraisers and users carry them out.

Developing the Performance Management System

Any organization's overall performance management system has three sequential stages:

1. *Planning.* Determining the behaviors and results that will be expected from every member of the organization.
2. *Execution.* Providing feedback, coaching, and guidance during the appraisal period to improve performance.
3. *Evaluation.* Identifying and discussing strengths and weaknesses during the appraisal period.

A fourth dimension, compensation or pay for performance, is based on the results of the evaluation made of the individual's contribution to the organization.

In developing the performance management system, the members of the implementation team will need to recommend the steps to be followed in the three phases—planning, execution, and evaluation—to meet the overall system parameters set by the senior management group. They may also be expected to recommend the procedure to follow in relating the appraisal system to the compensation system.

In the area of performance planning, the implementation team needs to assess and recommend the timing of the planning process, the way in which goal setting will be done, and the role of the employee in the planning process: Will he primarily be the generator of goals or merely the recipient of goals?

208   How to Create a Performance Appraisal System

In the performance execution area, the only major design decision will be whether the system should formally require interim reviews on perhaps a quarterly basis in addition to the annual review. While performance feedback and coaching are critical determinants of system success, most of the issues relating to coaching and feedback will be addressed during appraiser training.

It is in the area of performance evaluation that most of the team's work will be concentrated. Although designing the appraisal form is the most obvious requirement, a large number of procedural issues must be resolved in the course of creating the comprehensive performance management system:

- How many forms will we need to create to make sure that there are reasonable parallels between the nature of the various jobs and the forms that are used to assess how well those jobs have been performed?
- If a form is to have a section devoted to assessment of results, how many objectives or outcomes will be included?
- If a form is to have a section on work behaviors or competencies, which ones should be included?
- For each competency area or work behavior, how will the dimension be defined or described?
- Should the form provide for weighting the relative importance between work outcomes and work behaviors? If so, what is the appropriate weighting? Or should this decision be left up to individual appraisers?
- Within both work outcomes and work behaviors, should the form provide for weightings of individual goals or behaviors?
- Who should appraise performance? Should the immediate supervisor be the only appraiser, or should higher-level managers also provide appraisal input? What about peers and coworkers? Internal customers? External customers? Subordinates?
- Should the appraisal process provide for an employee to do a self-appraisal? If so, should space for a self-appraisal be included on the appraisal form? When should the employee review this self-appraisal with the supervisor?
- Should the process provide for upward appraisal?
- How many levels of performance should the form provide for?
- What should each of the levels of performance be called? What labels should be used?
- How will the individual's overall rating be determined? Should it be a mathematical average of the various ratings and weightings of the different dimensions, or a function of managerial judgment based on the overall performance of the individual?

- What will the appraisal period be? Will employees receive their annual appraisal on their anniversary date, or will all employees be appraised at the same time? If all appraisals are done at the same time, should this be at the close of the organization's business year or at some other time?
- How many meetings to discuss performance should there be? Should appraisers be expected to discuss the appraisal of the past year's performance, advise the employee of any compensation change, discuss developmental needs and plans, and set objectives for the upcoming appraisal period all during the same meeting, or should some or all of these tasks be done separately?
- What should be the linkage between pay and performance? Should the supervisor have discretion in making compensation changes, or should the relationship be direct (a rating of X generates an increase of Y)?
- How should unusual situations (new employees, transferred employees, matrix situations) be handled?

Creating the Performance Appraisal Form

"The appraisal form is a lightning rod that will attract all sorts of attention completely out of proportion to its importance," argues consultant Jack Zigon.[1] Performance appraisal experts almost universally contend that the form is not the most important part of the performance appraisal process, but users know better. Everyone will have an opinion, and demands for changes in the form will continue long after its designers consider it finally cast in concrete.

Use that phenomenon to your advantage, Zigon advises. Design the form early in the process, and get lots of feedback on it. The sooner you can get everyone's thoughts on the form and wade through all the revisions and fine-tunings that will always be required, the sooner you can concentrate on the aspects of the performance management process that will actually make a difference in people's performance: goal setting, effective feedback, periodic coaching, and others.

The most effective way for an implementation team to create a form appropriate for their organization is for them to analyze the organizational results they need to achieve, determine the number of forms required to help them achieve those results, and then review and analyze the actual forms in use in a variety of companies so they can identify what they like and don't like in the work their predecessors in other organizations have done.

In creating the performance appraisal form, the temptation is usually to err on the side of excess: including too much, asking too much of raters rather than too little. As they examine samples of appraisal instruments from a variety of other organizations, members of the implementation team are likely to discover many aspects of performance appraisal that they would like to incorporate in their own organization's approach.

Caution: Less is more.

The more work the performance appraisal procedure requires, the less likely it is that it will be done well. Although many organizations have had notable success in using a highly complex appraisal instrument, their success is less a result of the form itself than it is the organization's culture and senior management's commitment. It's easy to design page after page of appraisal instrumentation; the hard job is cutting back to the core.

Designing the Form Itself

Once the implementation team has received a thorough orientation to the subject of performance appraisal from the consultant or internal expert, it is helpful for them to have access to a variety of forms from other organizations as they deal with the questions they must answer for their own organization.

The role of the outside consultant or internal performance appraisal expert is not to tell the team what is right for their organization. The expert's appropriate role is the following:

- ▸ Identifying every question that needs to be answered
- ▸ Identifying the various alternative approaches that the team has available
- ▸ Identifying the pros and cons, the benefits and disadvantages of each alternative approach
- ▸ Providing insight and influence regarding which alternatives most closely meet the organizational parameters for the system set forth by the senior management group
- ▸ Helping team members make use of their knowledge of the organization—its history, culture, members, goals, and needs—in deciding which alternative to recommend

Reviewing the design decisions other organizations made in creating their forms (the boxes to check, the blanks to fill in, the competencies that are presented for evaluation) will help the implementation team in their form design efforts. Greater benefits will result from showing them how the samples they are reviewing serve to create a performance management system appropriate to the expectations of senior management and the goals of the organization. In other words, the design of the appraisal form must match the thrust and direction of the organization. If primary stress is to be placed on customer service, then a results-oriented, MBO-type appraisal system is probably not the best choice. What is needed in this case is an appraisal system that focuses on specifying the desired customer service behaviors and evaluates organization members on the degree to which those behaviors are exhibited.

Similarly, a results-driven organization might be served better by an appraisal process that requires each member to set specific and measurable targets at the beginning of the appraisal period and then evaluates precisely the degree to which each objective was accomplished. If implementation team members can see several examples of forms that support the purposes and direction they are trying to bring about, they will have a basis to begin their efforts.

How Many Forms Are Needed?

This is usually the best question with which to begin the forms development process. The results of the analysis—paperwork audits, interviews, surveys and questionnaires, focus groups—usually provoke a decision that more than one form will be required for the variety of different jobs in the organization. In a hospital setting, for example, there may be very few meaningful results measures or work outcomes available that accurately assess the performance of a nurse. Almost everything the nurse does is best measured in behavioral terms. For a claims processing clerk in the same hospital, however, the opposite may be true. Here results measures abound: claims processed per hour, percentage of claims processed accurately, number of claims settled at the first review, and so forth. For the hospital administrator, both results and behavior measures may be of equal importance.

One of the first decisions to be made by the implementation team, therefore, is the number of different forms to develop. The temptation is initially to have too many rather than too few. In one organization six entirely different forms were required to match significant differences in job content. A large food processing business has three performance appraisal forms: one for route sales representatives, another for district sales managers (route sales representatives' immediate supervisor), and one for everybody else in the company. In this case, the sales department held firmly to the belief that the jobs of route sales representatives and district sales manager were sufficiently distinctive to justify the effort to create a unique form for each position. The result was that for these two positions, there was a significant and immediate performance improvement following introduction since the performance appraisal form was entirely results oriented, specified exactly what the organization expected, and provided for a tight pay-for-performance schedule.

Most organizations find that four forms suffice to distinguish among the various job families in the organization: management/supervisory, professional/technical, nonexempt, and executive. Alcon Laboratories, the pharmaceutical subsidiary of Nestlé, uses one almost encyclopedic form for all jobs. The thirteen-page document is filled out completely for individuals at management and executive levels; with nonexempt and professional positions, only portions of the form are used.

Utility Fuels, a Houston-based energy company, developed separate forms for exempt and nonexempt employees. We then created a separate supervisory appraisal that was completed and added to the regular appraisal for exempt employees with supervisory responsibilities.

One way to help the implementation team come to a decision on the number of forms that will be necessary is to ask, "What purposes are we expecting the system to serve?" The decision on the number of forms necessary and what those forms will contain is a function of two factors: the number of distinct job types or families that are so different in content that one form alone could not reasonably be used to assess the performance of incumbents in these different jobs and the various results that the system itself is expected to achieve.

Here is final caution in determining the number of discrete forms required to achieve the purposes of performance appraisal: Not only will each additional form increase geometrically the amount of administrative burden in managing the system, but the risk of creating a corporate caste system arises. When in doubt, err on the side of one size fits all.

What Should the Form Contain?

In most cases, the performance appraisal form for most jobs will ask for two different kinds of information about the employee's performance: what he achieved (results or work outcomes or objectives) and how he went about doing the job (work behaviors or competencies or performance factors). Most appraisal forms designed for management and exempt positions place the emphasis on accomplishments or results; most forms aimed at service or nonexempt positions stress behaviors.

Work Outcomes or Objectives

Chapter 4 of this book analyzed the most effective process for creating performance objectives or work outcomes. When the manager and the subordinate have agreed on the most important outcomes to be achieved by the subordinate during the appraisal period (rarely fewer than three

Figure 10-1. Sample Results Section of a Performance Assessment Form

Accountability:

Objective/Goal:

Results:

APPRAISAL:

or more than seven) these typically are written in the appropriate blanks on the appraisal form. At the end of the appraisal period, the manager completes an assessment of the degree to which the objectives were achieved, indicates the rating for each, and in most cases determines an overall rating for the section on performance outcomes or objectives.

In most cases, the portion of the form that deals with results will be blank, except for the instructions that ask the appraiser to write in the various goals that were agreed at the beginning of the appraisal period, the summary of results achieved, and the evaluation of performance against that goal. Figure 10-1 provides a sample. The number of possible ratings and the labels assigned to each one of those positions will usually be the same as the ratings and labels used to evaluate overall performance at the end of the form. Two other questions arise in constructing the work outcomes section of the performance appraisal form: conditions and weightings.

Conditions Affecting Performance

Two salesmen working for the same manager set goals of a sales increase in their territory of 20 percent in the upcoming year. At the end of the year, salesman A has achieved a sales increase of 40 percent; salesman B has achieved only a 10 percent increase. Which one has done the better job?

Without further information, it is obvious that A has far outperformed B. But a review of market conditions indicates the opposite. One of A's customers decided to decentralize purchasing, abandon its national accounts program, and assign all buying to local managers. In B's case, his primary customer filed for Chapter 11 and closed all locations in B's territory. A's response to the changed conditions in his market was to relax, decrease his efforts, and simply write up the orders as they come in. B, on the other hand, reacted to the disappearance of his major customer by immediately beginning a major effort to locate and woo replacements. Now which one has done the better job?

The manager of A and B will undoubtedly take the changes in market conditions into account in assessing their performance; on the face of it, A has succeeded admirably, and B has failed to achieve the objective. Since the conditions under which individuals perform rarely remain static over the course of a year, the implementation team needs to consider whether including a segment to indicate the conditions under which performance was achieved should be included on the form or whether this aspect should merely be covered in training and left to the discretion of the raters.

Number of Objectives to Include

Few organizations expect an individual to develop fewer than three or more than seven specific objectives to be accomplished over the appraisal period. Three or fewer suggests that broad statements of accountability are being recorded rather than specific and measurable statements of actual work outcomes to be achieved. More than seven probably indicates job fragmentation and will lead to a loss of focus on the small but significant number of activities that will produce a disproportionate amount of job success.

On the master appraisal form in Appendix A, the section of the instrument devoted to assessment of goals and objectives provides for five to be appraised (three on the front and two on the back of a single sheet of paper, with space for an assessment of the individual's performance in the overall area of achieving job objectives). Small spaces are provided for the identification of the broad area of accountability, the specific objective within that accountability area, and the individual assessment of the success achieved in meeting that job objective. The largest part is provided for the analysis of the actual results achieved. If more than five objectives need to be identified, a separate sheet can be added. It rarely is needed.

Weighing Performance Objectives

The final issue to be resolved in designing the work outcomes section of the appraisal form is whether each performance objective should be weighted. Obviously not all objectives are of equal importance to the organization. Should the form reflect the fact that some objectives are more vital than others?

During the objective-setting discussion we can assume that the manager and subordinate gave some attention to discussing the relative importance of the items to be accomplished in the upcoming year. Developing a specific index of relative priority might help the worker make good decisions when faced with conflicting priorities, but the ultimate accuracy of these weightings is questionable, particularly since individual situations requiring discretional judgment cannot be predicted in advance and the likelihood of a change in priorities during the appraisal period is high.

The primary benefit of specifying the relative priority among different objectives may be in providing general guidance to the subordinate on where to concentrate efforts over the year rather than providing a formal multiplier for use in assessing the overall performance rating and recommending the resultant salary change ("Let's see, Fosdick, on your first objective I rated you as Superior but since that had only a relative weight of 0.3 it becomes ultimately less influential than the Barely Meets Standard I assigned you on the second objective with a priority value of . . ."). No value is gained through this exercise in managerial numerology.

Assigning different weights to different objectives can indicate clearly that some are more important than others and can also perform the more important task of highlighting objectives whose importance changes during the course of an appraisal year, but if weights are to be assigned, it is best to keep the process simple and optional if possible. Appraisers, in the course of setting objectives and entering them on the form, might be asked to come up with no more than A-B-C or 1-2-3 indications of relative priority and enter them on the form.

The Performance Factors Segment

For the assessment of work behaviors, the task is more complex. First, the specific behaviors to be evaluated must be determined. Of the dozens or even hundreds of skills, behaviors, competencies, proficiencies, and talents that could possibly be offered up for assessment, how can the team best determine the limited number of most critical items?

One place to start is by examining the core values of the organization. A great many sophisticated organizations have a mission statement or a declaration of their vision and values. What comprises this statement? What would an individual organization member need to do to demonstrate that he was living up to those core values? Seeking performance factors here will make the job of justifying their inclusion easier and serve to reinforce the importance of the organization's mission statement.

Another source of behaviors to include on the performance appraisal form is to identify the attributes and characteristics that will be required for the organization to succeed in the future. Another approach is to ask line managers to think about their best and worst performers in a given job and identify what the top performers do that the worst do not.

Job incumbents can play a helpful role. No one else knows a job as well as the person who is doing it. Why not ask a group of job incumbents to identify the critical work behaviors or performance factors that they feel lead to success? Job incumbents can also be helpful in defining the characteristics to be assessed and, more important, recalling examples of effective and ineffective behaviors to use as examples on the form itself or in appraiser training. Finally, involving incumbents in determining work behaviors or competencies to be assessed will increase the ease of implementation and acceptance of the new performance appraisal system, since those who will be appraised under it will have had a hand in its actual development.

Finally, recognize that work outcomes and work behaviors are related. If results are not being achieved, to some extent the cause of the deficiency is the failure of organization members to engage in those behaviors that bring about favorable outcomes. What are those behaviors? The answer to that question will generate additional items whose inclusion on the list of work behaviors to be appraised can easily be justified.

Describing Work Behaviors

Another challenge in identifying the behaviors to include on the assessment form is not so much with choosing individual factors but in adequately defining or describing them so that each assessor agrees on their presence or absence in the performance of a subordinate. The obstacle here arises from the difficulty in defining the meaning of teamwork, for example, or motivation, as opposed to describing what someone who is effective in this area tends to do. The difference between describing and defining a behavior is significant. An appraiser presented with only a definition asks, "Does this definition fit the person I am assessing?" and comes up with a yes or no response. On the other hand, given a description of desired performance or behavior, the appraiser asks, "How often do I see this individual acting in this way?" This shift from definition to description not only simplifies the process of explaining and portraying the characteristic; it also allows for appraisers to change from judging the extent to which the individual possesses the attribute to reporting how frequently the individual performs in the desired manner. Figure 10-2 illustrates the use of describing a performance factor in behavioral terms and asking for a report of the frequency of desired performance as opposed to the more conventional definition of the trait and judgment of the individual.

This procedure of describing behavioral frequency makes feedback

Figure 10-2. Sample Description of Behavioral Performance Factor

Adaptability/ Flexibility:	Meets changing conditions and situations in work responsibilities. Accepts constructive criticism and suggestions and uses them to advantage. Deals with anger, frustration and disappointment in a mature manner. Maintains objectivity in conflict situations. Seeks solutions acceptable to all.

INDIVIDUAL ➔																
		OCCASIONALLY		SOMETIMES		FREQUENTLY			USUALLY							
APPRAISER ➔																

Analysis: _____
_____
_____

discussions easier. In areas where an individual has been performing poorly, managers often have difficulty being straightforward when the form requires them to label the individual as "marginal" or "needs improvement" or "unacceptable." On the other hand, it is much easier to discuss a subordinate's poor performance if the instrument gives examples of ideal performance and the opportunity to say, "Bob, I indicated that I see you performing this way occasionally [the lowest point on the scale]. Let's talk about what you need to do so that next year I'll be able to report that I observe this frequently."

Priority of Work Behaviors

In discussing the merits of weighing the relative importance of different objectives or work outcomes, I recommended that any prioritizing included on the form be simple and probably left to the informal discussions between appraiser and appraisee. This is equally true with work behaviors.

Certainly some attributes are undoubtedly more important than others, but assigning a space to record relative importance is usually unproductive. The weighing is probably best left to the one-on-one discussion between the two.

A separate question arises about whether the relative importance of the assessment of work outcomes or objectives compared with the assessment of performance in the performance factors or work behaviors area should be required on the form. My informal polls of managers indicate that most believe that a minimum of one-half and more frequently two-thirds of the overall appraisal judgment should be based on the subordinate's performance in achieving predetermined work outcomes or objectives, with the rest devoted to the way in which the subordinate went about doing the job. Although these allocations necessarily vary depending on the nature of the job itself, the implementation team needs to recommend one of the following approaches:

1. The form itself assigns predetermined weightings to the work outcomes and objectives section and the work behaviors and performance factors section.
2. The form requires managers to indicate the relative importance of these two areas in coming up with their final assessment grade.
3. The form requires no formal weightings but allows managers to use their individual judgment to assign weightings to different parts of the form or to consider each part to be of equal importance.

Allowing managers a free hand in assigning weights increases the opportunity for bias and error to creep in. But no performance appraisal system can be made entirely bias free. The more that is done systematically to eliminate the possibility of bias and error, the more the system chips away at the manager's ability to use good judgment. The wiser course may be to allow greater rather than lesser discretion and monitor for problems by spot-checking appraisal forms and listening closely to employee complaints.

Boilerplate Information

In most cases, the greatest amount of space on the form will be taken up by the sections assessing the individual's performance against the goals and objectives set at the beginning of the appraisal period and the analysis and evaluation of how the person went about achieving those objectives—the performance factors or work behaviors sections. But few appraisal forms stop there. Certainly the form must capture some demographic data. In addition to the names of the appraiser and appraisee, other demographic items that might be included are:

- Job title
- Division, department, and other work group information
- Social Security number
- Pay grade or salary classification
- Evaluation period
- Number of months and years the rater has supervised the employee (with, occasionally, a minimum restriction of perhaps ninety days before the rater can complete the appraisal)

- The employee's starting date with the organization and in the current job
- Reason for appraisal (regular annual, employee request, voluntary or involuntary transfer, probationary, etc.)
- Current salary and position in range
- Date of next scheduled evaluation

Other Major Categories for Analysis and Assessment

Besides appraising the individual's effectiveness in achieving objectives and performing appropriately, several other areas are often covered in appraisal forms. Including every one of these in the appraisal instrument for one organization may make the process unworkably laborious, but each contributes to a fuller understanding of the individual's performance of the job and overall contribution to the organization.

Major Achievements and Contributions

In addition to assessing the individual's performance against the objectives set at the beginning of the appraisal period and the various work behaviors, here the appraiser is instructed: "In the following section, list the individual's three major achievements during the appraisal period. Consider the action the individual took to make the organization more effective, more profitable, or more admirable."

A section like this on the appraisal form forces the appraiser to move back from the microanalysis of the individual components of the job and look at the overall contributions that the person made. This may be one of the most significant additions to most appraisal instruments in use today.

Management authority Tom Peters argues that the most important element that should be examined in assessing a person's overall contribution to the organization involves "resuméability": what the individual did over the course of the appraisal period that was of such significance that it forced him to rewrite his resumé. If a person puts in another year and nothing has happened that would require a resumé update, then it's one more year of the same. Peters tells the cynical story of two executives discussing the departure of a purchasing manager who had been with the company eighteen years. "It's tough to lose eighteen years' experience," one said. "We didn't lose eighteen years' experience," the other replied. "We lost one year's experience repeated seventeen times."[2]

If the individual has not contributed anything that would require him to bring his resumé up to date, then he probably has not contributed a significant amount to the overall success of the enterprise, no matter how well he achieved individual objectives or exhibited exemplary performance in producing the work behaviors the company specified.

If the appraiser, evaluating the performance of an acknowledged superior performer, can't put her finger on exactly what the individual did to make the overall organization more effective, profitable, or admirable, perhaps it is the appraiser who needs confrontation with what is really important in organizational life.

Attendance Record

When I address a group of supervisors and ask them to identify what the most common people problem they face is, their answer is predictable: absenteeism. Getting people to come to work, every day, on time.

For jobs in which regular attendance is an important issue, the performance appraisal form represents a major underutilized tool in confronting attendance problems. Most appraisal forms, if they address the issue of attendance at all, simply ask the appraiser to make the same kind of judgment that is called for in every other area of work behavior. The sample in Figure 10-3 has several items worthy of note:

- ▸ *Attendance/punctuality.* Both issues that concern supervisors—attendance (coming to work every day) and punctuality (showing up on time ready to begin working)—are addressed.
- ▸ *Description.* The narrative provides a description of what the organization considers to be ideal performance. Describing desired perfor-

Figure 10-3. Assessment of Attendance

Attendance/ Punctuality:	Is present for work every day. Is fully ready to work at beginning of work schedule and continues until work day is done. Makes appropriate arrangements when adverse weather conditions or other problems might cause a delay in arriving at work on time. Conforms to work hours and schedule.											
INDIVIDUAL →												
	OCCASIONALLY			SOMETIMES			FREQUENTLY			USUALLY		
APPRAISER →												
Attendance Record:	Number of days absent in past twelve months:____ Number of days late in past twelve months:____ Personal attendance percentage:____% Organizational attendance percentage____%											
Analysis: _____ _____ _____												

mance instead of merely defining the trait makes it easier for the supervisor to discuss exactly what is expected with the individual.

► *Rating scheme.* The ratings provided are written in terms of behavioral frequency. The narrative describes exactly what the organization wants; the rating scheme allows the rater to assess how often the employee performs exactly as desired.

► *Attendance record.* One of the great failings of most appraisal instruments is that they fail to ask for the exact data about the individual's attendance record and instead ask only for an opinion of whether it is good or bad. In almost every organization, the four pieces of data asked for here are easily available (and, if they are not, the organization has not earned the right to complain about attendance problems).

Note that the form does not ask about causes or reasons for absence. It simply asks two factual and unarguable questions: How many days was the employee absent? How many days was the employee late? Later, in the analysis section, the reasons and excuses, if important, can be discussed. In this section, just the data are required.

Far more important than the number of days absent or late is the employee's attendance percentage compared with the organizational (company or department or team) norm. Assessing attendance in terms of the individual's average absence rate greatly eases the burden of improving performance through coaching. The supervisor does not have to be concerned with the causes of absence or whether they were excused. He simply has to request that the individual so improve his record as to be just slightly above average, a reasonable request.

If encouraging regular attendance is a significant issue for the organization, the use of an attendance assessment section can dramatically highlight the urgency of the issue.

Development Needs, Plans, and Goals

The issue for the implementation team is whether to include a section on the appraisal form for describing the development needs and plans for the individual. Most forms have one; few are effectively used. For the most part, the narrative contained in the majority of "Development Plans" boxes in most appraisal forms is some variant on "More time in grade" or "Additional exposure," both meaningless phrases.

If the appraisal form is to have a section on development needs, the implementation team should consider including more than just a blank space in which to write down whatever the manager believes it will take to fill the space. This area might ask for specific objectives and timetables. It might also consider referencing the information included in this section of the form with that described in the next area, developmental achievements.

Developmental Achievements

Most forms ask for an indication of the individual's development plans for the next year. Few, however, ever ask what happened to the good intentions recorded on last year's form.

If organizations are serious about development, the implementation team should consider whether it is appropriate to include a section asking the appraiser to assess how well the development plans created during last year's appraisal process were carried out. Did anything come of them? Is the individual now able to do something that a year ago she couldn't have done? What difference did the achievement of the development plan make to her overall effectiveness? How is the company better off as a result of her having acquired this skill?

Stakeholder Input

GTE Telephone Operations asks the appraiser to include information from other people who have a direct interest in the effectiveness of the performance of the individual under appraisal. "Contact four to six of the employee's stakeholders and comment on how others perceive the employee's strengths and limitations," the appraisal form instructs the rater. "These comments may or may not portray real job performance; however, they are important for the employee to understand. *It is also important to obtain information regarding the application of the skills/behaviors identified as critical attributes for Telephone Operations.*"

It may not be feasible or desirable to create a formal 360-degree feedback process as part of the performance appraisal system, but GTE's use of stakeholder inputs contributes a significant additional dimension to the process and gives both rater and ratee the benefit of a wider view of the individual's performance.

Team Objectives

With a growing number of organizations moving toward restructuring work in order to minimize the number of individual contributor positions and maximize the formation of self-directed or semiautonomous work teams, the traditional performance appraisal with its almost exclusive focus on appraising the contribution made by a single individual in becoming less appropriate in many companies. The implementation team creating a performance appraisal procedure in most organizations has to take into account the fact that most employees have some team involvement and some have almost exclusively team-based assignments.

In fact, each member of the implementation team is devoting a significant part of work to accomplishing a major objective, not through individual effort but through the working of the team. Since the creation and implementation of a performance management system is a major undertaking, it is likely that most members of the team are devoting enough hours to the project that it should be included as part of their annual performance appraisal. Therefore, in determining how to assess team performance as part of the performance appraisal system, team members need only look to themselves to generate many of the issues and challenges that they will face in creating a process to be used by other teams in the company.

The initial issue is to determine the extent to which the use of teams requires a separate appraisal form or even a separate process. If teams are occasionally used to address a specific need, the section of the form devoted to objectives and work outcomes is probably sufficient for analysis of how the person did as a team member. If service on a team is a major part of the person's work life for the year, the form needs to reflect it.

Probably all of the items in the part of the form devoted to skills, competencies, and work behaviors are appropriate for any person whose primary work involves being a team member rather than solely an individual contributor. Additional items relating specifically to team member performance (e.g., sharing resources, sacrificing personal objectives for team goals) will need to be added to make the process complete.

Approvals

The usual procedure is for the individual's immediate supervisor to complete the assessment form including the final performance appraisal rating, then have it approved by his immediate superior. It may then be forwarded to the human resources manager for review and approval, particularly if notice of compensation change will accompany the discussion of the appraisal and almost certainly if the raise requested is outside any established guidelines. Once all approvals have been collected, the form is returned to the immediate supervisor, who then schedules the meeting with the individual to review the appraisal form.

The benefits of this approach are obvious. Upper managers provide a check-and-balance function to make sure that the perceptions they have of the performance of individuals two or three levels down in the organization are shared by those who directly supervise those individuals. If there is a discrepancy, they can discuss and resolve it with the individual's supervisor before the appraisal is discussed with the individual.

Upper managers get an insight into how their juniors go about the appraisal process: how seriously they take it, how skilled they are in observing and recording performance, how defensible the judgments they make about subordinates are. Finally, for inexperienced or semiskilled supervisors, the upper manager can provide coaching and guidance on how to conduct the appraisal discussion.

There are disadvantages with this approach. Once she has achieved her boss's blessing, the appraiser is highly unlikely to be willing to entertain the possibility of changing the appraisal, even if the employee is able to present solid evidence and persuasive arguments about why the appraisal narrative and rating, though approved, is inaccurate.

Employees may also be reluctant to expend much energy discussing an appraisal with which they disagree, since it has already been seen and signed off on by the boss, the boss's boss, other bosses, and personnel too. "You can't fight city hall," they say to themselves. "It's better to grin and bear it."

A possible alternative is to charge the appraising manager with the responsibility of carrying out the entire performance appraisal procedure: writing the narrative, making all of the evaluations and ratings required, and discussing it with the subordinate before submitting it to her supervisor and personnel for review and filing. This approach will probably be comfortable only in organizations where the performance appraisal grade is just one factor in making the compensation change decision, where a high degree of trust exists throughout the organization, and where supervisors, managers, and human resources specialists at all levels are sophisticated and experienced.

The benefits of this approach include the genuine empowerment of lower-level managers to act in a highly sensitive area of the organization's operation, the increased probability that the ultimate appraisal document will reflect a genuine understanding (if not complete agreement) between rater and ratee, and a far greater likelihood of open discussions about performance and the areas where change and development are needed. The risks, however, are real: If an upper manager disagrees with the appraisal that a junior has assigned to a subordinate's performance, that junior manager will be in the uncomfortable position of having to go back to the employee and admit that he couldn't get the appraisal past his supervisor. Conversely, upper-level managers may be reluctant to recommend obvious and necessary changes in the form since it has already been reviewed with the individual.

Employee Comments

An almost universal part of almost every performance appraisal form is a section for employee comments on their reactions to their assessment. Whatever they write, from a legal defensibility standpoint the organization is better off since it demonstrates that the form was given to the employee with the opportunity to respond. Handwritten comments from a terminated appraisee preclude any argument of, "But I never saw this. They stuck it in my file without my ever seeing it!"

Encouraging the employee to make serious additions to the appraisal form does far more than just increase defensibility. A major marketing company, for example, devotes one full page of a three- or four-page form (depending on whether the appraisee is exempt or nonexempt) to soliciting employee comments. The questions the company asks the ratee to respond to are comprehensive:

1. Please list what you believe to be your job strengths: _____.
   Please list what you believe to be your job weaknesses: _____.
2. Please describe both your short-term and long-term career plans: __
   _____.
3. Please discuss how your supervisor and/or the company can help
   you achieve your objectives:_____
   _____.
4. Please note any additional subjects you would like addressed as part
   of your evaluation:_____
   _____

In its appraisal form for exempt employees, ARCO Oil and Gas Company does not go into this extent of detail; it simply provides a space labeled "Employee Comments." But immediately following the lines on which the employee is invited to write comments comes the statement: "The contents of this form have been reviewed with me. I understand that this form will be used by the company in connection with salary administration, development and placement activities. I also understand that whether I agree or disagree with this evaluation, I may enter my opinions here or on an attached sheet of paper and also discuss them with my Employee Relations Representative." The form provides a space for the employee's signature, followed by the supervisor's initials under the heading "Employee Comments Reviewed."

More important, the form continues with a printed heading, "Employee Disagreements Reviewed," and the initials of the second-level supervisor and the date, together with the closing space for overall employee relations review. Ratees at ARCO thus know that the company is serious about wanting to identify and deal with any employee disagreements with the appraisal, since review of employee disagreements by the appraiser's direct supervisor is specifically provided for on the form.

Promotability and Potential

Few performance appraisal forms have a section devoted to assessing the individual's long-term potential or immediate promotability. The reason is that indicating promotability is likely to create immediate expectations of advancement if the verdict is positive and discouragement if the employee discovers that the organization does not see him swiftly ascending the steps of the hierarchy. Indicating an assessment of an individual's promotability may also lessen defensibility if a highly promotable individual ever turns sour, is discharged, and then challenges the termination.

Promotion is always a function of many factors, only one of which is the performance appraisal rating. In this regard, the performance appraisal may be considered a threshold factor; without an exemplary rating, the individual doesn't even get her name thrown in the hat, but just having it in the hat is no assurance that it will be pulled when a plum job opens.

Rating Schemes

More energy may be expended over answering two questions than anything else in the entire design process. How many levels of performance should there be? What will we call each level?

The overwhelming majority of performance appraisal forms provide for either three, four, or five levels of performance. Rarely does an appraisal system operate on the basis of pass-fail, with only two levels of ratings, or provide for no final evaluation of performance at all. Equally rarely does an appraisal call for finer distinctions than five levels.

A major oil company developed an assessment form for nonexempt employees that ended with a six-position rating scale; it is shown in Figure 10-4. With six positions to choose from, there is no middle rating available, so the appraiser must rate the employee either above or below the midpoint. The narrative for the position immediately below the midpoint, however, always uses the term, "consistently meets," thus providing four categories of positive ratings and only two negative ones.

A defense contractor provides what appears to be a standard five-level rating scale: Unsatisfactory, Questionable, Satisfactory, Excellent, and Superior. But this nominally five-position scale, shown in Figure 10-5, becomes a nine-point one since the company allows raters to choose among three different levels of performance within the Satisfactory classification and two each in the Questionable and Excellent categories.

For the most part, unless there is easily quantifiable and objective

Figure 10-4. Six-Position Rating Scale

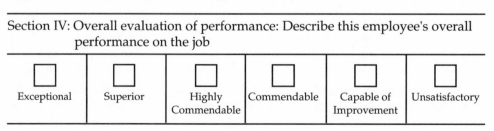

Section IV: Overall evaluation of performance: Describe this employee's overall performance on the job

| ☐ Exceptional | ☐ Superior | ☐ Highly Commendable | ☐ Commendable | ☐ Capable of Improvement | ☐ Unsatisfactory |

Figure 10-5. Expanded Five-Level Rating Scale

WORK OUTPUT	☐	☐ ☐	☐ ☐ ☐	☐ ☐	☐
Consider the volume of work produced under normal conditions, disregarding errors. Does it meet standards established by the Company?	Productivity below the minimum standard. Does small amount of work. Wastes time.	Productivity just enough to get by. Could get more work done. Slow and/or erratic.	Produces the average amount of work. Works steadily.	Productivity well above average. Works effectively and does more work than expected.	Productivity outstanding. Exceptionally fast worker. Makes effort count. Always working.

information, together with a clear standard of performance—sales results or widgets per hour, for example—a scale of more than five points makes a claim to precision that may be difficult to justify. The alternatives typically are three, four, or five performance levels. Figure 10-6 lists the arguments for and against each. As it indicates, however, no matter how many rating levels are provided, appraisers always tend to use fewer than they are offered.

A critical and often overlooked issue in determining the number of levels to include is whether there should be a midpoint position. If an even number of performance levels is employed—four, perhaps, or even six—then there is no middle position in which the great majority of appraisers are likely to end up. This eliminates the problem of central tendency by removing the centers but invariably results in positive skew. When in doubt, virtually ever appraiser finds it easier to give the subordinate the benefit of the doubt and place her in the category just above the midpoint than just below it.

In most cases a five-point rating scale provides for sufficient gradations in performance to be acceptable to most raters, without the removal of the middle position that a four-point scale produces or the lack of discrimination allowed by a three-point scale. As William Swan points out in *How to Do a Superior Performance Appraisal*, "Repellent as some of us may find it, a time comes when we just can't escape making an evaluative judgment. It is a process we have grown accustomed to from school—A, B, C, D, or F, and most people continue, in every area of life, to be evaluated according to some sort of scale; and with remarkable regularity, it turns out to be a five point scale (the ABCDF of our early schooling was a five point scale)."[3]

Swan notes that three-point scales (Unsatisfactory, Satisfactory, Outstanding) regularly become five-point scales, since raters can't resist putting notches between the three points. They find that some employees are better than Satisfactory but not quite Outstanding, while others are a little less than Satisfactory but not quite Unsatisfactory. Because three-point scales become five-point scales anyway, why not simply start that way?

Figure 10-6. Performance Levels Analysis

Number of Levels	Advantages	Disadvantages
Three	It fits most closely with total quality management assumptions. Managers can easily identify performers who far exceed standards and those who fail completely. Most people end up in the middle category, reducing the emphasis on the rating judgment. Appraisers, given fewer choices, tend to be more consistent. Some jobs are more amenable to pass-fail assessment. The middle category usually connotes "expected" performance, not "average" performance.	It may not allow for fine enough discriminations in performance. The lowest (Unacceptable or Noncontributor) level is rarely used. Managers may unofficially alter the system to provide a category between the top two levels. It does not allow for identifying the truly outstanding 2 to 5 percent. It does not distinguish between those who can improve and those who should be terminated.
Four	It eliminates a midpoint position, thus eliminating the "average" rating. It provides for sufficiently fine discriminations for most jobs.	It may cause an upward shift in appraisal ratings. Managers may resent not being able to rate average performers as such. The lowest level is rarely used. It may not distinguish between those who can improve and those who should be terminated.
Five	Most managers believe they are capable of making five-point performance distinctions. It allows for truly outstanding performers to be recognized. It is more consistent with bell curve distribution. It has the highest degree of familiarity and acceptability among appraisers and appraisees.	Appraisers may not be able to explain specific differences in performance between levels. The lowest level is rarely used. The middle rating is frequently considered as representing average or mediocre performance. It may encourage central tendency.

Rating Scale Labels

However many positions on the scale there may be, the positions must be labeled. Some designation for the various points on the rating scale must be made. There are four alternatives:

1. A *numerical rating*: 1, 2, 3, 4, 5.

2. A rating based on *behavioral frequency*, as described earlier in the

discussion on the assessment of work behaviors or performance factors. Here are some examples for five-, four-, and three-point scales:

Always
Usually
Frequently
Sometimes
Rarely

Regularly
Often
Occasionally
Seldom

Consistently
Frequently
Rarely

3. A rating based on the *evaluation concept*: a judgment made by the rater on the quality of performance. This is the most common rating method. Some examples for three-, four-, and five-point scales might include:

Distinguished
Superior
Competent
Fair
Marginal

Outstanding
Commendable
Acceptable
Needs Improvement

Superior
Fully Satisfactory
Unsatisfactory

4. A rating based on the *performance of the individual against a standard* or the requirements of the position—for example:

Greatly Exceeds the Standard
Exceeds the Standard
Meets the Standards
Partially Meets the Standard
Does Not Meet the Standard

Far Exceeds Requirements
Meets Requirements

Partially Meets Requirements
Fails to Meet Requirements

Exceeds Expectations
Meets Expectations
Does Not Meet Expectations

Figure 10-7. Advantages and Disadvantages of Rating Systems

System	Advantages	Disadvantages
Numerical	Has no inherent meaning connected with numbers May make it easier to determine a final rating from ratings of various earlier segments	Appraisers may resent being "classified as a number" May provide an illusion of precision that does not actually exist
Behavioral frequency	Rates frequency of performance, not value of individual Reduces defensiveness in appraisal discussions Provides a direction for performance improvement Specifies in advance what the desired performance is	Requires raters to be aware of frequency of performance Increases expectations that raters will be able to provide examples Applies only to performance factors stated in behavioral terms; may not be appropriate for results measures
Evaluation concept	Uses terms most users are familiar with Offers large number of rating labels to choose among	Increases defensiveness at being judged May be seen as a judgment of the worth of the individual, not the quality of performance Meaning of labels may not be clear
Performance against standard concept	Focuses on performance, not the person Uses less emotional terminology Indicates an expectation of performance improvement	Increases expectations that raters will have determined and discussed standards or requirements in advance Uses terminology that may be unfamiliar

Figure 10-7 summarizes the advantages and disadvantages of each approach.

There are other rating system considerations. Examine the two sets of rating schemes listed below. Both are four-point rating systems, but the choice of terminology leads to significantly different ratings:

Far Exceeds Expectations	Far Exceeds Expectations
Exceeds Expectations	Fully Meets Expectations
Fully Meets Expectations	Partially Meets Expectations
Does Not Meet Expectations	Does Not Meet Expectations

Each case is a four-point scale beginning with Far Exceeds Expectations and ending with Does Not Meet Expectations. But the middle positions of the two scales are significantly different. In the first set, both of the middle ratings describe the performance of an individual who at least fully meets the standards of the job. In the other, only one of the middle positions represents the fully satisfactory performer; the other would be used for the individual who is falling short to some degree of doing what the company wants.

Figure 10-8 shows the four-point rating scale used by an international food products manufacturer, together with the definitions. It is apparent that there are three categories that describe fully acceptable performance while in only one case is the performance faulty.

However many positions there may be on the scale, it is important to make sure that they accurately convey the message the organization wants to send about performance. The team can test various statements of performance rating before arriving at a final decision. Ideally, all users of the system should feel that the labels actually mark significant differences in performance and that the qualitative distance between the different labels accurately represents significant differences in actual performance.

Figure 10-8. Four-Point Rating Scale

Rating	Definition
Distinguished Performance	Results achieved far exceeded the expectations for the job. This year's contribution clearly moved the business forward.
Superior Performance	Results exceeded expectations. This year's contribution is clearly identifiable.
Competent Performance	Fully met expectations in all key areas. No major errors of execution or strategy.
Provisional Performance	Did not fully meet expectations.

TQM and Rating Schemes

Most TQM advocates, skeptical of the notion of performance appraisal as a whole, are particularly uncomfortable with the perceived ability of managers to make five-point discriminations of the performance of subordinates. With some justification, they argue that most managers are able to assess who in their work group is performing at a far superior level and who in the group is an anchor on the team's progress. Other than those clear distinctions, they argue, the rating of Satisfactory should apply; although there may be some differences in performance between one satisfactory performer and another, few independent observers would always agree on which one was higher. Perceived differences are as much a function of sampling error as real differences, and system deficiencies are far more important that human performance variables anyway. Why bother with more than the three obvious categories anyway?

For organizations committed to incorporating formal TQM principles into their performance appraisal system, the best approach may be to adopt a three-position rating scale with the expectation that almost everyone will be rated in the middle category since the great majority of any organization's members are, in fact, satisfactory. Appropriate TQM designations might look like one of the following:

Outstanding	Leader
Fully Competent	Contributor
Unsatisfactory	Noncontributor

Does "Fully Competent" Equal a "C"?

The final challenge in constructing a rating scheme that appraisers and appraisees alike will be comfortable using may be the most difficult, particularly for the majority of organizations that use a five-point scale. It is to eliminate the perception that the middle rating (Competent or Satisfactory, Fully Acceptable, or Meets All Expectations) is the equivalent of receiving a C in school.

The experiences of two different organizations are instructive here. At one of PepsiCo's most profitable divisions, it was common knowledge among up-and-comers that the clearest indication that their careers were stalled and that their competence was in question was to be rated Competent in their annual appraisal. Competent, the middle position on their five-point rating scale, was the grade usually assigned to those whose jobs were in jeopardy or who had achieved a position of "terminal placement." Almost every individual, immediately upon being rated Competent, started sending off resumés. The opposite experience comes from Alcon Laboratories, the highly successful Texas-based pharmaceutical division of Switzerland's Nestlé. Its five-point system has Distinguished Performer and Superior Performer as the higher designations and Needs Development and Unsatisfactory Performance at the bottom of the scale. The central point on the scale is labeled GSP (Good Solid Performance). The great majority of Alcon employees are rated GSPs, and the term has lost any pejorative connotation, primarily because of the proselytizing about the importance of good solid performance to corporate success by CEO Ed Schollmaier.

Schollmaier, who annually uses the company's elaborate appraisal form to assess his own performance and mails it to the Nestlé CEO, wrote an article for Alcon's employee magazine about his view of what good solid performance involved. "The last four years," Schollmaier wrote, "I've given myself a GSP. Heck, I'm proud of it. I've done a darn good job. I consider GSP to represent very good performance. If you achieve good performance over a number of years, then you've compounded good performance. As a youngster, I played on a lot of sports teams. A few were really good. I think that what differentiated the good teams from the others is that the average players really came to play every game, that the routine plays were made almost without fail, that occasionally the big play succeeded, and that committed teamwork made everyone perform a little better than you would expect. GSP performance from everyone wins games. Without it, a lot of superior performances by a few players will be wasted."[4]

Who Should Appraise Performance?

The individual's direct supervisor has historically been the primary, if not the exclusive, appraiser of performance. Even in organizations that provide for the supervisor's supervisor to review the completed appraisal form before it is discussed with the individual, the role of that upper manager has been less to provide input to the appraisal narrative and the ultimate rating as it has been to ensure that the report and rating were consistent with what he had seen from a different perspective. The one-over-one review of the performance appraisal served as much as an appraisal of the reviewer as it did the reviewee.

Over the past few years, particularly with the recognition brought about through the TQM philosophy, the emphasis has shifted away from viewing the supervisor as the sole determinant of the good and bad of performance and instead toward viewing her simply as one of many customers served by the individual being appraised. The supervisor carries important perspective, TQM advocates argue, but not the only perspective (and not even the most important perspective, many feel, since the most legitimate appraiser of any individual's performance is the individual's internal and external customers).

Figure 10-9. A Comparison of Potential Performance Appraisers

Rater	Advantages	Disadvantages
Immediate supervisor only	Greatest amount of knowledge of the job and performance expectations Usually has the most information about quality and quantity of work Greatest stake in producing an accurate appraisal of performance Having only one information source promotes simplicity and ease of administration Immediate supervisor has historically been sole assessor	The supervisor may be less familiar than others (coworkers, customers) about the quality of the individual's performance. In a matrix or project-based organization, another supervisor or project leader may have better information than the functional supervisor. The supervisor may be unduly or unwittingly influenced by the nature of the personal relationship with the subordinate. Employees may be skeptical of the fairness of the process if the supervisor is the only source of information.
Peers and coworkers (in addition to supervisor)	Adds broader perspective and balance Allows broader participation Reduced likelihood of bias or political ploys if all coworkers receive peer assessments May increase perception of fairness May generate teamwork-related strengths and weaknesses that otherwise would have been overlooked	Competitive coworkers may perceive a political advantage in lowering a rating of a peer. It increases paperwork and adds administrative complexity. It takes longer to collect and incorporate data. During appraisal discussion, the supervisor may be unable to justify ratings or assessments for which he was not the source. It requires greater supervisory skill to incorporate information. It requires development of a separate assessment process for use by coworkers. It raises concerns about confidentiality and privacy.

Figure 10-9. *(continued)*

Rater	Advantages	Disadvantages
Internal and external customers (in addition to supervisor)	Congruent with TQM philosophy Adds input from what may be most important source of data Increases attention paid to customers Provides for an objective check on customer service and quality assurance May increase perceived fairness	Customers may be reluctant to provide data. Customers are unlikely to be skilled in making objective assessments. It requires greater supervisory skill to incorporate information. It requires development of a separate assessment process. It increases paperwork and adds administrative complexity. It takes longer to collect and incorporate data.
Subordinates (in addition to supervisor)	Adds information from often-neglected source May provide data unavailable from any other source May encourage upward feedback and more effective discussions May reveal important supervisory strengths and deficiencies that otherwise would have gone unnoticed	It requires greater supervisory skill to incorporate information. It requires development of a separate assessment process for use by subordinates. It increases paperwork and adds administrative complexity. It takes longer to collect and incorporate data. Subordinates may be reluctant to provide accurate appraisal information for fear of retribution.

The implementation team must consider whether anyone other than the individual's direct supervisor should have a responsibility for appraising the performance of the individual. Who are these others? Senior managers, for one. Another group includes the individual's peers and coworkers. Another is the person's customers or downstream users of the products and services he generates. Finally there are the individual's subordinates. The implementation team must determine for each of these groups whether they should have a formal role in the appraisal process and, if so, what their role should be.

Figure 10-9 lists the various potential other contributors to the appraisal process with the benefits and disadvantages of the inclusion of each. The first row describes the advantages and disadvantages involved in the classical approach: The immediate supervisor alone is the only source of input to the performance appraisal process and judgment. The other rows consider the pros and cons of allowing information collected from other individuals and groups to be added to that of the immediate supervisor in developing the final appraisal document.

Self-Appraisal

A growing number of organizations are including formal self-appraisal as part of their performance evaluation system. The master performance appraisal instrument in Appendix A has formal provisions for appraisee self-evaluation. Individuals are also encouraged to complete appraisals of their own performance in the section on "Appraisal of Accountabilities, Goals, and Objectives" as well as provide information on developmental achievements and plans for the upcoming appraisal period.

The benefits of asking for a subordinate self-appraisal in most cases far outweigh any disadvantages produced by the requirement, as described in Figure 10-10.

Figure 10-10. Advantages and Disadvantages of Self-Appraisal Analysis

Advantages	Disadvantages
The incumbent is probably the best source of information about the quality of job performance.	Individuals may be fearful of retribution.
Assuming that accuracy and truth-telling are not punished by the organization or the supervisor, individuals provide extremely accurate data about the quality of their performance.	Individuals may deliberately rate themselves low in order to avoid disagreements with supervisor.
Self-appraisal increases the perception of fairness.	Individuals may deliberately rate themselves high in order to influence supervisor unduly.
Areas where appraiser and appraisee disagree are highlighted.	If substandard performers rate themselves high, they may feel that the supervisor's rating is a result of bias or prejudice.
Self-appraisal ensures that individuals are fully prepared for the discussion.	If individuals are required to submit their self-appraisal in advance of the meeting, they may feel that the supervisor has unfairly taken advantage of their self-disclosure.
The period spent by the individual doing the self-appraisal may produce valuable insights into personal performance.	

One additional issue arises regarding the timing of self-appraisals. Companies using the approach are divided in their opinion about when the self-appraisal should be completed and given to the supervisor. In almost every case, the organization expects the supervisor to review the appraisal form with the individual in advance, including both work behaviors or performance factors as well as the goals or objectives. The employee is then asked by the supervisor to complete the self-appraisal. Once the employee has completed writing the self-appraisal, one of three different procedures is followed:

1. The employee writes the self-appraisal and sends it to the supervisor, who uses it as an additional source of data in constructing the official performance appraisal. When the supervisor receives the employee's self-appraisal he then prepares (or revises) the appraisal he has prepared, has it reviewed and approved, and then meets with the employee to review the final appraisal document and discuss any variances or insights resulting from the individual's self-assessment.

2. The employee writes the self-appraisal and then meets with the supervisor to review it before the supervisor writes the official appraisal. The goal of the meeting is for the supervisor to gain an understanding of the employee's perception of his own performance and additional information for use in writing the formal appraisal. The accuracy or merit of the employee's perceptions is not the topic for this meeting; the goal is simply to understand how the individual evaluates what he has done during the appraisal period.

3. The employee and supervisor write their appraisals independently. At the beginning of the meeting (or just before the actual meeting begins), each reads what the other has written. During the meeting, any differences in perception between the employee's self-appraisal and the supervisor's official performance appraisal are reviewed and clarified.

Should the supervisor review the individual's self-assessment before writing the official appraisal, or should they read each other's appraisal at the time of the meeting? Figure 10-11 summarizes the advantages and disadvantages of each approach.

Upward Appraisal

Upward appraisal is the converse of self-appraisal: The individual is asked to complete a performance appraisal on his boss. The question is whether, as part of the organization's procedures for performance appraisal, employees should have the opportunity to assess the performance of their manager.

Figure 10-11. Comparison of Approaches to Timing of Self-Appraisal

Process	Advantages	Disadvantages
Employee prepares and submits prior to meeting	Supervisors have access to employee self-assessment before preparing official document. Supervisors may gain important information before preparing formal appraisal. Supervisors are prepared in advance for areas where significant differences lie. Employee preparation is ensured since formal appraisal cannot be prepared until self-appraisal is received.	Supervisors may be unduly influenced by employee's self-assessment. Employees may be reluctant to be honest. Substandard workers may feel that their own assessment may be used against them.
Employee and supervisor prepare independently	Employee's assessment cannot color supervisor's evaluation. Supervisors are required to be independent in their assessment. The power relationship is balanced; employees perceive this process as fair.	Supervisor may not be prepared to discuss significant differences. Employee may not complete the self-appraisal in advance of the meeting. With both parties seeing each other's document for the first time, a lot of time will be spent in reading. The comparison may lead to a situation of negotiation and trade-offs. The focus of the meeting may be on the rating rather than on the performance itself.

Many organizations are beginning to incorporate upward appraisal as part of their formal appraisal process. In most cases, the feedback from subordinates is anonymous, collected by human resources staff from all of a manager's subordinates after the appraisal cycle has been completed and fed back to the manager in aggregate form. As in other rating processes where a group of individuals independently and anonymously assesses the performance of a person, the highest and lowest ratings may be thrown out to prevent halo or bias from skewing the result. The manager is then presented with the mean response of the subordinate group and either told the actual distribution of the various scores or provided with the standard deviation so he can tell how much variance there was among all of the respondents.

One organization using upward feedback is Microsoft, named by *Fortune* magazine as the most respected company in America in its ability to attract, motivate, and retain employees. Figure 10-12 shows Microsoft's Manager Feedback Form, which all employees complete after their performance appraisal discussion with their manager. In addition to its obvious purpose of collecting data on managerial performance for use as a developmental tool, the feedback instrument serves to reinforce core values of the organization. At Microsoft the complete feedback form, with or without the name of the feedback provider, is sent to the appraiser's immediate manager. In most other organizations using upward feedback, human resources professionals are the process administrators.

Determining the Overall Rating

Most performance appraisal forms contain a dozen or two preliminary ratings before the final appraisal grade is arrived at. Between three and seven different objectives or goals may be assessed, and a dozen or more behaviors or competencies may be evaluated. There may also be an overall rating of the person's performance within the broad area of achieving objectives, as well as a separate overall score that evaluates performance against the work behaviors or job factors as a group. There may be other categories or sections on the form that also call for specific appraisal. At the end of almost every performance appraisal form, however, there is a space for the overall rating of performance.

How should that overall rating be determined? Should it be entirely a function of managerial judgment, where the appraiser is called upon to consider every aspect of performance and arrive at a defensible summary synopsis label? In this case, the assessor is implored to use his best judgment in weighing momentous accomplishments against the trivial and balance those deeds that were performed in an extraordinary way with those whose achievement was merely pedestrian.

Figure 10-12. Manager Feedback Form

NAME: _____   MANAGER _____
     (Optional)

DEPT.: _____   DATE: _____

The Manager Feedback Form plays an important role in Microsoft's performance review process. The objective is to provide constructive feedback on the manager's leadership skills and abilities. This is an important part of the manager's own performance self-management plan. The form should be completed for all lead, supervisor, and managerial positions.

Each employee should complete the Manager Feedback Form after your review discussion and forward the completed form directly to your manager's immediate manager.

Indicate your response to each of the following statements:
Strongly Agree (SA); Agree (A); Disagree (D); Strongly Disagree (SD)

My Manager:
    Empowers me to do my job. _____
    Identifies clear, attainable goals and objectives, by stating what needs to be accomplished and why. _____
    Provides an environment that motivates me to achieve my goals and objectives. _____
    Provides challenging opportunities that maximize the use of my skills. _____
    Acts as a sounding board for ideas. _____
    Recognizes and rewards innovation and creativity. _____
    Enables good performance by clearing roadblocks and providing support. _____
    Provides opportunities for professional development and improvement of skills. _____
    Demonstrates flexibility in management style. _____
    Communicates corporate and departmental goals and objectives. _____
    Acts as coach and mentor. _____
    Builds a cohesive team. _____
    Provides honest and constructive feedback about my performance. _____
    Delegates effectively. _____
    Conducts regular one-to-one feedback meetings. _____

Overall Comments:

Or should there be a formula provided, where mathematics supplants judgment and the individual scores on each of the appraisal's subsections, perhaps multiplied by the weights assigned to each and divided by the number of separate entries, lead to a final score that accumulates the series of assessments made throughout the form?

The process of assigning weights combined with the ratings for each item produces an appraisal system that provides the appearance of a high degree of objectivity, even if that objectivity is gained merely by applying an arithmetic formula to a series of subjective—and perhaps indefensible—human judgments. Although a process created in this way may end up looking more like a creation of the industrial engineering department than the human resources section, it has the advantage of forcing raters to place greater emphasis on those areas that the organization or the individual's boss has determined to be of the highest priority.

Administrative Issues

In addition to creating the form and making all of the decisions and recommendations directly connected with its design, there are administrative issues that the team must consider. For example, should there be an appeals procedure? (This important question is fully discussed in Chapter 15.) Who should have access to performance appraisals? Where should they be kept? How long should they remain on file? Can the employee be given a copy? Who needs to approve the appraisal before it is discussed with the employee? Who needs to review it afterward?

Most of the administrative issues can be decided fairly easily by looking at what the organization has done before and the particular preferences of the human resources function, usually charged with administering the process. The initial data collection efforts that were done may also have pointed out areas where tightening administrative requirements is necessary. The implementation team needs to be sure that all problems initially discovered get explored, if not fully resolved.

Several administrative questions do require the attention of the implementation team.

Identifying the Appraisal Period

When should employees be scheduled for performance appraisals and salary reviews? Note that I am not raising the question of whether the discussion of the person's performance over the previous twelve months and the discussion of the merit increase should occur in the same meeting. We'll discuss that thorny issue separately. The issue raised by this question is whether appraisals or merit reviews should be staggered throughout the year or whether they should all happen at the same time.

In general, almost every organization selects one of two alternatives regarding when the performance appraisal and merit review event occurs:

1. On the anniversary date of each employee's hiring or last promotion or salary action. This approach of reviews staggered throughout the year is commonly referred to as an *anniversary date* review.
2. At one specific time, usually at the end of the business year. This approach, where all reviews are clustered at the same time, can be referred to as *focal point* or *focal date* reviews.

Each approach has its advantages, but each also has a disadvantage so serious that it is seen as a fatal flaw by those who use the other approach. For the anniversary date approach, coordinating individual increases and pay rate administration with pay structure adjustments—managing the system so that no one is paid under the range minimum and the salaries of newer employees do not leapfrog those of more senior members—is a major challenge and administrative burden. For the focal point approach, on the other hand, the fatal flaw is that managers with large numbers of subordinates and low commitment to the performance appraisal system will not give a high priority to investing the time required to produce high-quality evaluations.[5]

Figure 10-13 illustrates the advantages of each approach and the environmental conditions conducive to its use.

The focal date approach is currently used in a majority of organizations. The administrative burden in changing from one approach to the other is high. The primary job of the implementation team in this area is to identify the organization's current practices (which may be some mixture of the two systems), determine where additional administrative attention is required to alleviate any problems, and plan for full explanation of the process and its administration in the course of appraiser training and employee orientation.

Handling Special Situations

Special situations include newly hired employees, employees transferring in and out of the work group during the appraisal period, individuals who are promoted, and matrix or network situations.

New Employees

The easiest way administratively to handle new employees is to fold them into the existing group and give them a performance appraisal at

Figure 10-13. Anniversary Date Versus Focal Date Reviews

	Advantages	Conducive Conditions
Anniversary date (staggered) reviews	Managers with a large number of subordinates are not required to review all of them at the same time. Reviews are based on a full performance period; those newly hired and those promoted have their performance appraisals and salary reviews adjusted and annualized. Employees are less likely to engage in comparisons of performance ratings or salary increases with others. Human resources staff are not engulfed with paper or required to chase down large numbers of appraisals at once.	Managers have a large number of subordinates. Work is not tied to a specific cycle. Line managers believe appraisals and salary reviews are important and are committed to doing them well. A results-oriented appraisal methodology is in place (ranking or forced distribution is not used). Lean staffing of the human resources function is a priority. Compensation is not directly tied to fiscal year results.
Focal date (clustered) reviews	Managers can project the impact of salary increases on budgets before informing subordinates. There is lower risk of midyear business shifts' creating uneven impact on employees with later review dates. Managers are less likely to be affected by mood, workload, and other factors unrelated to performance. All reviews can be compared, thus improving internal equity. Human resources staff are not required to monitor review dates and completions. Human resources staff can plan for additional workload since the review schedule known in advance. Reviews can be scheduled when the best financial/performance data are known and are current.	Personnel costs have a critical impact on results. The organization wants to tie rewards closely to results each year. The organization is subject to short-term swings in performance or cash flow. Managers are unskilled at appraisal. As a result, intensive training can be provided immediately before reviews, and ranking of forced distribution can be used to make compensation decisions. Human resources staff are better able to process all reviews at one time than to monitor reviews continually during the year.

the same time it would come up for everybody else (at the completion of their first year if an anniversary date approach is used; at the close of the business year if a focal date approach is used), but the benefits conferred by administrative simplicity are offset by drawbacks in performance management. Too much time may pass between the newcomer's entry into the organization and the receipt of the appraisal. Even if they are performing well there is no formal mechanism to advise them of that. A more effective approach is to formalize an interim review period. Typically at either ninety days (the close of the traditional probationary period) or six months, an interim assessment is completed. This provides required feedback, reduces anxieties, and gives people a dose of performance appraisal before it is connected to salary action. Interim reviews, particularly if they are scheduled more than once during the first year, do create additional administrative work, but most organizations and most managers find that it is worth it.

Transferred and Promoted Employees

Employees who are promoted or transferred in or out of the unit bring a different set of dynamics than do new employees. The individual transferred or promoted into the work group is already familiar with the organization and the appraisal process. This newcomer to the unit may be an organizational old hand, and the ordinary day-to-day coaching and feedback done by the manager in fulfilling his leadership responsibilities is usually sufficient to meet performance management requirements.

The primary challenge with transfers and promotions is access to information. An individual is promoted into the work group four months before the annual appraisal is due. The new supervisor is most familiar with her current level of performance, but two-thirds of the appraisal period was spent working under the direction of someone else. Who should bear the responsibility for completing the performance appraisal?

The easy answer is for the sending supervisor to complete a performance appraisal on the individual if six months or more have passed since the last regular appraisal was conducted. At the time of the next regularly scheduled appraisal, this interim appraisal is used as a primary data source in developing the regular appraisal. It ensures that information is up to date and that a full year's performance is considered. It also provides a mechanism for performance feedback from the sending supervisor just before the transfer or promotion takes place, a time when the individual may be particularly open to receiving this information, since a new job is beckoning and no salary action is connected with the information being transferred.

The downside is the additional administrative burden and the fact that the sending supervisor may give the process short shrift since the appraisal is done primarily to satisfy administrative requirements and produces little personal benefit to the sending manager. The whole exercise may seem to be nothing more than a personnel drill, since the employee is usually eager to leave and the manager is equally eager to see her off and get the replacement up to speed.

Matrix Situations

Matrix situations are particularly difficult. They require one man to serve two masters; injunctions back to biblical days warn us of the folly of this technique. A matrix or network situation arises in project-oriented organizations where an individual has a functional manager to whom he reports for administrative purposes (a senior software engineer reports administratively to the manager of software engineering) but is assigned for operational purposes to a project manager (the senior software engineer, together with his counterparts from marketing, industrial engineering, production and finance, reports to the Project Apollo manager). The matrixed individual may see his administrative boss only rarely and may even be geographically removed.

Unless the entire organization is run on a matrix or network basis, the easiest way to administer this organizational disorder is on an ad hoc basis, with both administrative and functional managers bearing shared responsibility for contributing to the appraisal.

Determining the Number of Meetings

In the course of the entire performance management cycle, there could be as many as six transactions about performance between the appraiser and the appraisee:

1. Manager and subordinate discuss the self-appraisal requirement of the process and set a date for the subordinate to submit the self appraisal. (*system inauguration*)
2. Subordinate and manager review the subordinate's self-appraisal in advance of the manager's completing the formal performance appraisal form. (*self-appraisal*)
3. Manager and subordinate discuss the subordinate's performance during the appraisal period. (*classical performance appraisal*)
4. Manager and subordinate review compensation change that will result from the quality of the subordinate's performance. (*merit/salary review*)
5. Manager and subordinate discuss developmental needs and create a development plan for the subordinate to complete during the upcoming year. (*development plan*)

6. Manager and subordinate set goals and objectives for the upcoming year. (*objective setting*)

The agenda for meeting 1, kicking off the process and discussing the self-appraisal procedure, is never combined with other meeting agenda: It is the brief session (if it is held at all) that inaugurates the annual performance appraisal program. Meeting 2 may not be held if the organization chooses not to use self-appraisal or incorporates the discussion of the self-appraisal as part of the manager's formal performance review. The agendas for meetings 3, 4, 5, and 6 are often combined. In fact, it is rare that any organization would hold four separate meetings to cover the four issues described above. But each of those issues is different. Each has a significantly different focus, though each is a regular part of the overall performance appraisal procedure. The task of the implementation team is to recommend which, if any, of the agendas should be covered in the same meeting.

The arguments for combining issues 3, 4, 5, and 6 into one meeting are obvious. The manifest benefit of combining everything is efficiency: Everything gets done at once. The manager and subordinate sit down, review the performance appraisal (or appraisals if the subordinate has completed a self-appraisal not reviewed earlier), and discuss the individual's performance over the year and the rating that the manager has applied to the individual components and the overall assessment. The manager then reveals the amount of salary increase that the subordinate will receive, and they discuss the implications of that decision. The discussion then moves to goal setting. They revise and update the current year's objectives; they set new ones based on changed corporate and competitive conditions. Development planning swiftly follows. The manager and subordinate discuss the subordinate's developmental needs and create a plan of action for the subordinate to follow to become even more efficient and effective than he is at present. Finally, dazed and dumbstruck, the poor fellow wanders out of the manager's office, grateful that the process has been completed one more time.

Efficient it is. Effective? Doubtful.

As I have argued several times in the course of this book, the biggest hidden problem with performance appraisal is that we expect an inordinate amount from one modest system. Nowhere is this problem more obvious than in the way too many managers and organizations go about completing the process, lumping every agenda item and issue into the space of one forty-five-minute transaction. If any real good and lasting change, any genuine increase in organizational effectiveness comes of this, it will be entirely a function of chance and happenstance.

The fundamental question for the implementation team to answer is this: How serious are we going to be about this whole process? While it is easy to scoff at the scenario portrayed above—the managerial equivalent of cramming a gallon of stuffing down the gullet of a quart-sized turkey—it is also obvious that requiring managers to conduct an entirely separate meeting devoted to each of the separate issues is probably not going to happen.

What is feasible? What will actually work? What will the organization sit still for? Just how many meetings can we reasonably expect managers to hold in order to meet their performance management responsibilities both economically and thoroughly?

The easiest way to resolve this issue is to start with the core transaction: the meeting between the manager and the subordinate to discuss the subordinate's performance during the appraisal period—classic performance appraisal. Now ask whether there is any other issue for the manager and subordinate to address during that meeting. What are the advantages and disadvantages of including this issue with the actual appraisal discussion? Then add another item to the meeting's agenda and determine what effect that will have.

Identifying the pros and cons for all of the possible permutations is laborious, and the message will quickly start to become apparent to all: The more that we expect to accomplish in one meeting, the less likely that anything will be accomplished at all.

Figure 10-14 identifies some of the benefits and risks inherent in combining the discussion of various issues in one meeting.

Ensuring an Appropriate Distribution of Ratings

Not everyone is a superior performer, and not everyone can be rated Superior. Many raters, if left entirely to their own devices, would be likely to rate all of their subordinates as superior performers in order to maximize their pay increases and minimize squabbling. Another task for the implementation team is to determine whether a mechanism to ensure a reasonable distribution of performance appraisal ratings needs to be created.

If the organization already has a performance appraisal system in place that the implementation team is revising or replacing, one useful activity is to find the answers to these two questions:

1. What has been the actual distribution of performance ratings over the past two or three appraisal periods?
2. What do people in the organization think the distribution has been? (There is frequently a significant difference between perception and reality.)

Whatever the actuality and perceptions regarding past distributions

Figure 10-14. Assessment of Issues to Be Discussed During the Performance Appraisal Meeting

Meeting Agenda	Benefits and Advantages	Risks and Disadvantages
Evaluation of subordinate's performance during appraisal period (classic performance appraisal)	Allows for undivided attention to be paid to performance without distraction of compensation concerns Reduces time pressure that would be present if other issues were also on the agenda Communicates organization's belief that a meeting devoted exclusively to reviewing job performance is appropriate Suggests that performance appraisal rating is not the exclusive determinant of compensation changes	It makes at least one more meeting necessary. The employee may not be as receptive to suggestions if compensation discussion does not accompany performance discussion. It may imply that pay and performance are only weakly related.
Performance appraisal plus compensation review	May encourage both manager and employee to take discussion more seriously Confirms strong linkage between pay and performance. Most individuals believe that pay and performance should be linked and discussed at the same time.	The subordinate's attention may be directed exclusively toward pay issue. Subordinates may set lower goals for upcoming appraisal period. Separate meetings to discuss performance and pay allow the manager two separate opportunities to influence subordinate.
Performance appraisal plus compensation review plus development planning and/or objective setting	Kills all birds with one stone Allows entire process to be completed in short period of time. Allows managers to accomplish several objectives in one meeting. Since all topics are related, there is some rationale for discussing all in one meeting.	It may not kill any bird completely; may just stun and annoy. It requires highly skilled managers to be effective. If any miscommunications occur, the absence of other meetings decreases possibility of correction. The employee is likely to suffer from information overload; retention of most critical messages may suffer. An employee who receives a lower than expected rating may not be open to discussing development or improvement needs.

of appraisal ratings, the question still remains whether the organization should construct some mechanism for ensuring a reasonable distribution of performance appraisal ratings or leave it entirely up to managers to make the recommendations that they believe honestly fit the facts of each case.

One approach is to create a forced-distribution system so that the percentage of people at each rating level reasonably approximates the distribution of a bell curve. In this case, about two-thirds of all appraisees would be rated at the midpoint rating—perhaps, for example, Fully Satisfactory. An additional 30 percent would be divided between the rating one position up and one position down from the midpoint: about 15 percent rated Superior and the other 15 percent rated Fair. Finally, about 5 percent of the population would be rated at the extremes: 2 or 3 percent labeled Distinguished, the other 2 or 3 percent branded Unacceptable.

Although this approach would achieve a statistically balanced distribution of performance appraisal ratings, a bell curve is appropriate only for very large random populations, not to the mix of individuals we find in organizations creating performance appraisal systems. No matter how large the company, the population to be assessed by any one appraiser—or department or division—is not particularly large, certainly not large enough for the statistical certainty of a bell curve distribution to prevail. And assuredly the distribution is not random; the organization does not hire and promote at random but rather hires and promotes the best it can find. There is no reason to think that the performance of employees in a given company or unit of that company parallels the performance of the population at large.

Another difficulty with the insistence on a forced distribution, particularly when it is combined with a fairly rigid percentage allocation scheme for allotting increases (an "if X, then Y" approach, where a rating of Fully Satisfactory generates a salary increase of 6 percent), is that improvement within a rating category cannot be recognized. It may well be that an individual who last year was barely rated Fully Satisfactory this year almost earned a rating of Superior. The improvement in performance has been significant, but the ultimate rating is unchanged.

Another approach is to provide guidelines or percentages. Just as allowing a range of percentage increases within a given performance appraisal rating gives raters more flexibility (e.g., a rating of Superior will result in a salary increase of between 6 and 11 percent), so allowing a range of performance ratings will help maintain an overall distribution of ratings in various categories while at the same time not force raters to allot people rigidly into categories. While even this approach of recommending that the organization expects that about X percent of employees will be rated Competent and Y percent rated Superior will not work with very small groups, it provides a logical perspective of the organization's expectations and is accepted as reasonable by most appraisers and appraisees.

Microsoft, for example publishes its specific expectations about the distribution of performance appraisal ratings. The Microsoft performance rating scale ranges from 5 (exceptional performance) to 1 (unsatisfactory performance). While communicating the expectation that performance appraisals should be "fair, objective, related to job performance, and used consistently," the company provides a general guideline that "approximately 35% of the employees in your division should receive performance ratings greater than 3.5; 40% should be at 3.5; and 25% should have ratings of less than 3.5."

The final alternative is to provide no formal guidelines or restrictions and allow raters, as long as they can convince those who have to approve their appraisal grades, to assign whatever rating they feel is most appropriate. This allows for the greatest exercise of managerial judgment, and as long as managers are sophisticated and well trained in performance management it will probably produce similar results to what a forced distribution system would generate. There will be more individual variances, however, and the administrative burden of ensuring reasonable corporate outcomes will increase.

Completing the Work of the Implementation Team

The task involved in designing a performance appraisal system is mammoth, as the length of this chapter should indicate. There are dozens of critical decisions that must be wisely made. Political considerations must be taken into account. The need for thoroughness must be balanced by the need to create a system that people will actually use.

During the development process, implementation teams usually find it helpful to schedule periodic focus groups or field application meetings in order to serve two purposes: (1) to get feedback from future users of the system to make sure that the assumptions they are making are sound and that the process they are developing is one that will work and (2), equally important, to develop a cadre of supporters who can be influential among other system users in paving the way for a smooth implementation.

No matter how good the system may be in theory, no matter how academically grand or legally solid, if it is not used, the entire development process has been a waste of time. The next chapter concentrates on the process for successfully implementing a new performance appraisal system.

Notes

1. Jack Zigon, "Performance Appraisal: Lessons From Thirteen Years in the Trenches," *p&i* (July 1994).

2. Tom Peters, *The Tom Peters Seminar* (New York: Vintage Books, 1994), p. 95.
3. William S. Swan, *How to Do a Superior Performance Appraisal* (New York: John Wiley, 1991), p. 91.
4. Ed Schollmaier, employee magazine at Alcon Laboratories, 1990, p. 5.
5. Robert J. Greene, Howard L. James, and Ann D. Scott, "Salary Review Timing: What Fits Your Organization?" *Compensation and Benefits Management* (Spring 1995): 24–27.

Chapter 11
Implementing a Performance Appraisal System

When human resources management system fail, the fundamental cause is rarely a flaw in the system itself. Most of the time, systems fail because of inadequate implementation. This chapter explains how to implement a performance appraisal system in such a way that it maximizes all of the benefits that were anticipated in its creation.

It might be useful to think of the creation of a performance appraisal system as similar to the creation of a new car. When an automobile manufacturer decides to invest the resources required to create an entirely new automobile, that decision is based on a recognition that there is a market for this vehicle and that its development and distribution will increase the overall profitability and success of the company.

Experts on automobile design look at every other car to determine what features and characteristics should be included. A great deal of consumer research will be done to find out what potential cutomers want in a car, how much they are willing to pay, and what trade-offs they are willing to make in price versus performance. Research and development experts explore every possible means to gain a technological advantage with this new vehicle. Prototypes are constructed and tested. The entire development process is marked by the attempt to incorporate the greatest amount of value at the least amount of cost.

Finally the car is ready. The work of research and development and design engineering has been completed; manufacturing is fully underway. But simply producing a superior automobile is insufficient to bring about the benefits that were anticipated when the top management of the company gave the green light to the production of the new car. Success will now be a function of entirely different groups: marketing, sales, distribution, maintenance, and customer service.

The same phenomenon is true for the successful development and implementation of a performance management system. When the implementation team has finished its design of the form, when all of the administrative guidelines have been determined, and all of the procedural questions resolved, only half the job has been done. The new performance appraisal system must be marketed to the organization and sold to users in the same way that the new car will be sold. Arrangements must be made for required maintenance and administration of the system. Finally, the more technologically advanced the system is, the greater the need will be for driver training.

The Role of the Implementation Team

The job of implementing the new performance management system does not begin at the point that the new appraisal form has been designed, any more than the job of the automobile manufacturer's marketing department begins once R&D, engineering, and manufacturing have finished their work and the new cars are rolling off the assembly line. Automotive marketing begins with the initial decision that there is a need in the market for a new car. Marketing is intimately involved throughout the entire design process. Similarly, the marketing of the new performance appraisal system begins with the initial decision to create a new approach.

In convincing senior management of the need for a new appraisal system, a great deal of marketing activities were conducted. Users of the organization's existing system were probably surveyed to determine what they liked and disliked about the current procedure, what they'd like to keep and what they'd like to abandon. Focus groups of system users may have amplified those survey or questionnaire findings. The implementation team used this information to design a system that met all of the demands and expectations at minimum cost.

Now the task is to market that system to build organization-wide understanding, support, and acceptance among system users. The specific questions that need to be answered during this stage of the implementation process include these:

- How will we determine that the new system actually produces the results we expect it to and operates the way we predict?
- How should we position the implementation and inauguration of this new system? As a major new program with all of the attendant bells and whistles? An incremental improvement to what we have already been doing? In software terms, is this a completely new product: Version 1.0? Is it a major upgrade to an existing product: a change from Version 2.2 to 3.0? Or is it a fine-tuning of an existing

product that has a secure market niche: a move from Version 3.1 to 3.2?

▸ What communication has already taken place about the development of the new system? What expectations (accurate or erroneous) exist about what's coming their way? What's the word on the grapevine?

▸ What should be the timing of communication? How often do we need to communicate? What resources and media are available?

▸ What misunderstandings about the performance management system are likely to arise? What will cause these? What do we need to do to put them to rest?

▸ What is the appropriate role of top management during the implementation process? What involvement should they have with training and orientation programs? What will be their role once the system is in place?

▸ Should there be an appeals process? What recourse does an employee have in the event of a perceived inaccurate or biased appraisal?

▸ What training will we need to provide to make sure that the system is used appropriately by appraisers? What orientation will appraisees need in order to gain the maximum benefit from the system?

Pilot Testing the New System

The most effective way of ensuring that the system does what it is supposed to do and creates no unforeseen problems is to pilot-test the new performance management process before installing it throughout the organization. The following criteria are useful in selecting the department or oranizational units to be used for the pilot test:

▸ The senior managers in these units are willing to invest the resources required to do the pilot test. They recognize that there may not be an immediate payoff to them and that regular operations of the unit may be disrupted.

▸ Managers in these departments are reasonably flexible and willing to try new things.

▸ The population of appraisers and appraisees is sufficiently large as to allow for a valid sample size.

▸ The nature of the jobs within the pilot-test departments is reasonably similar to jobs throughout the company.

▸ The units selected do not bear a stigma. If the reaction of the rest of the organization to favorable pilot-test results from a particular department is either, "Of course it worked there; they're in such bad shape that anything would work there," or, "Of course it worked there; they're the fair-haired boys and nothing ever fails to work in that department," even highly favorable results will be renounced. The pilot-test departments should mirror the rest of the organization.

► The units selected are in relatively stable periods. No unusual demands are being placed on organization members or management; no other major projects or experiments are distracting people's attention.

► The work being done in the pilot-test departments is not of such a critical or sensitive nature that the inevitable problems that the pilot test is intended to surface and identify will cause major damage to the unit's operational mission.

The purpose of the pilot test is to gain information from users on how well the system works in practice. For that reason, one more critical decision is whether to fire blanks or real bullets. Will the results of pilot-test appraisals count? Will the appraisal forms be placed in employee personnel files? Will actual salary decisions be made on the basis of pilot-test results?

As one study of appraisal implementation procedures points out, "Employees may express concern over whether the 'test' performance appraisals will actually count in terms of their eligibility for raises and promotions. Opinion is usually divided on this question. Some managers argue that a 'fail-safe' performance evaluation test will avoid a lot of unnecessary anxiety on both the interviewers' and the employees' parts. The skills involved in the new program may take a while to learn, and no one can be expected to perform them flawlessly the first time around. Everyone will feel better if there are no 'report cards' issued."[1]

On the other hand, the study continues, it is vital that there be formal accountability, for both individuals and the department involved. If nothing demonstrably better of different happens, there is little other than anecdotal evidence to convince top management to proceed with organization-wide implementation. Obviously, there is merit in keeping track of the following:

► Results achieved versus results desired on an individual basis
► The degree to which the work behaviors included on the assessment were effectively rated and the degree to which ratee bahavior changed
► The degree to which goals and objectives were achieved
► The difficulties and unforeseen obstacles that arose and how the participants in the pilot test dealt with them

- The recommendations pilot-test participants have for improving the system
- The personal reactions of those involved in the project—what happened to them or for them that might not have happened without the system

Top Management Involvement

Throughout the design process, an effective process will provide for regular communication between the implementation team and top management. The senior executive group needs to be aware of the direction the team is going in and the decisions that are being made along the way.

If the senior management group has done an effective job of laying out the parameters of the project and made clear the specific expectations they have of the final product, it is unlikely that the implementation team will wander too far afield. During the course of the team's design efforts, however, new and unexpected issues will continually arise, and decisions may be made in passing that should receive some scrutiny from senior organization leaders.

Most effective implementation processes provide for regular meetings between the chairman of the implementation team and either a member of senior management or a review board of several top executives who specially take on the task of representing the entire senior management group in making interim decisions and making sure that the team's activity is on target. This senior executive or review board can be extremely helpful too in convincing the appropriate operating managers to participate in the pilot test of the prototype of the system.

Whether or not a formal pilot test of the system has been conducted, when the implementation team has completed its design work, the system will be presented to top management for approval. If a pilot test has been conducted, these results should be reported:

- A complete description of the system itself, how it was developed, what it entailed, and its intended benefits
- Brief details on the pilot test procedure: the selection of locations, the methodology employed to test the system
- The tangible or measurable results of the pilot test—both good and bad—together with the team's recommendations on how the negative aspects can be corrected
- The reactions, verbatim if possible, of the managers and employees who participated in the test
- Recommendations on exactly what steps need to be taken next, by whom, when, and why

As the authors of the recommendations for presenting the pilot test results to management wisely urge, "Make it as easy as possible for the decision-makers to decide."[2]

Building Senior Management Support

Along with presenting all of the details of the system itself, the administrative procedures recommended, and the pilot-test results, the following agenda items also are valuable to cover in building senior management support:

- ▸ The planned positioning for the new system: a major, high-profile new program, a quiet example of the organization's commitment to continuous improvement, or something in between
- ▸ Communication plans to ensure complete understanding and support
- ▸ Sufficient details of the administrative and maintenance system so that top managers recognize that appropriate control systems have been put in place
- ▸ The recommendations of the implementation team regarding appeal procedures
- ▸ The recommendations of the implementation team regarding the role of top management in the implementation and maintenance of the system
- ▸ The plans for training appraisers and orienting appraisees
- ▸ Any other specific details of the planned rollout of the new system

Communicating the New System

To ensure a successful implementation, the implementation team needs to design a thorough communication plan. The team's task here is to become a mini-advertising agency for the new performance management system. Every member and stakeholder in the organization, inside and outside, is the market; the creation of complete understanding, acceptance, and support is its mission.

The specific mechanics of the communication plan depend on the organization's culture, history, and resources. Ideally, every communications vehicle available will be used to inform organization members fully about the development of the new approach. Particular events that might be described include the following:

- ► The formation and composition of the implementation team, with requests to pass on to members of the team suggestions for them to consider in developing the new system
- ► The project timetable and anticipated major events along the way
- ► Information about the subject of performance management and its importance to organizational effectiveness
- ► The results of initial employee surveys and focus group results
- ► Preliminary design decisions
- ► Pilot-test group selections and results
- ► Final plans for rollout, training, and orientation

Even after the system has been fully implemented, the need for communication about results and activities continues. Immediate results after the first appraisal cycle, including user testimonials, can build support for the system. After the completion of the first full year of use of the system, communicating to organization members the measurable improvements in organizational effectiveness can continue the positive reaction toward the performance management process.

Overcoming Barriers to Communication

In their book *Designing Performance Appraisal Systems*, Allan Mohrman and his colleagues report that social psychologists studying attitude formation have determined a number of principles that will help ensure that a message will be received, considered, and retained:[3]

- ► *Participation principle.* The fundamental concept is that people support what they help create. This principle forms the basis for the recommendation that an implementation team be used to design the process. It also supports frequent use of surveys, questionnaires, interviews, and focus groups.
- ► *Reward principle.* According to the old platitude, people are always tuned in to radio station WII-FM: "What's in it for me." Effective communications about the new appraisal system will have at its center a clear message about how the individual will personally benefit from the system.
- ► *First-is-best principle.* It is easier to create an attitude where none already exists than to change one that has already been formed. Communicate early, before people acquire negative opinions about the performance appraisal system.
- ► *The-facts-don't-speak-for-themselves principle.* Raw information alone does not communicate. Instead of simply providing the facts about the performance appraisal system and letting listeners draw their own conclu-

sions, it is far more effective to present the facts and then explain what the facts mean. Don't be subtle.

▸ *Print credibility principle.* The written word, with few exceptions, is more powerful than the spoken. People believe that anything in print, where it can be closely examined and challenged, is more likely to be true.

▸ *Reinforcement principle.* All communications vehicles should be used, and all should send a consistent message. Since some people will see and trust highly some media while ignoring or rejecting others, every available medium should be employed: bulletin boards, paycheck stuffers, employee orientation meetings, memos, letters to the home, videos, top management presentations, posters in the cafeteria, scripts for supervisory briefings, and others.

▸ *Credible-source principle.* Communications have the highest credibility when delivered by those whom we already trust. When implementing a sensitive change in its performance management system, one organization filmed a highly experienced old-timer in front of a flipchart explaining the system. His delivery was awful, but his credibility was so high that everyone believed his message about the value of the new system.

▸ *Repetition principle.* Communication must be constant and continuous. New employees will have missed early messages. To keep a performance appraisal system alive, communication about it must be ongoing and not limited to the time of initial implementation.

Communicating System Mechanics and Instructions

I clearly remember two of the organizations that have engaged me to help them redesign and update their existing performance appraisal forms and procedures. One was a large defense contractor, the other an electric utility. Although their business and their performance management procedures and forms were entirely different, the two firms had one striking commonality: In each one, the instructions to appraisers on how to complete their existing performance appraisal form were typed on one sheet of paper with single-spaced lines, scanty page margins, and no paragraph indentations. Worst of all, the typist who had prepared the instructions had typed everything on the page IN ALL CAPITAL LETTERS, the typographic equivalent of screaming. It was almost impossible to read. The information may have been complete and important, but it was incredibly punishing to attempt to read the instructions and decipher how the process was supposed to work.

A good appraisal process, in addition to the communication that is done during its development and in the training and orientation of system users, also provides instructions on the appraisal form itself that are clear. They are clear to the point that someone who has never completed a performance appraisal form and is unfamiliar with this particular company's procedures and mechanics could read the instructions and then complete an assessment of a subordinate's performance so accurately that his own appraisal would be rated as Fully Satisfactory or equivalent in the category, "Appraises performance appropriately."

The title or cover page of the appraisal form can be used for two purposes: recording demographic information about the rater and ratee and providing the rater with detailed instructions on how to complete the entire performance appraisal process, not just fill out the form.

Figure 11-1 shows the cover page of the appraisal form used by the Arlington, Texas, manufacturer of precision weighing equipment, Milltronics, which includes a complete set of instructions. Even without seeing the appraisal itself, after reading these instructions an untrained appraiser would be likely to do at least a competent job.

Rating Terms

The Milltronics instructions set not only tells the rater what steps to follow; it also defines each scale position on a five-position rating category. One of the most frequent sources of arguments among implementation team members is whether to provide specific definitions of the terms used for the various rating categories and, in particular, exactly how those definitions should read.

If the team runs into difficulty crafting the definitions, the easiest approach is to get the two (or three or even more) disagreeing parties to write down their versions of the definitions together with a brief explanation of why they prefer their approach or terminology. If after providing their sets of definitions and their rationales to the entire team for review the implementation team cannot come to a consensus decision about which of the sets is clearly superior, it is best to avoid divisive voting procedures, though this may seem the most expedient path to a resolution. Instead, they can submit the sets of definitions and rationales to the senior management liaison or the review board with an explanation of the dilemma. Senior managers will rarely have difficulty in making a final and binding decision.

Monitoring and Evaluation

In addition to its communication responsibility, the implementation team must create a mechanism to make sure that the system is used effectively following implementation. The two most logical checkpoints to ensure system operating effectiveness are immediately after the first appraisal cycle and after one full year of system operations.

Figure 11-1. Cover for a Performance Appraisal Form

PERFORMANCE APPRAISAL

Name:
Job Title:
Department:
Appraisal Period:
Length of Time in Position:
Appraiser:

INSTRUCTIONS TO THE SUPERVISOR

1. Give the employee a blank copy of this appraisal form in advance of the appraisal interview. Ask the employee to complete the form appraising his or her own performance for discussion during the interview. Set a date and time for the interview.

2. For the "Appraisal of Job Skills and Competencies," place an "X" at the point which best reflects how often the individual performs in the manner described. Provide comments and examples in support of your judgment for each item. Finally, provide an overall appraisal of the individual's job skills and competencies.

3. For the "Appraisal of Key Goals/ Objectives/Performance Standards," write an appraisal of the results the person has achieved for each and evaluate the person's performance. At the end, provide an overall rating of the individual's performance against goals/objectives/performance standards based on your individual ratings of each.

4. For the "Supervisory Skills Appraisal" (if used), complete the individual assessments, write a narrative summary of the individual's supervisory skills, and provide an overall rating.

5. Write a narrative summary for each section on the last page.

6. Provide an overall appraisal of this individual's performance based on your appraisals of job skills and competencies; goals/objectives/performance standards; supervisory skills (if used); and the narrative summary. Use the following definitions for your overall appraisal:

   "O" Outstanding   — Consistently exceeds all expectations.
   "E" Excellent   — Exceeds many expectations and meets all other expectations.
   "G" Good   — Meets all expectations.
   "F" Fair   — Meets most, but not all, expectations.
   "U" Unsatisfactory — Fails to meet many expectations.

7. During the appraisal interview, compare and discuss the individual's self-appraisal and your appraisal. Explain the reasons for your appraisal, review the individual's strengths and development needs, and come to a common understanding.

8. Ask the employee to write any comments about the appraisal he or she wishes to and sign the form indicating that it has been reviewed. Offer the employee a copy of the form.

Immediately after everyone in the organization has had an initial appraisal under the new system, there will be no data on the system's actual effectiveness since it has not yet had time to produce results. There is, however, a great deal of data that can be collected fairly easily to determine if the performance appraisal process is working as intended:

- ► What percentage of people who were eligible for appraisals actually got them?
- ► What explains why those who did not get appraisals failed to receive them?
- ► What was the distribution of appraisal ratings? Was this distribution consistent with the distribution produced by predecessor systems? Is the distribution what was expected?
- ► Is there any evidence of appraisal error? In particular, are there obvious examples of positive or negative skew or central tendency?
- ► How much narrative do appraisals contain? Does what is written appear to be the product of thoughtful analysis, or is it short and perfunctory? Does the written analysis tend to confirm or contradict the rating assigned?
- ► Have all mechanics been followed? Are all boxes and blanks completely filled out? Do all appraisal forms bear the appropriate signatures indicating review by the appraiser's manager and human resources if that is required? Has the ratee signed the form to acknowledge receipt if that is a system requirement?

In addition to reviewing the forms themselves to confirm accuracy and thoroughness, it is useful to survey the population of system users. Whether done through a questionnaire or interview, the convening of focus groups, or informal discussion with users about their experience with the process, a lot of information can be gained that will be useful in training new appraisers and providing refresher training before the next appraisal cycle begins.

At the end of the first full appraisal cycle, it will be possible for the organization to gain more than just user reactions and assessments of whether the technical requirements of the system were met. Now the focus is on the effectiveness of the performance management process. Did the system produce worthwhile business results? Are people performing better? Are noncontributors being identified and systematically eliminated? Are people clear on exactly where they should be concentrating their time and resources? Have supervisor-subordinate communications increased in frequency and quality?

If the organization used a survey at the beginning of the process to identify the need for revising the performance management system, it would be appropriate to readminister the same survey to determine if any significant changes have occurred and where additional work is still required. The survey instrument provided in Chapter 9, originally proposed as a data collection device to support the need to create a performance appraisal system, could now be used again to see how far the organization has come.

Management Accountability

The most important factor in determining whether appraisers will take their performance management responsibilities seriously and devote a substantial amount of time to the system and its requirements is whether they themselves are held accountable for using the system well.

One of the issues explored in a study of performance appraisal practices in Fortune 100 companies was how much time is spent on performance management activities. The researchers found that an average of eight hours per employee per year is spent on appraising executives, six on professional employees, and fewer than four on nonexempts. These figures are inclusive of all performance management activities: observing and documenting performance, completing the actual evaluation, and conducting employee feedback and coaching sessions. These figures are also quite inflated, the researchers reported, since they found that a handful of firms that paid a great deal of attention to performance management significantly raised the average responses.

Why isn't more time spent on appraisal? The researchers found that "one reason is simply that managers are not commonly held accountable for how well they conduct performance appraisal on their subordinates. In only 22% of the Fortune 100 sample managers were evaluated on how well they conduct performance appraisals. Basic motivation theory as well as common sense suggests that managers will devote little effort to a somewhat unpleasant chore for which they are not held accountable."[4]

Appeals Procedures

Regardless of the quality of the performance appraisal form, the logic and good sense of the administrative procedures, the completeness of the communications process, the skill of the trainers, the sincerity and commitment of the appraisers, and the thoroughness of the review, there will always be some employees who are unhappy with their performance appraisal rating. Even in organizations that provide no final report card grade, there will still be employees unhappy with the way the appraisal was written or the performance events that the manager chose to highlight or disregard.

Even when performance appraisal is used exclusively for feedback, coaching, and development, and salary administration is a function of seniority, job analysis, or some other function, not all people will be happy with their performance evaluation.

And that is the way it should be.

One of the most accurate indicators of an ineffective performance appraisal system is an absence of complaints about it. If even the poorest performers have no complaints about their organization's performance appraisal system, then the system is probably failing to distinguish and reward high performers and identify and eliminate poor performers.

When complaints arise about performance appraisal, the first question to ask is, Who's complaining? If the complaints are primarily coming from those whose performance is generally agreed to be bungling and inept and the nature of their complaint is that the boss is unreasonably demanding in his expectations, then all is well and the system is functioning effectively. Even if those incompetent performers are members of a sheltered caste—black, Hispanic, disabled, female, homosexual—and are couching their complaints in the tired rhetoric of discrimination, still the first question to ask is, How good is their performance? If they are not performing up to expectations and the organization is telling them so, their complaints are confirming the system's effectiveness. Ignore them.

But if the complaints are from those who are bearing the larger share of the burden—those whose performance is exemplary—then it is wise to listen and seek those places where the amelioration of the system is required.

Types of Complaints

Complaints about performance appraisal fall into two unrelated categories: judgment and administrative. Judgment issues deal with whether the appraiser's assessment was valid. Did he give appropriate weight to all areas of the individual's performance or concentrate only on those where performance was weak? Did bias or halo or recency or some other appraisal error color the evaluation? Did he intentionally lower a performance appraisal grade in order to reserve salary dollars for his favorites?

Administrative issues concern whether company policies were followed. The policy provides that every employee will have a performance appraisal and salary review during the month that the individual joined the organization. Sally started in April; it's now June a year later and she still hasn't received an appraisal. The policy says that employees who are rated Superior will be eligible for a salary increase between 5 and 8 percent. Harry's performance was rated Superior, but he was given a 3.8 percent increase.

Administrative complaints are usually easy to rectify. If the policy indeed says that employees will receive an appraisal during their anniversary month and a manager has let an individual's anniversary date slip by unnoticed, a word in the ear will probably be sufficient to bring about a correction. Similarly, if the salary system says that a rating of X will produce an increase of Y, and it produces instead an increase of Z, then the manager is dead wrong and senior management or human resources staff will have little difficulty in bringing him to heel.

The implementation team must decide whether to recommend that the organization create an appeals procedure that individuals who believe that they have been aggrieved by some element of the system can use to have their misfortune corrected.

In some organizations, employees have no appeal recourse available if they feel that the organization has slighted them in some way. This approach avoids wasting time on frivolous complaints, but the absence of a mechanism for dealing with employee concerns is not going to eliminate those concerns. It will simply confirm employee suspicions that there is a significant disconnect between the philosophy engraved on the mission statement plaque in the reception area and the actual workings of the organization in the back room.

The Human Resources Role

Most commonly the human resources function serves as the arbitrator, mediator, intercessor, ombudsman, umpire, referee, policeman, peacemaker, and father confessor for the system. Given the enormous number of roles human resources professionals are expected to play, the function has difficulty serving any one master well. While it is easy enough for personnel to arrange a rectification when a formal policy has clearly been violated, it is far more difficult when an employee with a stellar record and a new boss complains that the reason for his sudden wretched appraisal is that there are political games afoot. If senior management believes in backing its juniors when they are compelled to make a tough call, personnel may be in an untenable position in attempting to require the line organization to do the right thing when opinions vary greatly on what the right thing is.

The two most appropriate roles for human resources staff to play are policeman and coach. In administering the formal policies and procedures of the system, it is the personnel department's role to ensure compliance with the rules. If the rules are wrong, they should be changed. But until they are changed, the personnel department owns the responsibility for making sure that everyone plays by them.

In the domain of judgment, the personnel department's role is that of coach. It is still the line manager's decision how the performance of a subordinate will be assessed. If that subordinate is unhappy and believes that the appraisal judgment was outside the boundaries of "reasonable men may disagree," then the role of personnel is to gather whatever facts may be available, bring them to the attention of the line managers responsible for the initial assessment, and urge reflection and reconsideration. Even when the error seems blatant and potentially indefensible in the event of an external challenge, the organization must still resolve the core issue: Who is to make the final decision, line or staff? If human resources staff have veto power over line decisions, then the performance appraisal system will be seen as the tool of the personnel department, and operating managers are likely merely to go through the motions in order to minimize the personnel nuisance.

Open Door Policies

Many organizations provide for an open door policy, a procedure whereby employees have specific permission to bring a complaint or grievance to the attention of the CEO or other senior manager for review and resolution. The dilemma with open door policies is that they guarantee only review, not resolution. The employee has the absolute right to complain; nothing in the policy, however, says that management is required to reverse itself if an error has been made.

Open door policies work well when senior managers are committed to making them work well and are willing to reverse their juniors when they err. But the cards are stacked against that happening. Ask any manager what she wants in a supervisor and she will tell you, "Someone who will back me up when I've made a tough decision." One of the fundamental lessons taught in Management 101 is the importance of supporting subordinates when they make a tough call. The difficulty of reversing a junior manager's appraisal judgment is exacerbated since the typical procedure requires that junior manager to get her boss's blessing about the appraisal rating before reviewing it with the subordinate. When the subordinate, unhappy about the unexpectedly low rating he has just received, says, "I'd like to be able to talk with the big boss about this," the immediate supervisor can easily agree, since that manager has already been co-opted. Even if the CEO is appealed to, he is faced with overturning not just the decision of an employee's immediate supervisor but a decision that supervisor's supervisor has reviewed and assented to.

Open door policies tend to be marvelous in theory but mischievous in practice.

Peer Review and Other Procedures

Peer review is the most popular of a growing number of internal alternative dispute resolution (ADR) procedures that organizations are adopting to provide a mechanism for employee complaints and grievances to be addressed quickly and resolved permanently.

Virtually all of America's unionized employees have access to a formal grievance process that allows an employee's complaint to achieve final and binding resolution through appeal to an outside unbiased arbitrator. Virtually no unionized employees, however, are subject to the operation of a performance appraisal system.

The reverse is true for the overwhelming majority of individuals—now almost 90 percent of the private sector workforce—who are not represented by a union. Most of them are the beneficiaries of a performance appraisal process. When complaints arise, however, few have access to a formal problem-solving procedure that allows a final and binding resolution by an unbiased third party.

Peer review provides that mechanism. The peer review problem-solving procedure was initially devised at General Electric a decade ago as a union avoidance technique. It is now the most popular corporate ADR procedure. A large number of other major organizations have installed peer review to review and resolve employee complaints.

The operation of the system is straightforward. If an employee's complaint—whether about the misapplication of a personnel policy, or the unwarranted receipt of disciplinary action, or, most commonly, the individual's termination from the organization—cannot be resolved through discussions with human resources representatives and senior line managers, the employee can elect to use the peer review procedure for a final and binding resolution.

The individual presents his case to a panel made up of both fellow employees—people just like himself—and managers. He explains the situation and tells the panel what he feels should be done to correct it. Panel members (typically three peers and two managers selected at random from a pool of trained volunteers) ask questions, interview witnesses, research precedents, and review policy. When the panel feels sufficiently well informed, each member casts a secret ballot to grant or to deny the employee's grievance. Majority rules.

A letter explaining the panel's decision is then sent to the employee. All panel members sign; no minority opinions are permitted. Everyone gets back to work. The issue is resolved.

In an organization that has established a formal peer review or similar mechanism for the resolution of grievances and disputes, should an employee unhappy about a performance appraisal rating be permitted to take it to the arbitrator or panel? The instinctive answer is, Why not? If the company has elected to create such a mechanism, why should employees who have a complaint about the fairness of their rating be prohibited from using it?

The answer, however, is less simple than it appears. One question that arises is the jurisdiction of a peer review panel. What complaints will be allowed to come before the panel? What employee concerns are inappropriate for panel review?

Issues involving discipline and discharge are almost always considered appropriate for peer review panel scrutiny. On the other hand, questions concerning rates of pay, benefits, working conditions, and similar policy decisions are never grist for the peer review mill. But the question of whether it is appropriate for a panel to review a performance appraisal complaint is ticklish.

What makes it difficult is not that it requires the panel to decide between a supervisor's assessment and the opinion of the employee. The problem arises because it is impossible to give the panel the information it needs to decide whose assessment is correct. Questions involving disciplinary action require the panel to determine whether the company had just cause to take the action that it did. That is a fairly straightforward issue that can be fairly decided by an impartial panel. The data on which the decision was based are easily available.

To determine whether a supervisor's rating of an employee's performance is accurate, on the other hand, requires the panel to have all the information, impressions, and details that the supervisor has collected, consciously and unconsciously, over the entire appraisal period—an impossible task. For that reason, typically the policy is that employees have the right to file a grievance if the mechanics and procedures of the performance appraisal system have not been followed, but complaints about the fairness of a specific rating are not eligible for panel review. For example, if the organization's policy states that all employees will receive a written performance review at least once every twelve months and Harry has gone fifteen months without a review, he has legitimate grounds to file a grievance. Or if the policy says that employees who are rated Superior will be eligible for a merit increase of between 4 and 8 percent and Julia received only a 3 percent raise despite her Superior rating, she too is eligible to use the grievance machinery. But Norman, who was rated Satisfactory when he believed he deserved at least a Commendable rating, is out of luck as far as being eligible to use the grievance procedure. There's no way a panel could get the data it needed to tell what rating his performance deserved. He must find another outlet for his complaint.

Where peer review panels provide powerful benefits is in their ability to review the grievances of employees who have been terminated. Almost every organization with a peer review procedure actively encourages terminated employees to file a grievance, knowing that the great majority of panels—on the order of almost 90 percent—uphold the termination decision. In the small number of cases where the panel votes to overturn the discharge and return the individual to work, the evidence strongly suggests that an arbitrator, compliance officer, or jury would have come to exactly the same conclusion. The difference is that the panel does the job far more quickly, far more cheaply, and without any dirty laundry hung out to view.

Most implementation teams decide to provide some mechanism for third-party review of employee concerns about the process. If the concern deals with an administrative issue, using a peer review panel will ensure swift and defensible decisions together with a demonstration of fairness and the sincerity of the organization's mission statement in day-to-day practice. If the concern regards whether the rating itself was appropriate, that issue is best referred to human resources professionals for discussion, coaching, and, if necessary, review with the manager and department to ensure proper appraisal process are in use.

Providing the employee with access to an appeals process is as much a matter of reducing exposure to legal challenge as it is a matter of effective management practices and good employee relations. In Chapter 15, one of the important recommendations made for reducing legal exposure is to create some process for employee appeal.

Training: The Ultimate Communication Process

More than anything else, the training provided to raters will determine whether the appraisal system works as it is supposed to. No matter how appropriately the form matches organizational requirements, no matter how intelligently the process has been designed or how thoroughly tested, and no matter how much top management support there may be, if raters do not do a proper job of appraising and managing performance, the system will fail. Chapter 12 describes the process of creating an effective performance appraisal training program.

Notes

1. *BLR Encyclopedia of Performance Appraisal* (Madison, Conn.: Business & Legal Reports, 1990), p. I-79.
2. Ibid., p. I-80.
3. Allan M. Mohrman, Jr., Susan M. Resnick-West, and Edward E. Lawler III, *Designing Performance Appraisal Systems* (San Francisco: Jossey-Bass, 1989), p. 133.
4. Steven L. Thomas and Robert Bretz, "Research and Practice in Performance Appraisal," *SAM Advanced Management Journal* (Spring 1994), p. 31.

Chapter 12

Creating a Performance Appraisal Training Program

In developing a performance appraisal system tailored to meet the exact needs of the organization, the implementation team has had two responsibilities: developing the system itself, including the forms and all administrative procedures and policy guidelines; and ensuring that the system, once implemented, will be understood, supported, and accepted by everyone on whom it has an impact. The training provided to raters (and the orientation or formal training to ratees) will largely determine how successful the implementation ultimately is. In this chapter we examine the procedure for creating a performance appraisal training program as part of complete design effort. (This chapter is equally useful to a human resources manager, training director, or outside consultant who is called on to design and deliver a training program to an organization's appraisers based on an existing and ongoing appraisal system.)

Training for appraisers serves two purposes. The more obvious is to provide the knowledge and skills necessary to use the system well, to get all the benefits it was designed to provide. The second reason is defensive. A 1982 study, frequently confirmed, found that providing appraiser training was one of the primary causes for companies to be successful in winning legal cases when employees charged them with illegal discrimination resulting from performance appraisal.[1] Companies that train appraisers well not only can expect far fewer claims of discrimination; they also increase their chances of prevailing if discrimination claims are ever made.

Not much training actually happens in organizations though. The Bretz and Milkovich study described in Chapter 1 determined that although 90 percent of organizations reported having trained managers in conducting appraisal interviews and providing feedback, most of the training occurred when the systems were originally designed and installed. Few companies provide ongoing training on a regular basis, and since most of the programs they encountered were over ten years old, few managers benefited from the training that was done.[2]

Who Needs to Be Trained?

When a system is first introduced there will be a major training requirement for all appraisers. In addition, personnel representatives and human resources managers who may not have been directly involved with the work of the implementation team in designing the system will need specific coaching, since managers in the line organization—their customers—will be looking to them when questions about system administration arise. Finally, many upper-level managers will wear the hat of appraiser for their direct subordinates and approver for the appraisals their subordinates create on those who report to them. In addition to those receiving formal training, appraisees will have to be oriented, and if system success is to be maximized, an investment in training ratees on how to get the most out of the system would be resources well invested.

Once the system has been fully implemented, the need for training continues. New managers, recruited from outside the company or promoted from within, enter positions where they are required to write and review evaluations. Refresher training, particularly in organizations using a focal date approach where everyone receives an appraisal at the close of the business year or some other specific time, can provide significant benefits in renewing skills that have atrophied over the past eleven months.

The Role of Senior Management

When senior management has approved the new system, plans for conducting training, already in progress, can be made final. One of the first issues to resolve is the appropriate role for senior management in the training process.

If the system is to be fully effective, senior management need to see themselves as active users of the system and not as exempt from its provisions. The specific system for senior management appraisal may be different from the system used to appraise the performance of the middle management, technical, nonexempt, or other populations. But allowing senior management's role in the new performance appraisal system to be merely one of "do as I say, not as I do" will bolster organizational cynicism about just how serious management is about this new approach.

But top management does not need to go through the training program as anybody else does. Expecting them to spend a day being trained in how to apply a procedure that they are highly knowledgeable about and probably have the skills and experience to use well without any formal instruction at all just to parade their commitment is unwise. The presence of the most senior managers in any mixed group is likely to have a dampening effect on the participation of the rest of the attendees. The session will come off as a trainer-dominated lecture.

But there is a key role for the organization's senior managers to play in appraiser training. Every person in the classroom, listening to the facilitator explaining how to fill out the form and deliver the feedback, will silently be asking, "Does my boss really go along with this? And what about his boss?" The boss needs to speak. And what he needs to say is, "I believe in this. I use it myself. I will hold all of my direct reports responsible for using it and using it well. And one of the things I will appraise *them* on is exactly how well they use it." If senior managers say this and follow up on their words, not much more from the top needs to be said.

But there still is more that top managers can say that is important. They need to tell their juniors why they support the system and why they believe an effective performance management system is vital to accomplishing critical business objectives. For maximum impact, the senior manager in a session introducing the new appraisal process should relax, unwind, take the audience of juniors into his confidence, and talk not just from the head but from the heart about issues everyone in the room needs to hear him address:

- ► Why he personally feels it's important to give people clear direction about what they are expected to do.
- ► Why people need to know exactly where they stand, even when where they stand isn't where they think it is or where the organization would like them to stand.
- ► Why the company wants to make sure that it clearly recognizes and rewards those who make the biggest contributions to the enterprise and confronts those whose contribution is marginal with the need to shape up or ship out.
- ► How he knows that it's difficult to confront someone who isn't meeting expectations but, "By George! that's what you're getting paid to do and we expect you to do it well."

If the senior manager who is kicking off the session can leaven the message with personal experiences, it becomes an even more satisfying and memorable performance. Telling the group about the difficulties he once faced in working for a boss who didn't provide honest feedback can have a much greater impact than merely urging the troops to do the right thing.

Who Should the Trainer Be?

The default decision is to leave training up to the trainers: the training department, if there is one, or the human resources management function. While understandable, this is not the ideal approach.

What trainers bring is training skills, platform skills. What human resources professionals bring is administrative expertise. What line managers bring is inherent credibility.

The implementation team will usually have been made up of a majority of line managers. Using them as the primary trainers can create organizational credibility that staff specialists, no matter how skilled, can't generate. Regardless of their platform skills, what is important is their ability to talk about their individual commitment to the system and why it looks the way it does. During the training sessions, questions will inevitably arise about why the form was constructed the way it was or why one procedural decision rather than another was made. If members of the implementation team are doing the training, they can address and resolve those questions easily.

The larger the organization and the more comprehensive the performance management system, the greater the benefit from equipping line managers to handle the complete job of implementation. Amoco Corporation, the Chicago-based integrated petroleum and chemical company, replaced its appraisal system and built a new performance management system as part of a cultural renewal process affecting all 29,000 of its worldwide employees a few years ago. Implementing the new procedure was one of the largest internal projects it had ever undertaken.

More than 600 line managers participated in a five-day, train-the-trainer program. These managers, in turn, held two-day training sessions for employees and supervisors. "We felt that line managers would have more credibility than professional trainers," Jerry Mount, Amoco's director of performance management, explained. "We found that using line managers as trainers contributed to employee acceptance of the program and helped break down any skepticism employees might have been feeling. Line managers will continue in their role as trainers for new employees and roving ambassadors for the process."[3]

What Needs to Be Trained?

A combination of skills is required to allow supervisors to conduct performance appraisals successfully, notes Jack Zigon: "To do performance appraisal well, supervisors need technical expertise in performance planning and designing feedback and reward systems. But at least as important are the people skills of negotiating, coaching and motivating as well as basic interpersonal skills like attending, asking questions and explaining."[4]

Technical skills and people skills aren't the total requirement. People also need to know the philosophy of the system and why the company is doing this. What was wrong with the old way? they will ask. How does it fit with our goals and plans? What's in it for me? If these questions haven't been addressed in the kickoff by a senior manager, they need to be raised and addressed early on.

The administrative procedures of the system are also critical to system success. Managers need to know exactly what they are supposed to do and when. They need to know every step of the process.

Just because they need to know every step of the process doesn't mean that they have to be taught every step. There are many aspects of the system or new procedure that learners are capable of figuring out for themselves, thus increasing both the inherent interest in the training session and greatly escalating the chances of long-term retention.

High participation throughout the training process will facilitate both interest and retention at the possible cost of time. A workshop that is learner centered and instructor led will take longer to conduct than an instructor-centered seminar where participants get only minimal opportunities for interaction, discovery, and practice.

Discovery activities can occur throughout the course of training. In one case, I asked a group of reasonably experienced appraisers to talk for a minute or two in their teams about the experiences that they had had as recipients of appraisals as well as deliverers of them, and then construct a checklist of the five most important attributes of a good appraiser. While there were many overlaps ("fair," "good listener") each team had its own individual insights on what made a good appraiser. The checklists they created had more meaning to them than any list of good appraiser behaviors given to them.

The Two Key Requirements for Appraisers

In addition to learning all of the administrative requirements of the system, appraisers need to become as expert as possible in two other areas: performance managers and feedback deliverers. As *performance managers*, their tasks are:

- ▸ Recognizing various levels of performance, good and bad
- ▸ Keeping consistent performance records
- ▸ Helping subordinates identify the key accountabilities of their job
- ▸ Helping subordinates develop reasonable goals and measures or standards of performance

▸ Coaching subordinates before and after important events
▸ Adjusting objectives when appropriate
▸ Appraising performance accurately and objectively

As *feedback deliverers*, managers need a different set of skills:

▸ Listening well
▸ Being able to recognize different emotional reactions on the employee's part and responding appropriately
▸ Anticipating sensitive areas and dealing with them effectively
▸ Focusing their descriptions on observable behavior and providing specific examples to support their assessments
▸ Describing discrepancies between desired and actual performance without resorting to generalizations, judgments, or attitudinal concerns
▸ Mustering the courage to confront performance that is less than desired in a straightforward, unapologetic way
▸ Setting and communicating high standards of performance
▸ Gaining employees' agreement to meet those standards

The Mechanics of Training

The specific mechanics for achieving each set of objectives vary with the needs of the organization and the content of its appraisal system. Two techniques frequently used in performance appraisal training are worth particular note: role plays and behavior modeling.

Role Plays

Role plays may be the most disliked training technique by management training participants. Often they approach them as "little theater" performances, where they are called on to act in a way that is unnatural. In other cases their aversion to role plays comes from being forced to perform in front of a group and then, worse, having their performance critiqued by an audience of their peers.

But role plays do permit learners to prepare for situations they will encounter on the job. It allows them to practice behaviors and try new approaches in a risk-free environment, without the adverse consequences that could follow if they tried the new approach unsuccessfully with a subordinate in a real appraisal interview. It gives them the chance to rehearse tough conversations and, as much as learning what to say, learn what not to say.

Here are some guidelines for using role plays productively in performance appraisal workshops:

- *Conduct multiple role plays.* Instead of inviting two participants to come to the front of the room and act out their roles in front of everyone else, get everyone involved in role playing simultaneously. That takes the performance pressure off.
- *Use trios, not pairs.* Using trios helps to maintain a more businesslike atmosphere, particularly if some of the participants have a tendency to take the role play less seriously than is appropriate.
- *Use coaches, not observers.* The third person in the trio is to be a coach, not merely an observer. The role of the coach is to concentrate on the supervisor and restrict his comments to identifying and reporting back things that the supervisor did that were particularly effective. Having the coach instructed to look only for effective behaviors will reduce some of the performance anxiety. Later, coaches report on the single best thing they saw or heard the supervisor do.
- *Use short time frames.* Never ask participants to role-play an entire performance appraisal; it's far too long and they will get so caught up in the drama of it that they will forget about the specific skills they are supposed to be practicing. Instead, make role plays extremely short. Tell the participants that they will be practicing getting the meeting off to a good start, for example, and have them role play only the first fifteen to thirty seconds of the meeting.
- *Give goals, not tips.* Minimize any tips to role players on how they should play the role. Instead, tell them the goal that they should be striving for—for example, that their objective in this next role play is to get the employee to agree to take over the training of new college recruits even though the employee already feels overworked.

Behavior Modeling

Behavior modeling is a form of imitative learning where learners see a model performing a task in an ideal way and then rehearse doing that task in the same ideal way. By seeing an ideal model and then imitating that model, trainees gain practice and skill in performing exactly as they should.

For use in performance appraisal training, the organization can create videotape models internally or purchase prepared tapes from commercial vendors like DDI or Zenger-Miller. Each videotape is short and addresses one critical skill area. Between four and six learning points are presented by the live facilitator, who then plays the tape, asking the group to observe the actors using the skills just described. The learning points are always followed exactly in sequence by the actors; the results of the transactions are always successful. The models avoid generalities or theories, instead concentrating on showing step by step how to do a supervisory task.

After trainees watch the videotape and review the learning points they have just seen modeled, they practice through role play. Depending on the behavior modeling approach used, a pair of participants may conduct the role play in front of the group, with the trainer actively involved in guiding the supervisor through the use of the learning points or key steps during the role-play transaction. The practice session may be videotaped. In other approaches all participants may do the role play concurrently. Whatever the structure, the concentration is always on providing positive comments and ensuring that the learners use the key steps or learning points exactly as they are presented and are successful in doing so.

Studies of behavior model techniques generally concur that this approach of watching a master model appropriate behavior, learning the key steps that the model employed during the demonstration, practicing the activity through role play, and receiving positive feedback and an assured, successful experience can be dramatically effective in changing supervisory behavior.

If formal behavior modeling is not feasible for the organization, having participants model effective behavior using the scripts provided in Chapter 7 will increase the likelihood that they will use more effective approaches when they actually conduct their performance appraisal discussions.

Explaining System Mechanics

If the performance appraisal training program is serving both to introduce a new performance management system and train appraisers how to use it, a great deal of material will need to be covered. Frequently questions about the system come up that have the effect of sparking discussions that, though interesting, are sideshows that take attention away from the main attraction. These questions can be considerably distracting when they deal with elements of the system that either have not been finally decided or raise issues that have not previously been addressed.

If members of the implementation team are not doing the training themselves, it is critical to have at least one member of the team as a participant in every training session with the task of responding to questions that arise about form design and administrative requirements.

Another way to avoid training session problems is to arrange for the implementation process to include one final meeting of the implementation team immediately after the last training program. The purpose of this meeting is to consider and resolve all issues that arose during the training programs.

At the start of each training program, the trainer can post a flipchart page labeled "Issues to be Resolved" and explain to the participants that questions are bound to arise that have not yet been resolved or even considered by the team. To avoid spending time speculating about possible answers during the training session and thereby neglecting work on the formal items on the agenda, any questions that arise that cannot be immediately answered will be posted, along with any recommendations session participants may have, on the chart and reviewed with the implementation team at their final meeting. In addition to increasing the degree of control the trainer has over the session, the posting of an "Issues to be Resolved" chart helps generates worthwhile issues.

Appraisee Training

Particularly when a new system is being introduced, it is important that not only the appraisers are trained but that everyone who will be appraised under the system is at least oriented to the procedure and reasonably comfortable about what to expect. The ideal implementation process involves a significant amount of time—a half day perhaps—devoted to training appraisees on what to expect and how to get the most out of the system. Following are some of the items that could be included in an appraisee training session:

- How to talk to your supervisor about his or her expectations of your performance
- How to conduct a self-appraisal
- How to prepare for the interview
- How to keep track of your own performance
- What to do if you feel that the appraisal you receive is inaccurate

Ensuring Ongoing System Success

Once the system has been fully implemented, the need for ongoing and refresher training continues. At the end of the first appraisal cycle, a paperwork audit of the forms will indicate areas where additional training is necessary. The same interviews with supervisors and subordinates, focus groups, and questionnaires can be helpful in determining where additional training (or system revision) is necessary.

After the initial cycle of the performance management system has been completed, annual training can be done fairly quickly to get the skills of all appraisers back up to where they were at the time of initial implementation. Since they are now familiar with the system, they will be able to bring draft copies of actual appraisals to the training session so that they can work on real forms that they will be using for subordinates rather than case studies.

New managers need to get as much of the original training as possible. An annual session aimed at training all members of the organization who are responsible for appraisals and have not completed the training can be made voluntary or mandatory, depending on how strictly the organization wants to control the procedure. Or an organization can do what one company elected to do to preserve the autonomy of its managers while still getting the message across to all that taking performance appraisal seriously and doing it well was a very important corporate value. It announced that there would be a performance appraisal training session held on a given date for all managers who had not formally been trained. Attendance at the session was entirely voluntary, the company announced, but no one who had not been trained would be allowed to conduct a performance appraisal conversation or recommend a subordinate for an increase. This "voluntary" approach resulted in 100 percent participation by all eligible managers.

Notes

1. H. S. Feild and W. H. Holley, "The Relationship of Performance Appraisal System Characteristics to Verdicts in Selected Employment Discrimination Cases," *Academy of Management Journal* 25 (1982): 392–406.
2. Steven L. Thomas and Robert Bretz, "Research and Practice in Performance Appraisal," *SAM Advanced Management Journal* (Spring 1994): 31.
3. Hewitt Associates, "Amoco Implements 'Performance Management' Worldwide," *On Compensation* (February 1991): 1.
4. Jack Zigon, "Performance Appraisal: Lessons From Thirteen Years in the Trench," *p&i* (July 1994): 5.

Part IV

Critical Issues in Performance Appraisal

Chapter 13
Employee Development

How do successful people get to be that way?

Most of the factors that influence an individual's ultimate effectiveness have been firmly established by the time the person is a member of an organization and a participant in a performance appraisal system. His basic genetic endowment; early family, school, and other experiences; influential teachers, coaches, pastors, and priests have long since had their influence.

Harold Hook, CEO of several life insurance companies and wry observer of organizational effectiveness, cautioned against optimism in development efforts. The week that a manager spends going through a management development program may represent forty hours of the finest executive education available, Hook acknowledges. But what does that forty-hour experience stack up against? No matter how valuable that forty hours may have been, for somebody who's thirty-five years old, it represents less than 0.0002 percent of his total waking life experience. Hook's message? Don't get your hopes up too high on how much influence it will have.[1]

Hook's caution about conventional development approaches is echoed by the studies conducted since 1982 by Michael Lombardo and Robert Eichinger of the Center for Creative Leadership on the ways in which successful executives acquire their skills. Their research has determined that successful and effective leaders become that way "by responding positively and adaptively over a long period of time to diverse but specific experiences."[2] There are five broad categories of experiences they found to be developmental, as reported by several hundred managers who analyzed and identified the factors that resulted in their own growth:

1. *Challenging jobs.* Challenging jobs teach the subtleties of leadership. Dealing with crises, starting up an operation from scratch, fixing up troubled operations: These situations require individuals to cope with pressure and learn quickly. In absolute terms, challenging assignments are the best teacher. They are the most likely to be remembered and teach the greatest variety and largest number of lessons.

2. *Bosses and other people*. Bosses serve as models for values. "Exceptional people seemed to create a punctuation mark for executives, either by representing what to be or do, or what not to be or do. Whether by serving as models of integrity or acumen, poor ethics or avarice, certain bosses exemplify how values play out in management settings."[3]

3. *Hardships*. Hardships teach us about our limits. Making mistakes, getting stuck in dead-end jobs, enduring life's traumas: These events caused managers to look inward and reflect on their humanity, their resilience, their flaws.

4. *Coursework*. Coursework, the standard regimen of management development activities, is valuable less for what is learned directly than for the opportunity it presents managers to build self-confidence by sizing themselves up against peers from other organizations. Coursework is valuable as a forum for trading tips, picking up different problem-solving methods, and comparing themselves with others.

5. *Off-the-job experiences*. Experiences off the job, primarily community service, often served as primers of persuasion.

The Center for Creative Leadership's research confirms Hook's observation: Approaching the issue of development as simply a matter of finding the right program and running the individual through it will produce little developmental effect. Coursework can be used to provide specific skills that an individual is lacking, but just the fact that a course is available on a topic might suggest that the topic is not one that will be important in bringing about long-term success. Hardly a day passes without a brochure or flyer arriving in the manager's in-basket announcing a new program in presentation skills or finance for the nonfinancial manager or solving people problems or some other easily taught, easily learned skill. But genuine development does not come from easily taught and learned skill sessions.

Genuine development comes from the job. Robert Eichinger analyzed eight benchmark studies of executive development, including those done over fifteen years by his colleague Michael Lombardo at the Center for Creative Leadership, a thirty-year AT&T study, the studies done by Jim Kouzes and Barry Pozner that resulted in the highly regarded book *The Leadership Challenge*, and five others. In examining these studies, Eichinger and Lombardo asked, What are the competencies that are determinants of executive success? They found sixty-seven, each supported by research. Their list includes such items as strategic agility, political savvy, integrity and trust, intellectual horsepower, sizing up people, and standing alone.

Eichinger reported that although there were variations on where and how managers acquired competence in various areas, there was always a congruency within the reports on the source for a specific competency. That is, whatever the specific competency in question, there was a great deal of correlation in the reports from different managers about where they had acquired that particular skill. For example, Eichinger pointed out, managers gain competence in written communication skills very differently than they gain competence in strategic planning. However, all managers gained competence in written communications in the same way. And all managers gained strategic planning competence the same way. People develop street smarts in a different way than they develop interpersonal skills, but everyone with street smarts develops these skills in the same way.

Eichinger's work supports the idea that few important competencies are actually capable of being developed through traditional training and educational programs. The great majority are experience based. Most of the experiences that result in competence development are directly job related. Most of the rest are a function of special assignments. Few result from conventional development efforts.

The Development of Competence

The research by Eichinger and Lombardo generated sixty-seven discrete competencies required for organizational success, most of which come directly from on-the-job experience. Personnel Decisions International, the highly regarded Minneapolis firm of organizational psychologists and consultants, developed a similar inventory of skills and competencies needed for effectiveness in a variety of positions, levels, and organizations. Their inventory, called Profiler®, identifies nine core factors critical to success, each with several skill dimensions, providing a total of forty-eight components.[4] PDI's factors, with examples of some of their skill dimensions, include these:

1. Administrative (planning, developing systems, working efficiently)
2. Communication (speaking and writing effectively, listening, making presentations)
3. Interpersonal (building relationships, managing disagreements)
4. Leadership (leading courageously, coaching others, fostering teamwork)
5. Motivation (drive for results, showing work commitment)
6. Organizational knowledge (technical expertise, ability to use financial data)
7. Organizational strategy (focus on customer needs, promoting corporate citizenship)

8. Self-management (acting with integrity, self-development)
9. Thinking skills (thinking strategically, analyzing issues, using sound judgment)

The Individual Management Development process (see Appendix B) identifies the various major competencies required for success in a management or professional position together with the skill factors that make up each component. Each of the three dozen IMD factors is accompanied by a set of statements identifying the behaviors one might observe in someone who was highly skilled in the area.

Where Is Development Needed?

Identifying the learning and development needs of the members of an organization can be approached from two perspectives. A macro-assessment determines the universal, generally shared needs of a large population of organization members. It answers the question, What are the overall needs to address in management development efforts?

Information on the broad needs for development can come from examining performance appraisals to find common response threads in the section devoted to development plans. Few answers of genuine value usually result from this analysis, however, since most managers are not skilled in accurately identifying what it is that a subordinate needs to do in order to increase effectiveness. Another difficulty in using broad reviews of performance appraisal responses is that the needs that most managers can recognize are determined by the answers they have available. "Improving communication skills," "developing leadership," and "time management" are perennial pop-ups in lists of development needs coming out of performance appraisals, because answers are easily found. But few assessors recognize that what a highly successful subordinate may really need for accelerating her development is the chance to take charge of a turnaround effort or to move from a staff leadership position to a line position where genuine profit-and-loss measures will indicate exactly how well she is doing.

Organizational needs assessments can provide additional information on development needs, the results of which can be compared to the recommendations made on performance appraisals. One-on-one discussions with senior managers about the areas where they see deficiencies in organizational bench strength may be even more fruitful.

Identifying Individual Needs

A study of performance appraisal results may demonstrate or confirm the existence of broad organizational areas where development is needed, but the primary value of performance appraisal in development is the identification of individual needs. Organization-wide assessments, senior management perceptions, and strategy-driven issues may be more useful in identifying organization-wide areas that need to be addressed.

Where performance appraisal can be of most use is on an individual basis, identifying the specific areas that need strengthening and the deficiencies that need correction.

Concentrating Developmental Attention

The results of the performance appraisal will be the initial source for development ideas and possibilities. Certainly any area where current performance is insufficient must be immediately addressed and corrected. But addressing deficiencies is not where the value of development lies. The greatest return comes from addressing the growth potential of those who are already making a superior contribution to the organization. If the time a manager has available for coaching and development is limited, as it always is, it will be far more advantageous to allocate that time toward those who need help the least rather than those who need it the most. When resources are scarce, as they always are, put them where they will do the most good: with those who have the most to offer to the organization's long-term success, not to those who need shoring up in order to arrive at a point of adequacy.

Examples of the wisdom of polishing diamonds instead of polishing coal abound. The track coach, needing a 100-meter-dash runner to fill out the team's roster, lines up every candidate at the starting line. He fires the gun and checks the results. Who does he pick to direct his coaching efforts toward? Not the runner who needs the most help, the one who is running the dash in 12 seconds. The coach works with the person who needs help the least, the runner whose time is already 9.7. He's the one who may have the potential to develop into a world-class sprinter. Similarly the gardener thins out the weakest plants, keeping and fertilizing only those that start out robust. And the breeder sells off the runt of the litter cheap.

Only in managing people in organizations do our egalitarian notions—our belief that everyone is entitled to equal treatment in all areas of organizational life, including opportunities for development—crowd out our common sense. We know, in spite of operating under a social contract that insists that "all men are created equal," that everyone is not created equal. Some men and women are better than other men and women. Some have more potential than others. Some are smarter than others; some are more dedicated, more diligent, more willing.

But often, and unwisely, managers invest developmental energy on

everyone, committing time and assets to those who produce the least return on managerial investment, thereby neglecting those who are doing
fine on their own but would profit exponentially from being afforded serious developmental attention. The successful organization is the tough-
minded one that realizes that not everybody can make the team and that
not everybody who's on the team can hold a starting position. The most
effective manager, in terms of long-range contributions to organizational
survival, is the one who consciously neglects the development needs of
some in order to concentrate on the few who have the greatest chance of
outperforming the pack.

Concentrate on your keepers.

Identifying Individual Development Needs

The assessment of performance and the appraisal discussion between the
manager and the subordinate usually highlight the most important areas
where developmental attention could profitably be placed. Two other techniques can also be valuable in determining where enrichment efforts will
produce the greatest returns: 360-degree feedback and individual development reviews.

360-Degree Feedback

Over the past few years the literature on 360-degree feedback has prolifer-
ated, and every organization has by now discovered it. No personnel journal or management magazine worth its salt can go more than three months
without running another laudatory story touting multirater feedback's
ability to solve all performance appraisal woes. No language is too immod-
erate to describe the potency of this latest organizational panacea.

360-degree feedback certainly does have the ability to improve the
quality of information individuals receive about the quality of their performance. Details of various organizations' approaches vary, but the core is
essentially the same. Instead of (or in addition to) being solely evaluated
by his or her manager, the individual is assessed on a variety of dimensions
by an assortment of individuals with whom the person interacts: the immediate boss, other organizational superiors, peers and coworkers, internal
and external customers. The list can grow to include vendors and consultants, human resources professionals, even friends and spouses (only pets
have yet to be included).

With pencil and paper or on their computer, each individual fills out
a lengthy anonymous questionnaire about another. Everything can be
probed: personality, the way the person deals with others, leadership skills,

talents, values, ethics. A week or two later, the person being assessed is given the results and the chance to compare how her self-perception squares with those who know her best.

"Most people are surprised by what they hear," claims *Fortune* writer Brian O'Reilly.[5] "Only a fraction of managers have a good grasp of their own abilities. Those with certain kinds of blind spots are routinely judged less effective by co-workers." About a third of all managers are able to produce self-assessments that match what their coworkers concluded. Another third are "high self-raters" with an inflated view of their own talents. These are the people most often judged least effective by coworkers. The final third rate themselves lower than others do; these self-doubters get better scores because they may work harder and rely more on others.

After anguishing, rejoicing, or simply agreeing, the recipient does something about the evaluation. The feedback deliverer, particularly if that person is an outside expert or a skilled management development specialist, can help the recipient decide what—if anything—to do about the results. Most of the time the steps to take are apparent. Willingness is the primary determinant of how much change will result.

Implementing 360-Degree Feedback

After deciding to proceed, most organizations begin the process by determining which characteristics or attributes will be assessed. The organization can develop a home-grown instrument or look to many dozens of outside providers that offer an array of paper-and-pencil or computer-assisted instruments.

The number of items assessed can vary greatly. A tool offered by Pratt & Whitney contains 19 questions; another, William Steinberg Consultants' Managerial Self-Assessment Tool software, asks 500. Among other major off-the-shelf providers, ODT's Prime Search asks 50 questions, Personnel Dimension's Profiler has 135. The Center for Creative Leadership offers two different devices: Benchmarks with 156 questions and Skillscope's 98. Stylus, an offering from Human Synergistics, asks 240.[6]

Internally developed instruments have the benefit of concentrating on the specific items that are most important to the organization but lack the normative and validation studies offered by the best outside providers. Administration may be more difficult with home-grown devices, particularly if confidentiality is a major concern.

The sophistication of instruments varies. Many are little more than traditional trait scales gussied up to capture a collective pool of biases and ignorance from a host of friends and adversaries, rather than reflecting just the prejudice of the boss himself. Others are highly refined and validated, reflecting important organizational values.

The Bank of Boston is one of several large organizations, including

General Mills and PepsiCo, that retained consultants Sherbrooke Associates to help identify the leadership practices it wanted to inculcate among the organization's managers. It arrived at eight, among them, "A Big Picture Perspective," "Commitment to Results," "Appropriate Controls," and "Positive Feedback." For each practice it identified the behavioral indicators that would suggest that the individual was indeed proficient in that practice. For example, the "Commitment to Results" practice included such indicators as "Demonstrates personal commitment to achieving unit's goals" and "Inspires subordinates to give their best effort." Similarly, markers for "Positive Feedback" included "Demonstrates personal concern for the success of your people" and "Recognizes subordinates for good performance more often than criticizes them for performance problems."

The bank's managers assessed themselves; underlings filled out the forms on their superiors. Questions were posed, "To what extent do you/does your manager . . ." with the list of the thirty-two separate behavioral indicators they had come up with and a 1 to 5 scale for indicating whether the individual acted in the ideal way from a very small to a very great extent. The Sherbrooke consultants gathered the data, put together the reports, and guided the managers in sorting through all the "so what" and "next step" questions.

Electronic 360-degree assessment instruments will probably replace paper-based systems before too long. Computer-developed assessment processes allow for the input of far more raters to be collected and analyzed than is feasible manually. They allow for a wide variety of sorts to be made on the data to distinguish whether, for example, people who have known the ratee for a long time see him differently than do people who are recent acquaintances (and thus confirm or deny the defensive reaction, "Well, once people get to know me they don't feel that way").

Voices®, a Lominger Limited product, may be the most sophisticated computer-based system available. Voices draws on the Lombardo/Eichinger Center for Creative Leadership studies and relates the feedback to the sixty-seven competencies and nineteen career stallers and stoppers their research discovered. The Voices instrument controls for many of the problems inherent with paper-based systems and first-generation computer models and suggests what the next generation of 360-degree software will bring:

▸ *Central tendency and positive skew.* Raters using any 360-degree process tend to rate on the high end of the scale and cluster their responses in a very narrow spread. To overcome this, the Voices software is programmed to give raters continuous feedback on how much of the scale they are using in order to force them to spread out more of their ratings and use more of the scale. Not all raters like it, but Lominger argues that "we would rather have slightly uncomfortable raters with better data than comfortable raters with inflated data."[7]

▸ *Limited demographic information.* Most paper-based systems allow for separating raters into only a few groups: perhaps subordinates, coworkers, customers, immediate supervisor, and self. Electronic systems can offer raters the option of indicating demographic information about themselves that will then allow for the testing of suppositions, hypotheses, and defensive routines in addition to checking straightforward data. Raters can indicate how long they have known the individual; the context in which they know the person (at work, off work, previous job); and their own race, age, and sex. This information allows the ratee to formulate questions like "Does my style work better with older people/women/people like me?"

▸ *Limited follow-up questioning capability.* All instruments, computer or paper based, ask the basic question, "What's your opinion of this individual in this area?" Sophisticated software allows the collection of follow-on information to assess the degree of sureness that raters have about their responses, raters' assessments of where the ratee would score himself, whether the ratee has made any progress in the area in the past year, and the importance of the area for success in either the organization as a whole or the ratee's specific job.

▸ *Rater fatigue.* In paper-based systems, all questions are in the same order. The more extensive the instrument, the greater the likelihood is that raters will start running out of gas before they get to the last question. Since every questionnaire is identical, the same final questions will always be affected. Rater fatigue may not be preventable, but if the software can randomize the question sequence for every rater, the fatigue effect will be disbursed.

▸ *One-size-fits-all instrument construction.* Paper-based systems provide an instrument with only one set of questions. Computer-based systems can easily provide unique questionnaires for high potentials, the recently hired, or people from different departments. Ratees could construct their own surveys to get information of particular interest or importance to them.

▸ *Limited information.* One way to define a weakness is to consider it as a strength used to excess. A strong results orientation (a strength), if overused, can generate fatigue, burnout, and high turnover. Advanced software allows a rater to indicate that not only is this an area of strength (normally good news) but actually one of excessive strength—a good thing on its way to going bad.

▸ *Limited response opportunities.* Most instruments ask only for the specific responses to the questions. Comments can be written in, but they are difficult to administer and manage in the absence of computer assistance.

An electronic tool makes it easy to collect and feed back any narrative notes, tips, and developmental suggestions raters may provide.

The Source of 360-Degree Feedback

The impetus behind the explosive growth of multirater assessment can be tracked to several sources. Quality guru Dr. Deming is one. Deming's widely reported criticism of traditional appraisal techniques, where the supervisor rates the employee, stirred a search for new models. The quality movement has been a strong force in promoting the notion that those closest to the work are in the best position to evaluate how well it's being done and how it can be done better. Coworkers can often see better than the manager how well a colleague is pulling her weight.

The growing use of teams has also sparked interest in multirater assessments, as has the growing focus on customer satisfaction; customers, both inside and outside the company, are commonly included as feedback providers. Susan Gebelein of Personnel Decisions points out that new organizational structures caused by right-sizing, cross-functional collaboration, downsizing, matrixing, and flattening are another generator of interest. "In one of our client companies, a person may have as many as five bosses," Gebelein reported at the Society of Human Resource Management annual convention in 1994. "This stimulates the need for obtaining feedback on an individual's performance from multiple sources."[8]

360-degree feedback can have enormous power, perhaps more than any other technique, to bring an individual's shortcomings to his attention and confirm that areas of perceived strengths are actual and recognized strengths. Jack Welch, CEO of GE and widely considered to be America's toughest boss and most accomplished manager, is an unabashed proponent of 360-degree reviews: "When you make a value like teamwork important, you shape behavior. If you can't operate as a team player, no matter how valuable you've been, you really don't belong at GE. To embed our values we give our people 360-degree feedback, with input from superiors, peers and subordinates. These are the roughest evaluations you can get, because people hear things about themselves they've never heard before. But they get the input they need, and then the chance to improve. If they don't improve, they have to go."[9]

The Future of 360-Degree Feedback

360-degree feedback, particularly as computer technology enables it to be tailored to fit the specific needs of individuals and small work groups, will have enormous power to identify areas where development is needed and suggest how feedback recipients should start the process. But with the exception of the use of peer review in the appraisal of team members (discussed in Chapter 16), 360-degree feedback is unlikely to replace conventional, manager-driven performance appraisal. There are plenty of good reasons. As Jane Layman of Milwaukee's DL Associates, a consultant in 360-feedback processes, observes: "To turn the current anonymous employee evaluations into a formal appraisal tool does more than encourage biased responses on the part of some of the respondents; it poisons the entire well in terms of the original objective. Instead of providing information to assist someone to become a better manager, employees are now passing a significant judgment, and they will approach the task differently. It seems particularly inappropriate to tie pay, promotions or termination to anonymously provided evaluations. It is not a question of whether employees can provide relevant information. They can. Rather it is whether they should be allowed to provide information in a context in which they cannot be held accountable."[10]

Layman's observation is accurate. I may be willing to accept feedback on my development needs from a group that includes the office screwup and my rival across the hall, but once they start deciding about the size of my paycheck, I've got reservations.

The value of 360-degree feedback will remain in the area of employee development, not in its potential for replacing the traditional performance review. Some managers would prefer to have a multirater process lift the burden of assessing and discussing subordinate performance from their shoulders. These managers will be, and should be, disappointed. Susan Gebelein was clear in the position that Personnel Decisions, a major provider of multirater instruments, takes about the use of their product to replace conventional boss-down appraisals: "We DO NOT advocate multirater feedback taking the place of a manager's review. It does not respect the nature of multi-perspective feedback, does not hold the supervisor accountable for making the organization's judgment, and violates the employee's request for some time, just a little, devoted to them."[11]

Individual Development Reviews

The other procedure for identifying the specific areas where developmental energy should be focused is the structured individual development review.

The Individual Management Development (IMD) instrument was developed twenty years ago for a Fortune 50 consumer goods firm. The purpose was to enhance an already muscular environment. The company had a culture that encouraged and rewarded excellence in performance, risk taking, breaking boundaries, and thinking outside the box. It had a training function that was one of the first in the country to recognize that conducting training programs was a secondary concern—a means, not an end—and that improving organizational performance was the mission.

High-potential managers were identified and routinely moved into new jobs to create developmental challenges and broaden their experience. Performance and hiring standards were high; talent was nourished; the mediocre were identified and quickly shown the door.

After the completion of one annual review cycle, it became clear that the biggest deficiency in the performance management process was the development portion. There was no formal mechanism to help managers assess their subordinates from the perspective of their development needs, not just in terms of their current performance. Even for managers gifted in spotting what a subordinate needed to work on to make him ready for a next-step opening, there were no routine procedures for explaining how to do people development and coaching through the process.

The IMD process was created to fill that void. The assessment instrument was constructed by asking groups of managers to identify the major, broad areas of management responsibilities. Seven emerged:

1. Knowledge of the business
2. Priority setting
3. Problem solving and decision making
4. Interpersonal skills
5. Communication
6. People development
7. Achievement orientation

Within each of these core categories, the components comprising it were determined. For interpersonal skills, for example, the components were:

- Expresses emotions appropriately
- Initiates friendly interactions
- Provides positive and negative feedback
- Interacts effectively with superiors and senior managers
- Accepts positive and negative feedback
- Faces and resolves conflict

In every case, the individual components were identified that fit under the broad competency heading.

Finally, and by far the most important and most difficult task, three or four behavioral indicators for each component were determined. What would a person have to do to demonstrate genuine skill in this area? What distinguishes a high performer from a low performer? What does somebody who's good at this do that somebody who's not so good doesn't do? What's the yardstick?

In every case a couple of behavioral indicators were created that anyone could use to benchmark an individual's performance. How do you know, for example, that someone understands the performance measures for her job? Simple: She can state her job accountabilities, can state specific measures for each accountability, has reviewed and discussed quantifiable performance measures with her supervisor, and measures her own performance regularly and accurately. There's no guesswork involved; there are no judgments, no speculation. The person has either done those things or has not; she either can do them or she can't. In each case, they are observable and measurable.

The development process was not completed without a great deal of argument, debate, and controversy. But when the arguments were settled and the form went to press, there was agreement throughout the organization that it captured what was important and, even better, had identified how to know it when you see it. The IMD form told managers what to look for; it told subordinates what the company expected.

The Individual Management Development Process

The first step in using the IMD process is mutual agreement. The process is voluntary. Both the individual and the manager must commit to the time demands and the sacrifice of other areas that will be demanded when a project to make a significant impact on a person's development is launched. There is more required than just rearranging the schedule to allow Joe to be away Tuesday and Wednesday attending the time management course.

For the individual, embarking on a worthwhile development effort will consume a couple of hours a week ordinarily devoted to getting the job done. For the manager, the requirements are even more demanding. Not as much time is required, but a high degree of commitment to the process is. Even more than in classical performance appraisal, straight shooting and telling the truth are essential. If a manager fudges performance appraisal results to get a subordinate a slightly better salary increase than he might otherwise have deserved, no real harm is done. If the manager fudges the assessment of the subordinate's actual performance and capabilities as part of a developmental needs assessment, the individual's career may be jeopardized.

Before they can determine where the subordinate needs to go, they need to find out where the individual is right now. The IMD process starts by asking both the individual and his supervisor independently to complete the IMD assessment instrument. This requires making the scaled assessment for each of the three dozen items on the form and then identifying the five items that each believes are the most important for success in the subordinate's job.

The two then get together. They lay their two forms down side by side and compare their assessments. As they quickly go through the individual assessments for the first time, they mark two kinds of items to return to for fuller discussion: items on which they both agree that the subordinate's performance or competence is low and ones where the scores show a significant difference in perception, regardless of who rated the item higher.

When that preliminary review has been completed, their next step is to review the five items that the manager selected as being the most important for success in the subordinate's job and the five that the individual selected. Ideally there will be a great deal of overlap in their choices. If there is not, this fact is worth serious discussion. My boss and I may both agree that I'm doing a good job in most of the areas on the form, but if the five items he has picked as the most important don't square with my selections, I may be doing a very good job of doing something other than what he sees as my job. Analyzing the reasons for the selections of the various items and clearing up any misconceptions about what either one of us believes the critical aspects of the job to be can be momentous development experience all by itself.

The next step is to return to the assessment instrument to discuss the items that have been marked as worthy of closer inspection. One of the strong benefits of the way the instrument is constructed is that it provides observable and measurable behavioral indicators of exactly what competence in any area looks like. Discussions are easier when the manager doesn't have to struggle to support an opinion or speculation about the individual. Instead, most managers report that specific examples are returned to memory by reviewing the behavioral indicators listed and using them to spark recollections of things the manager has actually observed the subordinate doing over the past few months.

Defensiveness is also significantly reduced by following this procedure. One of the greatest advantages of the IMD process is that because it is an activity undertaken voluntarily and unconnected with the organization's formal appraisal system, there is no reason for both parties not to be entirely frank with each other. Managers often report that some of their comments to subordinates began, "Well, I hesitated to bring this up, but one thing I've noticed is . . ." Subordinates are far more willing to accept distasteful information when they know that the manager's purpose in passing it along is to help the subordinate increase effectiveness and eliminate any career anchors that are impeding progress.

Trust between the two parties is required. What often emerges is the development of a much higher level of trust and confidence in each other following one round of the complete IMD process. Once the individual and his boss have talked turkey, shot straight, and worked together to strengthen the subordinate's current and future organizational contributions, it is far easier for that trust level to continue in the future when sensitive situations prohibit the full disclosure of information. "Trust me on this," the manager can say, and the subordinate will.

The final step in this first meeting is to select the single item on which the subordinate will concentrate development energy. In the absence of an item that clearly provokes consensus regarding its urgency, the pair can select an element that both agree is important to job success and where both agree that room for improved performance exists.

It may turn out that instead of one specific item listed on the IMD form, the two of them come up with a different area that has emerged in their discussion as important for the individual to work on. No problem. The only caution is to make sure that it is small enough so that a reasonable degree of change can be achieved in a few months and that it is defined specifically enough that both parties know exactly what the current status is and what will be different once the individual has successfully developed.

Creating the Development Plan

Once they have reviewed the IMD assessment instrument, discussed the five items that each felt were the most important components of the job, and selected the one on which the subordinate will concentrate, the meeting ends. It now becomes the job of the subordinate to create a development plan.

"Think small" is the watchword here. One common temptation is to create too grand a plan to be accomplished in too short a time. The other snare is to think in terms of an annual development plan. Performance appraisal forms almost invariably set mischief afoot when they ask about an annual development plan or request information on what areas the individual needs to improve in over the next twelve months. The reason? Twelve months is too long a period of time.

The key is not to make annual development plans but instead to concentrate energy on doing a greater number of smaller things in a shorter period of time. If significant improvement cannot be achieved in an area in ninety days, then the area for concentration is too large. Break it down into its component chunks. Short-term, low goals is the key.

Constructing the Action Plan

In helping individuals figure out what the first step of their action plan should be, my advice is always the same: Find out where you are right now. No matter which area the individual and superior have agreed is the highest-priority target for development, the subordinate begins by collecting baseline data. Where do I stand right now in this area? the subordinate should be asking.

Most action plans that are successful in bringing about important and lasting change are constructed on a week-to-week basis. A week is a short enough period to remain a priority item and not be shuffled off into the "one-of-these-days" stack. Planning on a weekly basis encourages the individual constructing the plan to make a conscious decision about when to schedule the one to three hours appropriately devoted to development each week.

For the first week, and perhaps for the first two or three, the individual should take no action other than collect data on how often the developmental area arises in her job and how she handles it when it does arise. Collecting baseline data will achieve several results: It may confirm to the individual that indeed her supervisor was right when he recommended that this be an area for concentration. Awareness of the area may immediately generate ideas on how performance could be improved. Collecting baseline data will help demonstrate later that development has occurred. Whatever the developmental need may be, ultimate effectiveness will be greater if the first thing the person does is collect her own data to confirm that this is an area that requires some attention.

Once the data describing the nature and extent of the developmental need have been gathered, the next step in the development process is to create the action plan. Again, working on the basis of a week-to-week plan maintains an urgency for action while allowing activities to be broken down into workable pieces.

Management Commitment

After the initial meeting where the assessments of the IMD instrument are reviewed and the selection of a target area for improvement is made, it falls appropriately to the subordinate to create the action plan. During the assessment meeting or later when she is actively constructing the plan, she may need to ask her supervisor for suggestions on the steps she might take that would produce change in an area. The supervisor can freely make any suggestions, but the responsibility for developing a systematic, logical plan is the subordinate's. The supervisor's appropriate role is first to bless the plan: to review it, ask questions, make suggestions for improvements, provide counsel and advice. The other responsibility is to fund the plan by providing whatever resources are needed for the plan to be carried out.

The resources required are frequently but never exclusively financial. If the individual needs to attend a training program or educational experience, the funds will need to be allocated. If the individual needs to purchase a book or computer software to learn skills, somebody will need to write the check. If an offsite visit to another operation is required, somebody will have to spring for the trip.

The more important resource required is time. First, the supervisor will need to commit personal time for any checkpoints during the action plan period and in a final review at the end. Second, the individual who is carrying out the action plan has another task added to her list. She is in the position of needing to drop something that's currently on the list or take the development plan on as another "do-more-with-less" opportunity. Either way, how the individual is to find the time needs to be made explicit, particularly if the project is weighty and no existing work can be passed off or delayed.

Another resource, and frequently the most difficult, is arranging opportunities. If an employee and manager agree that an area of deficiency that must be addressed is "Faces and resolves conflicts," just keeping track of the conflict situations one finds oneself in and how they are handled isn't enough, nor is adding a training program in conflict resolution to the mix going to result in complete plan. What must happen is that the individual needs the opportunity to face and resolve conflict so that she can learn how to do it and start doing it better. One resource the manager may need to make arrangements to provide is situations rife with conflict for the subordinate to handle. While purposely generating conflict in order to allow her the chance to resolve it may be asking too much, the manager must still look for situations where conflict is a common element. Perhaps a short-term assignment of helping with customer complaints or negotiating grievances with the union might provide the opportunity.

The subordinate creates the plan; the manager blesses the plan; the subordinate then goes to work.

Using Training Experiences for Development

If attendance at a training program is part of the individual's development plan, whether it is a half-day course delivered by the organization's training officer or attendance at a six-week, university-based executive development program, there are several guidelines for making training coursework experiences generate the maximum return on investment. First, training should never be scheduled as one of the first activities in the plan. At the very beginning, most learners don't know what they need to learn. They have no internally tested data that tells them that, yes, this really is an area I need to learn something about and do something different in.

It is the latter phrase, "do something different," that is far more important than the former, "learn something about." The objective of a development plan is to change behavior, not to increase knowledge. A manager has no interest in whether a salesman can list the steps involved in prospecting for customers or pass a test in how to make productive sales calls. The goal is for him to prospect effectively and make productive sales calls. It may well be true that in order to do this he will have to learn what the steps are, but the objective is not to change what he knows; it is to change what he does.

What is it, as a result of the training program, that the individual will be able to do that he is not now able to do? That is the question to ask of training programs—not, What will he learn? not, What will he appreciate? but, What will he do differently? Without some initial data on what the individual is doing right now, it is difficult to formulate worthwhile behavioral change objectives.

While it may seem obvious, the next step in choosing the educational or training experience is to select the program best suited for meeting the needs of the learner. In some organizations, attendance at a multiweek university-based executive development program is a perquisite that has nothing to do with any identified developmental need. If an organization always sends every new director-level appointee to a strategic management program, acknowledge it (but still work with the individual to get the greatest benefit; even vacations can be learning experiences).

Too often, the selection of the program to attend is determined by the flyer that most recently went across the manager's desk. But likelihood is remote that an identified developmental need will arise just as a brochure for exactly the right training program arrives.

The most useful source for identifying both specific training and educational programs and worthwhile suggestions for on-the-job development is Personnel Decisions, Inc.'s *Successful Manager's Handbook*.[12] This 800-page manual is invaluable in matching the right program with the right person, particularly because all of its listings are tied directly to PDI's Profiler competencies, making it easier to match the skill development need with the best offering.

Another recommendation for using training effectively is to make arrangements that as soon as the individual returns from the training experience he be required to teach the main points, key concepts, and critical techniques to a group of colleagues. Sharing the learning experience maximizes the investment that the organization makes in the individual. More important, anyone who attends a training program with the knowledge that he is going to have to sift the wheat from the chaff and then serve the wheat to a group of colleagues will be a far more active participant in the learning process than will be someone who is just being dipped in the vat in the hope that some change will result.

The need for the manager and the subordinate to conduct a postprogram assessment is obvious but often ignored. More subtle, and perhaps even more important, for maximizing the value someone gets from attending a training program is always to conduct a preprogram assessment: writing out her objectives, calling the facilitator, and asking if those objectives will be met. They will be.

Concluding the Action Plan

During the period that the individual is actively working on achieving the action plan, he and the supervisor will usually have regular meetings, scheduled at the time the plan was created by the individual and blessed by the supervisor, to keep the supervisor up to date on the individual's progress, raise any red flags about failures to make progress or get needed resources, and enable the supervisor to meet his coaching responsibilities. Having prescheduled meetings also helps ensure, in a not-too-subtle way, that the development action plan will not get lost in the day-to-day shuffle of crises and high-priority distractions.

When the final event in the plan has been concluded, it is important for the individual and the superior to review what was done with particular reference to the IMD item that triggered the decision to concentrate development activity here. Is Jerry now regularly initiating friendly actions? Is Lorraine more willing to face and resolve conflict, and has she built her skill in doing so?

There is no need for any written assessment or any amendment to the performance appraisal other than a note in the manager's critical incident file about the successful completion so that when performance appraisal time rolls around again, the details will not be forgotten. With a successful development experience under their belt, the individual and the manager can then move on to the next item. As they proceed, the tangible action plan document will probably become less important as their skills in development increase.

Organization Development Efforts

The recommendations made in this chapter on individual management development concentrate on the often neglected one-on-one, supervisor-subordinate development process. On an organizationwide basis, an abundance of efforts can be undertaken to increase the overall effectiveness of organization members. Organizations like Weyerhauser and Motorola have become renowned for creating their own internal universities; General Electric sees its Work-Out and action learning programs as fundamental to achieving strategic objectives. But too often overlooked in performance appraisal is the question of what one manager can do working with one subordinate to bring about genuine individual development. The answer is, "An enormous amount." Following the recommendations in this chapter will make it a reality, regardless of any broader organizational efforts.

Notes

1. Private conversation with author.
2. Michael M. Lombardo and Robert W. Eichinger, *Twenty-Two Ways to*

Develop Leadership in Staff Managers (Greensboro, N.C.: Center for Creative Leadership, 1990).

3. Michael Lombardo and Robert Eichinger, *Eighty-Eight Assignments for Development in Place* (Greensboro, N.C.: Center for Creative Leadership, 1989).

4. PDI's list of competencies appears in *Successful Manager's Handbook* (Minneapolis: Personnel Decisions, 1996).

5. Brian O'Reilly, "360 Feedback Can Change Your Life," *Fortune*, October 17, 1994.

6. Information is drawn from Robert McGarvey and Scott Smith, "When Workers Rate the Boss," *Training* (March 1993): 34.

7. Michael M. Lombardo and Robert W. Eichinger, Voices User's Guide (Greensboro, N.C.: Center for Creative Leadership, 1994).

8. Susan Gebelein, "Multi-Rater Performance Appraisal" (presentation at SHRM National Conference, 1994).

9. Joyce Dean, "Managing," *Fortune*, December 19, 1993, p. 83.

10. Jane A. Layman, "360° Feedback Can Turn on You," *Fortune*, November 28, 1994, p. 45.

11. Gebelein, "Multi-Rater Performance Appraisal."

12. *Successful Manager's Handbook.*

Chapter 14
Pay and Performance Appraisal

A survey of 106 industrial psychologists identified the top ten uses for performance appraisal data.[1] Although the information generated by appraisals was typically used for multiple purposes, in order of importance performance appraisals are used for:

1. Salary administration
2. Performance feedback
3. Identifying individual strengths and weaknesses
4. Documenting personnel decisions
5. Recognition of individual performance
6. Identifying poor performance
7. Assisting in goal identification
8. Promotion decisions
9. Retention or termination of personnel
10. Evaluating goal achievement

As might have been predicted, salary administration was the primary use for performance appraisal data. However, cautions Edward E. Lawler III, a leading researcher on pay and performance, "Unless performance appraisal can be done well, it is foolish for an organization to tie the performance appraisal system to the pay system. The positive advantages of tying it to pay are more than wiped out by the potential negatives of tying pay to a poorly done performance appraisal."[2]

Organizational Reward Norms

The relationship between employer and employee can be viewed in its simplest form as an exchange relationship: Employees exchange their time and talent for organizational rewards.[3] The nature of this exchange relationship between employer and employee can be viewed in one of four possible ways. In pure form, each leads to a significantly different reward distribution system:

1. *Profit maximization.* The objective of each party is to maximize its net gain, regardless of how the other party fares. A profit-maximizing company attempts to pay the least amount of salaries and wages while attempting to extract maximum effort. Conversely, a profit-maximizing employee seeks maximum rewards, regardless of the organization's financial well-being, and leaves the organization as soon as a better economic deal is offered. The obvious examples of the *profit maximization norm* are the sweatshop on one hand and the striking labor union that holds out for a lavish contract settlement that threatens the employer with bankruptcy.

2. *Equity.* According to the *reward equity norm*, rewards should be allocated in proportion to contributions: Those who contribute the most should be paid the most. Basic principles of fairness and justice drive the equity norm. Common examples exist in almost every organization whose compensation procedures include some form of pay-for-performance, competency-based, or skill-based pay.

3. *Equality.* The *reward equality norm* calls for rewarding all employees equally, regardless of their comparative contributions. The best example is the union shop, where each worker receives exactly the same wage, regardless of any variations in production, seniority, or other factor.

4. *Need.* This norm calls for distributing rewards according to employees' needs rather than their contributions. While essentially a Marxist formulation, this norm might well work successfully in a family-owned and -operated business.

Conflicts regarding the compensation system frequently arise over the fairness of reward allocations because of disagreement about norms. To be effective, the reward system at a minimum must be based on clear and consensual norms.

Most organizations subscribe primarily to the *reward equity* norm. The theory that if an organization identifies good performance and then awards bigger paychecks to the good performers than to their weaker brethren, the organization will increase the amount of good performance, is certainly not new. The concept was codified in 1913. Educational researcher Edward L. Thorndike observed that a cat dropped in a small box with a secret trip lever that would open a door behaved wildly and randomly until it accidently tripped the lever and escaped. From then on, he observed, every time he put the cat back in the box it instantly returned to the lever. From that unpretentious observation came Thorndike's Law of Effect: Behavior with favorable consequences tends to be repeated, while behavior with unfavorable consequences tends to disappear.[4] From a cat in a box developed the key concept of contemporary salary administration: pay for performance or merit pay. Reward what you want, and you'll get more of it. Simplicity itself.

From the original simplicity of a cat in a box, the technique of salary administration became vastly more complex about thirty years later. For General Foods in the 1940s, Edward Hay concocted a corporate wedding cake of twenty to forty job tiers, each with a strict pay range, that mirrors the hierarchy exactly. The system assigns each job a number of points based on its level in the hierarchy. This scheme, dubbed the Hay system, or some variant on it, has been used by almost every large organization for the past fifty years to administer salaries. In describing the approach, *Fortune* writer Jaclyn Fierman observes that companies are eagerly seeking to replace the clunky Hay system because it accentuates the turf consciousness that most companies are trying to eradicate. The essential problem is that employees are urged by superiors "to be creative, entrepreneurial, boundaryless team players, but are being paid like felt-hatted organization men of the Fifties."[5]

The frustration with contemporary pay systems results from the attempt of compensation systems to quantify and set pay for the competency requirements of jobs—but it is not jobs but people who are paid. As Lyle and Signe Spencer explain in their book, *Competence at Work*, numerous issues today indicate the need for an approach to compensation that moves beyond the rigid classification and stratification of the Hay system and its clones:[6]

- ► The inability to attract people of higher competence to the organization
- ► The perception that people with certain competencies add more value to the firm than those without them in identical jobs, even when the possession of these competencies cannot be directly measured in organizational outputs (the ability to speak several languages, for example)
- ► The perception that job-based pay systems are becoming meaningless because change is occurring so fast that the traditional concept of a stable job is disappearing. One significant workplace transition is the replacement of jobs with roles. Organizations are realizing that the value added to the firm depends more on the competencies of the individual doing the job than it does on any definitions and demarcations contained in a traditional job description.
- ► The need for incentives to motivate, enhance, and retain state-of-the-art skills. Often an employee's future value is worth significantly more than his present position or performance.

▸ The need to redirect the emphasis of the traditional job evaluation system away from the things the organization is trying to reverse or avoid—empire building, for example, or big budgets. These traditionally win large numbers of factor points in conventional job evaluation systems but are the opposite of the transformation that many organizations are trying to achieve.

▸ The need to compensate equitably knowledge workers who don't manage many people or assets

▸ The perception that highly structured compensation systems promote bureaucracy: rigid hierarchies, narrow job descriptions, and restrictive job classifications that reduce organizational flexibility and are incompatible with the movement toward flat organizations and empowered employees

The ultimate frustration with traditional job-based pay systems is that they treat organization members as fungible commodities instead of as individuals who are valued for their differences, diversity, initiative, creativity, flexibility, and ability to change as organizational needs demand. Traditional job evaluation will not go away, but the future of compensation systems will involve far more than simply computing how much a specific job is worth to the organization based on objective and quantifiable point factors, and then paying the job incumbent a given amount, with variations determined almost exclusively by his time in grade and his supervisor's assessment of how well he did what he was told.

What Pay Can Do

Before exploring how pay and performance should be tied together (and whether that tying is in itself a good idea) let's back up and ask an ancient question: Does money motivate?

The world's developed countries are, in the fullest sense of the word, cash societies, as a Commerce Clearing House primer on wage and salary administration explains.[7] The distinction is not between cash and credit but between cash (including credit) and barter—the trading of goods and services without the use of money as a go-between.

It is beyond dispute that in a cash society, every individual must have cash (or the means to obtain it) to survive. Money talks, we say, and indeed it does. What it says is, "Without me, almost nothing else matters." While a company's employees may reflect a diversity of talent, color, background, and satisfaction with their jobs, they share this common denominator: With few exceptions, none can afford to be unemployed for long. In a cash society, each of us must have a source of cash.

So money is a priority—a basic need. But once that need has been met and essential necessities satisfied, money's leverage becomes trickier and more complex. Research has produced evidence that there are certain areas in which money has a significant impact:

▸ *Hiring people.* Assuming two different employers are offering similar work, the amount of money paid in salary, commission, or wages is probably the single biggest determinant of an individual's choice of which offer to accept. If it is high enough, pay will attract good job applicants.

▸ *Retaining people.* Money, in sufficient amounts, will keep people on the payroll. It may not motivate them, but it will make them reluctant to leave.

▸ *Motivating people.* Now the research starts getting interesting. Money can be a powerful motivator of performance, depending on how it's used. If it is used as an expression of recognition, it has the power to generate more and better effort. That's the whole idea behind the merit increase. Particularly when money comes in the form of a genuine, unscheduled, unanticipated merit increase that reinforces specific and observable exceptional performance, pay will be a powerful motivator—doubly powerful, in fact, because it provides both a reinforcer to the lucky recipient and an incentive to everyone else who discovers that this employer reinforces good performance with generous wads of moolah.

▸ *Avoiding dissatisfaction.* Here's the flip side of motivation. If managers can't get genuine motivation, they would at least like to have people who are not discontent. Avoiding dissatisfaction is a worthy and meritorious goal: Employees who are dissatisfied waste time, money, and physical and emotional energy. They don't work as hard as they might, and they quit when the organization would prefer that they stay. And if they become gravely dissatisfied with their paychecks, they can usually find a union organizer with a shoulder to cry on. Pay, when perceived as unfair, is a frequent source of organizational malaise. Keeping pay fair inside the organization (*internal equity*) reduces dissatisfaction. Keeping pay competitive with what other employers are paying (*external equity*) helps avoid resignations and dissatisfaction among those who stay.

What Pay Can't Do

An old film illustrating the basic concepts of reinforcement theory provides a classic example of what pay can't do: generate happiness. In a seven-second vignette we see a manager beaming with pride, who sits behind his desk wrapping up his annual appraisal of an employee's performance.

"And that's why," he says to her, smiling as he slides the form across his desk, "I'm able to award you this 6 percent raise."

The subordinate reacts as if stricken. She slams her hand on the desk, starts to stomp out, then whirls around and howls, "You call *that* a raise!"

We may be able to eliminate dissatisfaction with pay. We may even be able to influence motivation. But we cannot make people happy. No matter how big the increase, it's never enough. And even if somebody is thrilled at the moment, within a day she'll probably decide that in truth she was underpaid all along and that the organization's apparent munificent increase actually served merely to make her whole.

Satisfaction and Dissatisfaction

It has been almost forty years since Fred Herzberg declared that the opposite of "job satisfaction" is not "job dissatisfaction." It's "no job satisfaction." There's no semantic sleight-of-hand involved. In simple terms, the absence of dissatisfaction is not the same as the presence of satisfaction. The factors that control one are significantly different from the factors that affect the other. Job satisfaction is mainly a function of the work itself: the opportunities for achievement and accomplishment, the amount of discretion the individual exercises, recognition for achievement, real responsibility, and the opportunity for learning and growth. Job dissatisfaction results from entirely different factors: primarily deficiencies in working conditions, benefits, salary, supervision, interpersonal relations, and status.

Awarding a person a salary increase will generally not escalate the individual's satisfaction with the job unless the pay raise is clearly a true merit increase awarded as a means of providing tangible recognition for genuine achievement. As long as the increase is not so meager as to be perceived as insulting—the organizational equivalent of nickel-tipping an arrogant waiter—what the pay raise will successfully do is remove a significant amount of any unhappiness a person may be feeling. The content of the job is unaltered; only the job context has been changed. The conditions of work have been ameliorated; the work itself remains the same.

A pay raise will generally not motivate the employee to produce more work or better work. Genuine merit increases have the potential to motivate, but these types of pay changes will not:

- The regularly scheduled and anticipated annual increase
- A cost-of-living increase, whether scheduled or not
- An increase in the commission paid to salespeople
- An increase in the piece rate paid for piecework
- An increase in a regular bonus paid to employees

If we label these "merit increases," will that work? No. Dagwood will be delighted to receive a raise of any kind, whatever label Mr. Dithers may put on it. His dissatisfaction with his pay may be completely obliterated. "But if the raise is not truly in recognition of an unusual effort, it will not motivate the employee to go out and make an unusual effort."[8]

Pay for Performance

What does pay pay for? What are we purchasing with the money we put out in pay? With any other corporate expenditure, it is relatively easy to answer the question, What did we get for the money we spent? But once we move much away from the purchase of direct labor at an hourly rate, or a sales commission based on number of widgets sold, or a Frederick Taylor scientific management piece-rate scheme, we struggle to make tangible the quid pro quo of compensation. Just what is it that salary dollars buy?

One expert on organizational reward systems proposes that there are three general criteria for the distribution of organizational rewards:[9]

1. *Performance results.* These are tangible outcomes such as individual, group, or organizational performance; quality and quantity of performance; or achievement of goals.
2. *Performance competencies, actions, and behaviors.* These are the factors that relate to how the individual does the job or how the results are achieved. Such items as teamwork, cooperation, risk taking, communication skills, and creativity fall into this category.
3. *Nonperformance considerations.* What is rewarded here are such customary or contractual considerations as the nature of the work, the level in the hierarchy, the amount of seniority, equity, budget responsibilities, number of people supervised, tenure, and other components unrelated to performance.

Another way to understand the variables at work in a compensation system is to recognize that, similar to the scheme described above, there are three key factors at play in any compensation system: job role requirements, person competencies, and results produced.

Traditional pay systems base compensation primarily on *job role*: the job's position in the organizational hierarchy, the technical knowledge required of job incumbents, the amount of problem solving required, the complexity of decisions to be made, the number of people supervised, and the dollar value of assets managed.

Pay-for-performance procedures supplement the base salary computed through job role analyses with additional pay for *organizational outputs*. In addition to the base pay computed on the basis of what the job itself is worth to the organization based on its technical demands, competitive or market requirements, and other nonperformer factors, the organization grants additional pay based on performer outputs: actual performance results, economic benefits generated for the enterprise. The pure example is the sales commission; the common example is the awarding of a higher-than-average merit increase for the exemplary achievement of all objectives set in an MBO-type system. Employees get paid based on their performance and in direct relation to the results produced.

Finally, competency-based systems pay for individual characteristics: the ability to add economic value to the enterprise at some time in the future. The possession of any particular competency (e.g., the ability to work cooperatively with others, a strong orientation toward achievement, the skills required to persuade and influence, the ability to speak Korean, the possession of expert-level technical UNIX knowledge, the willingness to share that information) may not produce an immediate economic benefit to the organization, but it is an organizational asset. Competency-based pay is compensation for individual characteristics, for skills or competencies over and above the pay a job or organizational role itself commands and the merit increase for actual results achieved. The presence of competencies does not generate organizational revenues today, but the absence of them guarantees a dim future.[10]

Why Merit Pay Systems Fail

Pay for performance, competency-based pay, pay for skills—all equity-based reward systems—frequently encounter difficulties in their administration. The cause usually lies not in the concept but in its implementation, execution, and administration by both line managers and compensation specialists.

Despite the soundness of the theories behind various equity approaches, experience demonstrates that the various approaches do not work with the elegant simplicity that the theories supporting them suggest. Small discriminations in salary treatment are made by managers regardless of major differences in performance. Even when managers do make salary adjustment discriminations, they are often based on factors other than the individual's performance—for example, future potential, length of service, recompense for lack of promotional opportunities, or perceived need to catch up.

In "How to Ruin Motivation with Pay," researcher W. Clay Hammer identifies many of the factors that cause merit pay or equity-based systems to flounder in the attempt to produce high motivation and performance:[11]

1. *Pay is not perceived as being related to job performance*. Many individuals are unable to perceive much relationship between how hard they work and how much they earn. In a study of 600 middle and lower-level managers, Edward Lawler found virtually no relationship between their pay and their rated performance. Those who were most highly motivated to perform their jobs effectively were characterized by two attitudes: pay was important to them, and they believed that good job performance would result in higher pay.

Several factors account for the lack of connectedness perceived between pay and performance. In some cases, the rewards are deferred payments, like stock options, that won't be realized for such a long time that their ability to motivate current performance diminishes. Second, people feel that the goals against which their performance is being evaluated are unclear or unrealistic. In one study, 86 percent of bosses claimed that goal attainment determined the amount of merit increase recommended; only 36 percent of their subordinates saw goal attainment as having much impact on their raise.

Finally, the lack of information produced by secrecy in which so many compensation systems are shrouded leads managers to conclude that their pay increases have little to do with their performance.

2. *Performance ratings are seen as biased*. Although most individuals in the organization may agree with the pay-for-performance theory, many are dissatisfied with their supervisor's actual evaluation of their performance. The cause of the problem is not with the system itself but with the lack of trust between rater and ratee. The situation is exacerbated by the fact that the supervisor's role in determining pay increases is a transparent reminder to the employee that she is dependent on the supervisor for rewards.

3. *Rewards are not viewed as rewards*. A combination of factors is at work here. First, what the manager may consider to be generous reward, the employee may see as an insulting pittance.

Second, employees will be skeptical of organizational equity when they perceive the merit increase to be unfair relative to their performance during the appraisal period. Even when the rater and ratee agree on the performance rating, the individual may well feel that the reward his supervisor has recommended is inappropriate given the quality of performance that both see the same way.

A related problem arises when an employee who is happy with his pay increase discovers that others in the organization whose performance is noticeably inferior have received a similar increase, or if he believes that other people whose performance is at the same level as his own are receiving higher increases. Lawler recommends that at a minimum managers explain to their employees how salary raises were determined (for example, 50 percent based on cost of living and 50 percent on merit).

Industrial psychologist Herbert H. Meyer concluded on the basis of his research that 90 percent of General Electric managers rated themselves above average. "The fact that almost everyone thinks he is an above average performer," he said, "causes most of our problems with merit pay plans. Since the salary increases most people get do not reflect superior performance, the effects of the actual pay increases on motivation are likely to be more negative than positive. The majority of people feel discriminated against because, obviously, management does not recognize their true worth."[12]

4. *Trust and openness about merit increases is low.* If managers treat every aspect of the compensation as secret; if most information about the way the system comes through rumor, chatter, and water-cooler gossip; if managers are not capable of explaining the specific determinants of the amount of a salary increase; if employees are overlooked when eligibility dates come and go; then organization members will assume the worst about the integrity of the system.

Developing an Effective Compensation Formula

Narrowly defined job descriptions and tightly structured pay scales may have worked well in yesterday's job market when it was important to define how the cogs fit into the wheel, explains compensation writer Shari Caudron.[13] Today with downsizing and the compression in middle management leaving fewer job slots and promotional opportunities, the emphasis has shifted in many organizations to making employees business partners by involving them in sharing both the financial risks and the rewards of doing business. The traditional annual increase, based on a combination of cost-of-living adjustment based on the annual rate of inflation plus a small and loosely defined merit increase premium, is being replaced by a new term: *variable pay.*

Shifting away from standard annual pay raises, variable pay links compensation to individual, team, and company performance. The new variable-pay plans keep fixed costs in line while rewarding employees in good years or for achieving corporate goals. With variable pay, a portion of the employee's paycheck is put at risk. This means that if certain business goals aren't met, the pay will not rise above the base wage or salary. Merit increases drive up base pay, thus increasing retirement costs, since pension benefits are typically pegged to base pay. Since bonuses usually don't count toward traditional pension formula—they are not added to base pay but have to be re-earned every year—they hold down fixed costs while providing an incentive for superb results.

A recent survey of 1,350 large firms by the consulting firm Towers

Perrin found that 41 percent offered some form of variable pay to employees below top executive ranks, up from 35 percent the year before.[14] A similar survey of over 2,000 U.S. companies by Hewitt Associates, another major consulting firm, reported that since 1988, the number of U.S. concerns offering variable pay—chiefly bonuses—to all salaried employees has jumped from 47 to 68 percent.[15]

What should be measured and rewarded? Opinions vary, as do the actual formulas companies use. Most use a combination of the performance of the entire company, business unit performance, and individual results.

AT&T, before its 1995 restructuring, had almost ten years of experience with variable-pay plans. Following its loss of monopoly status, the company moved to a plan that held down base pay compared with competitors but significantly increased bonus potentials. Bonuses were linked to AT&T's benchmark for measuring corporate performance, Economic Value Added (EVA), a complex and sophisticated measure of real earnings. Managers earned the first part of their bonus based on their individual or team performance and, depending on salary level, got a 5 to 10 percent bonus based on those results. The second component was based on the performance of the profit center or business unit, each of the thirty-five or so with an individual EVA target. Performance of the profit center can add another third of the total bonus.

Finally, AT&T's overall corporate performance kicks in to the variable-pay computation. If the company hit its EVA target, every manager got a 7.3 percent bonus, regardless of what bonus might have been earned by individual, team, or business unit performance. If it greatly exceeded the target, bonuses could reach 11 percent, giving the average manager a total of a 20 percent bonus on top of salary and top performers almost 30 percent. "If this were a sport, we'd be thinking about giving players a share of gate receipts," an AT&T spokesman said about the approach. "The idea is to encourage people to think of the enterprise as a profit-and-loss organization. If it succeeds, I have a share in that success. If it's failing, that will also have an impact on my pay, so I'll try to fix something quickly if it looks like it's not going well."[16]

Other organizations recognize that most managers are fairly impotent in their ability to have an impact or overall corporate results. General Mills, manufacturer of Wheaties and Betty Crocker brands, ties half its annual bonuses to business unit results, the other half to individual manager performance. A marketing manager commanding a $75,000 base pay could earn about $90,000 at a competitor. If his product and division results match the industry average, he's looking at a $10,000 bonus—still about $5,000 shy of the industry position. But if his product ranks in the industry's top 10 percent in earnings growth and return on capital, he'll collect a bonus of $40,500. That will bring total compensation to $115,500, about 28 percent above the market average.

Jan Vernon, corporate compensation manager at Texas Instruments, notes that the company, which has long had a profit-sharing plan, is moving aggressively toward variable pay. Beginning in 1996, half of TI's profit-sharing bonanza will be paid out in cash instead of putting it all in a tax-deferred account for the employee's later use. The company is also allocating more of its total compensation budget into variable pay and letting its business units decide how the specific allocations to individuals will be made. Wafer fabrication plants are linking pay increases to productivity goals, while the defense side of the business is keying a portion of pay to team performance.

Competencies or performance factors—how the manager went about accomplishing the results—are considered usually base pay factors. In most variable-pay schemes, only results count. Steve Gross, Hay Group's national director of variable compensation, argues that the best base pay systems include measures of behavioral competency in addition to the job factor components measured in traditional compensation schemes. The pay-at-risk component of the reward system should be tied to accomplishments, he says.[17]

What is the appropriate allocation between base pay and variable pay? In most organizations, the higher the individual is in the organization, the greater the percentage of pay at risk will be. At Chicago-based Ameritech Corp., all 68,000 employees are compensated using a variable-pay approach. "We believe that when the company does well, our employees should do well," according to Harry Malone, director of compensation. "Conversely, if they aren't contributing to the company's success, their compensation ought to reflect that as well."

Every Ameritech employee has a set of target incentives, and the higher one is in the organization, the more that total pay is allocated toward the variable segment. This ranges from a low of 5 percent of pay for entry-level jobs to 35 percent at senior levels.

And what about the allocation between individual and team effort? At one automobile company, the allocation is fifty-fifty. Of that segment of pay that is variable, half came as a result of individual competencies, while the other half depended on how well the team as a whole performed. At Ameritech, Malone explains, "Most people have a split of 60 percent for team achievement and 40 percent for individual achievement."

Like so much else in the sensitive area of finagling with people's paychecks, challenges abound. An emphasis on team rewards risks alienating individual contributors. But then, say some TQM gurus, individuals don't really control more than 10 to 20 percent of what they do on their jobs anyway.

The key to developing a variable-pay plan that works, according to Robert Greene of the Lincolnshire, Illinois, firm of James and Associates, is to evaluate and reward employees by three perspectives:

1. How they excel as individuals
2. How they function as part of a primary performance unit
3. Where they fit in as citizens of the corporation[18]

While the exact ratios of team versus individual rewards, results versus competencies, and base pay versus the amount at risk depend on the specific business objectives the company is trying to achieve, variable-pay strategies seem to be the replacements to the rigid job classification systems whose labyrinthine taxonomies many organizations are eager to replace.

When Should Pay Be Discussed?

In simplest terms, should an individual's salary increase be discussed in the same meeting as the performance evaluation discussion? Or should performance appraisal and compensation changes be discussed together? Some recent research supports the joint discussion. When pay is discussed together with the performance appraisal, researchers found, both the supervisor and the subordinate tend to take the appraisal more seriously and exchange better information about performance expectations and performance results.[19] The same research also suggests that most individuals want pay and performance discussions to be linked, so that individuals will have a chance to understand how the performance appraisal system affects their pay.

On the other hand, the researchers found that when pay and performance discussions are combined, little attention is paid to issues of career development and personal growth and development needs. The focus is almost entirely on past performance and how that resulted in the amount of increase awarded. There may also be a tendency on the individuals' part to withhold negative data about performance, to set lower performance goals for the future, and to be more conservative about what he feels he can accomplish.

Particularly when the performance appraisal rating is only one of the component of the ultimate "How much?" decision, separating the two discussions can be beneficial. While it be administratively cumbersome, concentrating the performance appraisal discussion on the appraisal itself and assigning the compensation discussion to a separate meeting can ensure maximum mileage from both.

For example, IDS Financial Services and Weyerhauser Co. insist on keeping pay and performance reviews separate. Harley-Davidson began holding performance reviews at year-end and merit increase reviews on employees' anniversaries. When the two are combined, says Margaret Crawford, training director for the motorcycle manufacturer, "money, rather than feedback becomes the driver of the discussion." Other opinions are equally strong. It is awkward not to tie the two issues, argues David Monteith, vice president of human resources for Dress Barn, Inc., since pay is based on performance. "It's logical to talk about it in the same conversation using the same process," he says. David Lynn of consulting firm Blessing/White says employees aren't open to feedback if the focus of the conversation is on what they are worth.[20]

Pay and Performance Appraisal Results

The compensation system often provides for pay to be directly tied to performance appraisal results. Many organizations have a published schedule that indicates the amount of salary increase to be awarded based on the combination of the individual's performance appraisal grade and position in the minimum-midpoint-maximum range for a job. If little flexibility is allowed, managers frequently are tempted to skew the performance appraisal rating to justify the amount of salary increase they want to award rather than candidly calling the performance as it is and letting the resulting rating govern the salary increase.

A further difficulty arises when the system ties the amount of salary increase directly to the performance appraisal rating. Consider the manager faced with making compensation decisions for two employees, both of whom are solidly and accurately assessed to have performed at the Superior level. One of the two is fairly new to the job, has enormous potential, has put in remarkably long hours, and has devoted an enormous amount of time to self-development in order to perform at the superior level. The other is exactly the opposite. Gifted but lazy, he has almost effortlessly coasted to his Superior rating. Assuming that both are at the same point in the salary range, do both deserve the identical amount of increase?

What if the first employee speaks Japanese and the company has confidential plans to move into the Japanese market in the next year or two? Japanese-language skills, now extraneous, will become critically important. Should this currently irrelevant competency be rewarded now in hopes that the employee will be persuaded to remain employed until the day when his skills will be needed?

And what if the second employee is black, in a field like microbiology or electrical engineering where blacks are scarce and the constant targets of efforts to recruit them away? Race may be irrelevant to quality of performance, but should the company's commitment to maintaining workforce diversity rationalize a bigger increase than the performance appraisal rating would suggest in order to facilitate retention?

One fairly consistent finding among performance appraisal researchers is that leniency and rating inflation is the most common appraisal error. Given the natural desire on the part of most managers to avoid conflict and avoid salary dissatisfaction, it is tempting for them to rate everyone Superior, award the resulting increases, and get on with the job.

Organizations often force raters to come up with particular distributions of ratings in order to avoid inflation and equal ratings for all employees, notes Edward Lawler.[21] "Ranking and forced distribution are commonly used. Ranking is particularly bad, because it creates differences that cannot be defended and ignores the absolute level of performance. Forced distribution is better, if it is well-designed and applied to a large enough group of individuals."

The key issue in forced distribution is what kind of distribution to force. The most obvious distribution is the bell-shaped curve. In a rating scheme with five possible performance outcomes (for example, Marginal, Fair, Competent, Superior, and Distinguished), raters will be instructed that 5 percent of all employees must be assigned to the Marginal and Distinguished categories, 15 percent each to Fair and Superior, and the remaining 60 percent to Competent. Requiring managers to force-fit people into a bell-shaped curve assumes a normal distribution, and a normal distribution assumes randomness, but performance in organizations is not random. As any manager who has suffered under a forced distribution system will point out, it is highly influenced by selection, training, and the other developmental activities that the manager has engaged in. Although it does achieve statistically balanced performance distribution, it applies only to large, randomly selected populations, not the carefully selected populations that exist in every organizational unit.

Furthermore, if the forced distribution scheme means placing half the employees on the "good" side and the rest on the "bad" side (as would result if managers were required to identify the top 15 percent, the next 35 percent, the next 35 percent, and the bottom 15 percent), it will cause a lot of individuals to feel poorly treated. As Lawler points out, "It is almost impossible to defend breaking up a distribution like this one in the middle. It becomes a very emotional issue and what separates someone who is just over the line from someone who is just short of it is hard to specify and communicate. Around the middle is where most people fall."

Rigid ranking systems have their supporters. T. J. Rodgers, celebrity CEO of Cypress Semiconductor Corporation, is adamant about the importance of using a rigid ranking system in allocating performance rewards: "Managers shouldn't expect outstanding performance unless they're prepared to reward outstanding performance."[22] His chief gripe is that managers aren't scientific about rating their staff; they may be able to identify the real stars and the worst laggards, but the vast majority of people get lost somewhere in the middle.

At Cypress a ranking committee, supplemented with sophisticated performance software data, reviews every possible two-employee comparison and determines who was the superior performer for the year. The same software then reviews the ranking committee assessments and recommends appropriate merit increases, making sure that twenty quality checks are complied with. Among the checks are monotonic distribution (any group member ranked higher than another must receive a higher merit raise, thus preventing managers from taking money away from a highly paid top performer to give it to a low-paid weaker performer) and forced differentiation (the requirement of a minimum spread between the largest and smallest raises in a group).

A much easier approach may be simply to identify the extreme cases: the top 5 to 15 percent whose performance genuinely is distinguished, and the opposite 5 to 15 percent whose services the organization would be better off without. Within the middle, managers can make whatever fine tuning of salary adjustments they may feel appropriate. This tactic would ensure that the genuinely deserving are not overlooked and the truly awful are eliminated.

Providing guideline percentages may be the most effective way of influencing overall performance appraisal ratings, guarding against rating inflation, and protecting against pockets of severe strictness or leniency. Based either on what the senior management of the organization feel an appropriate distribution of performance appraisal ratings should be or based on previous years' actual distributions, the organization communicates to raters the guidelines that should be used for the distribution of ratings. For example, the personnel or corporate compensation department might advise raters that based on previous years' statistics, an appropriate distribution might be Distinguished, 3 percent; Superior, 25 percent; Competent, 60 percent; Fair, 10 percent; and Marginal, 2 percent. This provides a useful guideline for novice raters and an organizational perspective on what an appropriate distribution of performance ratings should be. Any manager who believes that she is managing a unit that deserves to vary significantly from the guidelines can be encouraged to state her case, but for the most part, the approach should find a great deal of acceptance on the part of both appraisers and appraisees. There will always be some supervisors who will resent any form of guidance and no set of guidelines will be appropriate for very small groups, but the approach is sufficiently workable to cover most situations.

Merit Reviews and the Poor Performer

How should the organization handle the individual whose performance is not good enough to justify a merit increase but isn't bad enough to terminate? Should the increase be delayed until performance improves or withheld until the next regularly scheduled appraisal? And what about an across-the-board cost-of-living adjustment? Should that be awarded?

The individual whose performance does not justify a merit increase should probably receive no salary change at all, even if part of the increase is earmarked for cost of living. The poor performer needs to get a strong message in unmistakable terms that his job performance is unacceptable, and he must improve or leave. To award any pay increase will muddy the waters, and the fact that he got a raise will remain longer and stronger in memory than any words his supervisor might have said about the need to improve.

A further argument for not giving any increase at all, including a regular cost-of-living adjustment, is that should the employee later be terminated and challenge the decision, the organization's position is made stronger by having sent a consistent message. He got a bad performance review, there may be other documented evidence of conversations putting him on notice that change must occur, and he received no salary increase when everyone else in the organization did. An employee who got a raise, even one designed exclusively as an inflation adjustment, will argue that if the organization had really been concerned about the quality of his work it wouldn't have boosted his salary.

But withholding the increase until the next regular appraisal period, typically twelve months, may be counterproductive since there is little incentive provided for immediate change and twelve months is a *long* way off. The best approach may be to withhold any salary pending a significant and sustained performance improvement but agree to review the performance, together with the salary, after a reasonable period of perhaps ninety days.

What Does the Future Hold?

The one universal area of consensus among all compensation prognosticators is that pay for performance is here to stay and will become more prevalent as the business environment becomes more competitive and employers strive to reward their top performers adequately.

Pay ranges may widen as organizations begin to acknowledge that there are significant differences between the top and the bottom performers in any job. Although there may be a 100 percent difference between the contribution delivered by the absolute best individual compared with the average or standard (but still acceptable) job incumbent, the likelihood is that the pay differential will be closer to only 20 percent. In the future, the chances are good that the spread in compensation between the best and the rest will expand.

Another pay prediction that several experts make is the withering of cafeteria-style compensation and benefit systems. While the Bureau of Labor Statistics reported a steady increase in the use of cafeteria plans in the late 1980s, analysts now see their growth slowing. "Flexible benefit plans have received substantial attention because they are a way of containing the cost of benefits," says Robert E. Sibson, retired founder of Sibson & Co., a major human resources consulting firm.[23] "But I think implementing flexible benefits for that reason has been a mistake—it's rather devious. Employees are entitled to know up front why a plan is put into effect, and those plans are put into effect usually to cut the cost of benefits."

Another consensus judgment is a reduction in programmatic compensation systems. With organizations looking for more effective approaches than intricate and elaborate Hay style systems provide, combined with the move toward broadbanding (clustering jobs into wide categories, decreasing the number of job classifications, and increasing salary ranges), combined with the fact that computers and the databases they can access are capable of providing line managers with market and competitive compensation information that until recently was available only to compensation professionals, will allow managers more authority to make pay decisions. "The information revolution has given us direct information on what competitive salaries are," says Sibson. "We don't need to conduct surveys any more. We can get that information from our employment experience day by day, fed into computers and fed out again on our jobs."

The continuing influence of total quality management approaches will have an impact on compensation systems, particularly since the underlying philosophy of TQM is sharply at odds with the pay-for-performance mantra. John Whitney, executive director of the W. Edwards Deming Center for Quality Management at the Columbia University Graduate School of Business, feels that all employees should get the same percentage merit raise because it sends out the message that everyone in the system is important. "Quibbling over whether someone should get a 4.7 percent raise or 5.1 percent is a colossal waste of time," he says. "We're not talking about very much money."[24]

With TQM's emphasis on teamwork and team performance, compensation will become even more challenging. It's difficult enough to come up with rational pay structures that everyone accepts on an individual basis; developing team compensation programs will increase the challenge enormously.

Finally, count on continuing change. As a *Fortune* magazine writer put it, "Life won't be cozy in the brave new world of pay-for-performance, but at the end of the day, you'll know more certainly than ever before that you've earned your money."[25]

How to Make a Compensation System Work

Providing the complete mechanics of designing and administering a compensation is beyond the scope of this book. But following several guidelines and understandings will help to make the performance management and appraisal system work congruently with the compensation system.

1. *Minimize secrecy.* Too often the determination about what information an employee needs about the operation of the compensation system is made on a need-to-know basis. If an individual does not have a demonstrated need for specific information about a part of the compensation system, that information is treated as confidential. One of the most important steps line managers, human resources administrators, and compensation specialists can take is to reverse that model. Instead of asking, "Does the individual have a specific need for this piece of information?" ask the reverse question: "What good business reasons exist for withholding this information?"

One discovery many companies make when they consciously expand the amount of information they provide about the mechanics and philosophy of their compensation system is that most people already knew more than the organization suspected. "We tell each of our people how the ranking committee evaluated his or her performance, the percentage merit increase awarded by the focal group leader, and how the manager adjusted the merit increase for equity," explains T. J. Rodgers about Cypress Semiconductor's sophisticated system. "Most people will accept an outcome they are unhappy with so long as they understand the logic behind it."[26]

2. *Compare the compensation plan in principle with the compensation plan in fact.* Many companies cannot specify the formula they use for giving merit increases since there is no actual formula that is being rigorously followed. Managers may be given a range in which to allocate salary changes, and the actual decisions about why Mary got an 8 percent raise while Harry got 5 percent may have little to do with their actual performance, position relative to midpoint, months since last salary action, or other policy-related issue.

Here's an easy test to determine whether the merit increase system is really rewarding merit. Ask the question, "If the company had to reduce staff by 10 percent, could the decision be made exclusively and appropriately on the basis of the last performance appraisal and merit review?"

3. *Specify the components that create the amount and percentage of the raise.* At a minimum, each employee receiving a salary increase should know what percentage of it is related to an overall cost-of-living adjustment and what percentage is directly related to merit. If some of the pay increase

was determined by results-based pay measures (pay for performance or pay for achieving objectives in an MBO-type system) and another part of the increase was based on competency-based issues (performance factors or job behaviors or how the person achieved the results), this distinction should also be made clear.

4. *If you want to use money as a motivator, then use it as a motivator.* Money motivates when it comes in significant amounts, not occasional nickels and dimes. Too often the actual dollar difference between the salary increase awarded the highest performer and that awarded to Joe Average isn't enough to feed a family of four one meal at McDonald's. Money can motivate, but pocket change merely insults.

Notes

1. Jeannette N. Cleveland, Kevin R. Murphy, and Richard E. Williams, "Multiple Uses of Performance Appraisal: Prevalence and Correlates," *Journal of Applied Psychology* (February 1989): 130–135.
2. Allan M. Mohrman, Jr., Susan M. Resnick-West, and Edward E. Lawler III, *Designing Performance Appraisal Systems* (San Francisco: Jossey-Bass, 1989), p. 175.
3. The explanation of organizational reward norms is based on Robert Kreitner and Angelo Kinicki, *Organizational Behavior*, 2nd ed. (New York: Irwin, 1992), pp. 496–497, and Jone L. Pearce and Robert H. Peters, "A Contradictory Norms View of the Employer-Employee Exchange," *Journal of Management* (Spring 1985): 19–30.
4. Edward L. Thorndike, *Educational Psychology: The Psychology of Learning*, vol. 2 (New York: Columbia University Teachers' College, 1913).
5. Jaclyn Fierman, "The Perilous New World of Fair Pay," *Fortune*, June 13, 1994, p. 57.
6. Lyle Spencer and Signe Spencer, *Competence at Work* (New York: Wiley, 1995).
7. *Wage and Salary Administration* (New York: Commerce Clearing House, 1990), sec. 4205.
8. Ibid.
9. Mary Ann Von Glinow, "Reward Strategies for Attracting, Evaluating and Retaining Professionals," *Human Resource Management* (Spring 1985): 19–30.
10. For more information on competency-based pay see Spencer and Spencer, *Competence at Work*.
11. W. Clay Hamner, "How to Ruin Motivation With Pay," *Compensation Review* (Third Quarter 1975).
12. Herbert H. Meyer, quoted in ibid.

13. Shari Caudron, "Master the Compensation Maze," *Personnel Journal* special report (June 1993).
14. Diana Kunde, "What Happened to My Raise?" *Dallas Morning News*, September 4, 1995.
15. Survey data reported in Shawn Tully, "Your Paycheck Gets Exciting," *Fortune*, November 1, 1993, p. 83.
16. Burke Stimson, quoted in Kunde, "What Happened to My Raise?"
17. Linda Thornberg, "Pay for Performance: What You Should Know," *HR Magazine* (June 1992).
18. Ibid.
19. J. B. Prince and Edward E. Lawler III, "Does Salary Discussion Hurt the Developmental Performance Appraisal?" *Organizational Behavior and Human Decision Processes*, 37 (1986): 357–375.
20. Examples from various companies from "Mixed Message," *Wall Street Journal*, November 10, 1992, p. 1.
21. Mohrmans et al., *Performance Appraisal Systems*, pp. 182–183.
22. T. J. Rodgers, "No-Excuses Management," *Harvard Business Review* (July–August 1990): 84–97.
23. "Designing a Compensation Program," interview with Robert E. Sibson, from *Compensation* (New York: Commerce Clearing House, 1991), Section 4203.
24. Fierman, "Perilous World of Fair Pay," p. 64.
25. Shawn Tully, "Your Paycheck Gets Exciting," *Fortune* (November 1, 1993): 98.
26. Rodgers, "No-Excuses Management," p. 98.

Chapter 15

Performance Appraisal and the Law

Interviewer: Have you ever had to lay anybody off?

Scott Adams (creator of "Dilbert" comic strip): No. I've tried, but unsuccessfully. It was many years ago, but there was this individual whose skills were so low that I tried to have him removed from the group. But it turned out that he had gotten sterling performance reviews for 20 years. The people in Personnel said, "Well, maybe he only does have second grade capability, but it would be impossible to lay him off: He could sue you because of all of his performance appraisals." That's when I knew that management was not for me.[1]

Since the passage of the 1964 Civil Rights Act, performance appraisals and the law have been intertwined. In the eyes of the law, a performance appraisal is an employment test. It is thus scrutinized in a manner similar to that of other aspects of the employment process: initial recruitment, selection, and hiring; promotion; compensation; and termination. As a result, the legal requirements for performance appraisal systems are similar to those for other selection tests. They must normally be based on a job analysis that allows business decisions to be made with reliability and validity. *Job analysis* refers to a systematic procedure for identifying the behaviors that are central to performing the job well and the results that the job incumbent is expected to produce. *Reliability* refers to consistency or dependability in measurement. *Validity* refers to the extent to which a test or appraisal instrument actually measures what it purports to measure.[2]

Although courts have ruled that performance appraisals constitute tests under the requirements set forth in the Uniform Guidelines on Employee Selection Procedures issued by the Equal Employment Opportunity Commission (EEOC) and the Department of Labor, the courts have not applied as stringent requirements to appraisals as to selection tests. That is, the cases suggest that courts may judge performance appraisals to a somewhat greater degree on their *facial validity*—the degree to which the criteria seem to apply logically to the job in question. If there is not a strong logical relationship and if the appraisal system has an adverse impact on a substantially greater proportion of a minority group, then courts are much more likely to require specific validation evidence similar to that required in proving the validity of other employment tests as suggested by the Uniform Guidelines.

The Laws

Several major laws affect the process of performance appraisal.

Civil Rights Act of 1964

On July 2, 1964, the U.S. Congress passed the Civil Rights Act, which became effective a year later. Title VII of the act made it a violation of the law for employers, employment agencies, unions, and joint labor-management apprenticeship programs to discriminate on the basis of race, color, religion, sex, or national origin. The act created the EEOC to administer Title VII.

The first major Supreme Court decision regarding Title VII came in 1971, in what is one of the most important civil rights cases ever to reach the Court: *Griggs v. Duke Power Company*. Duke Power had employed only blacks in one department and only whites in the others. A high school diploma or a satisfactory score on two standardized pencil-and-paper tests was required for employment in the departments where the white employees worked.

The Court's decision turned the EEOC guidelines into law when it stated that they expressed "the will of Congress." The Court ruled that where employment criteria (e.g., educational requirements) operate to exclude proportionally more minorities than nonminorities, such selection requirements violate the law where the employer fails to prove a demonstrable relationship between the criteria and successful job performance. Even though the employment procedures were neutral in form and intent, the Court ruled that they could not be justified if they result in discriminatory effects in the absence of a showing of business necessity for the use of such tests.

An analysis of the Court's decision in *Griggs* notes that the Court's opinion suggests that quota systems are contrary to the Civil Rights Act and that it is equally illegal to discriminate against members of nonminority groups. The decision reads:

> Congress did not intend by Title VII to guarantee a job to every person regardless of their qualifications. In short, the Act does not command

that a person be hired simply because he was formerly the subject of discrimination or because he is a member of a minority group. Discriminatory preferences for any group, minority or majority, are precisely and only what the Congress has proscribed.

The closing statement of the Supreme Court's decision in *Griggs* speaks directly to the issue of performance appraisal:

Nothing in the Act precludes the use of testing or measuring procedures; obviously these are useful. What Congress has forbidden is giving these devices and mechanisms controlling force unless they are demonstrably a reasonable measure of performance. Congress has not demanded that the less qualified be preferred over the more qualified simply because of minority origins. Congress has made such qualifications a controlling factor, so that race, religion, nationality and sex become irrelevant. What Congress has commanded is that any test used must measure the person for the job, not the person in the abstract.[3]

In 1978, to make the exact requirements that performance appraisal systems must meet clear, the four major government agencies involved in civil rights enforcement (EEOC, the Civil Service Commission, the Department of Labor, and the Department of Justice) published the Uniform Guidelines on Employee Selection Procedures. They included the following items:

- ► The central point in determining discrimination is the use of any selection procedure that has an adverse impact on a protected group.
- ► Any procedure, test, device, and so forth that informally or formally assists in the selection process is covered by these guidelines.
- ► Any measures of job performance used to demonstrate the validity of tests should represent important work behaviors or outcomes.
- ► Employers are required to keep records to substantiate their employment selection decisions.

The Uniform Guidelines also provided a rule of thumb for assessing adverse impact: the Four-fifths Rule. The rule states that the selection ratio (e.g., the number promoted to the number eligible) of minorities must not be less than four-fifths (80 percent) of the majority selection ratio. For example, if 50 percent of the majority eligibles were promoted, then promoting less than 40 percent of the minorities would be considered evidence of adverse impact.[4]

Executive Order 11246

Also in 1965, the Office of Federal Contract Compliance Programs (OFFCP) was established as the administrative body responsible for ensuring that federal contractors comply with Executive Order 11246, which, like the Civil Rights Act, prohibits employment discrimination on the basis of race, color, religion, and national origin (and was later amended to forbid discrimination on the basis of sex). The OFCCP requires all federal contracts to include clauses agreeing to refrain from discriminatory practices and exercises significant power to compel compliance. The OFCCP can publish the names of violators, cancel their contracts, bar violators from bidding, and recommend legal action, including specific performance of the obligation and reinstatement and back pay to those discriminated against.

The power of the OFCCP extends beyond examining for violations in the specific area where a complaint has been made. In several cases, a specific complaint about a discriminatory practice in one division of a large company led to an exhaustive review of the entire organization's total employment practices, including hiring, promotions, training, layoffs, recruitment, and performance appraisal, with recommendations covering the entire corporation and not just the location where the initial complaint was lodged. As Gary Latham and Kenneth Wexley note, "Most organizations consider the possibility of contract cancellations so serious that OFCCP field officers frequently are able to exert more influence on the personnel practices of the organizations they review than is justified by their legal authority."[5]

Age Discrimination in Employment Act

The Age Discrimination in Employment Act was enacted in 1967 and amended in 1978 and 1986. Its purpose is to promote employment of older persons based on ability and not on age. The 1967 act protected people from ages forty to sixty-five; the 1978 amendment extended the upper limit to age seventy, and the 1986 act effectively removed all age caps for most private employers.[6] With very limited exceptions—airline pilots and top executives—there is no mandatory retirement age in America and it is illegal for an organization to set one. If an employee wants to work until he's 95, it's entirely his decision. He's entitled to work as long as he wants—provided that he actually works, of course, and works according to the quality and quantity and other performance standards that the organization sets for its members. As attorney Rita Risser explains, "If they can't perform, you can dismiss them. But as long as they perform, you have to consider them for promotion, training and pay increases just like anyone else."[7]

Rehabilitation Act of 1973

This act applies to only a small number of employers—for the most part, federal contractors with contracts of $2,500 or more. Both federal contractors and employers that receive federal assistance are prohibited from discriminating against people with disabilities. For the most part, the definitions and policies of the Rehabilitation Act are similar to those of the Americans with Disabilities Act.[8]

Uniformed Services Employment and Reemployment Act of 1994

Congress passed this law in 1994 to reinstate and revise and in some cases expand job protection for veterans returning to their jobs. Under this law, a reemployed veteran cannot be discharged without just cause for one year if the period of military service was more than six months.

Americans With Disabilities Act

The ADA was enacted by the federal government in July 1990; its provisions became effective for most businesses in July 1992. More than with most other legislation, there are a great many problem areas and an enormous number of horror stories, many apparently true, about unreasonable and irrational demands employers have had to contend with for the sake of "hiring the handicapped." Enormous amounts of effort have been expended in defining and litigating the meanings of such mischievous terms as "reasonable accomodation" and "undue hardship"; even determining what is and what is not a disability is perilous. Not for naught has the law been termed "The Lawyers' Full Employment Act."

The provisions of the ADA make it illegal to discriminate in all areas of employment, including performance appraisal. While most of the complaints and criticisms of the law have involved hiring and termination situations, performance appraisal is fully covered by the act.

Civil Rights Act of 1991

During the late 1980s, the legal climate began shifting in favor of the employer rather than the employee.[9] Various Supreme Court decisions required employees to identify the specific employment practice allegedly responsible for statistical disparities[10] and held that simply demonstrating that an employer has a higher proportion of minorities in low-paying jobs is insufficient in and of itself to prove discrimination.[11]

Finally, in a case that dealt directly with performance appraisal, the written appraisals of a female employee suggested that her sex played a significant role in the firm's decision to deny her a promotion to partner.[12] However, the Court ruled that "an employer may avoid a finding of liability by providing a preponderance of evidence that the organization would have made the same decision even if it had not taken the employee's gender into account."[13]

The 1991 Civil Rights Act was intended to reverse this trend. With specific regard to the performance appraisal case, the act provided that employers are liable for any reliance on prejudice in making employment decisions. Thus, a complaining party may establish that an employment practice is unlawful by demonstrating that a characteristic protected by Title VII (in this case, the sex of the individual) was a "motivating factor" in the decision, even though other factors also motivated the decision.[14]

Civil Service Reform Act of 1978

Although it does not apply to private sector employers, the Civil Service Reform Act is important because of the attention it gives to performance appraisals. As Latham and Wexley argue, "The act serves as a sound, straightforward model to performance appraisal for the private sector as well. Adherence to the act should minimize successful legal challenges to a performance appraisal."[15] Among the provisions and recommendations of the act are these:

- ▸ Agencies are required to create performance appraisal procedures.
- ▸ Appraisal systems will encourage employee participation in establishing performance standards based on critical elements of the job.
- ▸ The critical elements of the job must be put in writing.
- ▸ Employees must be advised of the critical job elements before the appraisal.
- ▸ An employee's performance appraisal must be based entirely on the individual's actual performance of the critical elements of the job. It "must not include any controls, such as the requirement to rate on a bell curve, that prevents fair appraisal of performance in relation to the performance standards."[16]
- ▸ Appraisals should be conducted and recorded in writing once a year.
- ▸ The appraisals must provide information that can be used for making decisions regarding the "training, rewarding, reassigning, promoting, reducing in grade, retaining and removing employees."[17]
- ▸ Each agency is required to provide training to those who create and conduct appraisals.
- ▸ The effectiveness of each agency's performance appraisal systems must be periodically evaluated to ensure its effectiveness.

Ensuring Legal Compliance

Certainly following the recommendations of the Civil Service Reform Act should minimize any company's exposure to legal challenge resulting from its performance appraisal system. Further recommendations for minimizing risk come from a study done by W. H. Holley and H. S. Feild.[18] They began by analyzing sixty-six legal cases that involved charges of discrimination, primarily racial discrimination, resulting from performance appraisal. Of those, the defendants won thirty five. Most of those that the defendants won, the judges ruled in their favor because the plaintiff had failed to make a prima facie case of discrimination.

But in five cases, in each of which the plaintiff had established a prima facie case of discrimination, employers were still able to defend their performance appraisal systems and prevail. Holley and Feild studied these cases to determine what led to the defendant's success. They identified several common characteristics of the successfully defended appraisal programs:

- ▸ Appraisers were given specific written instructions on how to complete the appraisals.
- ▸ Job analysis was used in developing the content of the appraisal.
- ▸ Appraisals focused on observable behaviors rather than traits.
- ▸ Performance ratings were reviewed in advance by upper management.
- ▸ Appraisers were trained in how to appraise performance and in how to conduct the appraisal interview.
- ▸ The results were discussed with the employee who had been appraised.

Guidelines for Avoiding Legal Challenge

No appraisal system is immune to legal challenge. But the risk of legal difficulties can be minimized if basic good management practices are followed.

1. *The performance appraisal should be based on an analysis of the requirements of the job.* Courts are skeptical of subjective, trait-based rating systems since they leave an enormous amount of room for the biases of raters to influence the outcomes, and they are not directly related to specific job responsibilities. Organizations, however, are not required to conduct exhaustive analyses of each job in the company as a condition of doing performance appraisal. A job analysis can be built directly in to the appraisal process itself.

When an individual and manager discuss the important goals and objectives that the individual will address during the course of the year and against which his performance will be appraised, that is a job analysis.

If a manager evaluates the specific behaviors and expected conduct and demeanor required to perform according to the company's expectations, and then discusses these expectations and their importance with each subordinate, that is a job analysis.

Completely objective measures of performance do not always exist. If they did, everyone would use them. In fact, if there were complete, objective, and quantifiable measures for every job, performance appraisal systems themselves would probably not be necessary; the data would speak for themselves. But with most jobs, there are few absolutely direct and impartial measures of an individual's performance, particularly when successful performance is less dependent on performing countable acts than it is on such vital but slippery responsibilities as the ability to recognize and take advantage of opportunities, the ability to build a committed work team, or the ability to recognize obstacles before they become serious interferences.

When a supervisor and subordinate together determine what results the subordinate should concentrate on producing over the upcoming year and they also discuss how the subordinate will go about generating those results—the behaviors and competencies that must be demonstrated—a legitimate job analysis has been conducted.

2. *Performance dimensions should be defined in behavioral terms and supported by observable, objective evidence.* Not every job is amenable to results-based, quantitative measurement. For many, success in such job dimensions as cooperation, dependability, customer relations, attitude, and other even more abstract attributes are what are of primary concern.

The issue here is not whether these attributes are important. No one would argue that they are not critically important. Who would want an employee who is uncooperative, undependable, hostile with customers, and surly toward everyone else? And neither is the issue the fact that they cannot be measured and described. Of course they can. The difficulty arises when the appraisal form merely asks the rater to assign a judgment to the individual's possession or absence of these characteristics without defining exactly what is meant in behavioral terms.

Attorney Rita Risser makes the point clear: "Appraisals sometimes are conclusory, rating on attributes like attitude, leadership and initiative. These are admirable characteristics and can be rated. But you must give the facts to back up your conclusions in these categories."[19] The American Society for Training and Development agrees. In its publication, *How to Conduct a Performance Appraisal*, it provides a list of guidelines for reducing bias and error. The third guideline specifically encourages the inclusion of personal traits in a performance appraisal system: "*Build in subjective ratings.* Leave some space for the evaluation of traits such as creativity or integrity or other traits that are especially valued in the organization."[20]

There is no argument that a performance appraisal can include subjective evaluations and the assessment of traits and characteristics and still be fully legal. But two serious problems commonly arise. The first is that the terms, traits, and characteristics themselves are not even defined, let alone described in ways that allow raters to know exactly what is meant by the label. Simply providing a label and letting the rater figure out what it means is bound to generate problems.

The second difficulty with the way many performance dimensions appear on appraisal forms is that they often are defined without being described. In other words, the appraisal form itself or (assuming there is one) the manual or instructions sheet simply gives a dictionary definition of the meaning of the attribute to be appraised instead of describing what the rater should look for in assessing the quality of the individual's performance against a standard. For example, consider the difference between the following definition and description of "Job Knowledge" lifted verbatim from the appraisal forms of two of America's largest and best-known oil companies:

▸ "Understanding of the duties, procedures and responsibilities of current job."

▸ "Embraces new technology and finds practical application for it in their job. Accurately diagnoses technical problems and therefore knows when to call for assistance. Forms opinions and conclusions which are technically sound and well-founded. Acts as a resource to others; is sought out by colleagues for technical advice and willingly shares new technology with others. Takes an active interest in increasing their technical knowledge by reading technical journals, attending professional conferences, holding discussions with experts, etc."

Although one is significantly longer than the other, the real difference between the two statements has nothing to do with their length. The difference lies in their *focus*. The first statement simply defines what the author of the form meant by the label "Job Knowledge." The second statement provides a large number of significant examples of the kinds of actions and behavior one would expect to encounter in an individual with a great degree of job knowledge. The second statement would be highly defensible; the first would be a bit suspect.

In addition to providing specific behavioral descriptions of the attributes and job dimensions to be measured in the performance appraisal, the legal defensibility of the form can be strengthened in another way. Instead of asking the rater to make an absolute judgment regarding the degree to which the ratee possesses the attribute in question, ask her to describe the frequency with which the individual performs in the way the organization envisions. In other words, don't ask the rater to decide whether Mary's job knowledge is Marginal or Fair or Standard or Superior or any of a myriad of other judgmental terms or phrases. Instead, ask the rater to describe how often Mary acts in the ways described in the example provided above. Does she act this way rarely, occasionally, sometimes, frequently, or always? By changing the rating scale to eliminate the requirement that raters come to absolute conclusions regarding the goodness or badness of performance and replacing it with a scale that reflects the frequency with which the individual performs in a highly desirable manner, the organization should reduce the possibility of legal challenge and increase the ability of the rater to conduct a more meaningful discussion.

3. *Keep it simple.* Complex forms that attempt to provide a total and complete evaluation serve only to frustrate managers and allow their biases to overcome their objectivity. Some organizations, particularly those like Alcon Laboratories that enjoy an enormous amount of top management support for their system and a long organizational history of commitment to the performance appraisal process, can make a highly complex, thirteen-page form work almost painlessly. But most organizations struggle when the number of pages mounts. In her book, *Stay Out of Court*, attorney Rita Risser presents a seven-item appraisal form that is a model of simplicity. After recording the date, the supervisor's name and the employee's name, the supervisor then writes down the answers to the following:

1. List present job requirements.
2. Describe how the employee has performed the job requirements.
3. State the objectives from last year's appraisal.
4. Describe how the employee has achieved the objectives.
5. Comment on the employee's strengths and weaknesses.
6. What career opportunities should the employee consider?
7. List the specific objectives to be accomplished during the next review period.

Risser points out that her form provides no numerical rating scale. "Numerical ratings are perfectly legal," she says. "It's just a matter of preference."

Her simple and sound advice continues:

- If your form has a rating scale, you should rate most employees in the middle of the scale. The middle is average. That's where most people should be by definition. It's more accurate.
- If the rating scale uses words, look closely at the words that are used. They can skew results.

- If an overall rating is called for, don't just average the scores of the different categories. Weigh the relative importance of the various categories with reference to the specific job being appraised. For example, "initiative" is very important for a manager, whereas good "work habits" are almost taken for granted. The relative importance of these categories might be the opposite for a production worker.
- Don't overemphasize areas that aren't legitimate job requirements. For example, leadership skills should be recognized no matter who has them. But nonmanagers shouldn't be penalized for not having leadership ability.
- If another manager wrote the last performance appraisal, your ratings may be very different. Employees who have worked under the same manager for years learn to do their jobs in a certain manner. When new managers come in, or when current managers take training courses, they often want to change old ways of doing things. Just note that on the form itself. "Your last manager rated you excellent even though you were 85% of quota. I rate employees excellent only if they reach 125% of quota." As long as you are consistent and have a legitimate business reason, you can change performance standards.

4. *Monitor and audit for discrimination.* Two areas need to be monitored to make sure that the organization faces the least amount of risk from legal challenge: the performance appraisal procedures themselves and the personnel decisions that are based on performance appraisal data.

The first area involves determining whether the average appraisal results of members of a protected class are significantly different from that of the majority. "It is the rare organization in which the usual tests for adverse impact will not establish a prima facie case somewhere in the organization," write Allan Mohrman and his colleagues.[21] "Given statistical probability, the number of protected groups, and the past poor practices of most organizations, it is almost inevitable that a case can be made in most large organizations." Even if the average appraisal results of a protected class are significantly different from that of the majority, it does not follow that the appraisal system is automatically illegal. Rather, the statistical disparity may serve to shift the burden to the employer to justify the use of the performance appraisal system as valid. If the company's performance appraisal system ends up with the assignment of each individual to a specific rating category (e.g., Marginal, Fair, Competent, Superior, and Distinguished), an analysis should be made to determine whether there is any significant difference in the ratings given to minority group members versus the ratings of organization members as a whole.

The second area to monitor derives from the first. In addition to making sure that the performance appraisals themselves are not discriminatory, it is equally important to make sure that personnel decisions that are based on data that the appraisals provide—compensation, promotion, selection for special training programs, termination—are nondiscriminatory.

Monitoring and auditing cannot solve problems, but they can bring troublesome situations to the light. Once the organization knows where it stands, corrective action can be taken where the need is greatest.

5. *Train raters to assess performance accurately.* Chapter 12 discussed in detail the contents of an effective appraiser training program. Ideally every organization would conduct a formal and comprehensive training program that all managers are required to attend as a precondition for their conducting performance appraisals. In the absence of this ideal, virtually every organization can afford the time required to conduct a one-hour briefing session to help raters carry out their responsibility with some minimal degree of confidence. Providing this minimal level of training alone, in addition to the actual benefits it will provide in ensuring more accurate appraisals, will also be useful if the organization is charged with discrimination growing out of a performance appraisal rating.

The contents of this briefing should include at a minimum a review of the form itself and the organization's expectations about the degree of completeness required, the formal mechanics and procedures involved in the system, an explanation of the way ratings are to be assigned, common rating errors, answers to questions about the process that have been raised by appraisers in past years, and a reminder of red flag areas to check before holding an appraisal discussion. Red flags areas might include these situations:

- The average appraisal rating of minority group members is significantly different from that of the group as a whole (either higher or lower).
- An individual's performance rating has significantly declined since the last appraisal period, particularly in cases of long-service employees with a record of at least satisfactory appraisal results in the past. Simply the fact that a person has worked for the company for a number of years suggests strongly that his performance has been at least acceptable to the organization.
- The performance appraisal of an individual who was recently involved in disciplinary action indicates overall satisfactory performance.
- An employee whose performance was rated unsatisfactory in the previous appraisal period has not improved. (By maintaining the employment of an "unsatisfactory" performer, the organization is in effect saying that continued unsatisfactory performance will not result in termination.)

- There is a larger than usual number of extremely high or extremely low ratings. Appraisers should certainly be instructed to tell it like it is but should also be encouraged to substantiate any ratings that vary greatly from the norm.
- Problems with central tendency, leniency, or halo effect crop up.
- The organization places too much emphasis on subjective criteria such as attitude or initiative without the use of more specific examples or guidance.
- Comments on the appraisal are inconsistent with the numerical rating of performance.

6. *Train raters to conduct effective appraisal discussions.* Even if comprehensive training cannot be provided, a briefing session or even a set of written guidelines sent out with the appraisal form itself should include the following fundamental suggestions for an appraisal discussion that reduces the organization's exposure to legal challenge:

- Be prepared to provide specific examples to support performance ratings, particularly where the employee is rated as less than satisfactory.
- Avoid any discussion that makes reference to a person's membership in a protected group.
- Maintain rapport and a positive atmosphere during the discussion, even when discussing problem areas and the consequences of failure to improve. Many discrimination complaints result not from direct acts of discriminating but from an individual's belief that she was treated unfairly or caught off guard by an unexpectedly low rating that was not fully explained and justified.

7. *Encourage a "no secrets/no surprises" environment.* Employees should certainly know what the performance expectations their supervisor and their company have of them. Ideally, they would be involved in setting the standards and be active participants in determining the objectives and results they will be working on during the appraisal period.

Self-appraisal, particularly when the employee's self-appraisal is submitted in advance to be used as an additional information source in the writing of the manager's performance appraisal of the subordinate, can help alert the appraiser to areas where significant differences of opinion will need to be addressed and resolved.

The entire appraisal should be reviewed and discussed with the individual. The employee should be asked to sign a copy of the appraisal to confirm that the discussion and review did in fact take place.

8. *Provide for upper management review before the appraisal is reviewed*

with the individual. Most organizations require that managers who complete the appraisal form have it reviewed and approved by their supervisor before it is given to the employee. This is a good idea. Managers who might be capricious or arbitrary (let alone directly discriminatory) in their appraisal assessments may tend to be a tad more cautious knowing that their direct supervisor must review and approve what they have written.

Upper managers too should be encouraged to do more than rubber-stamp the appraisals that are sent up to them for review. In the majority of cases, the supervisor's supervisor of an individual has a reasonably good idea of the overall quality of performance of the people in his department, even though they may be two organization levels down. Simply by taking one appraisal and asking the appraiser, "I was surprised to see that you ended up rating Patty as Superior [or Distinguished or Unsatisfactory]. Tell me more about how you came up with that," will enormously encourage increased diligence in performance assessment in the future. In performance appraisal as much as in any other area of management, the old saw remains true: We get what we inspect, not what we expect.

9. *Provide some appeal mechanism.* Today, virtually every employee of every organization has an appeal mechanism to use to contest a perceived unfair appraisal: the legal system. A study by the Rand Corporation Institute for Civil Justice a few years ago revealed that employees were now three times more likely to sue their employers than they were in 1980.[22] Since employees do in fact have a way to challenge unfair appraisals, providing them with a formal means to appeal what they believe to be an unfair performance appraisal without having to go outside the organization can be a cheap form of insurance against unnecessary lawsuits.

One immediate appeal mechanism simply involves allowing the individual who believes himself to be the victim of an inaccurate appraisal to state his side of the story as a formal part of the record. Most appraisal forms contain a space for employee comments. Employees should be encouraged to use it.

If the employee wants to submit a statement to be appended to the appraisal to provide a counterbalancing argument to assessments made in the formal appraisal itself, there is no advantage to be gained in denying the person the right to do so. Frequently serious problems can be headed off completely if the manager says, "I'm sorry we don't see eye to eye about this, Jack, though we've now discussed it in some detail. While I won't change the way I have written your appraisal, I certainly want to encourage you to write a statement to be attached to my appraisal if you genuinely feel that what I have written is not correct."

With union membership in this country approaching a mere 12 percent of the workforce, formal union grievance procedures are available to only a small number of individuals. The number is even smaller than it might be, since very few union members ever receive formal appraisals of their performance so there is nothing to grieve. On the other hand, a rapidly increasing number of employers are voluntarily creating formal grievance procedures for their nonunion employees. Alternative dispute resolution procedures that companies are setting up include allowing employees access to binding arbitration, creating corporate ombudsmen, providing mediation of complaints, and establishing peer review grievance procedures where panels of fellow employees and managers hear an employee's complaint.

Employees who feel they were unjustly appraised and are legitimately concerned about the impact that this apparently arbitrary decision will have on their future should be allowed their "day in court"—but without having to go to court to get it. Good managers do make mistakes, and there are still inept managers who allow their biases to color their appraisal judgments. The common argument against an appeal process—"It undermines the boss"—just doesn't hold up, Allan Mohrman points out. It is the bad decision, not the right of appeal, that undermines the boss's credibility. Letting the bad decision go unchallenged undermines the organization and ultimately the credibility of the entire human resources management system.[23]

Who should hear the case? Although a company's policy should certainly be open to complaints of unfair appraisal, too often employees are skeptical about the results that will come from an open-door appeal and nervous about reporting concerns with their own manager to a higher manager. If the open door policy doesn't exist or isn't trusted and a grievance procedure isn't available or appropriate, to whom does the employee turn without having to talk to a lawyer, government agent, or other third party?

Hearing complaints about faulty, unjust, and biased appraisals is one of the legitimate counseling and ombudsman functions of the personnel department. If an employee feels sufficiently strongly that her supervisor erred in determining her rating, she ought to be allowed—even encouraged—to talk to personnel staff. Their responsibility is to hear her out, sort the facts from the feelings (and the fictions), and make a professional judgment about whether they are dealing with a whiner who should simply be told to grow up and start doing what she is getting paid to do, or whether the aggrieved employee is actually serving as a valuable distant early warning system, alerting the organization of genuine potential problem areas that should be explored.

All the while that he is listening, however, the personnel officer must assume that in cases where employee and supervisor disagree, the supervisor acted correctly. To yield to the seductive temptation of neutrality—listening impartially to both sides and forming no opinion until all the facts are in—reinforces line management's frequent suspicion that personnel types are merely organizational sob sisters to whom every malcontent and misfit is allowed to run in hopes of overriding his boss's requirement that he must do what he's getting paid to do and actually work for the paycheck he's picking up. Whenever there is a question about whether a performance appraisal rating is fair, the burden of proof lies with the employee. The only appropriate assumption is that, in the absence of compelling evidence to the contrary, the manager acted properly. To make any other assumption is to undermine the leadership of the enterprise.

Notes

1. Bob Filipczak, "An Interview with Scott Adams," *Training* (July 1994): 32.
2. From Latham and Wexley, *Increasing Performance Through Performance Appraisal*, edited by James W. Wimberly, Jr. (Atlanta: Wimberly & Lawson, 1996), p. 12.
3. *Griggs v. Duke Power Company*, 401 U.S. 424 (1971), quoted in ibid.
4. J. Vernon Odom, "Performance Appraisal: Legal Aspects," in Lloyd S. Baird, Richard W. Beatty, and Craig Eric Schneier, *The Performance Appraisal Sourcebook* (Amherst, Mass.: Human Resource Development Press, 1982), p. 109.
5. Latham and Wexley, *Increasing Productivity Through Performance Appraisal*, pp. 15–16.
6. Cliff Roberson, *Hire Right, Fire Right* (New York: McGraw-Hill, 1992), p. 11.
7. Rita Risser, *Stay Out of Court: The Managers's Guide to Preventing Employee Lawsuits* (Englewood Cliffs, N.J.: Prentice Hall, 1993), p. 37.
8. Roberson, *Hire Right, Fire Right*, p. 147.
9. Latham & Wexley, *Increasing Productivity Through Performance Appraisal*, p. 37.
10. *Watson v. Fort Worth Bank and Trust Company*, 1988.
11. *Ward's Cove v. Antonio*, 1989.
12. *Price Waterhouse v. Hopkins*, 1989.
13. Latham & Wexley, *Increasing Productivity Through Performance Appraisal*, p. 37.
14. Ibid.
15. Ibid., p. 39.
16. *Federal Register*, 1979, p. 3,448.
17. Public Law 95-454, 1978, 92STAT., p. 1,132.
18. W. H. Holley and H. S. Feild, "Will Your Performance Appraisal System Hold Up in Court?" *Personnel*, 59 (1982): 59–64.
19. Risser, *Stay Out of Court*, p. 69.

20. American Society for Training and Development, "How to Conduct a Performance Appraisal," Info-Line series, May 1990, p. 11.
21. Allan M. Mohrman, Jr., Susan M. Resnick-West, and Edward E. Lawler III, *Designing Performance Appraisal Systems* (San Francisco: Jossey-Bass, 1989), p. 1.
22. Rand Corporation, *Annual Report—The Institute for Civil Justice* (Santa Monica, Calif.: Rand, 1988).
23. Morhman et al., *Designing Performance Appraisal Systems*, p. 170.

Chapter 16
Emerging Trends in Performance Appraisal

Performance appraisal has been standard management fare for over fifty years. What will the next fifty hold?

My bias is clear: I am unalterably convinced that performance appraisal is one of the few management procedures that is here to stay. In the predictable near future there will be several adaptations of performance appraisal to increase the alignment of this technique with the growth of newer management processes.

The future of performance appraisal will be affected by four major elements. The first three are the growth in the use of team-based organization structures, the continuing influence and appeal of total quality management, and computer-based software programs for automating performance appraisal. Finally, the future of performance appraisal will ultimately be determined not by technology or organization structures but by people who are pushing the envelope of performance appraisal. They are doing things that haven't been done before, often working in organizations that are unaware that they harbor in their midst someone who is redefining the state of the art of performance appraisal and developing systems and approaches that not only have never been used before but are giving the enterprise an unappreciated competitive advantage. At the end of this chapter, we meet some of those people and look at the directions their work is taking us.

Teams and Performance Appraisal

Teams are a management process that is here to stay. The use of self-directed or, more accurately, semiautonomous work teams represents one of the most significant changes in the overall technology of organizational structure and design in the past one hundred years.

Until recently, virtually every organization has structured itself the way Alfred P. Sloan organized General Motors when Woodrow Wilson was president. The development of team-based organizational structures is the single most important and dramatic change to classical organizational structure since Sloan, Henri Fayol, Max Weber, and Frederick Taylor taught us how to create large organizations that generate minimum friction and maximum output. Unlike matrix management, which merely lays a vertical bureaucratic structure across a horizontal bureaucratic structure, team-based organizations abolish bureaucratic structure. It is a genuine and revolutionary change.

Corporate America is having a hot love affair with teams; scores of companies are finding that self-managed teams can boost productivity by up to 40 percent. Besides their demonstrated productivity gains, teams seem to be the most highly effective way of coping after rounds of downsizings and reengineerings have left companies with far flatter structures and therefore far fewer middle managers to supervise day-to-day activities. If teams are genuinely self-managed, the need for managers diminishes.

Data on the growth of teams are swarming. The Center for Effective Organizations at the University of Southern California found that 68 percent of Fortune 1000 companies are using high-performance or self-managed teams. "Teams become commonplace in U.S. Companies," a page one *Wall Street Journal* headline proclaims.[1] The story reports the Hewitt Associates study indicating that two-thirds of 1,811 employers surveyed nationwide are using formal teams to conduct work. Edward Lawler and Susan Cohen indicate that while nearly all American organizations are using project teams brought together for short periods to solve problems or complete projects, just under half (47 percent) of all American companies are using permanent work teams as the way to get work done.[2] These teams are not outside the organizational structure, comments Jack Zigon about the Lawler/Cohen research. They *are* the organizational structure.

Some tasks are easy for teams to accomplish completely by itself: housekeeping, continuous improvement, cross-training, equipment maintenance and repair, and setting production and vacation schedules, for example. Some tasks are tougher: managing cross-functional team relationships, hiring new team members, budgeting, and equipment purchase and selection. Some are extremely difficult, like handling disciplinary action and setting compensation levels. Team performance appraisal is up there with the toughest.

Appraising Team Performance

The primary dilemma with performance appraisals and teams is that appraisal forms and processes were built with individuals in mind. Using an individually based instrument to measure the performance of a team is difficult. Where does the work of the individual stop and the team begin?

The appraisal job gets even tougher when the teams are cross-functional, not homogeneous. If a group of customer service representatives used to work solely as individual contributors, each reporting to the same supervisor and each basically doing what all the others are doing, firing the supervisor and empowering the reps to act as a self-managed team doesn't change the nature of their activities much. But creating a cross-functional team that includes representatives from sales and finance and engineering as well as a customer service representative can play havoc with the attempt to find a valid basis for appraising team performance.

The obvious remedy for team appraisal maladies is to measure both individual and team performance. Team members need a clear understanding of their responsibilities as individual contributors along with the team member burdens they are responsible for. In fact, an excellent team development activity is to have team members, as part of their process of building group decision-making skills, identify all of their team member roles and determine the appropriate weights or values that might be assigned to these roles for appraisal purposes.

A more sophisticated approach to measuring team performance is to start by focusing on the team's customers and explore the work processes the team uses to satisfy its needs. Swiping a tool from the reengineering kit, Jack Zigon recommends creating a "process map": a matrix that lists all of the members of the team down the side and all of the tasks to be achieved across the top. It then becomes a relatively simple process to fill in the individual cells, identifying the responsibility of each team member for each task to be accomplished. For certain tasks, some team members will have a whole catalog of contributions they will be expected to make; others will find their cell for a given task empty. In addition to providing a highly valid mechanism for appraisal, this process map can highlight team members who are carrying a disproportionate share of the load.[3]

The most appropriate approach to team appraisal may also be the most obvious: Train team members to create their own performance expectations and measures of how well those standards or expectations are being met. The more that the team is involved in determining what will be appraised and how it will be measured, the more likely the team will be to accept the legitimacy of the appraisal process and, more important, the more the team will behave in the ways that its members have determined to be ideal.

The performance factors portion of any existing performance appraisal form should be examined by any company using or planning to use teams. At a minimum, "Teamwork" must be one of the competencies listed. There should also be behavioral indicators of effective teamwork, in a way that describes to team members what the organization expects of them in their service on a team. Better yet is to put the task to the team itself. Their writing of the behavioral indicators will also create the behavioral norms for the team.

Making Team-Based Performance Appraisal Work

In 1992 Clark Material Handling Company of Lexington, Kentucky, pilot-tested on its management staff, and then implemented throughout its organization, a team-based, peer performance appraisal process. The new system consisted of two parts: review and feedback. During the review phase, members of the team, minus the member under review, discuss the individual's performance, agree on a rating, and produce a written review. In a subsequent session, team members discuss the rating with the review subject and encourage him or her to respond.

In creating the performance appraisal, team members start with the company's ten "standards of excellence":

1. Quality of Work
2. Job Knowledge and Skills
3. Work Performance
4. Adaptability and Flexibility
5. Customer Relations
6. Safety and Housekeeping
7. Dependability and Reliability
8. Initiative
9. Stewardship
10. Interpersonal Relations and Teamwork

To begin, team members discuss the team's expectations of the member being reviewed, as well as the team's expectations of itself. Team members may discover that they are not as familiar as they should be with each other's jobs. The facilitator, who is always present, instructs any team member who is unsure about a review subject's job to give an average rating at first and then adjust the rating based on observations and documentation provided by other team members.

Facilitators help guard team members against falling into rating errors, particularly recency effect and halo. In addition, they stress that ratings should be based on behavior that is the norm, not the exception—whether good or bad. Team members are required to provide actual behavioral examples of a team member's successes and derelictions. "He lets us down a lot," may be true but is hardly specific. "He's been absent twelve days this year," qualifies easily.

Team members often find that managers, active participants in the team appraisal discussions, have more specific input than do other members. Managers may have greater access to data and may also be more skilled at making accurate behavioral observations.

The facilitator helps the team reach consensus and emphasizes that there should be no surprises during a review. It's inappropriate, the facilitator advises, for teams to gunnysack their complaints about a fellow member all year and then dump them on the unsuspecting pigeon at review time. Instead, team members have a responsibility to help each other succeed once they know the performance expectations.

Team Reviews in Action

Clark's review process begins with the employee being reviewed chronicling his own performance over the past year to remind the team of his strengths and accomplishments. He either discusses his assessment of his own contributions with his teammates in a face-to-face session or hands over the documentation and lets the record speak for itself.

The team compares the employee's own documentation with the company's standards of excellence, then discusses and agrees on a team rating for each standard. One member records salient comments; the process can take from ninety minutes to four hours.

The recorder's notes are transcribed to form a written review. Team members review it, make corrections, and sign the original. They then schedule a face-to-face session with the teammate being reviewed.

In as informal a setting as can be arranged, a designated team member reads the team's comments for each standard. Team members encourage the reviewee to seek clarification and interject their personal views on how the decisions made were determined. Feedback sessions are difficult; rarely is the information all peaches and cream. But clarifying the team's perceptions and expectations leads to greater commitment and understanding from team members.

Members are trained before being turned loose to dissect each other. Using a highly creative training twist, regular Clark employees practice giving feedback by using a temporary employee as the recipient. Clark makes extensive use of temporaries so the performance of any given one is known; each volunteers for the guinea pig role. Participants have the benefit of practicing and fine-tuning a tough skill on a live subject whom they actually know.[4]

Enhancing the Team Review Process

Clark's procedure is one of the most sophisticated for providing team members with the opportunity for performance appraisal. But this advanced approach could be made even more productive.

While the Clark process encourages team members to define behaviorally the company's ten standards of excellence and the ways that they show up in team performance, an additional way of ensuring rater accuracy, competence, and commitment would be to spend some time working with the team in defining what constitutes a competent rater. In the Clark example, a rater with little direct information about a teammate's performance of a specific fragment of his job is urged to give the individual an average rating and then adjust that rating based on the "observations and documentation" provided by other team members. That might be a reasonable approach, yet team members might prefer that those lacking data simply refrain from providing any assessment at all and not be swayed, for better or worse, by the opinions of others. Employees may have strong feelings about how they want their performance to be evaluated by teammates. Enabling the facilitator to allow the team to come to consensus on issues of how rater competence will be determined will increase their commitment to the process.

Rater bias can be a central concern for reviewees, particularly when, as in the Clark situation, peer performance appraisals will influence compensation decisions and promotional opportunities. Peer appraisals may seem fairer than supervisory appraisals, yet peers are likely to have an interpersonal relationship with the ratee and are more likely to be in direct competition for organizational rewards. Besides merely monitoring for bias and rater error, formal training in these areas can mitigate human dynamics problems.

Finally, ratees may not automatically accord peers the same degree of perceived knowledge or competence that is often automatically accorded to supervisors. Because peer raters may be less educated and less sophisticated than supervisory raters, they may be viewed by ratees as less competent. Again, training for raters, particularly peer raters, can optimize a process that is already strong.[5]

Team-Based Appraisal and Compensation

Even more challenging than managing the complexities of team-based performance appraisals are the difficulties involved in applying the results of those appraisals to the compensation of team members. A 1990 report by consulting firm DDI indicated that the only activity more complex for a team to handle than disciplinary action was setting compensation levels.

It's a rats' nest, most managers agree. Pay the team as a whole, and the stars feel slighted while the duds are delighted with the free ride. So then just pay for individual performance. But that violates the corporate teamwork mantra. And genuinely effective teams are synergistic; they are able to accomplish more by working together than even the most talented individual luminaries toiling alone.

To work through the rats' nest, consider four basic approaches to team-based pay: the TQM approach, skill-based pay, gainsharing, and small group incentives. If teams are used in an exclusively TQM-based environment, the pay dilemma is virtually eliminated; TQM advocates argue for equal pay for all, since differences in performance are far more likely (according to their philosophy) to be a function of variables in the system than of variables in the performer.

Similarly, skill-based pay for team compensation is relatively easy to manage, since team members can readily determine whether their mates do or do not have the knowledge and skills required to qualify for a raise. The focus—and the flaw—of skill-based pay is that the performer is compensated for the capability of being able to do something rather than the actual performance of that something against a measurable standard.

Gainsharing is a third team-based pay scheme. Gainsharing plans pass on the benefits and cost reductions and increased productivity through regular cash bonuses to employees. They have received sufficient attention in other places as to merit benign neglect here.

Then we come to small group incentive plans. How do we construct compensation schemes in order to reward individual and team achievement in a way that all perceive as fair? Small group incentive programs, as Sam T. Johnson of the compensation consulting firm the Wyatt Company defines it, "is a pay method designed to deliver a uniform award, based on the achievement of a single or multiple predetermined goals, to all members of a work group who share responsibility for work process and output."[6] For small group incentives to be effective in a work team environment, Johnson argues, several considerations must be present:

1. Employees' tasks must be interdependent.
2. Group contribution and collaboration must be paramount.
3. The focus must be on team problem solving and action.
4. Group behavior and results must be measurable.
5. The line of sight must be close and unobstructed.

Regarding the final item, if the work group is a small team of machine operators, packers, and a maintenance mechanic but the amount of the award depends on the annual improvement in plantwide operating efficiency, the distance between individual and team effort and ultimate reward is remote, with a plethora of intervening variables. But for the same team, if the measure is the increase in number of cases per hour per team, the connection—the line of sight—is close and tight.

Under the small group incentive plan, awards are made contingent on the accomplishment of operational or financial goals. In the typical situation, the target award is 5 to 10 percent of base pay.

Team Appraisal Processes From Other Organizations

Five cross-functional employee task forces convened in 1991 at San Francisco's Levi Strauss to revamp its creaking pay system. The result was Partners in Performance, a pay and performance management process whose mission is to create a single incentive pay system that encourages employees to think like stakeholders; link individual and team performance objectives to the company's strategic business objectives; and pay employees for performance and reward both individuals and teams.

Their performance management process encompasses performance planning at the beginning of the year, ongoing performance coaching, mid-year performance updates, and year-end review. Levi's pay program consists of three components: base pay, annual incentive pay, and long-term incentive pay. The annual incentive pay rewards individuals and teams for meeting corporate, business unit, and individual goals on an annual basis; the long-term segment rewards achieving the same three factors, this time with a multiyear focus.[7]

But rats' nests remain, particularly when the specific rats involved are those who are not pulling the same weight as the others. "Freeloaders pose problems in compensation of work teams," a *Wall Street Journal* article trumpets.[8] More companies are tinkering with their pay plans, the *Journal* reports, to emphasize individual contributions to team efforts because of worries about free riders. Unisys Corporation of Blue Bell, Pennsylvania, sets annual base pay raises on performance reviews by a team coach and three peers chosen by the ratee. Besides their individual awards, team members can get up to 20 percent of base pay as a team bonus. ATT Universal Card responded to employee entreaties for greater recognition in the difference in their individual efforts by creating wider differences in base salaries.

As teams proliferate, sophisticated team-based appraisal systems will continue to develop. New compensation structures will reward individual and team accomplishment in the area of work objectives and for performance factors. And among the performance factors, whether one is a virtually monastic individual contributor or a 110 percent teamer, there will undoubtedly be a factor somewhere on the form called "Teamwork."

Performance Appraisal and TQM

Like team-based structures, the interest in a total quality management process is also here to stay, although the Deming dictum that performance appraisals are inherently satanic will be recognized—as it is by most serious TQM advocates today—as hyperbole. Performance appraisal is a producer, a generator of quality. TQM and performance appraisal, as many organizations entirely committed to a TQM effort have demonstrated, can not only coexist but can enhance each other's effectiveness.

TQM's Critique of Performance Appraisal

Performance appraisal focuses managerial attention primarily on person factors, TQM on system factors. TQM advocates argue that performance appraisal is used by management to pin the blame for deficient performance on lower-level employees rather than focusing attention on the system, for which upper management bears primary responsibility.

TQM is based on the fundamental principle that quality products are a function of the system in which they are produced. The system includes everything that influences the final product or service, such as the availability of raw materials and supplies, the leadership style of the supervisors, the efficiency of the manufacturing line, and the culture of the organization. TQM encourages managers to focus their attention on these system factors; it promotes system management and minimizes individual differences between employees.[9]

Deming held the performance appraisal practices of American industry to be a root cause of its quality problems. As Jai Ghorpade and Milton Chen explain, four charges keep recurring in Deming's analysis:

1. *Current performance appraisal practices are unfair since they hold the worker responsible for errors that may be the result of faults within the system.* Deming distinguished between common causes and special or local causes of variations in system performance. Common causes are flaws endemic to the system itself; local causes are derelictions attributable to operator deficiencies. Deming believed over 90 percent of the quality problems of American industry to be common causes. Assuming he was right, judging workers according to their output can result in gross injustice. Deming's argument was that the cause of poor worker performance lies not within the worker but within the organization.

2. *Current performance appraisal practices promote worker behavior that compromises quality.* This indictment is not unique to TQM. It is one of the litany found in every critique of the system. Deming's objection primarily focused on results-based appraisal systems that are tied to reward systems. Link results and rewards, Deming contended, and the outcome is the generation of a short-term, quota-attainment mentality.

But results-based programs, particularly those making effective use of goal setting, can generate the same outcomes that Deming postulated as the consequences of TQM. Workers' self-worth is enhanced, as are motivation generated by the setting and achievement of stretch targets. Particularly when the results–job outcomes side of the ledger is balanced by a separate performance factors–competencies component, the worthy goals of TQM are made even more achievable through the effective operation of its performance appraisal nemesis.

3. *Current performance appraisal practices create a band of discouraged workers who cease trying to excel.* The charge here springs from appraisal methods that fit workers into forced distribution rankings where managers are charged with becoming corporate chiropractors, forcing everyone in their unit into a predetermined bell-shaped curve. The tendency here, as Ghorpade and Chen point out, is the common one of equating "average" with "unsatisfactory."

The sources of this dilemma are sloppy thinking. If the average is the median, then fully half of whatever the population under examination will be below average. Examples of this cerebral inanity are not hard to come by. Raising the number of students—or welders or programmers or total quality management rhetoricians—who are "above average" is folly; raising the average performance of those students and welders is an admirable and achievable goal. The challenge is an educational one, particularly when the company uses numerical performance appraisal ratings. What is needed is not to abolish performance appraisal ratings but to explain that a rating of 3 or Fully Meets Standards or Good Solid Performer is a highly desirable outcome, particularly when the basis of comparison is not the general population but the particular assembly of organizational honor students the company has expended enormous efforts to recruit.

4. *Current performance appraisal practices rob workers of their pride in workmanship.* Deming's concern here parallels the previous one. The preoccupation with quotas and numerical counts, and using the existing average as the baseline with never-ending improvement the goal, may well force workers and their managers to neglect quality in order to play the numbers game. There is a certain validity to Deming's argument, and there is an untapped reservoir of pride and dignity that current management practices often slight. But it's a problem of polluted bathwater, not a flaw in the baby. What's required is not eliminating performance appraisal itself but cleaning up the conditions in which it exists so as to mobilize that reservoir of pride in workmanship that truly effective appraisal processes can encourage.

Linking TQM and Performance Appraisal

TQM's concentration on system factors and performance appraisal's concentration on the performance of the individual are in parallel, not in conflict. In well-managed organizations committed to both system quality and individual excellence, they can serve as dual pillars of organizational effectiveness.

There are specific processes and techniques that organizations can use to integrate their TQM and performance appraisal processes in order to maximize both and reduce any apparent conflict:

1. *In an organization with a primary commitment to TQM, focus of the appraisal system should be on helping employees to improve their performance.* One of the most injurious aspects to performance appraisal is the excessive multiplicity of purposes that one system is expected to serve. In companies with major commitments to TQM, it is even more important that the expectations of the performance appraisal system be concentrated on helping individual performers know exactly how well they are doing and how they can improve their contributions to the enterprise. In TQM organizations, the primary focus of appraisal needs to be employee development.

2. *Concentrate appraisal discussions on identifying and eliminating perceived barriers to higher quality.* A primary goal of the appraisal discussion in a TQM-committed enterprise is the determination of system problems or common causes that impede individual efforts toward quality, not on attaching blame for system failure to operators. Heed this caution, however: Concentrating excessively on system causes for individual failures may encourage inadequate performers to attribute their shortcomings to system constraints. If only one individual in a group reports system deficiencies to be the cause of performance derelictions, a local—individual performer—cause may well be the reality.

3. *Encourage all system customers to modify the system to incorporate TQM tenets.* Whatever the formal paper appraisal system may require, a company or even a smaller organizational unit can frequently modify the procedure to meet its needs for providing TQM support as long as the basic administrative requirements of the appraisal system are met.

In one major unit of a large hospital, a charismatic department manager decided that whatever the administration of the hospital did, he was going to run his facilities department on the basis of TQM. Well in advance of the hospital's annual tedious performance appraisal drill, he gathered his troops together, reviewed the hospital's sorry form, and then told them that what it represented was the starting point for them to practice their *kaizen*—continuous improvement—skills. "What do we need to do, given the fact that this basic form is mandated, in order to complete it well enough to keep the personnel monkeys off our backs but also get some good out of the process for ourselves?" he asked his team. He funded a series of weekly pizza meetings for a task force of facilities employees who were charged with developing an answer to his question that everyone supported enthusiastically.

4. *Train raters in both person and system factors.* Rater training occurs in many organizations, but too often the concentration of the training is exclusively on considering person factors rather than system factors—special rather than common causes. Because the goal of any appraisal system is to improve overall organizational effectiveness, increasing the attention devoted to system considerations will not only increase the TQM connection but will also increase the likelihood that the overall goal will be met.

5. *Downplay results; highlight competencies.* In a TQM-driven system, the focus of appraisal efforts should be less on results achieved (since these will be heavily influenced by common causes and system successes and failures) and more on performance factors and competencies. Behavior is most compatible with a TQM orientation; it is observable, it is measurable, it generates worthy outcomes, and it is entirely under the control of the individual.

6. *Collect performance data from multiple sources.* Subordinates are often in a better position to identify system factors than are managers. The customers of the employee are often better judges of the quality of her performance than is the supervisor.

7. *Ask employees to provide examples of task achievement, quality improvement, and team performance.* Whether or not the organization requires formal self-appraisal as part of its performance appraisal system, the manager in a TQM-oriented organization can strengthen the TQM efforts by asking each subordinate to come to the appraisal session with a formal document listing examples of behaviors or activities in three areas critical to a total quality management effort:

- ▸ *Task achievement.* What have you accomplished that has served to make this organization more effective, customer sensitive, profitable, or productive?
- ▸ *Quality improvement.* What have you done over the course of the year to improve the quality of your own personal work or the quality of the product or service you provide?
- ▸ *Team performance.* What have you done that increases cooperation, teamwork, collaboration, and harmony?

Typically only task achievement is stressed in traditional appraisal systems. By requiring team members to report on their success in improving quality and strengthening team performance, the likelihood of increased effectiveness in these areas will increase.

Deming was shortsighted in his inability to recognize the potential that performance appraisal can have in enhancing the success of quality management efforts. By incorporating the suggestions above and seeing the two systems as partners in helping the organization deliver quality products and services to its customers through both the joint and team efforts of its constituents, TQM and performance appraisal can exist in a completely symbiotic relationship.

Performance Appraisal and the Computer

Hallelujah! Here comes the cavalry, riding over the ridge just in time to rescue managers from the job they hate the most. Just as software programs can help minimize the anguish caused by the annual requirement to fill out tax forms, so can similar programs make it just as painless to do performance appraisal.

The parallel between tax preparation and employee software is close. Both provide help for a task that is generally disliked, highly complex, infrequently done, and rife with penalties if errors are made. Completing both performance appraisals and income tax returns involves gathering voluminous information and using those data as the basis for filling out a form.

The software packages are also similar. While the IRS provides the only form the taxpayer is allowed to use, both tax preparation packages and appraisal packages walk the user step by step through the completion of a form, the better ones offering the availability of expert help in any area where questions arise. At the end of both processes, the software runs a series of checks for completeness, internal integrity, and any areas where legal red flags might pop up.

The primary differences is that paying taxes to the IRS is required by law. Let it slip, and you're off to the penitentiary. Evade your performance appraisal duties, and the worst you'll get is fired.

But there is one additional and quite significant difference. When we call up a tax program and start playing with the numbers, it's only numbers that we're playing with. But blithely using a computer to assess the contributions and capabilities of a subordinate may seem a bit mechanistic at first. Doubtless, just assigning a number to a trait, then sipping coffee while the software concocts a packet of preprogrammed phrases is a godsend to the slothful supervisor. The fact is, however, that using a good package and treating it as a tool for generating a respectable first draft of what will be the ultimate appraisal can actually help managers be better at their job. These products, mechanical as they are, can help managers to define clearly an employee's responsibilities, evaluate his skills and contributions, and write and edit a personalized, legally sound appraisal.

Performance Appraisal Software

Three performance appraisal products, all running on Microsoft's Windows 3.1 or later, now define the market in this category. Norm Wu, a former partner in Bain & Co.'s technology consulting section, started his company, Avontos, when he realized that management often failed to take his recommendations and implement them well because of people management problems. Avontos released its first product, ManagePro, in 1992 and immediately won technology industry praise and management acceptance for its ability to help manage people by setting goals and giving feedback and coaching. Review Writer, the Avontos performance appraisal software product, is a companion product that employs such experts as the employment law firm of Orrick, Herrington & Sutcliff and consultant Bill Swan.

Employee Appraiser is a product of Austin-Hayne Corporation, like the others well vetted by both human resources professionals and employment law specialists before being released. Employee Appraiser may be the most intuitive program of the three. It avoids scaled ratings entirely. Instead of rating a specific skill by degrees, Employee Appraiser gives a statement with a list of defining factors. If the statement applies, the user selects it, and the program writes supporting text. The software provides management coaching for the reviewer and improvement tips for the employee built into the review process. Its high quality guidelines can turn the review process into a developmental tool for both parties.

KnowledgePoint, the third provider of sophisticated employee appraisal software, offers Performance Now! Like the others, it gives managers the opportunity to select among predesigned forms or design their own. A unique feature in this program is that giving a subordinate a low rating will trigger a recommendation that examples need to be added in case the ranking is challenged.

It would be folly to review the products comparatively or describe unique features that any one offers, since all are continually under development. Just in the time between signing the contract to write this book, for example, and starting the writing of this chapter on computer-based appraisal software, all three companies published significant upgrades to their products. Competitive advantages originally possessed only by one of the products are now offered by all; improvements in the next version released by Avontos, for example, will quickly be enhanced by KnowledgePoint and Austin-Hayne. All of the products offer important features and benefits to nervous or unskilled appraisers:

- ► Each has reasonably easy-to-manage interfaces that allow for constructing performance appraisals without significant difficulty and make the job far simpler than starting with a blank form.
- ► All have built-in legal checkers that will highlight such terms as *maternity* or *young* or *attitude*. (Sometimes the programs turn nervous-nellie in their legal checking. Performance Now flagged the word *pretty*, apparently concerned that telling Herman that he did a "pretty fair job" might be an assessment fraught with peril.)
- ► All offer a variety of forms and templates aimed at different job families so that the information and language can be made reasonably appropriate.
- ► All make use of various forms of tips and pop-up wizards that make suggestions to the manager to support praise and criticism with specific examples. All provide hints and recommendations about

the entire performance appraisal process, including conducting effective meetings and reducing employee defensiveness.

▸ The programs can be particularly useful to managers in helping them to be specific by giving them the opportunity to peruse a vast database of skill descriptions and rate their employees in relevant categories, forcing them to take into consideration issues that they could easily have overlooked.

▸ All can be used during the course of the year for capturing performance data that can be applied in the annual formal performance. Managers who find the software reasonably easy to use will probably find it comfortable to add regular performance notes.

But the products are not perfect. A significant flaw with all of the programs is that by necessity they slight the objectives, standards, and work outcomes of the performance management process, simply because this element is not nearly as amenable to computer assistance as cooking up a bunch of sentences reflecting various levels of performance for the competencies to be assessed. Another intractable problem is that the most important part of the appraisal can't be controlled by computer software at all, no matter how sophisticated: the quality of the meeting between the individual and the appraiser.

Their greatest failing is that they are essentially soulless. Click the mouse to indicate that Suzie is a "3" in critical thinking, and a paragraph of machine text will gush out, describing Suzie's approach to analyzing problems, generated by a gadget that knows nothing about Suzie or the organization for which she works. In every case the software runs on algorithms, not on any knowledge of the individual.

Three perils then result. The first is the obvious one of accepting sterile machine-generated prose as representing the essence of a human being. Many times the writing samples provided by the programs are excessively simple, repetitive, jargon laden, or merely insipid: "Kayla is ineffective at preventing the polarizing of positions during discussions, so she does not ensure that discussions remain objective." Although all the programs provide for correcting that obvious problem by actively encouraging managers to edit the language that the program algorithms produce, laziness is a powerful inducement to leave mediocre content alone.

A second problem is that trifling errors may slip through that will reveal the appraiser as having simply done a point'n'click without having invested any real thought or deliberation in the process of writing the appraisal. If Sandy has done a fully acceptable job of keeping up-to-date technologically, the software might provide the reasonably sounding narrative, "Sandy usually keeps up to date on new developments in her field by reading, attending seminars, and maintaining contacts with colleagues." But if in fact Sandy did not attend one seminar during the year, then the validity of the entire appraisal will come under a cloud of suspicion.

Can They Make Writing Appraisals Too Easy?

The third problem is curious: These programs may in fact make performance appraisal too easy. Thinking about the performance of a subordinate over the course of a year's accomplishments, assessing the value of that performance, struggling to find the best words to describe that performance is a difficult job, and perhaps that's the way it should be.

Although the litany of grievances over performance appraisal always includes the protest that the process is difficult, it might just be better to keep it as one of management's more difficult demands. It should not be made so easy that it ends up being done thoughtlessly.

Certainly no one will argue that tax computation software should make the job of generating tax forms as simple as possible. There is no justification for placing any constraints on how simple tax preparation software programs should be made. But maybe there is an ideal simplicity for performance appraisal software programs, and making them simpler than that will end up being deleterious to the process.

I believe that the manager, before delivering any performance appraisal in which a computer-generated narrative plays a part, should agonize just a bit over it. He should read carefully the text the machine has generated, assuring himself that he can defend the contraption's assessment of his subordinate. Is the English plain and natural? Does it sound like other things he would write by himself or is it significantly different in style, tone, voice, etc.? Assume that the subordinate reads aloud a particular phrase from the appraisal and asks, "Boss, I think I understand what you're driving at, but how did you happen to put it like this?" The manager should be prepared to explain the words the machine has put in his mouth.

Finally, none of the packages fits seamlessly with any corporation's culture. Each was designed to appeal to the broadest possible audience. The stronger the corporate culture, the less appropriate any of these programs is likely to be without sophisticated fine-tuning.[10]

The Future of Performance Appraisal

Several organizations have developed approaches to performance appraisal that are almost startling in their departure from conventional designs. The techniques they are employing may be of immediate use to an organization that is struggling with the same unique set of circumstances that led these developers to come up with their systems.

Peer and Supervisory Appraisal at NRL Credit Union

Linda Steger is the human resources manager of NRL Federal Credit Union, a $160 million operation in Oxon Hill, Maryland. She commissioned a 1989 organization development study that indicated that this otherwise highly successful organization was experiencing some pinches. People didn't like the compensation plan. Employees complained that there was no relationship between organizational goals and individual performance, combined with a lack of feedback to anybody.

A task force representing a diagonal slice of the organization changed the system. Four parts make up the new approach. One central feature of the new system is "Job Objectives": results-oriented, measurable, understandable, achievable, and controllable factors written by employees and supervisors. The second component is "Credit Union Standards": behavior-driven performance factors common to the entire organization. "Technical Skills" makes up the third part of the evaluation: cross-selling, job knowledge, problem solving, and half a dozen others.

"Peer Evaluation" is the unique component of the new system. "Each of us is a unique individual who brings personal experiences, talents, beliefs, communication styles and coping strategies to the workplace," says Steger. "Blending these unique characteristics to form a team of diverse, contributing individuals is the challenge confronting us. Effective teams do not automatically develop: it takes commitment, hard work, encouragement, and guidance. To encourage team development we include Peer Evaluation as one of the components in our performance appraisal system."

Peers focus on three areas of performance: teamwork, member service, and initiative. They describe how colleagues help and hinder them in doing their job by giving specific examples. They also request specific changes to improve performance.

At NRL, peer evaluations are not done just by filling out a form, and turning it in to the supervisor. They are given in one-on-one meetings to provide feedback in a constructive manner.

"What truly sets our system apart however," Steger says, "is the evaluation of supervisors by employees." Just as peers confront each other in one-on-one peer meetings, so their program provides for one-on-one, face-to-face appraisals of supervisors by subordinates as part of the process. These sessions are more than merely guided discussions. On a formal appraisal form, each employee rates her supervisor using a five-point scale of Outstanding, Above Average, Competent, Marginal, or Unsatisfactory and then delivers an overall rating of the boss's performance. Will employees genuinely shoot straight with the supervisor, given the power dynamics at play? Yes, Steger argues stoutly. Several factors make it work in practice the way it was designed in theory. First, "Active Listening" is the first of the twelve standards employees evaluate their supervisors on. That alone serves to focus supervisors' attention.

Since its inauguration in 1990, Steger reports, improved communications at all levels is obvious. Feedback is continuous; team relationships are more effective. The relationship between organizational goals and individual performance is clearly understood by all employees.

And is telling your supervisor just what you think of her now easy? "Of course not," Steger admits. "But I did do some close surveying, asking lots of people lots of questions about how the process is really working. And more than 50 percent of the people throughout NRL feel that when it comes to the boss, I can say anything I want."

Quorum Health Resources

Let's agree on a couple of things that are common to virtually every appraisal system. The process is initiated and guided by the supervisor. There is some system of measurement. The information is used for things like compensation and promotions, and maybe discipline. And the boss is the source of the feedback. Right?

Wrong.

Those are all the things that Cindy Nosky and her team at Nashville's Quorum Health Resources abolished. Nosky, a human resources consultant with the hospital, describes her performance appraisal process as an employee-led feedback model. The system does not contain any sort of measurement, objective or subjective. It isn't used for administrative decisions. And although the model involves the employee and the supervisor, feedback comes from other sources: customers, suppliers, and coworkers.

Nosky is an unabashed Deming devotee: "We have decided to use Deming's approach exclusively. Most organizations will do a little Deming, a little Crosby, a little Juran, a little of this and that. We're following Deming completely in our efforts."

In October 1990 she put together a task force made up of a half-dozen of Quorum's hospitals that were the most sophisticated in their system to design a process for them. "I was tired of listening to other people's speeches and reading other people's articles and discovering that they hadn't gone far enough in matching theory to practice," she says.

Their task force came to several common conclusions:

- ▸ The feedback process must be an ongoing one, not an annual event.
- ▸ The employee must be responsible for coming up with both a personal and professional development plan.
- ▸ Customer feedback is the most important aspect.
- ▸ People should not be ranked.

"One of the realities is that systems of ranking and checking boxes was accomplishing nothing. In focus groups people said the only place where people-ranking and box-checking works is where the employee has a good leader. If the leader is good, then the employees say the process is good, but it's a function of the leader, not the process." On the other hand, they still found that employees want one-on-one time with their supervisor or other leader.

Another key finding was the discovery that employees don't want peer review but they very much want customer feedback—at least twice a year.

The process has four phases:

1. *Plan.* The employee and the leader decide who the employee's customers are, what information the employee will need to collect from them, and how the employee will go about doing this collection (survey, interviews, etc.). Included in this process may be collecting customer perceptions on such questions as, What's the most important aspect of my job? Where do I most need to improve my service to you?
2. *Gather.* The employee gathers the data and customer input from any likely source. The employee is encouraged to ask customers directly to evaluate her work and suggest ways for her to improve. This phase also provides for identifying organizational barriers to quality performance and the identification of developmental experiences that will help improve performance.
3. *Meet.* In this is feedback discussion, the employee shares the collected data with the leader. They talk about the kinds of improvements the data suggest should be made. Together they work out a plan of action, devise a timetable, and determine how success will be measured.
4. *Evaluate.* Employee and leader discuss how the feedback session went and what they need to do to improve the data collection and feedback process in the future.

In interviewing Nosky, I assumed that the supervisor would have some influence in suggesting areas that the employee should collect data in if he felt that there was a problem area that the employee should become aware of. "There you go," she replied, pointing out that I was ensnared in the traditional mind-set that sees the supervisor as the source of employee evaluation. "Stop thinking about the boss as the boss," she replied. "Try to realize that the boss is a customer of the employee. The employee will collect data from the boss as a customer. And the boss-customer can't do his job if the employee doesn't send in the weekly report in time."

In reply to a question about how the system affects poor performers, Nosky again fell back on Deming and the TQM approach Quorum has embraced. Common causes and special causes, events above and below the control limits are the issues here, Nosky argued. An employee who is consistently below the lower control limit in performance is a special cause, just as an employee who is consistently above the upper control limit is a special cause. But it's a mistake to create human resources systems to deal with special causes; rather they need to concentrate on general causes. Users need to investigate and eliminate negative special causes and emulate positive special causes. This system makes both visible.

One decision was to eliminate tying compensation to performance appraisal. Instead, Quorum uses factors like prevailing market wage and additional skills to determine compensation changes.

In one hospital Quorum was in the process of eliminating merit increases in the course of making the overall change to the TQM approach and was concerned about the impact of this change on their best performers. "So we went to our best performers," she said. "We explained the TQM approach in detail, told them that we were going to be getting rid of merit increases, and then explained that since they were the people who were likely to be most affected, asked them what they wanted instead since they couldn't get merit increases any more. Their response? They reported wanting job enrichments—better computers, better tools." More recognition was not one of the high responses. They didn't want praise for doing a good job; they wanted the tools that would allow them to do a good job.

A major obstacle in initiating a system so dramatically different from conventional performance appraisal arises if the system is not emulated from the top down. If senior management does not support it, it can't work. "If you're in a situation where your boss doesn't give you an appraisal but demands that you give your people an appraisal, this system—any system—won't work."

Any other bumps? One final, minor one. In one hospital not long after it initiated the new process, the employees liked it so much they started surveying everybody. "They went out of control with surveying," notes Nosky. "We had to implement statistical process control training to get things back to normal. You don't have to survey everybody to achieve accurate, significant results."

A Major Independent Oil Company

Chuck Mills, vice president of human resources for one of America's largest and most successful privately held oil companies, stood up in front of a hundred of his colleagues at a roundtable to talk about his company's frustrations and solutions to their performance appraisal mess.

Their mess was no different from the messes found at most other organizations, Mills admitted. "But because of the nature of our business we had the added challenge of finding a way to motivate and compensate both the cowboy and the geophysicist."

The previous system was the traditional textbook approach: sections for goals; sections for performance factors; separate forms for officers, exempts, and nonexempts. Finally, in this highly fluid, nonbureaucratic organization, things reached a boiling point when Mill's fellow officers rebelled at this burdensome, time-consuming, worthless process. The problems were the same as a lot of other companies shared: low accuracy of information, low percentage of completion, human resources staff seen as the policy cops, inability to defend terminations when challenged in court, and an unequivocal absence of management support.

Chuck sat down with the president and owner of the company, whose reputation, like that of his firm, was as a sharp, shrewd, and savvy player. The two of them cooked up an appraisal process that modeled their technical prowess and managerial savvy. "What are we really interested in?" Chuck asked the president. Together they worked out a list of fourteen questions that the president wanted each manager to ask each subordinate once a year.

They made a couple of administrative decisions: All reviews would be done at the same time of the year; nothing would go in the employee's file; and the reason that nothing would go in the employee's file is that there would be nothing to put in it. The process would be entirely oral. If there was a specific performance problem that needed to be confronted (rare in this highly selective, dynamic organization) it would be defensively documented and filed in case of later need. For the great majority of employees, however, the process would be conversational only—they would just answer these fourteen questions:

1. What were the five most important accomplishments within your functional area(s) of responsibility during the last 12 months?
2. What are the three most important things you would do differently to improve results if you could turn the clock back one year?
3. What are the most important objectives (limit to five) within your functional area(s) of responsibility for the next 12 months?
4. What do you consider to be your most important qualifications and strengths?
5. What do you consider to be your professional traits that you need to improve?
6. What are your most important objectives related to self-improvement and dealing with others which you hope to achieve over the next 12 months?
7. What are the greatest hindrances for you to accomplish the

company's objectives and achieve your professional and personal goals and objectives?

8. What can your supervisor do to facilitate your job performance and help you achieve your objectives?
9. What actions are you currently taking to help develop your direct reports and/or coworkers?
10. What actions are you taking to develop teamwork and more effectively utilize all of the resources and expertise within the company?
11. What single individual (outside of your functional area[s] of responsibility) has helped you the most over the past year?
12. Who would you recommend to replace you if something happened to you tomorrow and you were no longer able to perform your responsibilities?
13. Is there anything else you would like to talk about or that we should address as a part of this review?
14. How effective has this discussion been in reviewing your job performance and setting objectives for your functional area(s) of responsibility?

The manager gives the list of questions to the subordinate and asks him to think about the responses over the next week or so. Jotting down notes is fine, but there's no official need to write anything. After a week of rumination on both sides, the two meet privately and talk their way through each of the questions, taking notes if they want.

Before implementing the system, the organization ran it by their lawyers. No problems, the lawyers agreed.

The results? 100 percent completion. How can they tell that they get 100 percent completion with a system that's 100 percent oral and has no paper trail to check? One of the system's few rules is that every manager has to go through the fourteen questions with each of his direct reports. When he has finished his last interview, he writes a memo to the president, copy to Chuck Mills. What does the memo say? Just one line: "This is to let you know that I have finished my reviews."

Other results include the elimination of 90 percent of all the paperwork that used to be generated by the performance management process. There's still some paper about performance, but it's initiated only on an as-needed and never a routine or system-demanded basis. Eliminating all the bureaucracy allowed Mills to eliminate half a job in the human resources department.

Mills reports a dramatic increase in review effectiveness and an increase in managers' willingness to confront performance problems with individuals without hesitation. And almost without exception, employees reported that they liked the informality of the process. "Now he's being completely honest with me since there's nothing written down," was the recurrent employee response.

Just as the organization eliminated the old appraisal system, it eliminated the old compensation system: ranges, midpoints, job descriptions, salary surveys. It benchmarked a couple of key jobs, eliminated most job titles, and reduced down levels.

To make sure that their best employees are getting good raises, the company eliminated its previous forced distribution system and developed a four-level rating system exclusively for salary purposes. "We just give each supervisor a bucket of money," Mills said. "He can allocate it any way he wants, as long as he can justify his allocation decision to his people, to the president, and to me. And they can."

Team Performance Assessment at Texas Instruments

As much as at any other company in America, teaming has been a way of life at TI. And Consumer Products Division has pushed the technology of teams one step further than almost any other company.

Jerry Brady, a TI reengineering consultant in the Information Technology Group, had been the team facilitator for an eight-member team that successfully reengineered itself to increase effectiveness. Brady then received the assignment to work with another Consumer Products Division team to create something different in peer assessment and compensation.

"We created our own questionnaires," Brady said. The questionnaire, a portion of which is reproduced as Figure 16-1, contains thirty-three descriptions of effective team behavior, all stated in behavioral terms, occasionally with a statement of the opposite of the ideal behavior so that the desired performance could be clearly delineated for all team members. Each behavioral statement has three possible ratings for team members to use in assessing each other's performance:

- − = seldom or needs improvement
- 0 = usually or satisfactory
- + = frequently or outstanding

At first, team assessments were anonymous. Team members filled out the questionnaires weekly on each other's performance and behavior; the team facilitator collected and collated the data; and every Friday team members received their anonymous summaries.

The next significant change in the process came with the development of the "hot seat circle," about three months after the team had started working together and members had gotten to know each other well. Each week one member volunteered to be in the hot seat, with the other team members circled around him or her. The same team behavior questionnaires that they had been filling out since the team started working together

Figure 16-1. Team Member Behavior Questionnaire

13. He/she at the appropriate times tests for agreement and commitment to decisions reached by the team. As opposed to assuming that all are committed if no one openly disagrees.   (−)(0)(+)

14. He/she effectively plans and organizes team situations, anticipating potential problems.   (−)(0)(+)

15. He/she regularly contributes new ideas and relevant concepts. As opposed to waiting for other members to establish directions or solutions.   (−)(0)(+)

16. His/her comments are relevant and pertinent to the real issues at hand in the team. As opposed to speaking just to be heard.   (−)(0)(+)

17. He/she keeps the team on track when it gets off topic. He/she reminds the team the purpose of the meeting and how the current discussion is not aligned with it.   (−)(0)(+)

18. He/she effectively executes roles assigned to them, such as discussion leader, note taker, presentation preparation, scheduler, etc.   (−)(0)(+)

19. He/she plans recognizes and considers long term strategic issues when making decisions. As opposed to being focused on only short term or tactical issues.   (−)(0)(+)

20. He/she approaches and defines problems systematically. As opposed to haphazardly   (−)(0)(+)

21. He/she gathers relevant information in an organized manner and considers a broad range of issues or factors before drawing conclusions.   (−)(0)(+)

22. He/she meets their commitments and deadlines to the team. As opposed to being late or not doing them at all.   (−)(0)(+)

23. He/she takes the initiative to solve problems or overcome barriers. As opposed to passively accepting or assuming that someone else will take care of it.   (−)(0)(+)

24. He/she volunteers for tasks. As opposed to avoiding or being pressured into doing them.   (−)(0)(+)

Score: (−) = seldom or needs improvement (0) = usually or satisfactory (+) = frequently or outstanding (Seldom, usually, frequently, relate to behavior questions) (Needs improvement, satisfactory, outstanding, relate to performance questions)

months before were still filled out, but now anonymity disappeared as the individual on the hot seat told his teammates about the reviews he had received from them.

Until this point, every person knew how the rest of the team as a whole had evaluated his behavior and performance since he had received weekly feedback results. And each member knew what he had said about every other member since he had filled out the reports on each person on the team. But nobody on the team, except for the team facilitator who did the compilations and arithmetic, knew what the exact reviews for each team member from the other team members individually were. Now the sharing began.

The instructions to the hot seat occupant were simple: Just answer three questions: What did people say about you? What do you think about what was said to you? What are you going to do about it?

Most of the time, the news was good—disproportionately good, but not inaccurately good. TI highly values teamwork; that value is shared and encouraged throughout the corporation. The lone wolf won't last long at TI. It would be unusual for team members not to get a lot of positive feedback from their colleagues.

Confidentiality was inviolable. The corporate instructions describing the elements of the process make that clear: "The sole purpose of the individual assessment by core team members is to provide feedback to each core team member on his/her teaming skills, behavior in the team environment, behavior that affects team performance, etc., that can be used by each member towards improvement in those areas. All members of a core Product Development team will participate in an individual assessment conducted by their peers on the core team. The intent of this process is to openly and honestly communicate with each other as to individual strengths and weaknesses in the teaming environment, and to generate individual development plans to work on during the next review cycle. The results of this assessment are Team Strictly Private and will go no further."

This was also a technically successful team; they were making a good product and working well together. And there were no team or individual crises. Problems that required critical action would have been dealt with and eliminated before this process was ever initiated.

Later the process became even more sophisticated and pointed. Each team member received a team member input form. At the top were listed the names of all other members of the team. Below that were two lists: one providing the team's answers to the question, "The strengths and qualities I have noticed about you are . . ." with a requirement that there be a minimum of one and a maximum of three answers. Below that was the opposite perspective: "The areas for improvement that I have noticed about you are . . ." Again, the requirement was for at least one and no more than three responses. An actual team member input form is reproduced as Figure 16-2.

"It's easy to talk about team assessment," Jerry Brady said, as he was describing one of the most intense and demanding processes devised by any organization and calling it "easy." "The compensation part is tough. We spent a *lot* of time on it." The compensation part, confidential at TI, involved team ranking of each team member, which was then tied to a percentage.

The final part of TI's team performance appraisal process was to de-

Figure 16-2. Completed Team Member Input Form

THE STRENGTHS AND QUALITIES I HAVE NOTICED ABOUT YOU ARE (MIN OF 1, MAX OF 3):

1. You do not critique ideas without careful consideration; and you make significant attempts to understand the other persons point of view, i.e., when we were discussing the need for a marketing person on the team, you patiently listened to all perspectives before concluding that marketing adds no value to any team.

2. You were always willing to take on whatever tasks the team needed to be done, even when it was not in your area of responsibility, i.e., when you installed the special software on my machine that generates winning lottery numbers.

3. You always seemed to be one step ahead of the team. You were highly sensitive to when the team was starting bog down and prevented it from happening. This resulted in the team being much more effective.

THE AREAS FOR IMPROVEMENT THAT I HAVE NOTICED ABOUT YOU ARE
(MIN OF 1, MAX OF 3):

1. You sometimes became defensive about your ideas and suggestions, which made me feel uncomfortable and stopped me from offering any additional comments; i.e., your position on starting meetings at 6:30 in the morning.

2. You are sometimes late with your commitments to the team, such as the metric data on the TI-99 project.

velop a performance appraisal document, directly linked to compensation, created jointly by the individual and the team and placed in the individual's personnel folder.

The process Brady and his team devised has not yet spread throughout TI. Radical even for a company renowned for innovative approaches, it may never become part of the overall corporate approach. But it stretched the limits of performance appraisal, and it worked.

Notes

1. *Wall Street Journal*, November 28, 1995, p. 1.
2. Edward Lawler and Susan Cohen, "Designing Pay Systems for Teams," *American Compensation Association Journal* 1 (1992): 6–18.
3. Jack Zigon, "Making Performance Appraisal Work for Teams," *Training* (June 1994): 58.
4. Information on Clark Material Handling Company's appraisal process provided primarily from Martin L. Ramsay and Howard Lehto, "The Power of Peer Review," *Training and Development* (July 1994): 38.

5. The insights on several of the problems inherent with peer raters were suggested by Julie Houser Barclay and Lynn K. Jarland, "Peer Performance Appraisals," *Group and Organization Management*, March 1995, p. 39.
6. Sam T. Johnson, "Work Teams: What's Ahead in Work Design and Rewards Management," *Compensation and Benefits Review* (March–April 1993): 39–41.
7. "Team Based Pay at Levi Strauss," *HR Briefing*, 6 (1995).
8. *Wall Street Journal*, November 28, 1995.
9. The basic description of TQM practices is based on Kenneth P. Carson, Robert L. Cardy, and Gregory H. Dobbins, "Upgrade the Employee Evaluation Process," *HR Magazine* (November 1992): 88.
10. Information on the computer-based appraisal packages was developed from personal examination and from the analyses provided by the following articles and reviews: Elizabeth Longsworth, *PC Computing* (October 1994): 52–54; Doug Stewart, "Employee-Appraisal Software," *Inc. Technology* (Spring 1995): pp. 104–105; Phillip Robinson, "3 New Examples of 'MBA-Ware Help With Performance Reviews," *The Boston Globe*, September 7, 1994; Edward C. Baig, "So You Hate Rating Your Workers?" *Business Week* (August 22, 1994): 14; Alison L. Sprout, "Surprise! Software to Help You Manage," *Fortune* (April 17, 1995): 197–200.

Appendix A

Grote Consulting Master Performance Appraisal Form

Part I: Appraisal of Job Skills

Teamwork: Works effectively with other employees. Shares credit and opportunities when appropriate. Displays an appropriate balance between personal effort and team effort. Helps others when needed.

INDIVIDUAL →																		
	OCCASIONALLY				SOMETIMES				FREQUENTLY				USUALLY				
APPRAISER →																		

Analysis: _____
_____
_____

Problem Solving: Recognizes and analyzes work related problems. Uses available resources to evaluate potential solutions. Not only identify problems but also recommends solutions.

INDIVIDUAL →																		
	OCCASIONALLY				SOMETIMES				FREQUENTLY				USUALLY				
APPRAISER →																		

Analysis: _____
_____
_____

Accountability: Displays professionalism in approach to work. Accepts responsibility for all areas of the job. Does not make excuses for errors. Does not blame others for mistakes.

INDIVIDUAL →																		
	OCCASIONALLY				SOMETIMES				FREQUENTLY				USUALLY				
APPRAISER →																		

Analysis: _____
_____
_____

Motivation: Displays drive and energy in accomplishing tasks. Handles several responsibilities concurrently and comfortably. Displays a contagious enthusiasm for the job and the company. Displays a positive attitude in completing work assignments and interacting with others. Sees to it that tasks are done *well*.

INDIVIDUAL →																		
	OCCASIONALLY				SOMETIMES				FREQUENTLY				USUALLY				
APPRAISER →																		

Analysis: _____
_____
_____

Job Knowledge:	Possesses sufficient skill and knowledge to perform all parts of the job effectively, efficiently and safely. Relates current problems to historical ones. Provides technical assistance to others. Is consulted by others on technical matters. Makes active efforts to stay up-to-date.

INDIVIDUAL →																	
	OCCASIONALLY			SOMETIMES			FREQUENTLY			USUALLY		
APPRAISER →																	

Analysis: _____
_____
_____

Planning and Organizing:	Plans and organizes work effectively. Identifies available resources required to complete projects. Sets appropriate deadlines and checkpoints and meets them. Develops both short and long term plans. Makes good judgements about time allocation and resources required.

INDIVIDUAL →																	
	OCCASIONALLY			SOMETIMES			FREQUENTLY			USUALLY		
APPRAISER →																	

Analysis: _____
_____
_____

Communications:	Presents ideas effectively in formal and informal situations. Conveys thoughts clearly and concisely. Listens well and asks appropriate questions. Communicates well in writing. Reviews letters, memos and reports to assure accuracy. Keeps supervisor and co-workers informed.

INDIVIDUAL →																	
	OCCASIONALLY			SOMETIMES			FREQUENTLY			USUALLY		
APPRAISER →																	

Analysis: _____
_____
_____

Work Quality:	Uses time effectively and with a minimum of error. Does work thoroughly in a reasonable amount of time. Brings quality concerns to the attention of the appropriate individuals.

INDIVIDUAL →																	
	OCCASIONALLY			SOMETIMES			FREQUENTLY			USUALLY		
APPRAISER →																	

Analysis: _____
_____
_____

Adaptability/ Flexibility:	Meets changing conditions and situations in work responsibilities. Accepts constructive criticism and suggestions and uses them to advantage. Deals with anger, frustration and disappointment in a mature manner. Maintains objectivity in conflict situations. Seeks solutions acceptable to all.

INDIVIDUAL →																				
	OCCASIONALLY				SOMETIMES				FREQUENTLY				USUALLY							
APPRAISER →																				

Analysis: _____

_____

_____

Attendance/ Punctuality:	Is present for work every day. Is fully ready to work at beginning of work schedule and continues until work day is done. Makes appropriate arrangements when adverse weather conditions or other problems might cause a delay in arriving at work on time. Conforms to work hours and schedule.

INDIVIDUAL →																				
	OCCASIONALLY				SOMETIMES				FREQUENTLY				USUALLY							
APPRAISER →																				

Attendance Record: Number of days absent in past twelve months: ____ Number of days late in past twelve months:____ Personal attendance percentage:____ % Organizational attendance percentage:____ %

Analysis: _____

_____

_____

Part II: Major Achievements / Contributions

In the following section, list the individual's three major achievements during the appraisal period. Consider the action the individual took to make the organization more effective/more profitable/ more admirable:

1. _____

_____

_____

2. _____

_____

_____

3. _____

_____

_____

Part III: Appraisal of Accountabilities, Goals and Objectives

| Accountability: |
| Objective/Goal: |
| Results:

Appraisal: |

| Accountability: |
| Objective/Goal: |
| Results:

Appraisal: |

| Accountability: |
| Objective/Goal: |
| Results:

Appraisal: |

Part III: Appraisal of Accountabilities, Goals and Objectives — 2

Accountability:
Objective/Goal:
Results: **Appraisal:**

Accountability:
Objective/Goal:
Results: **Appraisal:**

Appraisal of Accountabilities, Goals and Objectives

Marginal	Fair	Competent	Superior	Distinguished

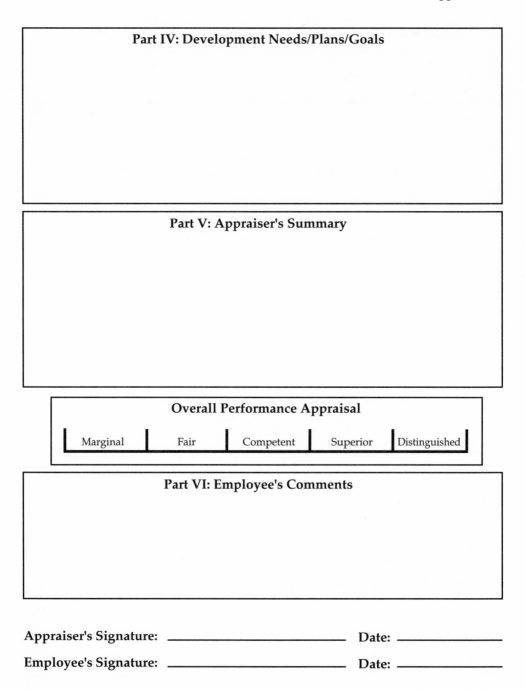

Part IV: Development Needs/Plans/Goals

Part V: Appraiser's Summary

Overall Performance Appraisal

| Marginal | Fair | Competent | Superior | Distinguished |

Part VI: Employee's Comments

Appraiser's Signature: _____ Date: _____

Employee's Signature: _____ Date: _____

Appendix B

Grote Consulting Individual Management Development System

INDIVIDUAL MANAGEMENT DEVELOPMENT

II. PRIORITY SETTING

A. SETS APPROPRIATE PRIORITIES
Can separate the important from the urgent.
Can describe rationale for priorities set.
Can separate "the wheat from the chaff" in job.
Can arrange priorities easily when circumstances dictate.

CIRCLE ONE	LOW		AVG.		HIGH
	1 2 3	4 5 6		7 8 9	

B. USES TIME EFFECTIVELY
Moves quickly from one activity to the next.
Makes use of "To Do" lists and other planning tools.
Makes good judgments about time allocation and requirements.
Sets appropriate deadlines/checkpoints and meets them.
Revises deadlines when necessary well in advance.

CIRCLE ONE	LOW		AVG.		HIGH
	1 2 3	4 5 6		7 8 9	

C. PLANS AND ORGANIZES WORK
Identifies all resources required to complete projects.
Develops both short and long term plans.
Spends minimum amount of time "fighting fires".
Structures work according to people's abilities.

CIRCLE ONE	LOW		AVG.		HIGH
	1 2 3	4 5 6		7 8 9	

D. CONTROLS AND FOLLOWS UP TO ASSURE WORK COMPLETION
Follows up to make sure job or task is accomplished.
Measures subordinates' productivity accurately and quantitatively.
Keeps costs within budget.

CIRCLE ONE	LOW		AVG.		HIGH
	1 2 3	4 5 6		7 8 9	

I. KNOWLEDGE OF THE BUSINESS

A. UNDERSTANDING OF THE PERFORMANCE MEASURES FOR HIS/HER JOB
Can state specific job accountabilities.
Can state specific measures for each accountability.
Has reviewed and discussed quantifiable performance measures with supervisor.
Measures own performance regularly and accurately.

CIRCLE ONE	LOW		AVG.		HIGH
	1 2 3	4 5 6		7 8 9	

B. EXPERIENCE LEVEL IN CURRENT JOB
Can relate current problems to historical ones.
Can identify resources required to do job.
Has handled all major activities engaged in by department.
Familiar with section and department history.

CIRCLE ONE	LOW		AVG.		HIGH
	1 2 3	4 5 6		7 8 9	

C. TECHNICAL KNOWLEDGE
Has sufficient content knowledge to perform all parts of the job.
Can provide technical assistance to others.
Is consulted by others on technical problems.

CIRCLE ONE	LOW		AVG.		HIGH
	1 2 3	4 5 6		7 8 9	

D. EDUCATION/TRAINING LEVEL
Has completed or is working on BA/BS.
Has completed or is working on MA/MS/MBA.
Has attended appropriate internal or external training programs.
Has been trained in content and performance expectations.

CIRCLE ONE	LOW		AVG.		HIGH
	1 2 3	4 5 6		7 8 9	

E. SELF-DEVELOPMENT EFFORTS
Reads extensively in both technical and management areas.
Is aware of new theories, approaches, developments, etc. in technical specialty area.
Attends professional meetings and seminars.
Seeks projects in areas outside immediate responsibility area.

CIRCLE ONE	LOW		AVG.		HIGH
	1 2 3	4 5 6		7 8 9	

III. PROBLEM SOLVING & DECISION MAKING

A. RECOGNIZES PROBLEMS AND OPPORTUNITIES
Can recognize potential problems before they arise.
Can see opportunities within problems.
Takes action on problems in early stages.
Can identify areas where problems are likely to arise.

CIRCLE ONE	LOW		AVG.		HIGH
	1 2 3	4 5 6		7 8 9	

B. USES RESOURCES IN SOLVING PROBLEMS
Doesn't try to solve all problems by him/herself.
Can identify all resources available for help (other departments, outside sources, etc.).
Involves peers in own and other departments in solving problems.
Uses boss appropriately as a resource.
Seeks subordinates' input to help solve problems.

CIRCLE ONE	LOW		AVG.		HIGH
	1 2 3	4 5 6		7 8 9	

C. SOLVES PROBLEMS SYSTEMATICALLY
Identifies a step-by-step sequence to solve problems.
Develops realistic time frames and meets them.
Develops specific measures to determine that problem has been solved.
Documents steps taken to solve problems.
Follows up to assure problem does not recur.

CIRCLE ONE	LOW		AVG.		HIGH
	1 2 3	4 5 6		7 8 9	

III. PROBLEM SOLVING & DECISION MAKING (Cont.)

D. FULLY RESOLVES PROBLEMS

Problems solved do not arise again.
Solutions do not create new problems.
All aspects of a problem are resolved.

CIRCLE ONE — LOW 1 2 3 4 AVG. 5 6 HIGH 7 8 9

E. MAKES GOOD DECISIONS

Lists all possible alternatives for decision.
Makes timely and logical decisions.
Does not try to make all decisions by him/herself.
Can make decisions on limited but adequate information.
Can state what potential problems decision can create.
Implements decisions effectively and follows up to assure results.

CIRCLE ONE — LOW 1 2 3 4 AVG. 5 6 HIGH 7 8 9

F. DEVELOPS NEW SOLUTIONS

Displays creativity in seeking solutions to problems.
Is able to integrate new ideas with current approaches.
Does not accept first possible solution.

CIRCLE ONE — LOW 1 2 3 4 AVG. 5 6 HIGH 7 8 9

IV. INTERPERSONAL SKILLS

A. EXPRESSES EMOTIONS APPROPRIATELY

Reacts to criticism objectively and non-defensively.
Deals with anger, disappointment, frustration, etc. maturely.
Displays loyalty to company and department.
Converses easily with others.

CIRCLE ONE — LOW 1 2 3 4 AVG. 5 6 HIGH 7 8 9

B. INITIATES FRIENDLY INTERACTIONS

Seeks out peers in own and other departments.
Converses easily with others.
Is included in group activities.

CIRCLE ONE — LOW 1 2 3 4 AVG. 5 6 HIGH 7 8 9

C. PROVIDES POSITIVE AND NEGATIVE FEEDBACK

Provides feedback objectively rather than personally.
Provides feedback immediately.
Provides both positive and negative feedback.

CIRCLE ONE — LOW 1 2 3 4 AVG. 5 6 HIGH 7 8 9

D. INTERACTS EFFECTIVELY WITH SUPERIORS AND SENIOR MANAGEMENT

Appears at ease in dealing with senior management.
Can make suggestions and/or disagree appropriately.
Displays corporate perspective in dealing with issues.

CIRCLE ONE — LOW 1 2 3 4 AVG. 5 6 HIGH 7 8 9

E. ACCEPTS POSITIVE AND NEGATIVE FEEDBACK

Reacts objectively rather than defensively.
Listens to feedback and learns from it.
Asks questions when feedback not completely understood.

CIRCLE ONE — LOW 1 2 3 4 AVG. 5 6 HIGH 7 8 9

F. FACES AND RESOLVES CONFLICT

Maintains objectivity in conflict situations.
Confronts conflict directly.
Avoids polarizing issues (i.e., us *vs.* them, win-lose, etc.).
Seeks solutions acceptable to all involved.

CIRCLE ONE — LOW 1 2 3 4 AVG. 5 6 HIGH 7 8 9

V. COMMUNICATION

A. PRESENTS IDEAS EFFECTIVELY IN FORMAL SITUATIONS

Is at ease in stand-up presentations.
Makes effective use of media (flip charts, slides, etc.)
Is not distracted by side comments, questions, etc.
Prepares and follows an agenda.
Begins and ends on time.
Sets and maintains pace.

CIRCLE ONE — LOW 1 2 3 4 AVG. 5 6 HIGH 7 8 9

B. PRESENTS IDEAS EFFECTIVELY IN INFORMAL SITUATIONS

Knows when to talk and when to listen.
Hears other speakers out.
Thinks before responding.
Follows up on decisions made.

CIRCLE ONE — LOW 1 2 3 4 AVG. 5 6 HIGH 7 8 9

C. KEEPS BOSS AND PEERS INFORMED

Advises boss when problems arise.
Does not withhold bad news.
Shares information on current projects.
Solicits assistance and review from others.
Prevents "surprises."

CIRCLE ONE — LOW 1 2 3 4 AVG. 5 6 HIGH 7 8 9

D. LISTENS WELL

Pays attention to speaker.
Takes appropriate notes.
Asks questions to clarify ambiguities.
Is able to summarize what has been said.

CIRCLE ONE — LOW 1 2 3 4 AVG. 5 6 HIGH 7 8 9

E. CONVEYS THOUGHTS CLEARLY AND CONCISELY

Speaks directly to the point.
Does not have to repeat statements.
Uses good grammar.

CIRCLE ONE — LOW 1 2 3 4 AVG. 5 6 HIGH 7 8 9

F. ASKS QUESTIONS OF OTHERS COMFORTABLY

Questions are concise, logical, and understandable.
Asks for exactly what he/she needs to know.
Questions don't irritate, belittle or intimidate others.
People feel comfortable answering questions asked.

CIRCLE ONE — LOW 1 2 3 4 AVG. 5 6 HIGH 7 8 9

G. ANSWERS QUESTIONS OF OTHERS COMFORTABLY

Answers questions non-defensively.
Does not hold back negative or unpleasant information.
Is able to say "I don't know, but I'll find out."
Follows up to get answers to questions.
Listens to both question and questioner.

CIRCLE ONE — LOW 1 2 3 4 AVG. 5 6 HIGH 7 8 9

H. COMMUNICATES EFFECTIVELY IN WRITING

Writing is clear and concise.
Knows when to write and when to call.
Reviews letters and memos to assure accuracy.
Purpose of letter or memo is clearly stated.

CIRCLE ONE — LOW 1 2 3 4 AVG. 5 6 HIGH 7 8 9

VI. PEOPLE DEVELOPMENT

A. SUBORDINATES KNOW WHAT IS EXPECTED OF THEM

Sets high, challenging goals for subordinates.
Develops specific, attainable, measurable goals.
Subordinates are able to state their accountabilities and measures.
Appraises subordinates'
performance objectively.
Conducts performance
reviews regularly.

CIRCLE ONE — LOW 1 2 3   AVG. 4 5 6   HIGH 7 8 9

B. NUMBER OF READINESS OF SUBORDINATES FOR PROMOTION

Subordinates are capable of filling in during manager's absence.
Discusses promotional opportunities with subordinates.
Subordinates work effectively with minimum supervision.
Actively seeks promotional
opportunities for
subordinates.

CIRCLE ONE — LOW 1 2 3   AVG. 4 5 6   HIGH 7 8 9

C. DETERMINES THE DEVELOPMENTAL NEEDS OF SUBORDINATES

Can identify specific strengths and weaknesses of each subordinate.
Delegates work to improve subordinates' skills in specific areas.
Judgments about development needs of subordinates are
supported by data.
Can describe developmental needs in terms of specific
situations and behaviors.
Has constructed a
development plan for
each subordinate.

CIRCLE ONE — LOW 1 2 3   AVG. 4 5 6   HIGH 7 8 9

D. EFFECTIVENESS OF DEVELOPMENT AND TRAINING EFFORTS

Results of development efforts are observable and measurable.
Has acquired reputation as a "people developer".
Establishes specific measures for development activities.
Percentage of people
promoted is higher
than peers.

CIRCLE ONE — LOW 1 2 3   AVG. 4 5 6   HIGH 7 8 9

E. PROVIDES DEVELOPMENTAL ASSIGNMENTS FOR HIS/HER SUBORDINATES

Allows subordinates to take risks.
Examines own job to determine parts that could be done
by subordinates.
Seeks special projects and assignments for subordinates.
Counsels and coaches
subordinates through
projects.

CIRCLE ONE — LOW 1 2 3   AVG. 4 5 6   HIGH 7 8 9

F. USES POSITIVE REINFORCEMENT AND FEEDBACK

Provides feedback quantitatively.
Uses reinforcement as a management tool to build or sustain
performance.
Constructively corrects subordinates so that they learn from mistakes.
Directs feedback toward
the task rather than
the person.

CIRCLE ONE — LOW 1 2 3   AVG. 4 5 6   HIGH 7 8 9

G. DELEGATES WORK APPROPRIATELY

Does not try to do entire job by him/herself.
Can state why he/she gives specific tasks to specific subordinates.
Follows up on delegated work to assure completion.
Delegates work in
accordance with sub-
ordinates' ability and
developmental needs.

CIRCLE ONE — LOW 1 2 3   AVG. 4 5 6   HIGH 7 8 9

H. TAKES APPROPRIATE DISCIPLINARY ACTION

Documents disciplinary action.
Uses good judgment in taking action.
Assures that "the punish-
ment fits the crime".

CIRCLE ONE — LOW 1 2 3   AVG. 4 5 6   HIGH 7 8 9

VII. ACHIEVEMENT ORIENTATION

A. ABILITY TO WORK INDEPENDENTLY

Pushes the limits of his/her job.
Makes good judgments about when to ask for help.
Does not need to have every detail of a job explained.
Keeps supervisor advised
of progress, changes,
problems with projects.

CIRCLE ONE — LOW 1 2 3   AVG. 4 5 6   HIGH 7 8 9

B. ASSERTIVENESS

Argues for what he/she believes in.
Knows when to stop arguing.
Speaks with conviction about his/her projects.
Questions policies and
decisions he/she does
not understand.

CIRCLE ONE — LOW 1 2 3   AVG. 4 5 6   HIGH 7 8 9

C. RISK TAKING

Makes good judgments about when to take risks.
Knows what dangers and penalties are involved.
Identifies potential problems
before acting.

CIRCLE ONE — LOW 1 2 3   AVG. 4 5 6   HIGH 7 8 9

D. RESULTS ORIENTATION

Displays a sense of urgency.
Does not accept excuses for failure.
Can state exactly what results
he/she is seeking.

CIRCLE ONE — LOW 1 2 3   AVG. 4 5 6   HIGH 7 8 9

E. IMPACT AND INFLUENCE ON OTHERS

Opinions and ideas are sought by peers in own and other
departments.
Ideas and suggestions are taken seriously by others.
Can persuade others to accept his/her point of view.
Knows how to plan and "stage" ideas and proposals
to gain acceptance.

CIRCLE ONE — LOW 1 2 3   AVG. 4 5 6   HIGH 7 8 9

F. RESILIENCE

Bounces back quickly from disappointment and frustration.
Is able to adapt to change.
Does not express inappropriate discouragement or
disappointment to others.

CIRCLE ONE — LOW 1 2 3   AVG. 4 5 6   HIGH 7 8 9

G. ABILITY TO MANAGE THROUGH A CRISIS

Willingly puts in extra time and effort required.
Does not take over subordinate's job in a crisis.
Coaches and counsels subordinates in crisis situations.
Does not lose sight of objectives.
Keeps communications clear.

CIRCLE ONE — LOW 1 2 3   AVG. 4 5 6   HIGH 7 8 9

H. ABILITY TO MAKE MISTAKES AND LEARN FROM THEM

Does not make same mistake twice.
Reviews and analyses mistakes with supervisor.
Does not make dumb mistakes.

CIRCLE ONE — LOW 1 2 3   AVG. 4 5 6   HIGH 7 8 9

Index